Jon E. Lewis is a writer and historian. His many previous books include the bestselling *The Mammoth Book of the Edge, The Mammoth Book of Polar Journeys, The Mammoth Book of True War Stories, World War II: The Autobiography, The Mammoth Book of Combat* and *A Brief History of the First World War*.

THE MAMMOTH BOOK OF

The Vietnam War

Edited by Jon E. Lewis

ROBINSON

ROBINSON

First published in Great Britain in 2015 by Robinson

Copyright © J. Lewis-Stempel, 2015

3 5 7 9 10 8 6 4 2

The moral right of the author has been asserted.

A CIP catalogue record for this book
is available from the British Library.

ISBN 978-1-47211-606-2 (paperback)
ISBN 978-1-47211-607-9 (ebook)

Typeset in Great Britain by Hewer Text
Printed and bound by CPI Group (UK) Ltd, Croydon, CR0 4YY

Robinson
is an imprint of
Little, Brown Book Group
Carmelite House
50 Victoria Embankment
London EC4Y 0DZ

An Hachette UK Company
www.hachette.co.uk

www.littlebrown.co.uk

Contents

Part II
Home Front

Part III
The End

Preface

War in the "Nam" long preceded American involvement. Following the defeat of Japan at the end of WWII, the "Good War", France tried to re-impose colonial rule on the country. The French met fierce resistance from Communist guerrillas in the north of the country, whose "hit-and-run" tactics steadily eroded Gallic morale. And General Giap, the leader of the Communist North Vietnamese Army, had more up his sleeve than irregular warfare. In 1954 Giap's forces surrounded the French garrison at Dien Bien Phu; the encirclement included heavy artillery dragged covertly over the mountains. When Dien Bien Phu fell to Giap after 57 days of siege the French commitment to stay in Vietnam fell with it. France immediately ceded power north of Ben Hai River (near the 17th Parallel) to the Communist Viet Minh; in the south rule passed to a Western-backed regime under the Catholic Ngo Dinh Dien.

If anybody seriously thought the Communists would stay north of the 17th Parallel they were mistaken. By 1959 Ho Chi Minh was sending his "Viet Cong" guerrillas below the border. The response of America was to deploy "military advisors" on behalf of the capitalist South. With the staged "Tonkin Gulf Incident", in which North Vietnamese allegedly fired on US naval forces American involvement in the Vietnamese civil war ratcheted up. By 1969 542,000 US troops and other military personnel were "In Country", and to keep the Army at full strength required a draft of eligible males. In other words, conscription, compulsory military service. Now every young American male had the chance of glory. Or was it death?

However raised, the numbers going into the green machine of US Army – who, really, did the bulk of the grunt's stuff, fighting up close with Charlie, way more than the navy and the fly boys – were never enough. Neither did technology turn out to be the infallible God of American dreams, though it came close to pulling off the miracle. Napalm and the defoliating Agent Orange had their moment in the Asian sun, had their backers, yet "Nam" was truly the war of the helicopter, the sound of rotor blades the war's theme tune. Well, that and The Doors. Vietnam was the first rock'n'roll war, with the bloody but intoxicating union of Mars and Caliope being perfectly conveyed by the "New Journalism" of Michael Herr. It was a good war for writers.

A good war for special forces too. Or at least, their proliferation. John F Kennedy is lodged in the mind as the man who smartly negotiated the Cuban Missile Crisis and created the Peace Corps. Offstage he birthed US special forces; DELTA, the US Navy SEALs, LRRPs all made their entrance in the world in the sixties. Working the Mekong, the rice paddies, the swamps and rivers the SEALs went out in three-men detachments to kill communists. To "Sat Cong".

But despite the concept and practice of heliborne recce and assaults ("airmobility"), despite SEALs, despite the smell of napalm in the morning and evening, the North had the will. The fanatical will of ideologues. As the war dragged into jungle skirmish after skirmish and the body bags started arriving stateside, the will of the American people, like the French a decade before, eroded. The war in "Nam" became a burning issue with the counter-cultural hippie movement of the sixties, composed for the most part of middle class white youth. A big tranche of American youth suddenly fell in love with protest politics. Peace, man. Universities, ironically, became battlegrounds. At Kent State protesting students were shot. Students chanted, "Hey, hey, LBJ [Lyndon B Johnson], How many kids you killed today?" in reference to reports of indiscriminate shootings, bombings, "napalmings" of Vietnamese civilians by US forces under the reign of Kennedy's successor. Vietnam: "The Bad War".

In retrospect, which is the historian's conceit, the military outcome in Vietnam was a close run thing. The North tried the big one, the Tet Offensive, in 1968 . . . to no great practical effect, and the loss of over 45,000 of its combatants. The shock of Tet was more terrible than the military consequences of Tet. Yet American nerves were rattled. It was Dien Bien Phu all over again. The will to fight and die in a far away land waned, disappeared. In 1973 America withdrew from its longest war. Perhaps 450,000 Vietnamese, north and south, lay dead. Thirty six thousand Americans had died with them.

And America had psychic wounds which remain unhealed to this day. There is no end.

Part I

In Country

War in Vietnam 1954–1967

Dien Bien Phu

Jules Roy

In 1953 the French Army High Command in Vietnam decided to garrison the hamlet of Dien Bien Phu in order to prevent Viet Minh excursions into neighbouring Laos. The hamlet itself lay in the middle of a geographical bowl, surrounded by a ring of small hills. On these hills the French placed eight strongpoints (allegedly named after the mistresses of the garrison commander, Colonel Christian de Castries).

At 1700 on 13 March 1954 65,500 men from the Viet Minh attacked the outlying strongpoints at Dien Bien Phu. The onslaught was stunning, not least because the Viet Minh, led by Vo Nguyen Giap, had dragged heavy artillery into the area undetected, which they positioned on the rear slopes of the mountains surrounding the French positions. Such positioning of the artillery made it near impervious to counter-battery fire. The first French outpost, Beatrice, fell on 14 March, Gabrielle on the following day. Thereafter Giap's force could pound the French garrison below with virtual impunity.

Against all the odds the 14,500-strong garrison held out until 7 May. The last French outposts only surrendered after days of fighting, some of it hand-to-hand, some of it trench-warfare in the manner of the Great War.

The battle cost the lives of 3000 French troops. It was also the de facto end of French rule in Vietnam.

This account of the last day of the French stand at Dien Bien Phu is by Jules Roy, a Franco-Algerian writer and air force officer.

THE NIGHT OF MAY 6–7, 1954

AT ISABELLE, ALL the 105-mm. guns but one had been destroyed. On Éliane, where a terrible storm of shells had just broken, Major Botella heard Langlais calling Bréchignac on the radio.

"Young Pierre calling Brèche, Young Pierre calling Brèche, who is that deluge meant for?"

"Brèche calling Young Pierre; it's for Éliane 2."

The shelling moved to Éliane 3, then to Éliane 4, while the guns on former Éliane 1 and Mont Fictif opened fire. Langlais sent three tanks still capable of movement over to the left bank, at the foot of the peaks.

At 1815, hard on the heels of their last salvo, the Viets, wearing gauze masks, hurled themselves against Éliane 2. Using radio communication between its companies and battalion command posts for the first time, the 98th Regiment was in position in front of the peaks of Éliane 4.

Botella replied with his mortars and his recoilless guns. The Viets got as far as his command post but were driven back by Vietnamese troops, who, when they had good officers and NCOs, fought as fiercely as their brothers on the other side, just as North Koreans and South Koreans had fought one another. One of their officers, Captain Phan van Phu, saw his company reduced to thirty men.

At 2100 hours, signals orderly Tran ngoc Duoï of the People's Army went into action with his unit. In the white light of the flares which had taken the place of the moon in its first quarter, he could make out the movements of the counterattacks. In spite of shell splinters in his head and right leg, he refused to allow himself to be evacuated, sheltered a wounded platoon commander and went on carrying out his orders with a limp. When a dynamiter was killed, he took his charge, placed it, lighted it and went back to his mission. The Viet troops were cut to pieces by the mortars, but the following waves covered them and went on.

On Éliane 2, which was held by two companies of the 1st

Battalion, Parachute Chasseurs, under Captain Pouget, a Viet jumped in front of Sergeant Chabrier, pointed an automatic pistol at him and shouted, "Give yourself up. You're done for –" then fell back dead. At 2300 hours a great silence suddenly descended on the position, and Pouget said to himself, "Perhaps they're going to let us have a bit of peace?" But then, like the spray of a huge black wave breaking almost noiselessly against a jetty, the earth was hurled high into the air by the thousands of pounds of explosive in the Viet mine, and fell with a thunderous din on the roofs of the shelters and into the trenches. The crater which opened under the defenders' feet and buried them still exists. The vegetation has not returned to it, but the rains fill it in a little every season.

The shock troops, who had been waiting for the signal of the explosion to go into action, felt the earth rumble and hurled themselves screaming at the shattered position. Section Leader Dang phi Thuong, under the orders of the commander of No. 7 Platoon of the 3rd Company of the 98th Regiment, advanced rapidly through the hail of bullets from automatic weapons toward the smashed blockhouses, but found his way barred by the fire from Sergeant Chabrier's platoon, which mowed the attackers down and toppled them into the muddy crater that the mine had opened. "What a sight for sore eyes!" cried one of the machine gunners. But the weapons ended up by jamming, the stocks of ammunition by running out, and the swarm of Viets overran the position. The 12.7-mm. machine gun on the tank "Bazeilles" was the last to fall silent.

At midnight, the five Dakotas which were to drop the last company of reinforcements asked, in the interests of their safety, that no more flares be sent up. Langlais and Bigeard hesitated. Even if it was dark, how could the pilots make out the tiny dropping zone in the midst of all the fires of the battle? Wouldn't the Viets take advantage of the darkness to resume the attack? Near the door of the Dakota, the pockets of his battle dress stuffed with whisky for General de Castries and brandy for Langlais, and worried in case he should break his bottles when he landed, Captain Faussurier waited for the green lamp to light up. Finally Bigeard queried Lieutenant Le Page on the radio.

"The flares must come first," Le Page replied unhesitatingly.

Langlais ordered the planes to turn back, and the men of the 1st Battalion, Parachute Chasseurs, returned to Hanoï, sick at heart. In the shelter of the camp headquarters where Geneviève de Galard was sleeping, sheltered under a table, on a mattress of parachutes, Bigeard felt a certain comfort at the thought that the sacrifice of that company had been avoided; a hundred men could no longer alter the course of events. Calls for help were jamming the lines to the artillery and the radio links with the strong points. As for the enemy radio receivers, they resounded with shouts of victory.

With one of his radio operators killed and the other hit by a bullet in the stomach, Pouget had stopped answering calls from the main position. He had been given up for dead and no more calls had been sent out to him. At four in the morning, he operated his transmitter himself and got through to Major Vadot.

"I've reoccupied all of Éliane 2, but I've only thirty-five men left. If we're to hold out, you've got to send me the reinforcements you promised. Otherwise it'll all be over."

"Where do you expect me to find them?" Vadot answered calmly. "Be reasonable. You know the situation as well as I do. Not another man, not another shell, my friend. You're a para. You're there to get yourself killed."

On the wavelength of the Éliane command network the Viets played the record of the "Song of the Partisans," and now and then their waiting voices took up the refrain:

*Friend, can you hear the black flight of the crows
In the plain? . . .*

"The swine," muttered Pouget, "the swine."

At Éliane, Botella had fifty mortar shells left and a few

cases of grenades. The loudspeakers of Bigeard's radio receivers vibrated: "Dédé calling Bruno, the ammunition's running out."

"Brèche calling Bruno, we're nearly finished."

On all the hills, the strong points changed hands several times within a few hours: The enemy hurled himself at any breach he made, then fell back in disorder. Dead and wounded dropped to the ground. On the west face, Claudine 5 was overrun, near a tank which could not fire any more.

Sitting out in the open near his radio set, Pouget watched the 120-mm. mortar shells pounding Éliane 4 where Botella was holding out. The ground was cracking open. Pouget saw some Viets running along the crest of Éliane 4, lit up by the flares, dropped by the planes. Down below, Dien Bien Phu was burning and fireworks were spurting from the shell stores. Now and then a few stars appeared through the clouds which filled the darkness.

At 0410, before his eyes, along the whole front of Éliane 2, the Viets stood up without firing. Pouget heard them shouting: "Di di, di di! Forward, forward!"

The survivors of Éliane 2 had one machine-gun charger and one grenade left. Pouget ordered the sole remaining lieutenant and those men who could still walk to return to the main position, and, falling back from one hole to the next, found himself reunited with them at the foot of the peak, in a trench full of corpses which they piled up to protect themselves.

Another shrieking tidal wave surged from the ground and broke over the 5th Battalion, Vietnamese Paratroops, covering Captain Phu; but a handful of Legionnaires and paratroops counterattacked again, recaptured some lost trenches, pushed aside the dead and dying to place their machine guns in position, and brought their fire to bear on the shadows in the flat helmets. Officers who were not yet twenty became company commanders or died when, like Second Lieutenant Phung, they called for mortar fire to be directed on them. Of the 6th Battalion, Colonial Paratroops, twenty men remained alive around Major Thomas. Sergeants gathered survivors together and rushed into the attack. Who would be victor or vanquished when this night came to an end? To help the men hanging onto the last peaks, Langlais withdrew some platoons from battalions in the center and threw them into the action among the burning eastern peaks. Everywhere men stumbled over shattered bodies. In the light of the flares which the wind carried toward the mountains, faces ran with sweat and with thick black ink. On Éliane 2, where since four in the morning nobody had answered Brèchignac's calls, the groaning of the wounded filled the dawn. Behind the eastern crests, the sky was turning golden.

MAY 7, 1954

On Éliane 10, at the foot of the peaks, day was breaking. The enemy was advancing everywhere, searching the shelters. Besieged in a block-house, Lieutenant Le Page managed to escape with a couple of men. The miracle was that Éliane 4 was still alive, that Brèchignac and Botella were still in command, calling for help. But what help could they be given? Lemeunier went into Langlais's shelter; he had gathered together a few Legionnaires and was ready to fight his way to the west.

"Not to the west," said Langlais. "To Éliane 4 where they're still holding out."

Langlais emerged from his shelter into the brutal light of summer. In the sky, Dakotas were dropping supplies. In all the trenches leading to the hospital, pitiful files of men trampled on corpses gradually being buried by the mud. Wounded men nobody could attend to any more were left where they lay. Turned loose by the Viets, who had told them, "Go back to your people and tell them we are coming," some battalion medical officers got through to Grauwin with the half-naked cripples who had returned to the fight a few days before.

On the other side of the river and the shattered ammunition dump swarmed the hundreds of men who had taken refuge weeks before in holes in the river banks in order to avoid the fighting, and whom Langlais compared to the crabs on tropical coasts. Dregs of humanity, deserters – Langlais could not find words sufficiently contemptuous for them. He could have mown them down with machine-gun fire or crushed them with a few 105-mm. salvos, but he turned away in disgust. Like Bigeard now, he was beyond all that. Like Béatrice, Gabrielle, Anne-Marie, Huguette and Dominique, Éliane had a new lover . . .

Under the bursts of automatic-pistol fire, Pouget had felt the corpses he was sheltering behind tremble. A grenade exploded near his helmet, stunning him. As in a nightmare, he heard a little nasal voice saying, "You are a prisoner of the Democratic People's Army of Vietnam. You are wounded. We shall take care of you. Can you walk?"

He looked up at his victor in the gauze mask.

"And my comrades?"

"We shall attend to them. Their wounds will be dressed. The medical orderlies are coming."

Pouget got laboriously to his feet. It was all over for him. He was stripped to the waist, with no weapons or marks of rank, hairy and haggard. Somebody helped him to walk. His radio operator leaned on his shoulder.

Friend, can you hear the muffled cry of the country
Being loaded with chains?

He was no longer strong enough even to hum the tune the Viets had been broadcasting all night. Defeated, he refused to resign himself. At the end of the suffering and humiliation that awaited him and were already escorting him, he knew that he was going to find the great explanation and salvation.

Suddenly the artillery in the east opened fire again and the shells started falling once more. Long, deep, whistling notes pierced the general din. Hope suddenly mingled with amazement. Captain Capeyron, Sergeant Sammarco, Corporal Hoinant and a great many others, surprised to see the first salvos fall between the positions, turned toward the west. Voices cried, "It's Crèvecoeur!" Faces revealed a joy which did not yet dare express itself freely, but which would burst forth a torrent ready to turn against the course of fate and carry everything with it. Yes, it must be the Crèvecoeur column, which the radiotelegraphers had been claiming to be in touch with for days and which they had said was approaching, which was swooping down from the mountains into the valley with an apocalyptic din. Men did not know whether to shriek or weep for joy. They were already hoisting themselves out of their holes when the range lengthened, reached the command posts and crushed the innocents getting ready to meet their saviors. They were expecting Crèvecoeur, but what they heard was the thunder of Stalin's organs.

Three men dressed in mud, haggard, their faces black with stubble and smoke, staggered up and collapsed on the ground. Bigeard bent over one of them and took his hand. Was he crying? It no longer mattered at this moment when everything had been surpassed, when the grandeur of the ordeal made them giddy, when words were no use except to those witnessing from afar the death agony of Dien Bien Phu. Bigeard, who had never been known to utter a cry of commiseration, simply said over and over again, "Poor Le Page . . ."

He was weeping for a whole body of knights massacred in vain because a general had flung his army into the enemy's trap, giving in to the bluster of those who had urged him to throw himself into the wolf's jaws. Among those who would be cited among the dead and the prisoners, how many names represented the flower of that army, sacrificed turn and turn about, for centuries past, for great causes and solemn idiocies! Bigeard had a vague suspicion that the disaster taking place had achieved nothing but a crucifixion, of which countless former high commissioners, secretaries of state or prime ministers were already washing their hands with affected delicacy. Obsessed by the idea of the coolie's pole on his shoulder, he could not yet imagine what was waiting for him. Who could tell? The diplomats were gathered together at Geneva; everything might be arranged at the last moment. He did not know that the men by whose fault battles are lost are not those whom they kill. Without suspecting it, it was himself that Bigeard discovered beneath the masks of clay and blood drying on his lieutenants' faces.

"Stop shelling . . ." Brèchignac had just asked Bigeard to spare Éliane 4 a bombardment that would kill off the wounded when he received a report from Botella that any further resistance was impossible. Botella then called Bigeard.

"Dédé calling Bruno, Dédé calling Bruno . . ."

It was the same metallic voice which used to announce, "Objective reached." Bigeard pressed the transmitter switch.

"Bruno here."

"Dédé calling Bruno. It's all over. They're at the command post. Goodbye. Tell Young Pierre that we liked him."

A click. A curter voice: "I'm blowing up the radio. Hip hip hooray . . ."

It was nine o'clock. On the heights surrounding Éliane 4, in the rice fields in the ravines, swarmed a host of little armed men, dressed in coarse green cloth, with sandals cut out of tires on their feet, helmets of interlaced bamboo decorated with the ruby of a red star on their heads, and gauze masks over their faces, who came running out of their hiding places in the forests and mountains. They reached the crests of Éliane in a huge roar which was carried along in waves by gusts of wind as they arrived on the summits. Spreading out over the sides and ridges of the Élianes, they uttered shouts of triumph and raised their weapons in a victorious gesture at sight of the yellow curves of the river and the plowed fields of the entrenched camp. On the double crest of Éliane 4, they could be seen jumping over the ruined trenches, crossing the tangled barbed-wire defenses, and stepping over piles of corpses lying on top of one another in the macabre reconciliation of death, or stretched out on their backs, their arms open, their faces eaten by flies, their mouths still full of a last groan, men fallen from their crosses, nailed to the pulverized ground among the wretched wooden supports of the shelters, or swimming in the slimy mud.

In the face of this swarm of human insects sprung up from all sides, the artillery of the entrenched camp, nearly out of ammunition and gun crews, remained silent. It had three hundred 105-mm. shells left and ten 120-mm. Fighters dived out of the sky, dropped bombs, fired their machine guns and spread disorder for a moment, but the swarm gradually resumed its advance when the planes disappeared after the ten minutes at their disposal. Botella decided to stay at his command post, but ordered Second Lieutenant Makowiak to rejoin the main position with a few uninjured men and a few wounded who could still walk. Soon afterward, the Viets surrounded him and took him into their lines. Section Commander Dang phi Thuong, second-in-command of Platoon No. 7 of the 98th Regiment, returning to the action to give Éliane the *coup de grâce*, saw him go by, surrounded by guards, bare-headed and balding, on his way to the first regrouping center where he would find Brèchignac and Pouget, mute with misery. At Opéra, Bizard was holding out and getting ready to launch a counterattack against the Élianes, but Langlais incorporated him into the defense system of the main position.

Capeyron, who was searching near Éliane 2 for some men from his company who had gone up there during the night, was hit by some grenade splinters which slashed his left wrist and groin like a razor.

At ten o'clock, from his office in the citadel at Hanoï, Cogny called Castries. The storms moving over the whole region crackled in the receivers. The conversation, which might be the last contact with the entrenched camp, was recorded in the radio room.

"Good morning, my friend," said Cogny. "What resources have you got left?"

Castries's voice was clear, slow, deliberate; a little shrill, as it always was on the telephone. Now and then, he searched for a word, corrected himself, repeated himself. Cogny punctuated his remarks with muffled words of acquiescence.

"The 6th Battalion, Colonial Paratroops, the 2nd Battalion, 1st Parachute Chasseurs, and what was left of the Algerian Rifles."

"Yes."

"In any case, there's nothing to be done but write the whole bunch off."

"Yes."

"Right ... At the moment, that's what's left, but greatly reduced of course, because we took, we drew on everything there was on the western perimeter in an attempt to hold out in the east ..."

"Yes."

"What's left is about two companies from the two BEPs put together ..."

"Yes."

"... three companies of Moroccan Rifles, but which are no use at all, you realize, no use at all, which are completely demoralized ..."

"Yes."

"... two companies of the 8th Assault ...

"Yes."

"... three companies of BT2s, but that's only to be expected because it's always that way, it's the Moroccan Rifles and the BT2s that have the most men left because they don't fight."

"Of course."

"Right, and out of the 1st Battalion, out of the 1st Battalion, Foreign Infantry, there're about two companies left, and about two companies of the 1st Battalion, 13th Demibrigade. It's ... they are companies of seventy or eighty men."

"Yes. I see."

"Well, there you are ... We're defending every foot of ground."

"Yes."

"We're defending every foot of ground, and I consider that the most we can do . . ."

Static suddenly interrupted the transmission.

"Hello, hello," Cogny repeated.

"Hello, can you hear me, General?"

". . . that the most you can do?"

". . . is to halt the enemy on the Nam Youm. Right?"

"Yes."

"And even then we would have to hold the bank, because otherwise we wouldn't have any water."

"Yes, of course."

"Right, So, well, that's what I suggest we try, I'll try to bring that off, ah, I've just taken, I've just seen Langlais, we're in agreement about that. And then, damn it all, I'll try, I'll try, conditions permitting, to get as many men as possible out toward the south."

"Good. That'll be by night, I suppose?"

"What's that?"

"By night?"

"Yes, General, by night of course."

"Of course. Yes."

"And I . . . I need your permission to do that."

"All right, fellow."

"You give me permission?"

"I give you permission."

"Anyway, I'll hold out, I'll try to hold out here as long as possible, with what is left."

Castries paused for a while, then intimated that he had nothing more to say.

"General?"

"Yes, all right."

"That's it . . ."

"From the ammunition point of view, have you . . . is there anything to be recovered?" Cogny asked very quickly.

"Ammunition. That's more serious, we haven't any."

"There isn't anything that . . ."

"We don't have any, you see. There are still a few 105-mm. shells, but . . ."

A sentence in the transcript is undecipherable. Castries may have referred to 155-mm. shells, for all those guns were unserviceable.

". . . they aren't any use here."

". . . for the moment. And as for the 120-mm., the 120-mm. shells . . ."

"Yes."

"I still have, I must still have, between 100 and 150."

"Yes."

"Which are all over the place, you see."

"Yes, of course." Cogny repeated.

"Which are all over the place. We can't . . . it's practically impossible to collect them. Obviously the more you send, the better, eh?"

"Yes."

"So we'll hold out, we'll hold out as long as possible."

"I think the best thing," said Cogny, talking fast, "would be for the Air Force to put in a big effort today to bring the Viets to a halt."

"Yes, General. The Air Force must keep up its support, eh? Nonstop, nonstop. Yes, and about the Viets, I'll put you in the picture as to how they stand."

"Yes."

"In the east the Viets have thrown in everything they've still got."

"Yes."

"Including two regiments of the 308th Division."

"Really? Yes."

"You see? On the western perimeter at the moment there isn't anything, there can't be anything but the 36th Regiment."

"The 36th, yes, I think so too."

"Just the 36th Regiment, eh? The 102nd Regiment . . ."

Suddenly he was cut off.

"Hello, hello," Cogny repeated in a panting voice while the technicians tried to re-establish contact.

"Can you hear me?" Castries continued.

"The 102nd Regiment, you were saying?"

"Yes, General."

"The 102nd Regiment?"

"Just that they've been thrown in on the eastern perimeter . . ."

"Yes."

". . . the 102nd Regiment and the 88th Regiment."

"That's it."

"You see? Plus what . . . plus what remained of the 312th . . ."

"That's it. Yes."

". . . and now the 316th."

"Yes."

"You see?"

"They've thrown everything in on the eastern perimeter," said Cogny.

"But you see, as I foresaw, the 308th, as I think I've already mentioned, escapes me, you see, as usual."

"Yes, that's it . . . Good, well, what about the withdrawal to the south?" asked Cogny. "How do you envisage it? Toward Isabelle or a scattered movement?"

"Well, General, in any case, in any case they'll have to pass south of Isabelle, won't they?"

"Yes, that's right."

"But I'll give orders, I'll give orders to Isabelle, too, to try, to try to pull out, if they can."

"Yes. Right. Well, keep me in the picture so that we can give you the maximum air support for that operation."

"Why, of course, General."

"There you are, my friend."

"And then, why, damn it all, I'll keep here, well, the units that don't want to go on it . . ."

"That's it, yes."

". . . the, how shall I put it, the wounded of course, but a lot of them are already in the enemy's hands, because there were some in the strong points, Éliane 4 and because ... and Éliane 10."

"Yes, of course."

"You see? And I'll keep all that under my command."

"Yes, fellow."

"There you are."

"Good-bye, fellow."

"I may telephone you again before ... before the end."

"There now, good-bye, Castries, old fellow."

"Good-bye, General."

"Good-bye, fellow."

Castries put down the receiver. Two hundred miles away, Cogny did not look at the officers standing silently around him. Sweat was running down his forehead. Hanoï lay crushed under the heat of the storm which refused to break.

At midday, Bigeard went to see General de Castries.

"It's all over," he told him. "If you agree, I'll get out of here at nightfall with my men. But we've got to make the Viets think that we're still holding out, and to do that the artillery, mortars and automatic weapons have got to keep on firing. Leave a good man here – Trancart, for instance."

"No," replied Castries. "I won't give that job to anybody. I'll stay, Bruno, old fellow. Don't worry; we'll keep on firing all night. At daybreak we'll cut our losses."

At 1300 hours, Captain Capeyron took up position on Junon with fifty-four Legionnaires. Sergeant Sammarco, at whose feet a 75-mm. shell had landed without exploding, said to a pal, "If we get out of this alive, we'll get blind drunk for a fortnight." In readiness for the sortie, Sergeant Kubiak emptied the flasks of rum in the "Pacific" ration crates into his water bottle. Langlais, Bigeard and their staff officers had some hot soup. Together they studied the situation and summoned the battalion commanders who were going to take part in "Operation Bloodletting." Tourret, Guiraud and Clémençon were unanimous in the opinion that it was impossible. However slim the chances of success, for they were completely cut off, they would have to make the attempt, but the Viets occupied the whole of the left bank, except for the bridge which they were trying to capture, and, like broken-down horses on the point of collapse, paratroopers and Legionnaires were at the end of their tether. One of the two boxers had been knocked out.

At 1530, accompanied by Bigeard, Lemeunier and Vadot, Langlais went to see General de Castries. He did not know that a telegram sent from Dien Bien Phu at 1400 hours had fixed the cessation of hostilities for seven the next morning. At Isabelle, where there were still two thousand shells left for a solitary 105-mm. gun, Colonel Lalande had permission to attempt a sortie. Castries was free to decide Langlais's fate and that of the remaining officers and men. He said to Bigeard, "You're going to pay dearly for all this, Bruno. You ought to try to make a break for it with a few men."

Who could possibly pull off that sortie? Perfectly calm and self-assured, Castries agreed that within five miles all of them would be overcome by exhaustion. Castries dismissed the officers and remained alone with Langlais. Exactly what they said to each other has been forgotten. Between the remarks exchanged with Bigeard, or by radio with Cogny, everything has become confused. Besides, what can they add to what was? Even monks end up, under the influence of communal life, hating one another.

These two men so different in character and methods no longer had any grounds for dispute. Who bore the responsibility for the fall of Dien Bien Phu? Neither of the two. Outstripped by events, Castries had failed to react at the right moment, but he had not wanted this post for which he was completely unsuited. He had not deceived anybody; others had been mistaken about him. He had been honest enough to warn Navarre, "If it's a second Na San that you want, pick somebody else. I don't feel cut out for that." And he had lacked the necessary humility to see that he ought to be replaced. Cynical and frivolous as he was, was it his fault also that he didn't like Langlais and Langlais didn't like him? Was

Langlais also to blame if, preoccupied with the patrols he had been ordered to organize every day, he had been unable to rehearse the counterattacks intended to recapture outposts which nobody expected to fall? To imagine that he should have demanded the necessary time and resources from Castries and Gaucher is to be wise after the event. It is necessary to go back in time, to breathe the atmosphere of optimism which reigned among the garrison, to hear the roar of Piroth's artillery when it fired its salvos into the mountains at the slightest alert. Who had had any premonition, at the time, of the disaster which had just occurred? As for his animosity toward Castries, that was only skin-deep. Langlais had made offensive remarks on several occasions about Castries's reluctance to leave his shelter, but if everybody paid homage to Langlais's spirit, who hadn't quarreled with him and suffered from his anger and bad temper?

"It's all over," said Castries. "We mustn't leave anything intact."

A brief access of emotion suddenly misted over Castries's eyes and froze Langlais's icy features. When Langlais saluted, Castries stepped forward with his hand outstretched, and Langlais, without saying a word, threw himself into his arms.

About 1600 hours, in the course of a radiotelephone conversation, Lieutenant Colonel de Séguins-Pazzis offered Colonel Lalande the choice between a pitched battle and an attempted sortie toward the south. Lalande was given no indication that the main position would not hold out until the following morning. He chose a sortie at nightfall, issued the orders prepared for that purpose, and sent out reconnaissance patrols toward the south, along both banks of the Nam Youm, to gauge the resistance the enemy was likely to offer. Since the direction of the sortie had been altered from the southwest to due south, there were no maps or guides available. Moreover, only one track seemed to be practicable, by way of Muong Nha, Ban Ta Mot and Ban Pha Nang, and Lalande had to change his plan.

On returning to his command post, Langlais gave orders

for the destruction of all weapons, optical and signals equipment. Bigeard remained aloof from all this. The news spread at once that surrender was imminent. Sergeant Sammarco had the barrels of rifles and machine guns thrust into the ground for the last cartridges to be fired. With incendiary grenades they soldered the breeches of the 105-mm. guns or melted the mortars and the bazookas. The ammunition was thrown into the river. The engines of the tanks which were still in working order were raced without any oil. The chaplains gathered together their chalices and holy oils. Grauwin buried a few bottles of penicillin with markers to indicate their position.

The fighting began again and the Viet battalions gradually advanced toward the center, surrounding paratroop units which fell immediately. There was no longer any question of fighting. Already, on the left bank, white rags were being waved among the Moroccans and the river-bank population. Dressed in green, with motley scraps of parachute material in their helmets and their duck trousers rolled up to the knees, the Viets appeared from all sides, in a silent, overwhelming flood. The river was crossed at 1700 hours. Hearing his battalion commander utter an oath, Sergeant Kubiak turned toward Castries's command post over which a huge white flag was waving. It suddenly occurred to Captain Capeyron that he ought to burn the 3rd Company's flag. Bending over the fire which his Legionnaires had hurriedly lit, he had just seen the last letters of the word "Loyalty" embroidered on the silk eaten up by the flames when the Viets arrived. A Viet officer gave the order: "Hands up!"

Capeyron did not obey. Some Viets came up and kicked him in the buttocks. Some Legionnaires broke ranks to intervene. Pale with humiliation, Capeyron restrained them.

"Don't move. It's too late."

In all the trenches on Éliane, the Viets began piling up the corpses from both sides and covering them with earth. On the summit of Éliane 2, they erected a sort of bamboo cenotaph, thirty feet high, which they decorated with white silk parachutes.

Algerians and Moroccans who had remained in hiding for days and nights on end came out into the open, waving rags and, naturally choosing the word which in all the armies of the world has always meant the end of fighting and the fraternization of former enemies, shouted, "Comrades!"

Company Commander Tho, entrusted with the task of establishing a clearing station, found the prisoners unusually docile; most of them stretched themselves as if they had been lying down for a long time and did breathing exercises. They were sent to the rear in groups of ten or so, without guards, simply being shown the way to the first collecting center. The head of the surgical block at Him Lam, Dr. Nguyen duong Quang, a pupil of Professor Tung, had tents made of parachute material put up to shelter the wounded, and started for the hospital.

"Here they come." These were the words you heard everywhere. In his shelter, Langlais hurriedly burnt his letters, his private notebook, the photographs of the woman he loved and even his red beret. He kissed Geneviève de Galard and gave her a message for his mother while his staff officers destroyed the command archives and the typewriters. He put on his old bush hat, which made him look like a melancholy sailor in a sou'wester. Why had he burnt his red beret when Bigeard had kept his? It was because he was afraid the Viets would use it as a trophy; unconsciously, he also wanted to spare what he held dearest in the way of military uniform the humiliation of defeat. Born for action, he suddenly found himself deprived of everything and at a loss as to what to do, whereas Bigeard, without decorations or marks of rank, but with his red beret pulled down over his head, was already preparing his escape; he rolled a nylon map of the highlands round his ankle and thought of hiding in a hole, under a pile of parachutes. Why shouldn't he succeed in escaping?

Little by little, the camp started swarming with activity, while clouds of smoke rose into the air and the ground shook with the explosions of material being blown up. Demoralized by the savagery of the fighting and by the bombardment which had gone on without stopping since the evening of May 1, thousands of haggard men, who had been drinking the yellow river water out of buckets since the purification plant had been destroyed, regained hope of surviving. Spontaneously, as if they had been slaves all their lives, they formed up in columns, knotted little squares of white material to the ends of sticks, and allowed themselves to be driven toward the northeast along the sides of Route 41 beneath the contemptuous gaze of the Legionnaires and the paratroopers. These were not the pictures of the disaster which would be taken a few days later by cameramen rushed to the spot to reconstruct, with docile North Africans disguised as paratroopers, the scenes the Vietminh had dreamed of. How many were there, at that moment, who preferred captivity to insolence? Ten thousand? And are we entitled to think that Dien Bien Phu would never have fallen if they had fought like the other two thousand who were preparing to force a way out?

The guns destroyed, the sandbags ripped open, the shelters in ruins, the burned-out trucks lying in puddles of yellow water – everything showed that the defeat was complete. Dirty parachutes covered the hills and the valley, hung on the river banks, clung to the parapets of the bridge and the barbed-wire entanglements like torn spiders' webs. There could no longer be any doubt about it: all was lost. Some, like Sergeant Sammarco, said to themselves, "It wasn't worth the trouble of killing so many people." Most remained silent. Corporal Hoinant, who had never seen anybody but his chief, Major Guiraud, could not understand anything any more. He had been told that it was essential to hold out until the Geneva Conference was over, and now they had just given in. As for hoping, he had abandoned all hope since he had been deceived with the assurance, repeated every day, that Crèvecoeur was on the way.

"Come out with your hands up . . ."

If the fortunes of war had gone the other way, Hoinant and Sammarco considered that the victory of the paratroops and the Legion would have been more harshly imposed on the defeated side. Neither of them had witnessed the humiliation inflicted on Captain Capeyron and, through him, on all the vanquished. They noted the correct behavior and lack of hatred of the Viets, who said to them, "The war is over." Perhaps. Commandos jumped down into the trenches, holding their noses because the smell was so atrocious, and ransacked the command posts in search of documents. Others, in token of their joy, threw grenades into the river, where they exploded with a muffled noise. Grauwin inspected the uniforms of his medical orderlies and distributed armlets on which red crosses had been painted with Mercurochrome.

"Whatever you do," Grauwin told his team, "don't leave my side."

In Hanoï, where he had heard Castries outline the situation to him once again, Cogny had the signal switched to the floor below, to General Bodet, whom Navarre had left on the spot to represent him and who wanted to bid Castries the official farewell, worthy of the Commander in Chief and his brilliant deputy.

Bastiani, Cogny's chief of staff, intervened.

"Wait a minute," he said to Cogny. "You didn't mention the question of the white flag."

Catapulted out of his seat by a terrible premonition, Cogny rushed downstairs and burst into Bodet's office just as Navarre's deputy, in his shrill little voice, was saying to Castries, "Good-bye, my friend. And all the very best. You've put up a good fight."

Cogny pushed him to one side and snatched the receiver from his hand. Navarre had never conceived the possibility that the white flag might be hoisted. In his directive of April 1, he had declared that under no circumstances was the idea of capitulation to be considered.

"Hello, hello, Castries? . . . Hello, Castries?"

"General?"

"Look, man, naturally you've got to call it quits. But one

thing certain is that everything you've done so far is superb. You mustn't spoil it all now by hoisting the white flag. You're overwhelmed, but there must be no surrender, no white flag."

Did Castries suddenly realize the extent of his blunder? Probably nobody will ever know, and General de Castries and Séguins-Pazzis will take their secret to the grave. What is striking about the recording of this conversation – and the copies I have heard have been cut at precisely this point – is Castries's embarrassment after Cogny's injunction and the argument he uses to justify himself. To justify himself for what if not for having hoisted the white flag?

"Ah! Very good, General," Castries replied after a pause, in a heart-broken voice. "It was just that I wanted to protect the wounded."

"Yes, I know. Then protect them as best you can, letting your [. . .] act on their own [. . .] What you've done is too fine to be spoilt like that. You understand, don't you?"

"Very good, General."

"Well, good-bye, fellow, see you soon."

There was no "*Vive la France!*" as the commander of the entrenched camp was reported saying. Radio operator Mélien, who was putting the signal through from an office near Castries's, concluded for the benefit of his opposite number in Hanoï, "The Viets are a few yards away. We're going to blow up the transmitter. So long, fellow."

The white flag which Sergeant Kubiak had seen flying over Castries's command post while Bigeard and Langlais were getting ready in their shelters to receive the Viets was hurriedly taken down.

Cogny informed Madame de Castries of the fall of Dien Bien Phu and asked her to keep the news secret. In Cogny's anteroom Mr. Hedberg, a journalist on the *Expressen*, was waiting.

There was the sound of feet running over the roof of the shelter. When Platoon Commander Chu ta Thé's squad reached the superstructure of Castries's command post at a gallop, did it unfold and wave the red flag with the gold star that day, or was the scene reconstructed later? On the French side, nobody knows. The only flag that Sergeant Kubiak saw flying over Castries's command post was the white one. He stated this in writing, and the official periodical of the Foreign Legion published his story in its issue of April, 1963, without anyone protesting.

When the Viets entered the command post and pushed aside the door curtain, Castries was waiting for them standing, unarmed, his sleeves rolled up. He had changed his shirt and trousers and, as usual, was wearing his medal ribbons. The parachutist Sergeant Passerat de Silans, who belonged to Langlais's signals section, maintains that at the sight of the submachine guns aimed at him Castries cried, "Don't shoot me." This doesn't sound like Castries, who may have said, in an attempt to change the squad's threatening attitude, "You damn fools, you aren't going to shoot, are you?"

Grauwin glanced toward the sap and caught sight of Castries, pale under his red forage cap, a cigarette between his lips, dazzled by the sunlight. He was promptly driven away in a jeep to be questioned by the Viet Military Intelligence. Did Grauwin also see, as he would subsequently write, Langlais, with his frozen, unseeing face, and Bigeard, his head bent under his beret, swept away in a crowd of prisoners? Langlais and Bigeard had come out together, without putting their hands up, but at a different time from Castries, whom they would not see again for ten days. Grauwin, his heart pounding, went down to the hospital. A Viet soldier, his legs covered with mud, his belt hung with grenades, appeared and gestured toward the sap.

"Outside!"

In the operating theater, where Lieutenant Gindrey of the medical service was bending over a torn body, men lay groaning on stretchers, waiting their turn. Followed by Geneviève de Galard and his medical orderlies, Grauwin came out onto the terreplein, where some wounded men, who had just been put down near some rotting corpses, watched him go by like salvation disappearing from sight.

In the vicinity of the command post, the Viets called for Langlais, who went toward them.

"That's me."

He was surrounded and Bigeard followed him, walking among his staff. The Viets also shouted, "Bigeard! . . . Where is Bigeard?"

His hands thrust deep into his pockets, Bigeard went on walking in the long column, anonymous and walled up in a silence from which he would not emerge for days, ready to seize the slightest opportunity to escape. They could look for the wolf Bigeard themselves. He carried nothing on him, not a single packet of cigarettes or tin of rations, while some prisoners were bent under suitcases stuffed with food. His faithful orderly, knowing what he was like, had taken a carton of Lucky Strikes for him from Castries's command post. No doubt Bigeard knew that he was down on the canvas, but he was already getting to his feet. The fight wasn't over. Nothing was over as long as life went on flowing through his veins. This business was not simply an affair between the West and the rebels, the Expeditionary Corps and the People's Army; it was a scrap between the Viets and himself. How had these little men, the youngest of whom looked like boys of fifteen and who had always avoided battle for fear of meeting their match, managed to win? How were fresh humiliations to be avoided in the future? What lessons were to be learned from this affair and from this army of ants which had fought on empty bellies but with their heads full of the ideas and the hope with which they had been crammed? These were the questions which haunted him. He, too, had heard the "Song of the Partisans" all night on the Viet wavelength. He felt sick at heart.

For the moment, shutting out everything around him, his shoulders hunched so as not to irritate anybody, he watched through half-closed eyes for any relaxation of the guards' supervision so he could escape into the mountains with a few companions, as Second Lieutenant Makowiak would do, reaching an outpost in Laos. From the generosity of the

People's Army, Bigeard expected nothing. Defeated, he would suffer the lot of the defeated, without ever accepting it. "Poor bastards." He kept repeating this insult to punish himself and the simpletons who had thought they were bound to win because their camp was stuffed with artillery and heavy machine guns and received supplies every day by air from Hanoï. Perhaps he remembered that at Agincourt, too, the French had despised the enemy and had prepared for battle with the same arrogant self-assurance. But above all else, there must be no tears such as he had seen on the faces of some of his comrades. Victory over the ants of the totalitarian regimes was won in other ways; as for the victory parade, led by a band through the streets of a capital, which some officers had vaguely dreamed of, once the Viets had been laid out in the barbed-wire entanglements, Bigeard laughed at the idea. Here it was, the victory planned by the staffs of the Expeditionary Corps and approved by the government. He did not know that in a few weeks the prisoners would be gathered together and made to march all day long, with bowed heads, in columns of eight, a procession of shame escorted by little men armed with automatic pistols, in front of the cameras of the Communist world; but when he was asked to take part in the reconstruction of the capture of the command post, he would reply, "I'd rather die." And the Viets would not insist.

If the Viets were calling for Bigeard everywhere, it was because they wanted to see at close quarters the wolf finally in captivity with the sheep. How could they recognize him with nothing to distinguish him from the men plodding like a procession of caterpillars toward the northeastern heights?

Under a sky suddenly empty of planes, the little group of doctors crossed the bridge. The last packages of the seventy tons which twenty-eight Dakotas had dropped during the morning were spread out; 105-mm. shells, food supplies, small arms, pharmaceutical products, canned milk, everything henceforth belonged to the victor. On the other bank the medical team was stopped and Grauwin was ordered to return to care for the wounded. Dr. Nguyen duong Quang had just inspected the hospital, which he had found far better equipped than his own; he had noted that the Vietminh soldiers were treated on an equal footing with the French. Touched by Grauwin's sadness, he had some coffee brought to him.

At 1755 a dispatch from Cogny asked Colonel Lalande at Isabelle to tell him his plans for the coming night. Lalande was still unaware that the main position had fallen. He learned it only at 1830 from the decoding of a message and the sudden opening of a bombardment which blew up his ammunition dumps, cut his telephone wires and set fire to his dressing station. After which the Vietminh radio told him on his own wavelength, "It is useless to go on fighting. The rest of the garrison are prisoners. Give yourselves up."

About 2000 hours, guided by the Thais who had not yet dared to desert and wanted to disappear into the country, the 12th Company of the 3rd Foreign tried to escape along the right bank, following the curves of the river. Radio contact was poor and it was difficult to follow its progress. From the firing which broke out, it was possible to locate more or less accurately the points where it had met Viet resistance. A little later, the 11th Company set off between the track and the left bank. About 2100 hours, silence seemed to indicate that it had succeeded. One by one, in the total darkness, all the units followed, laboriously extricating themselves from the barbed-wire entanglements and the muddy trenches. The noise of fighting came from the south, where the 57th Regiment was barring the way with one battalion on each side of the Nam Youm. At 2300 hours, Captain Hien, who with a third battalion was blocking the junction of the Nam Youm and the Nam Noua, where Route 41 met the track from Laos, was ordered to return. An attack created disorder among the bulk of the units, cut them off, split them up and overwhelmed them. Soldiers of the People's Army and the Expeditionary Corps mingled with one another. Voices shouted, "Don't shoot. You will be well treated." Colonel Lalande then decided to try to hold out on the spot and ordered his units to return to Isabelle, where utter confusion reigned.

In Paris, it was nearly five o'clock. M. Joseph Laniel, the Prime Minister, mounted the tribune of the National Assembly to announce, in a voice which he tried to keep steady, the fall of Dien Bien Phu. All the deputies, except those on the Communist benches, rose to their feet. The stupor of defeat suddenly weighed upon the city, where the papers were publishing dispatches which had arrived out of order, mutilated by the Saigon censorship. A special edition of *France-Soir* carried a banner headline spread over eight columns: "DIEN BIEN PHU HAS FALLEN." *Le Monde* announced that the plane of Bao Dai, who had been accused for some days of delaying the evacuation of the wounded by his stay on the Côte d'Azur, had narrowly escaped an accident. The weather was fine that Friday afternoon, and the chestnut trees in the Bois de Boulogne and along the quays were in flower. The theaters and movie houses would be open that evening as usual.

About one o'clock in the morning of May 8, a small group of French-speaking Viets waving a white flag advanced toward the command post of Isabelle. "Let us pass," they told the soldiers who stopped them. "We want to see your commander, Colonel Lalande." Colonel Lalande agreed to see these envoys, who told him, "All further resistance is useless. Don't be stubborn." Lalande then gave orders for a cease-fire.

For Bigeard and Langlais the darkness was falling, whereas it seemed to Captain Hien as if a long night had come to an end. Everywhere the news of the victory spread like wildfire from village to village. Professor Tung, on his way toward the hospitals in the rear, had learned it at 2000 hours. Already people were shouting, "It's all right. We know." The entrenched camp looked like a huge flea market where the victors were dividing their booty of bars of soap, flashlights and canned foods. Lights were shining in the basin, where there was no longer any fear of air raids which would kill as many French as Viets. Yet planes continued to fly over the region, ready to drop flares or bombs on the poor stars in the valley.

General Navarre's former aide-de-camp was marching with ten thousand prisoners toward the Tonkin camps. The Viets had tied his hands behind his back because he had refused to answer their questions. Throughout the world, where Waterloo had created less of a sensation, the fall of Dien Bien Phu had caused utter amazement. It was one of the greatest defeats ever suffered by the West, heralding the collapse of the colonial empires and the end of a republic. The thunder of the event rumbles on.

Death in the Rice Fields

Malcolm W. Browne

Browne reported the Vietnam War for AP and ABC, winning a
Pulitzer for journalism. Here he accompanies South Vietnamese forces on an anti-VC sweep in the Mekong Delta in 1961.

A drenching, predawn dew had settled over the sloping steel
deck of the landing craft, and I slipped several times climbing
aboard in the inky darkness.

Soldiers cursed sleepily as they heaved heavy mortar base
plates and machine guns from the pier onto their field packs
on the deck.

The night was still and moonless, and the air would have
been warm except for that unpleasant dew, sometimes laced
with raindrops. The French used to call it "spitting rain".

This was December, 1961, and I was going out for my
first look at an operation against the Viet Cong. There were
no American field advisors in those days (and no helicopters
and almost no communications), and I tried to stay close to
soldiers or officers who could speak French. Most of them
could.

The place was a town called Ben Tre in the heart of the
flat, fertile Mekong River Delta, about fifty miles south of
Saigon. Ben Tre, the capital of Kien Hoa Province, still takes
pride in the fact that it has produced some of Viet Nam's top
Communists. Ung Van Khiem, former Foreign Minister of
the Hanoi government, came from here. Kien Hoa is also
famous for its pretty girls.

It was about 4 a.m., and I was dead tired. I had been up late with the province chief, Colonel Pham Ngoc Thao, a cat-like man with short-cropped hair and a disconcerting walleye.

Thao had been an intelligence officer in the Viet Minh during the Indochina War, and had gone over to Diem after independence in 1954.

The night before, Thao had invited me to the opening of a theater he had had built in Ben Tre, and the curious town residents had turned out in their holiday best. The bill of fare was a traditional Vietnamese drama and some comedians, jugglers and singers. It lacked the glamour of a Broadway opening night, but it was about the fanciest thing Ben Tre had ever seen.

Two masked actors in ornate classical costume were inton-ing verses about a murder they were planning and the audience was murmuring expectantly when Thao leaned toward me.

"My troops are going out in the morning. We have intelli-gence that a battalion of Viet Cong is moving through one of my districts. I'm not going, but would you be interested?"

Just then, the action on stage reached a high point. Several actors in stilted, oriental poses were supposed to portray vio-lence, their brilliantly colored robes swishing. Applause rushed through the theater, and children put down their pop bottles to chatter. Thao, obviously pleased, warmly joined the applause.

He always liked the theater. A year or so later, when Diem sent him on a special mission to the States, he made a special point of visiting Hollywood, where he was photographed with actress Sandra Dee. The picture was sent back to Viet Nam by news agencies, but Diem's censors prohibited its publication, presumably because they felt it would be detri-mental to fighting spirit.

The three hundred or so troops on the pier that morning were an odd-looking bunch, a mixture of civil guards and self-defense corpsmen. Some were in neat fatigue uniforms with helmets, others in the loose, black garb of the Vietnamese peasant, topped with old French bush hats. There were no troops from the regular army on this operation. The commander was a crusty, French-trained captain with several rows of combat ribbons on his faded olive drab uniform.

The diesel engines of the three landing craft carrying our makeshift task force belched oily smoke and we were moving, the black silhouettes of palm trees sliding past along the edges of the narrow canal. Here and there a dot of light glimmered through the trees from some concealed cluster of huts.

For a few minutes, the commander studied a map with a neat plastic overlay, making marks with red and black grease pencils, under the light of a pocket flashlight.

One of the few things Western military men have taught Vietnamese officers to do really well is mark up maps. The Vietnamese officer studies his sector map like a chessboard. Even if he has only a squad or two of men under his command, he uses all the ornate symbols of the field commander in marking his deployment on maps. This love of maps has often infuriated American advisors, who feel more time should be spent acting and less on planning.

After a while the light flicked out. A few of the troops were smoking silently, but most had arranged their field packs as pillows and had gone to sleep amid the clutter of weapons. We were not scheduled to reach our objective until several hours after sunrise.

I finally dropped off to sleep, and must have been asleep about an hour when a grinding lurch and the sound of splintering wood roused me.

It was still pitch dark, but people were screaming, and on the deck of the landing craft, troops were rushing around. In the darkness, we had somehow collided with and sunk a large crowded sampan. Twenty or thirty sleeping occupants had been thrown into the canal, with all their worldly possessions. A few of them apparently were hurt.

The two other landing craft were chugging on down the canal, but we had stopped. Troops holding ropes were helping swing the people in the water over to the shore. When everyone had reached safety, we started up again, people still yelling at us in the distance. We must have destituted several large families at a blow, but there was no thought of getting their names so that they could be compensated by the government. I couldn't help feeling that their feelings for the government must be less than cordial.

The sky began to turn gray, and at last we left the maze of narrow canals and turned into a branch of the great Mekong itself.

The sun rose hot and red, its reflection glaring from the sluggish expanse of muddy water. We were moving slowly ("We don't want to make too much engine noise or the Viet Cong will hear us coming," the commander told me), and the dense wall of palm trees on both banks scarcely seemed to move at all.

It was nearly 9 a.m. when our little flotilla abruptly turned at right angles to the left, each vessel gunning its engines. We had reached the objective and were charging in for the beach. As we neared the shore we could see that the beach actually was a mud flat leading back about fifty yards to the palm trees, and it would be arduous hiking getting ashore.

The other two landing craft were going ashore about one mile farther up the river. The idea of this exercise, it was explained to me, was to seize two sets of hamlets running back from the river front, trapping the reported Viet Cong battalion in the wide expanse of rice fields in between.

We slammed into the mud, and the prow of our clumsy ship clanked down to form a ramp. We leapt into waist-deep water and mud and began the charge toward higher ground.

If the Viet Cong had even one machine gun somewhere in the tree line, they certainly could have killed most of us with no danger of encountering serious fire from us. Each step in that smelly ooze was agonizingly slow, and at times both feet would get mired. Little soldiers carrying heavy mortars and machine guns sank nearly to their necks. It happened that no one was shooting at us that day.

The first squads clambered up to high ground and began

firing. Two light machine guns began thumping tracers across the open rice field, and mortars began lobbing shells at random. Individual soldiers with Tommy guns (I was surprised how many of our group were equipped with submachine guns) were emptying their magazines into a string of huts or into the field. Off a mile or so to our right, noises told us that our companion party was similarly employed. It really sounded like a war.

I was standing on a high path running parallel to the river near a machine-gun position, looking out over the field where our Viet Cong battalion was supposed to be trapped. The green rice was nearly waist high, and there might easily be a battalion concealed in this field for all anyone knew.

Suddenly, a man leapt up about fifty yards away and began to run. This was it!

Every machine gun, Tommy gun, rifle and pistol in our sector poured fire at that man, and I was amazed at how long he continued to run. But finally he went down, silently, without a scream.

Our little army continued to pour intense fire into the field and several huts until it occurred to someone that no one was shooting back, and it might be safe to move forward a little.

Some of the troops began to move into the huts, shooting as they went.

Near me was a cluster of five Dan Ve (local Self-Defense Corpsmen) dressed in ragged black uniforms with American pistol belts and rusty French rifles. The group was detailed to go into the field to look for the man we had seen go down, and I went with them.

We found him on his back in the mud, four bullet holes stitched across the top of his naked chest. He was wearing only black shorts. He was alive and conscious, moving his legs and arms, his head lolling back and forth. There was blood on his lips.

The Dan Ve squad, all young peasant boys, looked down at the man and laughed, perhaps in embarrassment. Laughter in Viet Nam does not always signify amusement.

Perhaps as an act of mercy, perhaps as sheer cruelty, one of the men picked up a heavy stake lying in the mud and rammed one end of it into the ground next to the wounded man's throat. Then he forced the stake down over the throat, trying to throttle the man. The man continued to move. Someone stamped on the free end of the stake to break the wounded man's neck, but the stake broke instead. Then another man tried stamping on the man's throat, but somehow the spark of life still was too strong. Finally, the whole group laughed, and walked back to the path.

The firing had stopped altogether, and several old peasant men were talking to the officers of our party. Two of the old men had a pole and a large fish net.

The peasants – I think they were hamlet elders – walked out to the wounded man, rolled him into the fish net, and with the net slung between them on the pole, carried him back to the path. As they laid him out on the ground, two women, both dressed in baggy black trousers and blouses, ran up from one of the huts. One of them put a hand to her mouth as she saw the wounded man, whom she recognized as her husband.

She dashed back to her hut and returned in a moment carrying a bucket, which she filled with black water from the rice field. Sitting down with her husband's head cradled in her lap, she poured paddy water over his wounds to clean off the clotting blood. Occasionally she would stroke his forehead, muttering something.

He died about ten minutes later. The woman remained seated, one hand over her husband's eyes. Slowly, she looked around at the troops, and then she spotted me. Her eyes fixed on me in an expression that still haunts me sometimes. She was not weeping, and her face showed neither grief nor fury; it was unfathomably blank.

I moved away some distance to where the operation commander was jabbering into a field telephone. When his conversation ended, I handed him a 500-piastre note (worth about $5.00), asking him to give it to the widow as some small compensation.

"Monsieur Browne, please do not be sentimental. That man undoubtedly was a Viet Cong agent, since these hamlets have been Viet Cong strongholds for years. This is war. However, I will give her the money, if you like."

I don't know what happened to that money, and I didn't go near the place where the woman was sitting, but I walked into the hut I had seen her leave.

It was typical of thousands of Mekong Delta huts I have seen. The framework was bamboo, and the sides and roof were made of dried, interlaced palm fronds with a layer of rice straw thatch on top. The floor was hardened earth. A large, highly polished wooden table stood near the door. Peasants eat their meals on these tables, sleep on them and work on them. There were four austerely simple chairs. In a corner were several knee-high earthen crocks filled with drinking water. Just inside the door was the family altar, extending all the way to the ceiling. Pinned to it were yellowed photographs and some fancy Chinese calligraphy. On a little shelf a sand pot containing incense sticks smoldered fragrant fumes.

To the right, from behind a woven bamboo curtain, two children were peering with wide eyes. The eyes were the only expressive elements in their blank, silent little faces. Incongruously, one of them was standing next to a gaily painted yellow rocking horse, one rocker of which was freshly splintered by a bullet hole.

I walked out of the hut and down the path. By now, troops were strung all along the path between the two hamlets about a mile apart, and were stringing telephone wire and performing other military chores.

Snaking through the palm trees, a water-filled ditch about twenty feet across obstructed my progress. But a few yards away, a soldier had commandeered a small sampan from an old woman and was ferrying troops back and forth. I went across with him. As I continued down the path, scores of mud walls about five feet high obstructed progress. All were obviously freshly built, and most had gun slots. It was strange that no one had decided to defend these good emplacements against us.

I came to a small hut straddling the path, consisting only of upright bamboo spars and a roof. The little building was festooned with painted banners, the largest of which read "*Da Dao My-Diem*" ("Down with US-Diem"). A group of young women were dismantling the hut as soldiers trained rifles at them. I was told that this was a Viet Cong "information center".

Finally, the troops began moving out from the tree line into the field itself, converging from three sides: the two hamlets and the path itself. The battle would come now, if ever.

We moved single file along the tops of the dykes that divided the field into an immense checkerboard. The thought struck me that if there were guerrillas hiding in the tall rice we would make fine targets as we moved along, but no one seemed worried.

Progress was slow. The mud dykes were slippery as grease, and every time a soldier toppled into the muddy paddy, the whole column halted as he was pulled out. I was reminded somehow of the White Knight in Lewis Carroll's *Through the Looking Glass*. Superficially, we combed the field from one end to the other, our various forces finally meeting in the middle.

A little L19 spotter plane droned overhead, radioing what was no doubt useful information to the ground commander.

It would be difficult to search that field more completely than we did, and we found not the slightest trace of a human being. Of course, the rice could easily have concealed a thousand or even ten thousand guerrillas, without our knowing.

Viet Cong guerrillas have developed the art of camouflage to an incredible degree. In rice fields, they often remain completely submerged under the muddy water for hours, breathing through straws.

But by now the sun stood like a blast furnace in the sky, and the troops were tired. A few had tied to their packs live ducks and chickens they had pilfered from the hamlets, and were looking around for level ground on which to prepare lunch.

"It looks as though the Viet Cong got away again," the commander told me. "It's time to go. It's not a good idea to be moving around out here when the sun starts going down."

By noon, three hundred mud-drenched, tired troops were boarding the landing craft, and silence had settled over the hamlets again. We had suffered one wounded – a Civil Guard who had stepped on a spike trap, which had pierced his foot.

The three landing craft churned their way out into deep water, and the tension disappeared. Soldiers lighted cigarettes, talked and laughed, and spread their sopping clothing on the deck to dry.

All of them had a warm feeling of accomplishment, of having done a hard day's work under the cruel sun. The irregularity in the palm-lined shore that marked our hamlet receded into the distance.

And I couldn't help thinking of the old travelogues that end, "And so we leave the picturesque Mekong River Delta, palm trees glimmering under a tropic sun, and happy natives on the shore bidding us 'aloha.' "

Tonkin Gulf: Eyewitness

James Stockdale

The Tonkin Gulf incident led to America's unofficial declaration of war against Vietnam. James Stockdale was the commanding officer of Fighter Squadron 51, flying off the USS *Ticonderoga*. He was involved in a shoot out with Vietnamese PT boats on 2 August 1964; he was in the air again on 4 August, the day of the fake "Tonkin Gulf Incident", which gave Washington the pretext for war.

I had the best seat in the house, orbiting a few hundred feet above the two American destroyers, clear of the surface haze and spray that their crews' eyeballs and radars had to penetrate. And when, after a couple of hours, it came to light that no American eyeball, from the air or from the destroyers, had ever detected a PT boat or a wake or a gunflash, a steady stream of messages emanated from that same destroyer commodore who had sent the first [alert of a possible attack]: "Wait, there may have been a mistake, take no action until we have proof. Hold your horses." . . .

The whole scene was loaded for misinterpretation. You had people in Washington who had passed up the opportunity for a show of force two days before. You had a frustrated President who was getting heat on the back channels from Maxwell Taylor and the then current head of state in Saigon – heat for passing up that chance. You had a President who felt inferior and ill at ease in the office, and who had bearing down on him from behind in a hot presidential campaign,

Barry Goldwater, whose main plank was that Johnson was soft on Vietnam. And so when the messages started to come in saying that there was a second Tonkin Gulf event, he was elated because here was the reprieve: "My God, two days ago I made an ass of myself and now I can recover and win the election and happy days are here again."

... The visibility from the deck of the destroyers was nowhere near as good as it was for me circling around at a thousand feet, surveying the whole area. They later found sailors who claimed to have seen sparkling things in the water, but most of those "sparkling things" sightings were dreamed up a couple of days later, when re-debriefings were conducted after a message from Washington demanded "proof." I know of no responsible person who considers them anything but bunk. Two days before, I'd led the attack against real boats in the daytime and I saw my bullets hit them and even in bright sunlight I could see sparks as they glanced off. I could see their wakes were wider and more pronounced than the destroyers' wakes. Their guns flashed. People say, "Wasn't it a dark night?" Yes, it was dark as hell and that's why I could see so well. The wake would have been luminous. The ricochets would have been sparkling, the gunfire of the PT boats would have been red and bright. I'm sure I'd have seen anything within five miles of those boats during the hour and a half that I was there. No question about it.

No boats were there and when I got back to the ship, the commander of the destroyers had come to the same conclusion. He [cabled Washington,] "Please don't take any rash action until you verify this." In other words, a plea to disregard the [earlier] messages he'd been sending – that weather conditions, the sonar operator's lack of skill and other things had rendered the question wide open and not to take action on it. These cables were part of the same three-hour continuum. And Washington had those in their hands for twelve hours and I'm sure that important people were seeing them. They had twelve hours to change their minds and it still went on.

I went to bed laughing that night. I was very tired and I was laughing in relief. I'd nearly flown into the water and killed myself trying to find these boats. It was the third flight I'd had in one day, it was after midnight, and on the way out there I thought we were going to war and I'd said, "My God, I'm going to be telling my grandchildren about this night." And I finally realized there was nothing to find and came back and they read me the messages that had passed from the destroyers to Washington saying the same thing. And they also sent in my reports. Everybody was saying, "Well, that was the goddamnedest mess we've ever been in. Let's have a cup of coffee and forget about it." If this had happened in the nineteenth century, before radios, that would have been the end of it.

And then I was awakened about two hours later by a young officer and told that they have received word from Washington that we're going to retaliate. And I said, "Retaliate for what?" And he said, "For last night's attack." He didn't know any better. Well, I sat there on the edge of the bed realizing that I was one of the few people in the world that realized we were going to launch a war under false pretenses. And sure enough, the next day we did.

I led this big horde of airplanes over there and we blew the oil tanks clear off the map . . .

Now it is very important to understand that there was a tinderbox situation in the Western Pacific that was probably going to precipitate war, and a person might say, "What's all the fuss about. It was going to happen anyway, what is so wrong about picking the opportune time to trigger it? No big thing." But there is such a thing as moral leverage, which tilts the argument in the other direction. The Communists have a great nose for moral leverage. Any good bargainer knows the balance of authority has tipped when the other guy has performed some act of which he might be ashamed. And in the case of starting wars it is very, very important that you have that moral leverage behind you.

A leader who starts a war must face the fact that there will later be many times when he wishes he could get out of that war. Because as the caskets move by and grief emerges there is going to be a great temptation, unless he is just an Adolf Hitler, to get out of that. And "to get out of that" that way is a worse mistake usually than getting into it, because it lets everybody down, just like McNamara and Johnson bailed out and left a whole generation of Americans over there to pick up after them.

I'm a warrior and you can see I'm a hawk, but I'm going to tell you that when you get into a war you've got to be very sure that you are on honest, solid rock foundations or it's going to eat you alive. In a real war, you just cannot risk losing moral leverage, which he [Johnson] did. There was no question that Washington knew what they had done and not a lot of question about them knowing it as they did it. . . .

I could have sulked or resigned but I didn't. I would have been ground up like an ant. There would have been no satisfaction in being a martyr. Anyway, I told them what the truth was. A message went out from the ship to Washington right after I had landed, saying that I had seen no boats. But it was a great learning experience. I was forty-one and growing up. I had always thought the government worked just like Poli. Sci. One and Two said it did. And now I realized that this was a goddamned fiasco and I was a part of it. And I thought, "Well, live and learn. This is the way the ballgame is played."

The Tonkin Gulf resolution passed on August 7. That was two days after the flight I'm talking about. And the State Department said that was the functional equivalent of a declaration of war. But it passed on the coat-tails of the second – the false – incident. And McGeorge Bundy later said that Johnson was so much a child of Congress that when he got the resolution he thought the war was over. If Congress was behind him, then it was just a matter of waiting for the curtain to fall.

He signed that thing on August 11. And that day we read

at the breakfast table that the Harris poll showed LBJ's popularity jumped fourteen percentage points. And just before noon that same day I was sitting at my desk doing paperwork when suddenly the ship's yodel-horn blared the welcome-aboard honors appropriate for a vice admiral. I remember wondering how that happened out there in the middle of the ocean. And then the phone rang. It was Captain Hutch Cooper. He said, "Jim, a couple of guys just came aboard and say they want to talk to you. I'll send them down with an escort." There were two guys in sports shirts and slacks, one about my age and the other younger. The older one introduced himself as Jack Stempler, special assistant to Secretary McNamara. And he said, "The day before yesterday, I was down with my family at the cottage at Nag's Head. About four in the afternoon I was walking back to the beach and what do I see but a government staff car in the driveway. I was to go right to Washington. So I picked up a bag and away we went. We were sent out here just to find out one thing. Were there any fuckin' boats out there the other night or not?" And this is four hours after they'd signed the "declaration of war."

Below are the US President's Address to Congress of August 5, 1964, and the resultant "Tonkin Gulf Resolution":

Text of Joint Resolution, August 7, Department of State Bulletin, 24 August 1964.

"To promote the maintenance of international peace and security in Southeast Asia.

"Whereas naval units of the communist regime in Vietnam, in violation of the principles of the Charter of the United Nations and of international law, have deliberately and repeatedly attacked United States naval vessels lawfully present in international waters, and have thereby created a serious threat to international peace; and

"Whereas these attacks are part of a deliberate and systematic campaign of aggression that the communist regime in North Vietnam has been waging against its neighbors and the nations joined with them in the collective defense of their freedom; and

"Whereas the United States is assisting the peoples of Southeast Asia to protect their freedom and has no territorial, military or political ambitions in that area, but desires only that these peoples should be left in peace to work out their own destinies in their own way: Now, therefore, be it

"*Resolved by the Senate and House of Representatives of the United States of America in Congress assembled,* That the Congress approves and supports the determination of the President, as Commander in Chief, to take all necessary measures to repel any armed attack against the forces of the United States and to prevent further aggression.

"Sec. 2. The United States regards as vital to its national interest and to world peace the maintenance of international peace and security in Southeast Asia. Consonant with the Constitution of the United States and the Charter of the United Nations and in accordance with its obligations under the Southeast Asia Collective Defense Treaty, the United States is, therefore, prepared, as the President determines, to take all necessary steps, including the use of armed force, to assist any member or protocol state of the Southeast Asia Collective Defense Treaty requesting assistance in defense of its freedom.

"Sec. 3. This resolution shall expire when the President shall determine that the peace and security of the area is reasonably assured by international conditions created by action of the United Nations or otherwise, except that it may be terminated earlier by concurrent resolution of the Congress."

PRESIDENT'S MESSAGE TO CONGRESS, AUGUST 5, 1964

To the Congress of the United States:

Last night I announced to the American people that the North Vietnamese regime had conducted further deliberate attacks against U.S. naval vessels operating in international waters, and therefore directed air action against gunboats and supporting facilities used in these hostile operations. This air action has now been carried out with substantial damage to the boats and facilities. Two U.S. aircraft were lost in the action.

After consultation with the leaders of both parties in the Congress, I further announced a decision to ask the Congress for a resolution expressing the unity and determination of the United States in supporting freedom and in protecting peace in southeast Asia.

These latest actions of the North Vietnamese regime have given a new and grave turn to the already serious situation in southeast Asia. Our commitments in that area are well known to the Congress. They were first made in 1954 by President Eisenhower. They were further defined in the Southeast Asia Collective Defense Treaty approved by the Senate in February 1955.

This treaty with its accompanying protocol obligates the United States and other members to act in accordance with their constitutional processes to meet Communist aggression against any of the parties or protocol states.

Our policy in southeast Asia has been consistent and unchanged since 1954. I summarized it on June 2 in four simple propositions:

1. *America keeps her word.* Here as elsewhere, we must and shall honor our commitments.
2. *The issue is the future of southeast Asia as a whole.* A

threat to any nation in that region is a threat to all, and a threat to us.

3. *Our purpose is peace.* We have no military, political, or territorial ambitions in the area.

4. *This is not just a jungle war, but a struggle for freedom on every front of human* activity. Our military and economic assistance to South Vietnam and Laos in particular has the purpose of helping these countries to repel aggression and strengthen their independence.

The threat to the three nations of southeast Asia has long been clear. The North Vietnamese regime has constantly sought to take over South Vietnam and Laos. This Communist regime has violated the Geneva accords for Vietnam. It has systematically conducted a campaign of subversion, which includes the direction, training, and supply of personnel and arms for the conduct of guerrilla warfare in South Vietnamese territory. In Laos, the North Vietnamese regime has maintained military forces, used Laotian territory for infiltration into South Vietnam, and most recently carried out combat operations – all in direct violation of the Geneva agreements of 1962.

In recent months, the actions of the North Vietnamese regime have become steadily more threatening. In May, following new acts of Communist aggression in Laos, the United States undertook reconnaissance flights over Laotian territory, at the request of the Government of Laos. These flights had the essential mission of determining the situation in territory where Communist forces were preventing inspection by the International Control Commission. When the Communists attacked these aircraft, I responded by furnishing escort fighters with instructions to fire when fired upon. Thus, these latest North Vietnamese attacks on our naval vessels are not the first direct attack on armed forces of the United States.

As President of the United States I have concluded that I should now ask the Congress on its part, to join in affirming the national determination that all such attack swill be met, and that the United States will continue in its basic policy of assisting the free nations of the area to defend their freedom.

As I have repeatedly made clear, the United States intends no rash-ness, and seeks no wider war. We must make it clear to all that the United States is united in its determination to bring about the end of Communist subversion and aggression in the area. We seek the full and effective restoration of the international agreements signed in Geneva in 1954, with respect to South Vietnam, and again in Geneva in 1962, with respect to Laos.

I recommend a resolution expressing the support of the Congress for all necessary action to protect our Armed Forces and to assist nations covered by the SEATO Treaty. At the same time, I assure the Congress that we shall continue readily to explore any avenues of political solution that will effectively guarantee the removal of Communist subversion and the preservation of the independence of the nations of the area.

The resolution could well be based upon similar resolutions enacted by the Congress in the past – to meet the threat to Formosa in 1955, to meet the threat to the Middle East in 1957, and to meet the threat in Cuba in 1962. It could state in the simplest terms the resolve and support of the Congress for action to deal appropriately with attacks against our Armed Forces and to defend freedom and preserve peace in southeast Asia in accordance with the obligations of the United States under the Southeast Asia Treaty. I urge the Congress to enact such a resolution promptly and thus to give convincing evidence to the aggressive Communist nations, and to the world as a whole, that our policy in southeast Asia will be carried forward – and that the peace and security of the area will be preserved.

The events of this week would in any event have made the passage of a congressional resolution essential. But there is an additional reason for doing so at a time when we are entering on 3 months of political campaigning. Hostile nations must understand that in such a period the United States will continue to protect its national interests, and that in these matters there is no division among us.

One to Count Cadence

Pfc James Crumley

Crumley (1939–2008) was born in Texas, and served for three years as an enlisted man in the US Army. Below is an extract from his novel *One to Count Cadence*. The setting is the Clark Air Force Base in the Philippines, where the 721st Communication Security Detachment is being trained preparatory to deployment in Vietnam.

TETRICK'S ADMONITION TO STEP EASILY with Lt. Dottlinger commanding the Company proved all too correct. During the set of days after my lengthy initiation into the seminal rites of Town, a small incident, the breaking of four cases of bottles, touched off the events known as The Great Coke Bottle Mystery, or Slag Krummel Rides, Howsoever Badly, Again.

It was a Wednesday or Thursday morning – without the limits of an established weekend period of rest, we seldom knew the day of the week. Lt. Dottlinger always checked the Day Room first thing each morning. He counted the pool cues and balls, and the shuffleboard pucks, examined the felt of the pool tables for new nicks or tears, and made sure the Coke machine was full. These things were nominally his responsibility since the equipment had been purchased from the Company Fund and the Coke machine was a concession of the Fund. All seemed well until he felt a bit of glass crunch under his spit-shined shoe. He picked it up, and found it to be the lip ring off the rim of a bottle. He knew the trick: two rims hooked together, then jerk, and a neat little ring of glass pops off one or both. He didn't see any others at first, but when he examined the trash in the houseboy's dust bucket, he found dozens of rings. Also, he noted, there were hundreds of cigarette butts, in spite of his standing orders against extinguishing them on the Day Room floor. He checked the four cases of empties. All except for one had been broken. Dottlinger took the dust bucket and dumped its contents in a neat pile in front of the innocently humming Coke machine. He shooed the houseboy out, closed and locked the double doors opening to the outside passageway, unplugged the Coke machine, which burped twice like a drunken private in ranks, rolled shut the louvers on both walls, turned off the lights, then locked the entrance from the Orderly Room.

He took the pass box from the 1st Sgt's desk and placed it in his desk which he always kept locked. Then he called the Criminal Investigation Division.

The CID officer who came was a heavy Negro captain in a baggy suit and 1930s snap-brim hat which shouted "Copper!" He nodded his head when Lt. Dottlinger explained the situation and showed him the evidence, but said nothing. The CID man dusted part of one case of bottles at Lt. Dottlinger's insistence. There were over two hundred partial, smudged and clear prints on them. When Lt. Dottlinger demanded that he run a check on the prints, the CID officer shook his head and said, "Lieutenant, they are Coke bottles. For treason, perhaps even for a murder, I might be able to run the ten thousand or so prints on those bottles, but for Coke bottles . . . sorry about that." He shrugged and left. Tetrick heard Lt. Dottlinger mumble, "Damned nigger cops. Can't expect them to understand the value of property."

Shortly before noon a notice was posted on the bulletin board. There would be no passes pending confession of the bottle-breaker.

In theory mass punishment is against the Uniform Code of Military Justice but since a pass is a privilege rather than a right, it can be denied at any time for no reason.

Most of the men were extremely annoyed at first, but they quickly settled down, thinking, as did Lt. Dottlinger, that the guilty party would confess. During those first few days they found it almost refreshing not to be able to go to Town. They had the Airman's Club and the Silver Wing Service Club to pass the nights, or they could bowl or go to the gym or the library. A new, exciting kind of party evolved in the large storm ditches on the edge of the Company Area, called Champagne Ditch Parties. Mumm's was cheap at the Club and did not count on the liquor ration. The ditches were concrete lined, about five feet deep and shaped like an inverted trapezoid. A man could sit in the bottom, lean back and drink Mumm's from a crystal glass, and hope it didn't rain if he passed out. A kid from Trick One broke both arms trying to broad jump a ditch one night, but took little of the fun out of the parties.

So they did these things for one, two, then three weeks, but no one ever came forward. I noticed that Morning who had been the loudest and longest griper at first seemed to be resigned to the lack of Town. By the end of the fourth week the only hope was the return of Capt. Saunders. Tetrick had given up trying to persuade Lt. Dottlinger, and had taken to playing golf three afternoons a week, drunk before the tenth tee. The men were quiet, but uneasily so. They, like Morning, had stopped talking about it. They gathered shamelessly around the older dependent girls at the pool; they who had vowed to a man at one drunken time or another never to sully their hands on a leech. Even Novotny shouted from the high diving board, strutted his brown body before them and let them pity his scarred leg. He had taken an eighteen-year-old one to the movie one night, but Trick Two was waiting in ambush and hooted him out of the theater. "There are some things a man just doesn't do," Cagle snorted when Novotny complained to him.

Every room had its personal copies of *Playboy*, and they were closely guarded. Closed doors were respected with a warning knock, and men took alternate cubicles in the latrine out of deference to the *Playboy* readers. All the seed which heretofore had been cast into the bellies of whores, now flushed down larger, wetter holes, until it was a wonder that the sewage system didn't clog or give birth.

I kept busy during this time, helping the sergeant from the Agency outfit who was going to coach the football team draw up plays and practice routines. He had asked me to coach the line as well as play. Tetrick and I had tried to go to Town twice. Both times we ended up at old movies and felt guilty for two days afterward. Oddly enough I had the best run of luck I had ever seen during this month. I won over seven hundred fifty dollars in four nights at the NCO Club playing poker, then went to Manila with Tetrick and took out three thousand pesos shooting craps at the Key Club while a quiet, fat Filipino dropped ten thousand on the back line against my string of thirteen straight passes. He looked as if he wanted to kill me when I quit after thirteen. But still I didn't have enough money to get passes for the men.

Then word came that Capt. Saunders was going to take a month's leave after the school. That meant another six weeks without Town, and that was unbearable for the men. It is one thing to be a soldier, to live in a world of close order drill, of Physical Training each morning, equipment maintenance, maneuvers, training lectures, and another thing to be a clerk, a changer of typewriter ribbons, a cleaner of keys. Being a soldier gives you the feeling of accomplishment no matter how stupid you think the whole idea is: you survive in spite of everything they can do to you. Being a clerk has all the stupidities, all the same injustices as being a soldier, but none of the pride: anyone can survive being a clerk. It is the same problem which attacks men on assembly lines and in paper-shuffling office jobs when they discover that their life is as senseless as their work. They take to the bottle, join lodges, coach little league teams, have an affair – anything to forget what they are. The men in the 721st had Town to cover all these areas of memory-killing. Oh, sure, some of them made their tours in the Philippines on library books, camera trips and butterfly collections, but most needed Town. That is why it was there. And Lt. Dottlinger had taken it away. So what happened had to happen. (Or at least I like to tell myself that it did.)

If Morning had come to me with his idea in the beginning, I would have, as he so aptly noted, stopped him, but he came near the end, when it was ready for enactment, and it was too late to stop him.

He came in my room the night before the mass confession, grinning and excited, popping his fingers and pushing his glasses back up on his nose. "We got him," he said, opening my door without knocking.

"Who?"

"Slutfuckingfinger, man. Lt. Big Butt Dottlinger. Pinned to the wall by his mangy cock. Betrayed by his own words."

"What? Who? . . ."

"I got every one of them, man, every last swinging dick." He danced around my room as if he needed to pee.

"Wait a minute. Slow down. Sit down and let me know who has got whom where."

He swung a chair in front of the bunk, straddled it, and said, "The man said, 'No passes until the guilty one confesses.' Right? Right! Tomorrow he is going to confess."

"You know who it is?"

"No, but it doesn't make any difference."

"You elected a savior to sacrifice?" I laughed. I wondered who.

"No." He smiled and rubbed his thighs as if he had a magnificent secret. "Tomorrow morning at 0700, beginning with the day-trick before it goes to work and ending with the mid-trick, every enlisted man in the Operations section will go see the commanding officer and confess . . ."

"Don't tell me. Not another word."

"What do you mean? We got that son of a motherfucker dead. Dropped him down, man."

"Don't tell me. Jesus, Morning," I said, getting off the bunk. "This kind of crap is . . . damnit, it's mutiny or inciting to mutiny or conspiring to mutiny or something. I don't know the name, but I do know it is Leavenworth talk. Don't you know that? Goddamn don't tell me. I don't want to know. I can't know. Get the hell out of here. Now!"

"What's with you? He can't touch a hair on our heads. He hasn't got the guts to court martial the whole outfit, and he can't get me unless somebody breaks."

"Morning, don't you understand, somebody will shit out. Somebody will! Somebody always does. Even a single trick couldn't pull this off, much less forty men. They're going to send you to jail, babe, forever."

"Somebody shits, they get busted!" He popped his fingers loudly, and I knew it would happen. There was no doubt in his voice. "Besides, it will never get that far. Dottlinger will blow his stack, hit an enlisted man or have a heart attack or something. I go in first, and you know how he hates me, and he hasn't got the brains to think that I've got the guts to organize this and still go in first. He thinks I'm crazy."

"What if he takes just you."

"So fucking what? I only have one stripe to lose for my country."

"But what about . . ." I moaned, waving my arm in the general direction of heaven and hell. "Do any of the other trick chiefs know?"

"You're not even supposed to know. But I thought you'd want to."

"How sweet. I don't know! I don't know you! Get your ass out of here!" I took the cigarette he offered. "At Leavenworth, kid, they got even a literary magazine, but no women, no beer, but lots of walls. You won't like it there."

"It'll work. What are you afraid of? It will work."

"Don't tell me. I don't want it to work. I hope you guys never get your passes back. Never. You're all crazy. I hope they lock you up forever. Jesus, what a mess. Don't do it. Don't do it."

"What!" he shouted. "And let that half-assed Arkansas farmer do this to us. Man, we have to fight back, and now!

What kind of men are we if we let him do this to us and we don't fight back."

"Write your congressman. Consult the chaplain. Shit in the air. But don't try to fight the Army. Don't." . . .

. . . Only Joe Morning had the personality, the voice and the gall to convince so many men to even agree to such madness, much less carry it out. But he did it. He talked in private to every enlisted man in the Operations section, and then hit them again with a band of converts. I learned from Novotny that Morning had first mentioned the idea during the wee hours of a ditch party, but only mentioned it. Then the next day, when everyone had forgotten, he spoke about it again in the back of the three-quarter going to work, and then again coming back. He convinced Novotny in a long talk that night. Quinn and Franklin wondered why they hadn't thought of such a great idea. Cagle was ready for anything. The rest of the Trick was easy to convince. Once he had the Trick, he had their close friends on the other tricks, then their buddies, then the whole damned Company. That they only had to use physical persuasion on two men is an indication of the mood of the Company. And keeping it quiet was even easier, since the men were already security conscious because of the work.

It was beautiful and funny and I loved and feared the whole idea, but stayed in my room, sleeping with the door locked, while it took place.

I was blasted out about midmorning by Lt. Dottlinger on the handle of a bull horn. It was so loud I didn't understand what had been screamed, and I charged out in my shorts, thinking partly of Pearl Harbor and partly of a public execution. Lt. Dottlinger stood at my end of the hall calmly announcing, "Company formation in fifteen minutes!" He had known what was up when he opened the door to Morning and saw the line, but he didn't say anything. He had already given a blanket permission for anyone knowing anything about the broken bottles to see him without going through the 1st Sgt.

He let them all in, asked questions about the bottles, made notes, and took names. Outside Tetrick was racing up and down the line, bald, sweat-shining head in hands, pleading with them to break it up and go away before they were all killed. He remembered a pile of heads he had seen in Burma left by the Japanese. But Lt. Dottlinger was calm and controlled through it all, though his control must have been the absolute hold which marks the final stage of hysteria. He quietly ordered each man back to his quarters after the interview. The men in the back of the line were frightened, as well they might have been, by this quiet approach of the lieutenant's. Many might have broken line, but Morning, intrepid, wily Joe Morning, had placed men he could trust on either side of those he couldn't; and he knew just exactly which were which. But he hadn't counted on Lt. Dottlinger's anger taking this form. More than men have hung on the nature of another man's mood in the morning. When I saw Lt. Dottlinger in the hall, speaking pleasantly into the electric megaphone like a daytime television game-show announcer, I knew Morning's plans had failed. I wondered what was going to happen, as I got into uniform; I should have wondered who was going to pay. When Lt. Dottlinger had first seen me in the hall, he had smiled, nodded, and said, "Good morning, Sgt. Krummel." How little he knew.

The Company had been assembled on the volleyball court between the barracks and the drainage ditches for nearly an hour before Lt. Dottlinger came out. He was walking from the waist down, a smug, arrogant strut like Brando in *The Wild One*. Ah, he was loose. I thought for a moment he might mumble too, but he had added an English undertone to his Southern accent to strut a bit more. He accepted Tetrick's "Hall pre'nt an' 'counted for, sir," with a salute of languid grace. I wanted to laugh. But it would have been a nervous giggle. I, the whole Company too, was caught by that creepy version of fear which only comes when you're faced with someone who is crazy. It isn't so much that you're frightened that you might come to physical harm, but that you're faced with something not human anymore. You don't know what it is, and you don't care because you realize what it isn't, and you can only run and run until you wipe the face of insanity from the deepest regions of your memory; but as you run, you understand that some unsuspecting night you will dream that tormented, twisted face, and wake, oh my God, scream for the savior you had forgotten, and scream again, for the face is yours. Dottlinger scared us like that. If he had taken a rifle and shot the first rank of men or snatched a rose from his shirt and sniffed, none of us would have blinked.

"Well," he began, striding along the Company front, his hands clasped casually behind him. For once he didn't have his ball-point swagger stick. "It seems we have a small mutiny and then make up the lost time by going to work at 0400 tomorrow morning." Nice move. The day-trick was going on Break, and my Trick would have to make up the time.

It wasn't good, but it wasn't disaster either. Then I heard another grunt from Morning, a furious exhalation, and he started to say, "Request permission . . ." But I overruled him.

"Request permission to speak to the Company Commander, sir," I sang out. Dottlinger wouldn't hold to his word about forgetting about the mutiny charges if he got hold of Morning. Why he hadn't figured it out by this time was a wonder to me.

"Certainly, Sgt. Krummel."

I said dreadful things to myself as I walked toward him, but I wasn't afraid of him anymore. I just didn't know what I was going to say.

"Could I speak to you in private, sir?" I asked after saluting. The sweat blackened areas of his shirt had grown, and his face was pale, but his eyes still glittered with fire enough for one more encounter. He told Tetrick to have the men stand easy. I followed him a few steps toward the barracks.

"Yes, Sgt. Krummel?"

"Sir. Sir, I know I'm off base, but the events of this morning seem to call for unusual actions."

"They are unusual events."

"Yes, sir."

"Well, sergeant, what did you want?" he inquired when I hadn't spoken for several seconds.

"Well, sir, it's about the restriction to the Company Area."

"What about it?"

"Well, sir, ah, I'm worried about the quality of the work at Operations. It is already low due to the tension, and this harsher restriction, sir, will probably lower it even further. The Filipino liaison officer has already threatened to go to the major if the work doesn't pick up." One lie. "And the men are terribly on edge, sir, already. Might even say they're horny as hell, sir." I giggled like a high school virgin. I was willing to be anything.

"I think the men can curb their physical appetites, sergeant. There's too much of that sort of thing happening in this Company anyway. And as for the quality of the work – send them to me if it doesn't pick up. This outfit is getting soft. It needs a little iron, and I intend to see that they get it."

"Yes, sir, I agree." Two lies. "But the men feel that if the man who broke the bottles . . ." (God, I thought, is this really about some broken bottles.) ". . . is in the Company, sir, then he has confessed and, sir, no matter how silly this logic sounds, or how much a play on words it is, that's the way the men feel, sir, and . . ."

"Well, if they think I'm going to be threatened . . ."

"Excuse me, sir, but they don't mean that, I'm sure." Three lies. "They're just desperate, sir, and I'm afraid, sir, that we might have a real mutiny on our hands. I saw one in Korea, sir, and it was bad." Four lies. "Everyone's record took a permanent blemish, sir."

He nodded. He knew who was threatening whom, and he didn't like it. He thought for a bit, then smiled slowly as if he knew something. "You're perfectly correct, sergeant, a real mutiny would be quite disastrous. But I don't see how I can go back on my word, do you?"

"Sir?"

"Well, everyone hasn't confessed."

"Sir?"

"You haven't confessed, Sgt. Krummel. You might have done it, for all I know." He smiled again, a smile which said, "I've got you Mr Master's Degree."

"Sir, I'd like to make a statement. I'm the one, sir, who broke your Coke bottles in the Day Room." Five lies. "I'll make restitution to the Company Fund, sir, and plead guilty to any charges you would like to make in connection with the actual destruction of the bottles, sir."

"Were you drunk, sergeant?" Oh, he was loving this.

"No, sir."

"Then why did you do it?" His best fatherly tone.

"Momentary loss of perspective, sir. The machine took my coin and refused me a Coke, and since the machine was unbreakable, I avenged myself on the innocent bottles, sir."

"Sounds as if you might be mentally unbalanced, sergeant." How he would like me to plead that.

"No, not at all, sir. Like all good soldiers, sir, I have a quick temper and a strong sense of right which, under the direction of competent officers, can be a formidable weapon in combat, sir."

For a second he had forgotten whom he was playing with. "Well . . . Well, this isn't combat. Return to your Trick, and report to me after this formation."

"Right, sir." I saluted sharply, whirled and marched back.

Lt. Dottlinger turned to Tetrick, told him to dismiss the Company after informing the men that all prior restrictions were lifted and the pass box would be open immediately. The Day Room would be reopened after proper cleaning. The men had already heard the lieutenant's words, and they cheered when Tetrick dismissed them. Most ran for the barracks to change for Town, but a few paused to ask unanswered questions of me.

I told Tetrick what I had done before I went in to see Dottlinger. He assured me that Dottlinger would not dare any more than an Article 15, Company Punishment. Tetrick seemed resigned that someone would be slaughtered for the greatest good, and seemed not to mind particularly that that someone was me. His attitude seemed to say, "It's for the best."

"To hell with it," I said. "Maybe I'll kiss the bastard and let him queer me out, or maybe bust his pussylick face for him and let him hang my stripes for teeth he ain't going to have."

"If you do, holler, so I can be a witness that he hit you first," Tetrick laughed.

But I had already thought of the worst thing he could do: ignore my confession, let me go, and then single out any enlisted man and bust him with evidence he would say I'd given; and if I didn't agree to this, then the Company would be back on restriction again. I was surprised how much I hated Dottlinger at that moment, but even more surprised to discover that I wasn't worried about my stripes and that I cared about the respect of my men. I had said, when I reenlisted back in Seattle, that God couldn't involve me with anything or anybody again; I wanted to be a happy, stupid payday drunk. But what God couldn't do, Joe Morning engaged.

Dottlinger did, as Tetrick had predicted, give me Company Punishment: two hours extra duty for fifteen days. One hour policing the Day Room and one hour marching in front of the barracks as an example with full field pack and blanket roll. "To begin immediately," he had said. He unlocked the Day Room, had me open the louvers, and gloated while I swept the floor with a short broom.

So for fifteen days no one spoke to me for fear I'd take their heads off. The whole thing was so public, marching in daylight, squatting in the Day Room like a recruit. Once at a particularly bleak moment Tetrick had said, "Tell him to fuck himself. He hasn't got a leg to stand on. He can't touch you within the regs."

"For a man with no legs, he's stepping on my toes pretty

heavily," I answered – but thought about his suggestion more than I care to admit.

I had nearly decided that what I had done wasn't worth it when the only good thing of the time happened. This kid from Trick One came out of the barracks one day when the sun was pouring into my fatigues like lava, and at that dark, sunblinded moment, had said, "Look at the little tin soldier. It walks, it talks, it's almost human." I don't suppose he intended that I hear him, but I had. Someone else had too. From the second floor above the door an invisible voice roared like the wrath of Jehovah. "Shut your wise mouth, fuckhead!" The kid jumped, looked around, then dashed back in the barracks, perhaps wondering if God hadn't spoken to him.

I glowed. I sparkled. I felt heroic for a change, instead of dumb. (I'm not ashamed: pride has turned better heads than mine.) Someone understood.

"Ah 'tis a kind voice I hear above me," I said, but only a deep laugh answered me.

But by the time my hour was over I had lost that quick lift under the sun. The sun wasn't merely in the sky, it was the sky. From horizon to zenith the heavens burned in my honor, and in my chest and back and head. And in the shattering light all clear things lost themselves. Colors faded into pale imitations of themselves and became dust.

I had come back to be alone, to find simplicity, and had found trouble, and in this trouble found I must fall back on that which I was, that which I would be, that which I had always tried not to be.

I am the eldest son of generations of eldest sons, the final moment of a proud descent of professional killers, warriors, men of strength whose only concern with virtue lay in personal honor. But I still misunderstood a bit that day, I still confused being a soldier with being a warrior. That small, mean part of me which had wanted to care about rank and security and privilege was dying, and with the death of order began the birth of something in me monstrous, ah, but so beautiful. My heritage called, and though it would be many long moons before I answered, the song had burst my cold, ordered heart and I hated in the ringing sweep of the sun, and I lived.

First Blood

John Laurence

John Laurence covered the Vietnam War for CBS News from 1965 to 1970; his documentary about a squad of U.S. troops, "The World of Charlie Company," received every major award for broadcast journalism. The extract below is from Laurence's memoir, *The Cat from Hue*.

October 17, 1965

Three days of introductions, briefings, medical checks, parachute fittings, emergency rescue instructions, interviews, drinks, bull sessions and we were ready to fly. Wilson, Funk and I had been invited to film a combat air strike with the U.S. Air Force. Preparations took place at Bien Hoa airbase, fifteen miles north of Saigon. Wilson filmed the air crews at work, rest and play. The pilots were a wild bunch – mischievous as small children, funny and egocentric, late adolescent boys in men's bodies who drove their fantastic machines like teenage kids racing souped-up cars in high school. The pilots' lives appeared to exist solely for planes and flight. When they weren't actually flying or getting ready to fly, they were talking about flying, thinking about flying, writing home about flying, dreaming about flying, or listening to one another tell stories about flying. Much of their time was spent waiting to take off on short notice in the operational ready room, the "ops shack," a cold prefabricated air-conditioned hut, sterile as a hospital waiting room.

The pilots were comfortable with our company – partly out of politeness, partly because of shared adventurous spirits, partly, I suspected, for our ability to get them on network television where their families and friends would see them. Waiting in the ops shack, Wilson and Funk told them about the helicopter crashes at Suoi Ca and Dong Den and our experiences with the Army and Marines. The pilots listened closely. They were interested to know what it was like on the ground: not only the fighting but also descriptions of the extreme heat, dust, rain, mud and biting insects – a war they did not experience themselves other than for the few seconds the ground flashed by on their bombing runs in a blur of flame and smoke. Their sympathy for soldiers and Marines fighting in the field was sincere.

"I'll do anything to help those ground doggies out of a jam," a pilot said. "I mean *anything!* Up to and including gettin my ass shot at." He paused for emphasis. "But I thank the good Lord every night of my life that they're down there" (pointing his finger down) "and I'm up here" (pointing up in the air). All the pilots laughed.

To the crew and me, the prospect of military flying provided fresh expectation, a new thrill, as daring as anything we had ever done. To the pilots, combat aviation was routine. They were mostly casual about it, as if the danger of getting shot down was part of their job, what they did for a living.

No TV crew, we were told, had been allowed this much freedom to film a bombing mission in Vietnam before. The Air Force was giving us an inside look at its tactical operations in South Vietnam. From the big airfield at Bien Hoa, as well as from bases at Saigon, Pleiku, Qui Nhon, Danang, Chu Lai and from U.S. Navy aircraft carriers in the South China Sea, American pilots were flying scores of missions each day. They struck preplanned targets and provided tactical air support for American and South Vietnamese infantry forces through the country. For this story, the unit chosen for us to cover at Bien Hoa was the 602d Fighter Squadron. Its pilots flew Douglas A-1E attack bombers, "Skyraiders."

TV news coverage of the U.S. armed services in Vietnam focused primarily on the Army and Marines because ground troops did most of the fighting and were more easily accessible to camera crews. Now the Air Force wanted a larger share of public acknowledgment. Senior information officers in Saigon who approved our project trusted us to report what we saw in a favorable or at least objective light. We had asked for permission to fly on a bombing mission over North Vietnam, but our request was denied.

Wilson, Funk and I were back together as a team. Since the Suoi Ca Valley incident the week before, a new bond existed among us. We had more respect for one another, for our abilities under pressure, for being able to work calmly in danger. Wilson was furious with Morley Safer for taking all the film of the crashed helicopter and dying soldier and using it without crediting McEnry, Hoan or me. Wilson swore he would never work with him again. He promised to find an even more dramatic combat story with me. He was serious. The day after the helicopter crash, Wilson flew all day with First Cav medevac pilots hoping to get shot down again. He did not succeed. But he did get an interesting story about two wounded Cav soldiers who were rescued by helicopter and flown to a field hospital for treatment. We shipped it to the States for broadcast with my narration, but it was not as dramatic as Wilson wanted. The three of us were once again looking for a story and this time treating one another more as friends. We had formed a kind of brotherhood in adversity, like the allegiance between children in a troubled family.

The bombing mission was being carried out by a flight of four planes. I sat next to one of the pilots, Major Charles Vasiliadis, a dark, square-faced veteran who had flown over 350 missions, more than any American pilot in Vietnam. Starting up, the giant gas-reciprocating engine that filled the nose of the A-1E crackled, coughed, sputtered and roared with such ferocity I feared it was going to blow up. Just the sounds of the Wright R-3350 engine attested that enormous forces were engaged. One at a time, the big planes rolled down the mile-long runway at Bien Hoa before struggling slowly into the air, bombs and napalm canisters heavy under their wings.

Skyraiders had been in military service since 1946, when they were known as "Able Dogs" after their original designation as AD-1 (Attack Douglas). Standing fifteen and a half feet high and forty feet long, with wings of fifty feet and tall straight-up tail assemblies, they looked like the cartoon drawings schoolboys copied out of war comics, muzzle flashes spitting from the wings. These E models carried four 1,000-pound bombs, eight 500-pound bombs, canisters of napalm and hundreds of rounds of 20 millimeter cannon. The 8,000 pounds of ordnance and fuel made up more than a third of the planes' total weight and pulled hard on them as they lumbered off the runway and gained altitude foot by foot. The clouds ahead of us were washed in solemn shades of gray and white.

Wilson, Funk and I flew separately in each of three planes, sitting on parachutes in the passenger seats to the right of the pilots. We were strapped to the seats by shoulder harnesses and seat belts that were joined by metal fasteners at the chest. The copilot's control stick had been removed from its base between our legs although foot pedals for the flaps remained. The instrument panel was a screen of lights, dials, meters and switches, incomprehensible to me except for speed and altitude. Wilson had a small silent camera that gave him more maneuverability in the confined space of the cockpit. Funk recorded the natural sound of the planes, the rushing wind, and the radio conversations of the pilots.

Major Vasiliadis was thirty-seven years old but the softness of his face, the short curly black hair, his large straight nose and the mole on his left cheek made him look younger. Some of the pilots in the squadron tended to flamboyance, but Vasiliadis had a modest, unpretentious manner. A graduate of Harvard University, he had twice been decorated with the Distinguished Flying Cross. The other pilots called him "Vas," pronounced Vazz.

At about three thousand feet, the planes climbed into a black cloud. Except for the dim red lights on the instrument panel, the cockpit was dark. Rain splattered hard against the windshield. The aircraft bounced and yawed and pulled with sudden jerks, hurtling it forward as through dense fog. Vas held his eyes on the maze of instruments moving in front of him and tried to steady the gyrating plane with his gloved right hand on the control stick that twitched violently between his knees. The thirteen-ton machine bored through the clouds like a snowplow. Vasiliadis had an expression of calm concentration. I breathed slowly in and out and tried to force myself to relax.

Higher up, the plane broke through the tops of the clouds and skimmed over puffs of gentle white fluff. The plane emerged in bright sunshine and clear blue air that reached to infinity. After the dark confinement of the clouds, the brilliant sky felt refreshing, liberating. Elation hit me at the same time as the warm sunlight and I lowered the sun visor on the hard plastic helmet. Vas joined formation with the other pilots and the flight turned west and south on a heading toward the border of South Vietnam and Cambodia.

Speaking on the internal intercom before each maneuver of the aircraft, Vas announced what he was going to do next: "Okay, turning left now. You'll hear a little more throttle," taking me through it step by step so that I knew what to expect and wasn't alarmed by sudden movements of the plane. I was no longer afraid. Vasiliadis seemed confident with what he was doing, as fearless as the young army officers who stood up straight during the sniper fire in the Suoi Ca Valley. *If he isn't scared*, I thought to myself, *why should I be?* Not knowing what emotion to feel, I borrowed his. Total calm. It did not occur to me that Vas and the other pilots were concentrating so carefully on the dozens of details they had to remember to fly the mission correctly – the actual mechanics of flying, navigating, communicating, targeting, attacking – that there was no space left in their conscious minds for fear. They were too busy. Nor did I consider the possibility that any serious fear they felt could not be revealed: to the other pilots, to the CBS crew, perhaps. to themselves. It had to be suppressed. Maybe the fear of something going wrong had become so familiar with them that it was part of the background by now, another detail in their long checklist of mechanical considerations, like the steady drone of the engines.

The flight leader was Jay Ledbetter, a thirty-six-year-old captain from Melbourne, Florida. The other pilots were Major Gale Kirkpatrick, 35, of Selma, Alabama, and Captain Adrian (Jack) Geraghty, 36, of Amityville, New York. All were experienced fighter jet pilots who had been switched to A-1Es for duty in Vietnam. The Air Force considered the prop-driven planes more useful than jets for some of the work in the guerrilla war. A-1Es could carry twice as much bomb weight as a jet plane, and could stay airborne four to five hours a flight, waiting on station to provide tactical support to ground troops on short notice. What they gave up in speed, the A-1Es gained in destructive power and time on target.

Kirkpatrick was a large handsome man with a slow drawl, a quick sense of humor and a gregarious disposition that fit his big frame. Ledbetter and Geraghty were thinner, wise-cracking, more like flying stuntmen. I had the impression that all four were pleased to be chosen by the Air Force to fly us, though they tried not to show it. They were exceptionally attentive to our needs in the air.

The flight to the border was long and slow. By the time the A-1Es arrived at the target, a forward air controller (FAC) was waiting. This was another Air Force pilot who circled over the countryside in a small single-engine spotter plane. His altitude was a few hundred feet. The A-1Es stayed above five thousand feet in tactical formation.

"Do you see the village just to the east of the river?" the FAC said on the radio. "Just off my left wing?"

"Roger, the village east of the river," Ledbetter answered.

"That's it. That's the VC village you're going to hit."

"Ah, roger that."

"On the west side of the village, you can consider that the border," the FAC said. "We don't want you to go past the buildings on the west side. So, if you make a left-hand pattern, it'll have to be tight into this village with a tight left break to stay a couple of clicks away from the border."

"That's affirmative, this side of the village."

"Okay, it's all yours. I'll get out of the way. Happy hunting," the FAC said.

The planes circled in a wide arc between scattered clumps of cotton-white clouds. Below, the countryside was a green-gray checkerboard: hundreds of square miles of flat farmland and long straight rows of rice fields and irrigation canals that reached to the horizon – part of the massive expanse of the Mekong River Delta. Rectangular pools of water, peaceful in the morning light, reflected the sun. Speaking on the radio, the pilots decided on the order of bombing. Vas would go third, after Kirkpatrick.

"If you have to throw up," Vas said, "try and do it in the helmet, okay?"

"Affirmative," I said, pretending not to be worried. At Bien Hoa, Wilson, Funk and I had been warned that we would probably be unable to keep our food down after the first couple of passes. Then we'd be all right. I had chosen not to eat breakfast.

"Okay, hang on. Here we go."

Vas flipped toggle switches on the controls to arm the bombs and jerked the control stick hard to the left and the plane rolled over on its side. The engine, wings and ailerons strained with the force. The horizon tilted suddenly to the right and then disappeared and all I could see was a great dark mass of earth rushing up toward us. The plane pointed almost straight down, turning from side to side on the axis of its nose. The engine roared with the added power of the dive and the air rushed past the canopy of the cockpit fast and loud. My body felt light, like a leaf, without weight.

I was off balance, disoriented, unable to tell up from down. The strongest sensation was one of rushing forward, complicated by the weightless twisting motion of the plane. I was frozen in the seat, too frightened to breathe or move or cry out. At the same time, I felt a strange exhilaration. My physical senses were warning of danger but my cognitive reason was saying it's all right, nothing is going to hurt you, this is thrilling.

Time stopped.

The straw roofs of a village appeared a thousand feet below, racing toward us fast. Sunlight flashed off a flooded rice field. Vas made sight adjustments and the wings came level for a second and the bombs fell away from under the wings with a metal *clank*. An instant later, he pulled the control stick all the way back and the aircraft shuddered with the competing forces of weight, drag, lift and thrust. The engine screamed and the nose came up and the plane strained into the sky. I felt the sudden pull of five times my weight sucking me into the seat. My chin was driven into my chest. All the strength went out of my arms and shoulders, making them heavy and lifeless, no longer part of me. I could not lift my head. Simultaneously, my vision went black around the edges and formed a tunnel around a circle of light that narrowed to a sharp solitary point and then went out. I was unconscious.

Time passed. As I came to my senses, Vas was talking on the intercom. I pulled my head out of my chest and turned to look. He was smiling.

"How did you like that?" he asked.

"Amazing," I said, feeling the breath come back.

"You feel sick?"

"No."

"Good. You're doing better than your buddies."

Kirkpatrick and Geraghty were talking on the radio about Wilson and Funk.

"Damn. I'm gonna have to open the canopy," one of them said.

"We got enough puke in here for a swim."

"Shit, I forgot my snorkel."

"He who barfs before lunch buys the drinks before supper."

Wilson's voice came on the radio. "At least the camera's still dry," he said, a laugh in his voice.

A minute later, Vas said, "Here we go," and the plane rolled over and turned a perfect pirouette on the tip of its left wing. The wing came back to the right and the plane dived straight at the village. The straw roofs were on fire now. Flame and smoke reached up to touch the plane. Vas released more bombs and a few seconds later the cockpit shook with explosive shocks. The plane climbed out of the dive and raced through clouds of black smoke.

The periphery of my vision faded, a dark circle formed around the edges of light, but this time I did not black out. Vas turned his head and looked at me with an expression vaguely suggesting approval.

On the fourth or fifth pass, I saw individual farmers – women and men – standing in fields outside the village in round straw hats with hoes in their hands. They looked up at the diving plane. Vas squeezed the trigger on the control stick and the cannons in the wings of the Skyraider fired a long burst of 20 millimeter shells – explosive metal missiles almost an inch thick. The shells struck the ground among the farmers, chopping the earth and sending up spouts of brown dirt and also striking the men and women farmers and tearing through the delicate assemblies of their bodies. The plane zoomed over and past before they fell.

"Why do they just stand there?" I said on the intercom. "Why don't they run away?"

"'Cause they don't know any better," Vas said. "Dumb bastards."

He said it with such authority I didn't doubt him. But I wondered, *If they're all VC as they're supposed to be, why don't they run for cover?*

When all of the bombs, napalm and cannon had been dropped and fired, the flight headed toward Bien Hoa. Vas slid the hard plastic canopy back to let in the cooler air. He switched the radio to a special air force frequency that was playing gentle instrumental music, mostly strings arranged in the style of Mantovani, aerial muzak. *How different from the last few minutes.* The tedium relieved the tension of the bombing strike. Vas and I did not talk much. Warm sunlight bathed the cockpit. The ride back to base was as easy as driving home from a Sunday afternoon ball game.

At Bien Hoa, the plane passed over the runway at 500 feet, flying level with it, the control tower just to the left. Suddenly, the plane flipped over on its right wing with such violent force I feared we had collided with another plane. I panicked. My hands reached forward and seized the edge of the control panel. Heart pumping, body rigid, I thought we were going to crash. But the plane only went around on its side in a hard right turn, 180 degrees, taking us back to the end of the runway for the final approach.

"What was that?" I said.

Vas turned his head to look at me. He was smiling – a wry, knowing insider's smile that seemed to say, "Gotcha." It was the look of a warrior, smug in victory, the only time I saw it. Maybe he had just forgotten to warn me, but I didn't think so. He had been meticulous in describing every other sharp movement of the plane in advance. Vas could have mentioned "the pitchout," the hard turn combat aviators make over the runway after a mission, showing their empty bomb racks to the control tower just before landing. He had managed to scare me in the last moments of the flight and I had shown my fear.

"That was the *break*," he said.

Later, in Saigon, Wilson and Funk described the scenes they had recorded and I wrote a story on the anatomy of an air strike, focusing on the skills of the pilots, the versatility of the vintage airplanes, the thoughts of the pilots from interviews at Bien Hoa. I wrote nothing critical about them or the mission. I did not draw attention to the farmers they killed. Wilson said his pilot had not strafed any farmers, so he had no pictures of it.

A day later a message arrived at the bureau from Russ Bensley, the producer in New York who was responsible for film coverage of Vietnam on the *CBS Evening News*. Bensley's message said that the UN representative from Cambodia was claiming that American planes had bombed and strafed a Cambodian village near the border with Vietnam. Bensley asked us to find out whether the Cambodian protest had anything to do with the air strike we had filmed and would soon be arriving in New York. It was only an off chance, he said, but we should check.

I called the Air Force public information office in Saigon and explained Bensley's query to the two officers who arranged our coverage of the air strike. Lieutenant Colonel Dave O'Hara and Lieutenant Colonel Dan Biondi were friendly acquaintances. We had lunch when I arrived in August and I was indebted to them for getting Wilson and me on the Air Force plane to the Philippines to cover the volcano eruption three weeks earlier. They said they were not aware of the official Cambodian protest but would find out what happened.

Biondi called back later in the day. His voice was strained. He asked to go off the record and I agreed.

"Ah, Jack," he said, "I've checked around about your request. I'd like to give you an answer, but I can't. I hope you'll understand, but we can't talk about this one. If you understand what I mean. We can't say anything."

His voice was worried, vulnerable, no confidence in it. I asked him several questions but he resisted answering.

"Jack, it would be better all around if you'd just keep this one quiet," he said. "I'm asking for a favor here."

I said I understood, thanked him and hung up the phone.

Biondi's honesty surprised me. He could have denied there was any connection between our mission and the Cambodian protest and that would have been the end of it. My superiors in New York probably would have accepted the word of the Air Force spokesman in Saigon and dropped the issue. Instead, Biondi chose to let me know something was wrong. But he had not confirmed that U.S. planes struck Cambodian territory. Nor could I quote him. He was enlisting my cooperation in covering up any trouble ("just keep this one quiet"). The truth, presumably, would have embarrassed the Air Force, the Pentagon and the U.S. government.

I thought about it all day and discussed it with the bureau chief. It was a tough call. On the one hand, it was a good story. U.S. planes bombing Cambodia would make headlines. I felt sympathy for the innocent farmers who had been killed. A big news story might help prevent it from happening again. But we didn't have confirmation. It would be impossible to prove where the planes had bombed without help from the Air Force. On the other hand, I didn't want to jeopardize our relationship with Biondi and O'Hara. Reporting a bombing of Cambodia would cause a major rift between the Air Force and CBS News, and it might seriously affect future news coverage. The story could also be inaccurate. *What to do?*

The next morning I composed a short message to Bensley saying that the Air Force could not confirm that any of its planes had struck Cambodia. That *was* the end of it. The A-1E story went on the air in its original form. The pictures were dramatic but it was just another air strike in South Vietnam.

Without realizing it, I had become a player in the official Saigon information/propaganda game. I had demonstrated my willingness to accept favors from the U.S. mission and also to return them. By broadcasting uncritical stories about American military activity, I earned special access to other military stories in return. Because I believed what I was reporting was accurate, I felt no guilt. Reporting everything I saw or was told or believed to be true in a spirit of full disclosure seemed less important than maintaining my good military contacts, keeping the information officers happy, and moving ahead in my career. I saw the war as an honorable cause, fought in the national interests of the United States and South Vietnam. I was still, as they said, "with the program."

Later in the month, I had lunch at the Rex Hotel again with my contact at the embassy. By now I knew that he was a senior officer in the Central Intelligence Agency, the Saigon station chief. Svenson and I talked about the war. He knew about the air strike on the Cambodian border but we did not discuss it. After lunch, we rode down to the ground floor in the narrow hotel elevator. There was enough room for three, possibly four, people. The third person in the elevator, a young Air Force captain in uniform, stared at me with curiosity, as though trying to place where he had seen me before. On the sidewalk outside, I was saying good-bye to the CIA man when the Air Force officer approached.

"Excuse me," the captain said. "Do you work for CBS?"

I said I did.

"Are you the reporter who went on that A-1E mission over on the border?"

"Yes I am."

He smiled, pleased with himself.

"I'm the FAC who was spotting for you on that one. Saw your report on TV. Thought I recognized you in the elevator." We shook hands.

"Do you remember that village we hit? Where the dinks just stood there and took it?" His tone was serious now.

"Uh huh."

"You know, it was driving me crazy that we might have got the wrong place. So, I went back on my own the other day to take a look. You know what? We hit the wrong target. I got the rivers mixed up. When I told you guys to bomb on the east side of the village we were already two clicks inside Cambodia. I read the map wrong."

"Yes," I said. "I heard that might have been the case." The CIA officer listened with interest but did not speak.

"Well, I just wanted you to know that," the captain said. "It's really been on my conscience."

The Relief of Plei Mei

Major Charlie A. Beckwith

Charlie Beckwith was the commanding officer of Project DELTA, a US special forces unit founded in 1964. In the October of 1965, Major Beckwith and Project DELTA were tasked with the relief of Plei Mei, a special forces camp 40km south of Pleiku city in the central highlands under attack from two regiments of the People's Army of Vietnam (PAVN).

I worked all night, studying maps, looking for LZs, determining routes. My bones told me this was not going to be any piece of cake. I talked to the Air Force forward air controllers who had been flying over the camp. There was a lot of our enemy down there. This was going to be an operation where a lot of our people would get hurt.

Bill McKean and I, the next morning, flew near the camp trying to find an LZ. The trick was finding one not so close to the camp that it gave our position away to the enemy, and not so far away that we would wear ourselves out working our way to the camp. As we were flying around looking at the proposed LZ the Hog (helicopter gunship) that was escorting us threw one of its rotor blades, crashed, and exploded in the jungle. A bad omen.

The two Vietnamese Ranger companies and fifteen American Green Berets from Project DELTA climbed into the helicopters at Camp Holloway and took off, flying south toward Plei Me. After the LZ had been prepped with two air strikes flown by bombers and gunships, we landed about

0900 of the 21st. The day was another hot one. Major Tut, who commanded the Ranger companies, and I agreed we'd go along very slowly, carefully. I didn't think we should sacrifice speed for security. The elephant grass we were moving through was shoulder high. In some areas, where the foliage was particularly heavy, we had to crawl on our hands and knees.

Around noon we crept up to a small Vietnamese village. We learned it was deserted, but that villagers had been there no more than eight to ten hours before. The cooking fires were still smouldering. Somebody had come through there and taken these people with them. This bothered the Vietnamese. I didn't give it much thought since it was only a matter of time before we hit something. About then Colonel Bennett, who was flying in a Bird Dog (0–1), one of those small forward control aircraft, came up on the radio. He first asked me to mark my position with smoke. I refused. Then he tied into me. "Major, you're moving too slow. You won't get there in a week the way you're going." I answered him respectfully, but thought, That's nice, but why don't you go to your room, boy, and let me get on with this operation. You're not on the ground, and you have no idea what we're trying to negotiate.

We continued to move through the jungle in single file. The column stretched out. Toward the middle of the afternoon I heard two shots up ahead of me. I ran forward and found one of my guys had shot an enemy soldier wearing a pith helmet and a khaki uniform. He'd been carrying a box of 75mm recoilless rifle ammunition. Another enemy soldier with him had managed to escape in the dense undergrowth. Major Tut came up and went through the dead guy's uniform looking for papers. Tut was getting nervous. He told me that this man was not a VC, but rather from a regular North Vietnamese unit. Our people had suspected the NVA had regular units in the south at this time, but this was the first time anyone had actual proof of it. The next time one of the communications planes flew over I got on the air and passed the news along.

Major Tut then came over and informed me he and the Ranger companies were going to turn back. This was as far as they were going to go. I told him my mission was to get into Plei Me, and I intended to do so with or without him. I preferred to do it with him, but I didn't really give a shit one way or another. I intended to reinforce the camp. Tut said that when we shot the NVA soldier it had become a new ball game. I didn't have enough sense to be frightened. Probably, I should have. It was getting late now so I didn't argue with him very long.

I called together the fifteen Americans and told them what had happened, and that I intended to push on. I told Major Thompson and my two sergeant majors we would lead the relief force.

I had with me the Group's sergant major, Bill McKean's right arm, John Pioletti. Sergeant Major Pioletti had convinced McKean to let him go. I had mixed feelings about this. I knew if anything happened to John, McKean would string me up alive; but I also knew that if I needed support McKean would not leave me and his sergeant major dangling out there. On top of it, Sergeant Pioletti was a first-class guy. I trusted my life with my own sergeant major, Bill DeSoto. I was glad he was along for the ride.

I also had with me a new operations officer. Tommy Thompson was to go home in two weeks, and Major A. J. Baker had just arrived in country. He was a great big boy we called Bo who had played football at the University of Arkansas. He had arrived in Nha Trang on the 19th and on the 21st he was with us in the jungle outside of Plei Me. What a way to get his whistle wet! I asked him to bring up the rear of our small column. We moved out.

At approximately 2000 hours we were close enough to the camp to hear the shooting. I got the camp on the radio and they came in clearly. Someone said to me, "Come on in and join the party." That made me angry. I knew people were dead and more were dying, and I didn't perceive this to be a goddamn party. I had also decided not to go into the camp that night. My sixth sense told me if I attempted to enter the camp, those inside might take us for the enemy; and if anyone on the perimeter was trigger-happy, it would end badly. I radioed back to Pleiku and informed Bill McKean that I would enter the camp at dawn. Bill DeSoto and I did a quick recon of the unimproved single-lane dirt road we'd been moving parallel to, which ran into the camp. When we returned to the column, Bo Baker ran up and said, "Major, Tut's back." I followed him – there were the two Ranger companies. Tut said words to the effect that he would have lost face if he'd left me.

We went on half-alert that night, that's half the force awake and half asleep. I slept for three hours and was awakened on the 22nd before the sun came up. After Bill DeSoto got the column up we eased on about 300 yards to our left flank and began to slowly go down the side of the road. We hit a ridge above the camp, maybe 800 yards out, and from there I could look down into the NVA positions. I noticed a position the Communists had set up to ambush any relief columns that tried to enter the camp. For some reason it was unoccupied. I was damn glad. I told my guys and Major Tut it would take us too long to reach the camp continuing through the jungle. "My plan is to veer off to the east, hit the road just as it goes over the hill, then run like hell to the camp gates."

We evidently caught the enemy by surprise. Once on the road we dashed for the camp and took some light fire. A Vietnamese lieutenant was killed. So, too, was a newspaper photographer who, without permission, had gotten on one of the choppers back in Pleiku and had come with us. He had long blond hair. The bullet took him through the side of the face. Four or five others received minor wounds. Within a half hour everyone was in the camp. The first thing I noticed on going through the gate was the Montagnard tribesmen who had been killed while defending the camp; they were still lying in the wire. I mean everywhere. Dead people. Oh, shit, I thought, there's going to be a lack of discipline in here. If they can't pick up that kind of thing then, man, there's some problems in here. I was right. There were about sixty other dead Montagnard soldiers stuffed into body bags and stacked up like cordwood. The smell was terrible.

The Special Forces captain in charge of the camp was Harold Moore. I let him know quickly that I was the new mayor of Plei Me. Shaped like an equilateral triangle, the camp sat in a slight bowl and was surrounded by barbed wire. There was a trench system that ran throughout the inside of the camp. About ten wooden buildings with corrugated metal roofs made up the interior. The outside of the camp was usually occupied by the Montagnard soldiers' families. Needless to say, under siege the families were now all inside. The camp was crowded and it was dirty. A thick red dust covered everything. It was in turmoil. The Vietnamese camp commander, Captain Moore's counterpart, stayed in his deep bunker. I never saw him once the whole time I was there. Outside the barbed wire there were a hell of a lot of Communists.

I called Pleiku and explained to them that we should fortify the camp first, to make sure we could hold it, and then find out how many of the enemy we were facing. We shouldn't do anything until we knew for sure. Bill McKean did not agree with me. He said, "I want you to get outside the camp, rummage around, clear the enemy out of there. Then, obviously, if you do that you can hold the camp."

I said, "Sir, that's not a good idea."

He said, "Well, Major, I'm ordering you."

In the afternoon we mounted up both Ranger companies. Captain Thomas Pusser, a West Pointer I thought a lot of, was the advisor to the Vietnamese Rangers. I got him and the other American advisors who were going out on the sweep operation together. "I want you all to be very careful out there. Don't take any chances you don't have to take." Then Pusser and I discussed the two Vietnamese companies. The leadership of one of them was stronger than the other. I suggested to Tom he go with the stronger unit. He felt because he could kick ass and get it moving he should go with the weaker one. I finally agreed with him. He went out with the weak company. I shouldn't have let him do that.

The plan was to begin to clear the northern slope area from which most of the heaviest fire was coming. The NVA waited for both companies to get outside the gate. Then they came out of their holes and hit us with everything they had. About fourteen men were killed, including Tom Pusser. Many more were wounded. I felt fortunate to get any of those Rangers back inside the camp. They had been very badly mauled. I immediately got on the radio, and got Bulldog to agree that we should fortify the camp. I then asked for an air drop of a couple hundred 5-gallon water cans, since we were running out of water, and a basic load of ammunition. I didn't know how much we had, but I wanted to make damn sure we had enough. I also asked for a couple of boxes of cigars, some cigarettes, and a case of whiskey. "I don't care what it is, anything assorted." This got McKean a little bent out of shape. Then I asked to have a chopper come in and get our dead. I felt that many dead were bad on morale. Reportedly, McKean asked for volunteers in Pleiku to fly in to us, but no American chopper pilot stepped forward.

The first Air Force resupply drop, in order to avoid the enemy .51-caliber machine guns that ringed the camp, flew too high and dumped most of its ammunition outside the wire. The second drop landed in the camp. It was all ammo. The third drop contained water, cigars, and the other things I'd ordered. It, too, landed on top of us.

Late in the afternoon of this first day, after the Ranger companies got back and we licked our wounds and took our resupply drops, I got together with Tommy Thompson, Bo Baker, Bill DeSoto, and John Pioletti. We were all beginning to realize that we would be damn fortunate to get out of this camp alive. We were receiving a lot of 81mm mortar and 75mm recoilless rifle fire. I was very concerned that we hold that first night. I had our people go out to all the crews manning the machine guns to make sure they knew what their instructions were. I didn't want them picking up and running away scared. That night I thought we were going to get hit. We took heavy mortar and recoilless rifle fire all night long, but were not probed.

The next day we began to strengthen the camp's fortifications. The mortar and recoilless rifle fire fell in spurts. Occasionally a lone enemy soldier would jump out of a hole and rush the wire throwing hand grenades. Around 1030 hours Bill DeSoto got hit. One of those heavy machine gun slugs nearly tore his arm off.

From the intensity of the fire Plei Me was absorbing, I made an estimate of the enemy force besieging us. When I reported I thought there were at least two, maybe three, large forces of regimental size surrounding the camp, I got some people in Pleiku really shook up. After that I got priority on all air strikes. I don't deserve credit for the damage those strikes did to the enemy. My deputy, Major Thompson, organized and directed the strikes. Air Force fighters and naval aircraft flying from the carriers off Yankee Station pounded the jungle around us. They hit the enemy with napalm and 250- and 500-pounders all day long. We learned later we were surrounded by two regular North Vietnamese infantry regiments, the 32nd and 33rd.

That night I received a telegram by radio from President Johnson. It said something like, "We're thinking about you. Hold out there as long as you can. God bless you all."

The nights were worse, far worse, than the days. Ropes of green and orange tracers flew into and out of the camp. Overhead, circling C-46 Flareships kept the area illuminated. Multicolored parachutes, which had been used to resupply us, were strewn here and there and gave the camp a raffish appearance. The pounding intensified. Mortars and recoilless rifles fired relentlessly. Amazingly, during these terrible nighttime hours the camp rats, oblivious to the havoc they were a part of, continued to come out and run over the ruins just as if everyone was asleep.

Bombers came over again on October 24th and began to eat up the NVA. I'd say our side flew seventy-five to one hundred sorties a day. We just walked these air strikes all around the outside of the camp. We used a lot of air, and we broke the enemy's back with it. Many of the strikes were so close to the wire we took shrapnel in the camp. One particular string of bombs hit very close. Major Thompson, who was calling in the strikes, kept hollering, "I like it! I like it!" Captain Moore had wanted to take a photograph of one of these strikes. I tried to warn him to keep his head down. A piece of shrapnel from one of the hard bombs ripped half his shoulder off.

During the daytime, between the air strikes. I tried to sleep. Besides the newspaper photographer who was killed during our run for the camp, I had two other unauthorized newspaper people with me in the camp. We taught them how to shoot a .30-caliber machine gun and gave them one to man in the south corner of the perimeter. They did a first class job for us.

The situation on the third day: We were putting in a lot of air strikes and I wasn't sure what was going to happen next. We learned by radio that a South Vietnamese armored column trying to reach us had been pinned down and stopped cold by an enemy ambush.

Sometime, I'm not sure when, Khoi, the Vietnamese helicopter pilot I thought so much of, flew into the camp. I told him he was crazy, and he should fly his ass out of there. "You know, Boss," he spoke perfect English, "your problem is you worry too much." He loaded up a lot of dead. We had problems keeping the Montagnards off. They wanted to get out too. Khoi made two flights in and out. He took fire the first time but not the second. His luck held that day. Sometime later, though, he was killed in Military Region I when his chopper crashed into a mountain in bad weather.

With the napalm and bombs doing their work, the NVA began to relax their hold on us. The mortar barrages fell off, so did the small arms and machine gun fire. It got so that even a couple of Huey slicks (small troop-carrying helicopters) flew in. We were then able to get a lot of the kids and women out. We also began flying out our dead. Some of the dead had been lying in the jungle heat for six days. They were ripe. I know that John Pioletti, while loading one of the choppers, was throwing up over the body bags.

There was another problem that worried me. The first day in Plei Me, Captain Pusser had been killed with the Ranger companies outside the wire; in the melee that followed, they hadn't brought his body back. I knew I had to recover his body. We mounted an operation. It was on either day four or five. I asked for volunteers. "The Vietnamese," Major Tut told me, "will get his body for you. We want to do this." Some Vietnamese went out and brought Captain Pusser's body back. He could only be identified by his dog tag. The heat had distorted his body terribly. It was a damn shame.

We received word by radio on Monday, the 25th, that the relief force of tanks, armored personnel carriers, and troops was on the move again. A slick arrived and left a forward observer in the camp who would help direct artillery fire down the road, walking it just in front of the slow, chugging armored column. As the sun went down the first tanks finally clanked into view and took up a defensive position around the camp's perimeter.

The following morning the 2nd Battalion, 1st Brigade, from the 1st Cavalry Division (Airmobile) was helicoptered into Plei Me. I was asked by their liaison officer where I would recommend he put his unit. I selected an appropriate area for the Cav to land in. Around and beyond the north slope there were a lot of dead enemy soldiers and the stench was terrible. Landing there would be an instructive introduction for the 1st Cav, which had only arrived in country a short time before. No better way to let them know war is hell. After the battalion landed, because his people were throwing up all over themselves, their CO asked if they could move somewhere else.

Before I left I walked around the outside perimeter of Plei Me. The ground was pitted by bomb craters and blackened as far as I could see by napalm. There were also a lot of dead out there. In one case I noticed two enemy soldiers who were actually chained to their machine guns. It was later estimated there were 800 or 900 dead North Vietnamese regulars in front of the camp. I don't know the exact number and I didn't run around counting them. Eventually a bulldozer came in and just covered everything up.

Ia Drang

Lt-General Harold G. Moore and Joseph L. Galloway

On November 14 1965 Lt. Col Hal Moore's 1st Battalion, 7th Cavalry conducted a heliborne assault into LZ (landing Zone) X-Ray in the Ia Drang Valley in the Central Highlands. So began the battle of Ia Drang – the first major engagement between US regulars and the PAVN. Moore's force was surrounded by 2000 North Vietnamese from the 33rd and 66th Regiments with assistance from Viet Cong elements; in turn Moore's force was reinforced by elements of 2nd Battalion, 7th Cavalry and 2nd Battalion, 5th Cavalry. Despite brutal fighting the "Cav" were able to hold against repeated attacks. During a tactical march to LZ Albany, two and a half miles away, on the 17th the 2nd Battalion was ambushed by the PAVN.

Journalist Joe Galloway was awarded the Bronze Star with Valor for carrying wounded men to safety at Ia Drang.

The North Vietnamese commander on the battlefield, Nguyen Huu An, has a keen memory of that bloody afternoon of November 17, 1965, on the trail to Landing Zone Albany: "My commanders and soldiers reported there was very vicious fighting. I tell you frankly, your soldiers fought valiantly. They had no choice. You are dead or not. It was hand-to-hand fighting. Afterward, when we policed the battlefield, when we picked up our wounded, the bodies of your men and our men were neck to neck, lying alongside each other. It was most fierce." That it was, and nowhere more fierce than along that strungout American column where the cavalry rifle companies had been cut into small groups.

Lieutenant John Howard was with Headquarters Company near the tail of the column. "At some point early in the battle I was situated next to a large anthill. A sergeant not far from me had received a nasty wound to his foot and he was screaming in pain. I crawled over next to him and started to bandage his foot. No sooner had I told him to try to quit screaming than I was hit by a bullet which spun me completely around on the ground. It had hit me on the right side of my stomach. I pulled up my shirt to see how bad it was and, luckily, it had cut through my flesh but had not gone into my stomach. I had a flesh wound about five inches long."

Bullets continued to hit all around Howard. He grabbed the sergeant and told him they needed to move around to the other side of the anthill. "On the other side we joined up with four other soldiers who were grouped together in the grass. We continued to fire at North Vietnamese soldiers behind trees and anthills and tried to figure out what we should do next."

Although they were now out of sight of each other, Lieutenant Bud Alley, the 2nd Battalion communications officer and Howard's friend, was not far away. "It was consternation," says Alley. "Men on either side of me were being shot. At that point I had not seen any of the enemy. All I could see was the trees and our guys. I tried to move up to my right. I moved into a hail of bullets. Everyone was trying to keep moving up toward the landing zone. I was at a big anthill, pinned down by a machine gun. Fellow on my right, a Puerto Rican, was wounded. I traded the Puerto Rican PFC my .45 pistol for his machine gun.

"I took the machine gun and moved around left of the anthill and tried to move forward, firing to my front. I crawled up on a man behind a little tree; then two enemy automatic weapons opened up, cutting that little tree down. He screamed and hit me in the back. I rolled over on top of him and he had both hands over his face. He told me: 'Don't worry about me;

I'm dead.' He opened his hands and he had a bullet hole right in the center of his forehead. He pulled two grenades and threw those grenades. I started crawling back to the big anthill where I had come from. I knew we weren't going forward. By the time I got back to the anthill, the wounded guy, a dead guy or two, another wounded guy, and my radio repairman were there all huddled behind that anthill. Which way do we go?"

William Shucart, the battalion surgeon, was also in that section of the column. "I got up and started looking for somebody, anybody. I ran on, and encountered a couple of enemy soldiers. This meeting scared the shit out of me and them both. I got the M-16 up and fired before they did. That was the end of that. Then I looked over and saw this sergeant leaning against a tree. He said, 'Can I give you a hand, Captain?' Calm as could be. That was Sergeant Fred Kluge of Alpha Company, 1st Battalion, 5th Cav. We went back to a larger group at the rear of the column, maybe fifteen or twenty guys, with several wounded. We were in an area with a lot of wounded and no supplies, only a few styrettes of morphine and some bandages."

Just forward of the headquarters section of the column, Charlie Company was beginning to die. Specialist 4 Jack Smith was with the lead elements in the Charlie Company formation, near Lieutenant Don Cornett, the acting company commander, when the company charged into the teeth of the enemy machine guns. In the first seconds Smith saw one of the radio operators fall dead with a bullet through the chest, his eyes and tongue bulging out. The men of Charlie Company were firing in all directions.

Suddenly, Smith says, he heard a low moan from Lieutenant Don Cornett. He tore off the officer's green fatigue shirt and saw a bullet wound in his back, to the right of his spine. He and another soldier began bandaging the lieutenant's wound. Smith thought how dependent they all were on this one man, now badly hurt, who was the only leader in reach. Then a man beside Smith was shot in the arm and a torn artery began spurting blood. Then a round tore through one of Cornett's boots, tearing away all the toes on his foot.

Now a North Vietnamese with a Maxim heavy machine gun appeared just three feet in front of Smith. The young soldier flicked the selector switch on his M-16 to full automatic and fired a long burst into the face of the enemy machine gunner. An exploding grenade took down another American close by.

Only a few minutes had passed, but Jack Smith's world was being shot to death all around him. Then, he says, something happened that convinced him to keep fighting. Lieutenant Don Cornett, in agony from his wounds, told Smith he was going to do something to try to get his troops organized. Cornett crawled away into the high grass. A brave young lieutenant died doing his duty somewhere out there in hand-to-hand fighting.

Smith recalls: "Within a span of perhaps twenty minutes everyone around me was dead or wounded, except me. You have to understand that in our area the elephant grass was chest-high; once you hit the dirt your world was about as big as a dining-room table. Your world was completely confined to that area and the six or seven men around you. At that point, we were isolated. Alpha Company was in the same shape. Then the North Vietnamese swept through. I believe they came between Alpha and our company and began to shoot people. We didn't know if the noise from five feet away, as they began to shoot people, was friendly or enemy."

Smith saw soldiers take machine guns, lie flat on the ground, and begin firing into the grass. "Often they were firing right into the muzzles of other American machine guns. People were screaming to stop the shooting. It began to have all the elements of a massacre. Nobody was in control because all the officers were to the front and our radio operators had fallen dead on their radio sets."

Just forward of Charlie Company, with the Delta Company mortars, PFC James Shadden was in agony from his two severe wounds. "By this time, some of the NVA were coming through the area killing all who were screaming and calling for medics. Snyder Bembry was killed in this manner by an English-speaking North Vietnamese, probably an officer. He shot Bembry, as Bembry, screamed, with a full automatic weapon, and then spoke these words in English: 'Wait a minute. Who are we shooting?' I almost blurted out 'Americans' in answer before I realized what was happening. He had an accent." PFC Snyder P. Bembry of Unadilla, Georgia, was twenty-one years old when he died.

Unable to fight back or do anything to save his buddies from the Vietnamese executioners, James Shadden took the last course left to him: He booby-trapped his own body. "The shot in the arm left me with nothing but a grenade, which I couldn't throw left-handed, so I refrained from trying," Shadden recalls. "And more of the enemy were coming my way from the other side. So I slid the grenade under my armpit, pin pulled. I figured if they got me I might get them."

Specialist 4 Bob Towles of the Delta Company antitank platoon had run into a grassy clearing, leading the way for a dozen of his buddies, several of them badly wounded. He stopped and looked back through the woods toward the column: "I peered through the grass and managed to locate our previous position. There were the North Vietnamese, rummaging what we had left behind. Then they fired bursts from their AKs into the ground. Now I realized what else we had left behind. All of us hadn't made it out of there. I considered shooting at them. Then I thought better about it. It would only attract their attention and we were in no condition to fight."

Most of the people with Towles were wounded, sprawling on the ground and lying on top of each other. "We couldn't function as a combat unit from this pile. At that moment, Sergeant Baker ordered me to move out again. I got up and headed for the wood line on the far side of the clearing. After covering about fifty yards, I noticed movement in the trees off to my right. Americans! I cut to the right and entered the clump of trees. Ten or fifteen yards into the trees two shots rang out. I heard them whiz by behind me. Sergeant Baker lurched and fell. One bullet struck his chest, the other his back. He was a half-step behind and to the left of me. I stopped, knelt, and scanned the trees. Nothing. Sergeant Baker clutched his chest and ordered me to keep going. Just then someone else reached him and helped him to get up." Towles rose and turned in the direction he had been heading before Baker went down. "I saw Sergeant [Miguel] Baeza kneeling behind a tree and got to him. It took a few moments to catch my breath and compose myself. Then I asked him for information about this sector. He wasn't sure. I informed him the enemy had wiped out the mortar platoon, then over-ran Charlie Company. Baeza pulled out his bayonet, slit my shirt sleeve, and bandaged my right arm. My hand had frozen to the pistol grip of my M-16, but my trigger finger still worked. No pain; my arm was numb.

"I looked around our position. It seemed pretty good. Trees large enough to give some protection formed an arc facing a clearing opposite the one we had just traversed. The other men formed up, facing the direction we just came from. A few men guarded off west and north. I noticed PFC Lester Becker off by himself facing east. His large tree could easily be occupied by two men. I told Sergeant Baeza I'd go over with Becker and help cover that area. I ran the ten yards to the tree and took position on the right side of it."

From behind that tree Bob Towles and Lester Becker heard moaning nearby in the tall grass of the clearing and decided to investigate. Towles remembers, "I went around the right side of the tree, Becker the left. Instantly two shots. I heard the chilling sound of the bullets' thump as they both hit soft tissue. I stared paralyzed with disbelief as Becker slumped to the ground grasping his stomach. I couldn't move. Others ran across and dragged him to the shelter of the tree. At that moment, Captain Hank Thorpe [the Delta Company com-mander] appeared behind us. He shouted for us to fall back to his position. We obeyed and carried Becker on a poncho. Once there, we left Becker with the medics. He survived to be medevac'd, but died later." Becker, twenty-five, was from Harvard, Illinois.

Towles's small group of Delta Company survivors had reached the Albany clearing. They joined the thin line of defenders in the cluster of trees where the battalion command post was located.

At the other end of the column, Captain George Forrest was now herding his men of Alpha Company, 1st Battalion, 5th Cavalry off the trail and into a defensive posture.

Alpha Company rifleman James Young remembers Forrest ordering their withdrawal across a grassy clearing that was under enemy fire and then asking for a volunteer for a dangerous mission. Alpha Company was taking incoming fire from a machine gun that, by the sound of it, was an American M-60. Forrest wanted someone to crawl out into the tall grass, locate the machine gun, and tell the gunners that they were shooting fellow Americans.

Young, who had grown up in the Missouri backwoods and knew something about stalking, said he would go. "Another rifleman, a PFC from Chicago, Ronald Fortune, said he would go with me. We started crawling with that machine gun firing over our heads. It was an M-60 and we all assumed it was Americans. When we got close, fifty or sixty yards away, we started yelling at them. Then I realized that they were enemy. It was as though someone told me: 'These are not our men. They are not responding to our calls.' "

Young told Fortune to stop yelling. "I continued to crawl in their direction, trying to locate their exact position. I intended to take them out. Then a bullet struck me in the head. I knew I was hit in the head, and I thought I was going to die. It dazed me good but didn't knock me out. I had my chin strap on so it didn't knock my helmet off. I asked Fortune if he would get in touch with my parents and tell them that my last concern was for them. I thought it was over for me. I asked him to bandage me. He took the bandage off my belt and he patched me up. He was telling me it wasn't too bad, that I was going to be all right.

"Then I tried to crawl in the direction of the machine gun again. Fortune thought I was out of my head and tried to stop me. We were both down low. Every time I would move he would grab me by my legs and hold me. After struggling with me for a while, he said, 'I'm going back,' and he left. I told him I was going to get that machine gun. What it was, I really was afraid to turn my back on that machine gun."

The machine-gun bullet had pierced Young's helmet and crushed his skull on one side of his head. But he was still determined to take out that gun. "As I moved I heard the Vietnamese calling out something. After that I never heard the gun fire again. What I heard were orders for them to pack it up and move. I moved to where I thought it was, still afraid to raise my head on account of snipers. There was lots of shooting. I never found the gun. They were gone."

Lieutenant Enrique Pujals – a Pennsylvania Military College classmate of Lieutenant Jack Geoghegan of Charlie Company, 1st Battalion, 7th Cav, who was killed at LZ X-Ray – was leading the twenty-four-man 3rd Platoon of Captain Skip Fesmire's Charlie Company, 2nd Battalion. His platoon, bringing up the rear of the company, was just ahead of the headquarters detachment. Pujals says he had his men in column formation, but not in single file, when the shooting erupted.

"Then I got the order on the radio: Deploy your platoon and maneuver right. I used hand and arm signals to get the platoon on line. When I looked back, I was several yards ahead, on my own, and the platoon was still in their positions. I went back, giving verbal commands to get on line and follow me, and to pass the word. Some were getting together when the radio operator called me and said the Company Commander had a message for me: "Hold where you are. Stop the maneuver and fire only at a target." I tried to get information on what the hell was going on, but he said, "Out."

"The firing was still going on up to my right front. Then bullets started to come our way. I thought they were from the lead American elements. Not many, but they caused me concern. I tried to raise anyone on the radio to get them to watch where they fired and to give me a situation report. Still nothing. I tried to form a perimeter of sorts. Meanwhile, up front, the screams kept on as part of the weird symphony of battle sounds."

Pujals couldn't believe that the entire battalion was firing everything it had just because of a couple of snipers. "I told my radio operator that I was moving up to find the weapons platoon leader. The vegetation changed as I moved. Where my platoon was there were trees and shrubs 10–15 feet apart and waist-high grass (for me, 5 foot 6 inches tall, sometimes it was nearly neck high). But the weapons platoon had entered a very thick spot with thick grass, and very, very tall clumps of bushes. We were moving in column. The weapons platoon was in file."

Pujals asked a couple of the men he met where their platoon leader was, and was told: Up ahead. Very few men were prone; very few were facing out toward the firing. Most were leaning on something or other, resting. Nobody seemed to know what was going on. "I moved ahead. I was on the outskirts of the thicket when I felt a stabbing shock on my left heel. I thought I had stepped on one of those infamous punji stakes. I grabbed my left leg to pull it off, when I felt like I'd been struck with a sledgehammer on my right thigh. I saw it out of the corner of my eye – a little puff of dust and the trouser leg split and I knew I was hit.

"My thoughts were silly, a little phrase we had used back in the world to signify something was amiss: 'There goes the weekend.' My right leg just twisted all out of shape and began to crumple under me. I tried to shove myself as far back as I could to avoid having it fold under me as I fell. I made it. My leg was stretched in front in a more or less normal position. My thigh was broken. No doubt about it. I was now flat on my back and useless and helpless. What could I do? Yes, call for the medic. But what if they killed my medic as he came to help me? I was bleeding and if I kept this up I'd bleed to death so I chanced it and called.

"He came over with one of my fire-team leaders. They patched me up. I had them splint my M-16 to my right leg, up high. Then the medic took out a morphine ampule. I refused, protested, tried to avoid it, but I still got stuck. They pulled me up to a tree and helped me take off my pack. I had 15 loaded magazines in it and 800 rounds extra I'd picked up at Chu Pong. The guys from the 1st Battalion 7th Cav had said to take as much ammo as you could carry, and then more. I asked for my two canteens and they got them for me."

Pujals called to his platoon sergeant and told him to take command, and as he did the firing shifted. "My platoon began to get it. The blades of grass were cut at the level of my chest and fell on me. Now the screams were from my men. I did not see them die, but I certainly heard them. One of them screamed, 'Oh my God, forgive me!' I still believed we were under fire by our own troops. I was extremely angry. My men were dying around me and I could do nothing. Those were my thoughts. Later I learned the truth and was ashamed."

At the head of the column, the small group of men and officers with Lieutenant Colonel McDade was locked in a heavy firefight with an enemy determined to overrun them. Captain Joel Sugdinis of Alpha Company, 2nd Battalion, still worried about his missing 2nd Platoon, had shifted to the southeastern side of the grove of trees to watch the area across the clearing where his men had disappeared.

Sugdinis recalls, "I could see movement, but I couldn't tell whether they were our people or the enemy. I saw one soldier stand up and start helping a wounded soldier hobble away from the battle. I picked up binoculars. When I focused in on the two, they were North Vietnamese and the more healthy one was firing his AK-47 from his hip at what appeared to be objects close to his feet. My thought was that he was executing our wounded. I fired one shot and they both went down. After the battle we removed many of our 2nd Platoon dead from that area and several had been shot in the head.

"Someone from the vicinity of the command group yelled

that the North Vietnamese were crawling up on us from the south. There was an open area on the south side with knee-to-waist-high grass. Those of us who were standing turned and began firing into the grass. Several North Vietnamese attempted to flee. One North Vietnamese stood up and continued to advance directly toward us firing his AK-47 from his hip, John Wayne style. I think everyone who saw him fired directly into him. I'm sure it was only a second or two, but it seemed he would never go down."

Lieutenant Pat Payne and his recon platoon had been in the thick of the fight around the Albany clearing since the beginning. "During the first hour, at least, we did not have any artillery coverage at all. We were learning a bitter lesson. The second thing is we had no helicopter coverage. We had no gunships overhead. For that first hour or two, it was belly-to-belly and man-to-man. It didn't make any difference if you were a major, captain, sergeant, or private; we were all standing shoulder to shoulder, shooting it out with the NVA. I can hear the cry 'Here they come!' and we would all rise up and cut loose. There was fear in the air, but I never sensed panic, at least not after the first ten or twenty minutes."

Payne thought the North Vietnamese had done a much better job of anticipating and preparing for the attack, "but the Americans who survived the initial onslaught began to rally. In one respect, you could think of it as the Little Big-horn; we were surrounded, with our packs in front of us, shooting it out. During the course of that long afternoon I never saw a soldier not do his duty. I never saw anyone who cowered in the face of the enemy. Our backs were against the wall and it was a matter of survival. Every person I saw rose to the occasion. Somewhere during the afternoon we started to get some sort of artillery support. However, since we were so spread out I don't recall us being able to use it effectively for close fire support."

The fighting had been under way for well over an hour when Lieutenant Larry Gwin, the Alpha Company executive officer, looked to the northwest, where Alpha Company's 1st

Platoon had disappeared in the first assault. He was stunned by what he saw: "Two men were staggering over to our position! They were Staff Sergeant Walter T. Caple, acting platoon sergeant, and Staff Sergeant [Rother A.] Temple, a squad leader. They had fought their way out of the trap. They were exhausted and they indicated they were probably the only ones left alive. They did say that some of the company mortar platoon were in position with the Delta Company people and were OK. But we had still lost our command."

Now came the event that would turn the course of the battle at the head of the column in the Americans' favor. Lieutenant Gwin describes what happened: "Captain Jim Spires, the battalion S-3, comes dodging into our position. He tells us that tactical air is on the way and wants to know where our people are. What's our situation? He asks if any men are still out there. We said nothing. Spires said: 'You mean everybody out there is either dead or captured?' The silence was eloquent. Spires said: 'You sure?' He was satisfied we were. He ran back to the battalion anthill. The air was on the way, but I don't remember any artillery or ARA. Nobody knew where anybody was."

Shortly afterward the command came over the battalion net: Throw smoke. Lieutenant Gwin moved a little way into the grass and the men in the Albany perimeter all began to throw smoke grenades. "I saw Skip Fesmire, Charlie Company commander, throwing smoke. I had no idea what the hell he was doing up here. Our perimeter was marked with all colors of smoke, delineating our positions, and shortly after, the air strikes started

"They were A-1E Skyraiders with napalm! The first napalm canisters fell right at the point where Sugdinis and I had left the jungle and came into the clearing. We could see masses of North Vietnamese on the other side. I was very sure they were going to come across at us. I think they were cleaning up over there, shooting down at the ground, dispatching our wounded. That first strike was right on target with two napalm cans. I saw them hit the tops of the trees and jellied napalm was coming down through the tree limbs and the NVA were jumping up trying to get away and being engulfed in the flames. I saw that time and time again."

The slow, reliable old Skyraiders worked their way around the tree line surrounding the hard-pressed defenders of the Albany clearing, first using their canisters of napalm – jellied gasoline – then their 250-pound bombs, and finally employing their 20mm cannons to strafe the swarming North Vietnamese.

Lieutenant Gwin remembers, "It cleaned out swath after swath. Those fuckers would jump up and try to run. They didn't make it. By now the Americans were cheering and laughing at each strike. The cheering stopped when they dropped two canisters directly onto the position where the remnants of the 2nd Platoon had been making their stand. It might have been me, but all I could hear was the crackling of the unexpended rounds burning in the flames that had engulfed our men. None of us know if there were any still alive at the time, but then none of us want to think about it."

Gwin and others noticed that the enemy firing had slackened, but that as each of the Skyraiders made its bombing run the jungle all around erupted with enemy fire as the North Vietnamese aimed everything they had at the swooping aircraft. Gwin says, "I marveled at how beautiful those birds looked, flying directly at our position and letting fly with all they had."

Then Gwin rolled over, looked up, and saw an A-1E heading his way. "It let go the canister and it was coming right at me. It passed so close overhead I could see the rivets and it stuck in the middle of that field. One North Vietnamese jumped up and ran towards us and we shot him dead. I guess they dropped fifteen or twenty cans of napalm. One aircraft dropped his napalm in the field to our front. I thought he'd made a mistake bringing it in so close, but as it crashed to the ground and the flames burst, about five enemy leaped up only thirty yards from our perimeter and were cut in half by our fire. The last incident involved one particular enemy-manned anthill to our front with a heavy machine gun behind it, firing at the A-1Es. The crew never faltered in the face of imminent death and continued firing until one of the last napalm cans dropped smack dab on that gun and cremated the entire anthill."

Lieutenant Pat Payne, the recon-platoon leader, remembers the blessed relief that the Air Force delivered. "They were a sight for sore eyes, and the cheers rang out as they made their first runs. The plane was so close that as the pilot flew by you could see his profile in the cockpit. He made repeated passes to strafe the advancing NVA; he would slow the plane, slow it down, shoot his guns, and literally chew the ground up in front of him. Other planes arrived and began to use napalm. You could see a large number of North Vietnamese, fifty or a hundred, quite a number, within fifty or seventy-five yards of us – massing to attack – when one of the Air Force planes dropped the napalm on a direct hit on them. We began to cheer."

Major Frank Henry and Captain Joe Price, the battalion's fire-support coordinator, not only got the Air Force on target but also, for the first time in the fight, began calling down artillery strikes around the Albany clearing on clearly visible clusters of North Vietnamese soldiers in the tree line. In those areas, at least, they were fairly confident no Americans were alive. The future of what was left of this battalion began to look a little bit better.

Although badly wounded, Sergeant Major Jim Scott remembers the moment: "After the air support arrived, the artillery started coming in. This was about two hours into the fight. They would see groups of the enemy and call down fire on them. All of this was within fifty yards of us. I could actually see from my position, on top of an anthill, the NVA attempting to charge the battalion. They would form up forty or fifty men; then Frank Henry or the artillery officer would adjust the fire on them. All of a sudden there was a lull in the battle, around four or five P.M. It got quiet. I knew the battalion would survive; up till then I didn't believe we could. We had radio reports coming in that the other companies in the column were cut off, in bad shape, taking multiple casualties. They were fighting in isolated platoons and squads. I knew the casualties had to be heavy, but I don't think anyone knew exactly what the situation was at that time. Everybody was scattered."

Lieutenant Colonel McDade was understandably concerned when contact was made with the A-1Es about where they would put down the napalm and how close. "We had to worry about the risk of hitting our other people. I had no idea where George Forrest's A/1/5 company was. I knew they were close and had some general idea which direction, but we had to use the napalm and the question was, Could we use it safely? We decided: Let's bring it in as close as we can to ourselves; that would mean we were backing it away from the other units. It worked."

Back in the column, Lieutenant Bud Alley continued to search for a secure perimeter but couldn't find one. "Lieutenant Butch Aull, Charlie Company platoon leader, and one of his guys came down a little slope; he was looking for his people. He slid right in front of me on his knees. I pulled him down. About then they opened up on us. He said: 'Look where they shot me.' He was wearing a .45 tanker rig holster. He had a slug in the holster and his .45 pistol, which was right over his chest. He said he was OK, 'but they almost got me.' I asked him what we ought to do to get out of this mess. He said we needed to move over to the left side of the column, that they had it under better control there."

There were six or seven in the group. Butch Aull told them they should count out loud and, on the signal, jump up and run. About then the A-1Es made a strafing run right over them. Aull said, "We better go now." Then, says Alley, "Butch took off first, in front of me. We were just going to go five paces and down. He jumped off. I jumped off. I said: 'Butch, where are you?' I never saw or heard him again. [Second Lieutenant Earl D. Aull, twenty-three, of New Orleans, Louisiana, was killed that day.] I tried to move again. Another strafing run by the A-1Es and I jumped up under cover of that and ran again. My mindset at the time was that it was better to get hit by your own than by them."

Forward in the Albany clearing perimeter the situation was improving by the minute. Specialist 4 Dick Ackerman, of the recon platoon, remembers: "Our artillery was supporting us so close we would occasionally get some shrapnel. There were planes flying close support. We started digging in whenever we could. My entrenching tool was still attached to my pack left out in the clearing, so I used my bayonet, my fingers and someone else's tool when it was available. The comfort of a trench just big enough to hold your body is unbelievable."

No more than two hundred yards away, in that tortured column of desperate Americans, one man prayed for a miracle and the U.S. Air Force delivered it. PFC Jim Shadden, Delta Company, who had booby-trapped his own body with a hand grenade, was badly wounded and unable to move. He was directly in the path of a group of North Vietnamese soldiers methodically sweeping the ground, killing his wounded buddies. "Before the North Vietnamese got to me, half a dozen of them, a pilot came over at treetop level, turned straight up, and dropped a canister of napalm dead center on them. I never cease to be amazed at the accuracy of that drop. The heat of the napalm rolled across my face and body like an open door on a furnace. I owe this pilot more than it is possible for a human to pay. May God bless all pilots!"

Specialist Bob Towles, also wounded, was now inside the small perimeter at the head of the column: "We learned of impending artillery fire. This helped us take heart. A minute or so later a violent explosion erupted inside the perimeter. Screams, shouts, and searing white phosphorus flew everywhere. I heard cease-fire being yelled. Finally high-explosive shells exploded in the tree line on the other side of the clearing. The entire jungle disappeared in flame, smoke, and flying dirt. No one could live through that, could they? Wrong."

Towles had one more adventure to endure: "I heard a rushing noise behind me. Staff Sergeant Ronald Benton, the recon-platoon sergeant, charged across the interior of the line and dove for cover. A single shot cut the tree limb directly over my head. The limb fell and hit my helmet. I turned to curse Sergeant Benton for drawing the fire, and saw a scorpion crawling up my leg. I forgot everything else and tried to kick it off. Then I stood up, flailed around and struck it with the barrel of my rifle and ground the thing into the dirt. I realized that what had just happened was absurd. I crawled back to my tree."

Lieutenant Enrique Pujals, badly wounded and with his grasp of reality fuzzed by the morphine injection, did his best to follow radioed instructions to guide the Air Force planes: "At one time I was told to pop smoke; [and] tell the distance and direction of the smoke. My platoon sergeant, off to our rear, also popped smoke to mark the limits of our positions. No air strike at least where I was. The firing increased in our area, off to our rear. My platoon was holding on. The fire changed; it had become a series of intermittent but very intense fire-fights."

Pujals heard the sing-song voices of the enemy soldiers getting closer. "They sounded excited, pointing out dangers or targets to one another, then short intense bursts of automatic fire. Screams, sometimes. We knew what it was and someone dared utter it: 'They are killing our wounded!' This was terrible. We had lost the fight, the enemy was mopping up and taking no prisoners. We were as good as dead."

Lieutenant Pujals decided to go down with as many of the enemy as he could take. "I had two .45 pistols. One I got from my radio operator. He hadn't cleaned it in a couple of days and I had trouble charging it, I was so weak. Someone else charged it for me. I was ready. I had already died, I figured. How many would I be able to fire off on the dirty .45? I told my radio operator that now he could see why we were always on their asses about cleaning their weapons; now his life might depend on how many rounds I could get off on his dirty .45 pistol."

Pujals thought he was only seconds from oblivion when a

huge black cloud formed up right where the voices were coming from. "Napalm, I thought. The Air Force made it! The voices ceased and the noise of battle resumed, only now it was concentrated off to my right. An air strike with all the trimmings. We had won. It was all over. Only a matter of time before our troops could get to us; an hour or so. I drifted off to sleep. But the battle raged. Really intense firefights; my platoon in deep shit."

Specialist Jack Smith's ordeal with Charlie Company, on the other hand, only grew worse: "The NVA were roaming at will shooting people, hurling hand grenades, and if they weren't doing it we were shooting each other. I moved away, napalm falling so close it was making the grass curl over my head. I went to another area and again I was the only man there who wasn't wounded. It terrified me. I was bandaging up a sergeant when all of a sudden some NVA jumped on top of us. I pretended to be dead; it was easy to do since I was covered with those people's blood. The North Vietnamese gunner started using me as a sandbag for his machine gun.

"The only reason he didn't discover I was alive was that he was shaking more than I was. He couldn't have been much older than me, nineteen at the time. He started firing into our mortar platoon; our mortar platoon started firing grenades at him and his gun. I lay there thinking, *If I stand up and say, 'Fellows, don't shoot me,' the NVA will shoot me. And if I lay still like this my own men will kill me.* Grenades started exploding all around; I was wounded, the North Vietnamese on top of me was killed, that sergeant was killed. I moved to yet another position and this went on all afternoon. Everywhere I went I got wounded, but I didn't get killed. All the men around me were dead."

Although the air strikes had broken the back of the assault against the command-post perimeter, there was no shortage of North Vietnamese along the column. The 2nd Battalion commander, Lieutenant Colonel McDade, was isolated in the Albany perimiter and the setting was hardly conducive to clean, clear, and factual radio reports from the embattled companies to the batallion commander, nor from McDade up the line to Colonel Tim Brown, the 3rd Brigade commander. McDade could see what was going on in his little perimeter, but he was dependent on radios for word of what was happening in the ranks of Charlie, Delta, and Headquarters companies, and there was only silence.

Help was on the way, but it would not arrive in time nor in the right place to be of much use to the Americans still trapped and alive in the column. The division journal notes that at 2:30 P.M. the 1st Battalion, 5th Cavalry on Landing Zone Columbus was "alerted to assist" McDade's column. Captain Buse Tully's Bravo Company, 1st Battalion, 5th Cavalry was assigned the mission of attacking "to relieve the pressure and attempt to link up with the beleaguered battalion."

At 2:55 P.M., the 120 men and officers of Bravo Company began marching overland from the artillery base at LZ Columbus toward the rear of the 2nd Battalion, 7th Cav column approximately two miles away. By four P.M. Captain Tully's company was within six hundred yards of Captain George Forrest's Alpha Company, 1st Battalion, 5th Cavalry perimeter. Tully held up there until the Air Force completed its strikes on the North Vietnamese; he then resumed the march. By 4:30 P.M. his company sighted American troops, "remnants of our Company A who had broken out of the death trap."

In an account of the operation written for *Armor* magazine, an Army publication, the following year, Tully said: "Along with them were elements of Headquarters and Charlie Company, 2nd Battalion 7th Cavalry. Company A had taken many casualties and was missing one whole platoon. You cannot imagine how happy Captain George Forrest was to see friendly faces. I got a great big bear hug from him."

Tully's reinforcements deployed to secure a one-helicopter landing zone at the tail of the column to bring in medical evacuation helicopters. The time was five P.M. "When the majority of the wounded had been evacuated," Tully wrote,

I gave the order to move out toward where I thought the remainder of 2nd Battalion 7th Cavalry was located. Our Company A was to follow in column as soon as the remaining wounded were evacuated. We had not moved 400 yards when the very earth seemed to erupt with mortar and small-arms fire. The company was deployed in a wedge and had just passed over a small ridge line. To our front was a densely thicketed wood line. All three platoons came under fire simultaneously.

The NVA were in the wood line. Two men were killed and three wounded in the initial volley. One of the wounded was my 3rd Platoon leader Lieutenant Emil Satkowsky. Another was PFC Martin,* who had only 14 days left in the Army and who the night before had burned his hands so badly on a trip flare that he had been evacuated. Before leaving he swore to his buddies he would be back the next day. Sure enough, on the first supply ship into Columbus on the 17th, there he was. He had talked the doctor into just bandaging his hands and letting him come back. He was the point man in the first platoon when we got hit and had his hip torn open. At this point there was no alternative except to press the attack and hope that by taking the wood line the fire could be stopped.

By now Tully's people were beginning to spot the enemy soldiers.

The M-79 grenade launchers proved extremely effective for blowing a man out of a tree. By the time we reached the wood line we had killed enough enemy and driven the remainder far enough into the jungle that the firing

---

* Two PFCs with the last name Martin served in Captain Tully's Bravo Company – PFC Roger Martin and PFC Flemming Martin. Both were wounded in action in LZ Albany and the authors have been unable to determine which of them is the PFC Martin of Tully's article.

subsided to an occasional sniper round. About the same time, Captain Forrest radioed that more wounded had come into the clearing from the west and requested that I hold up so he could med-evac them. This process repeated itself as stragglers continued to filter in. Battalion headquarters had been advised and at 6:25 P.M. orders were received to wrap up in a two-company perimeter and prepare to sweep north to link up with the 2nd Battalion 7th Cavalry at daybreak. At nightfall, we still had 22 wounded in our perimeter. They were made as comfortable as possible for the long wait until morning.

Reinforcements were also on the way for the battalion command perimeter at the head of the column. During the afternoon, Captain Myron Diduryk's battle-weary veterans of the fight at Landing Zone X-Ray, Bravo Company, 2nd Battalion, 7th Cavalry, got a warning to prepare for a night air assault into a hot landing zone. The Bravo Company troopers, delighted to have survived the hellish fighting on X-Ray and enjoying a well-deserved rest and a lot of cold beer back at Camp Holloway, were stunned when told that they were being thrown back into a desperate situation so suddenly.

Specialist Jon Wallenius, Bravo Company mortar observer, was doing some serious celebrating. He had not only survived X-Ray without a scratch, but this day, November 17, was his birthday. "I was twenty-two years old. We were fed and showered and new clothes were available. I spent the afternoon at the Enlisted Men's Club drinking beer with the platoon, exchanging stories and celebrating my birthday. Around four P.M. Diduryk came in and told us to 'saddle up.' We were going to rescue the battalion."

"At about 1600 hours," Lieutenant Rick Rescorla recalls, "Captain Diduryk walked up. 'Get the Company together. Battalion's catching hell. We may have to go in. You're the only platoon leader left in the Company. Help all the platoons get their shit together.' Men spilled out of the Clubs and double-timed to their equipment. They worked quickly, throwing on their harnesses. No protests, but their eyes filled with disbelief. Again? Diduryk then issued the shortest frag order in Bravo Company history: 'We'll be landing from the southeast. Open fire at anything on your left. Run to your right.' A hostile landing with one side of the landing zone held by the North Vietnamese. Sitrep [situation report] from the ground: Grim. Expect to be sandwiched between friendly and enemy fires."

At about 5:45 P.M., Rescorla gathered the platoons. "They pressed in close, listening intently for the word. [SFC John A.] Uselton, the mortar platoon sergeant, [Staff Sergeant William F.] Martin, [Specialist 4 Andrew] Vincent, [Specialist Jon] Wallenius, the towering [Sergeant Larry L.] Melton. Eighty or more. Young faces, old hollow eyes. 'You know the battalion is in the shit,' I said. 'We have been selected to jump into that shit and pull them out. If you fight like you did at X-Ray you'll come through it. Stay together. Come out of those choppers ready to get it on.'

"Across the field the first lift ships were sweeping in. 'Head 'em up,' Captain Diduryk growled. I turned and walked ahead, Fantino trailing with the PRC-25. The road stretched out past the permanent hooches of the rear echelon at Holloway. Word spread that we were on a suicide flight. Tumbling out of cozy bunks, Holloway's finest lined the road to watch us depart. Hawaiian shirts, aviator shades, jeans, beer cans in hands. Cooks and bottle washers, the shit-burners, projectionists, club runners. Same Army, different species. The Company picked up pace, a tight, dirty brown column."

A few of the men carried AKs, trophies from X-Ray. "No one had shaved," noted Rescorla, "but our weapons sparkled. 'What outfit are you?' one spectator asked. 'The Hard Corps of Bravo Company, 2nd of the 7th.' 'Where are you headed?' 'To kick ass,' I yelled back. A deep rumble ran through the ranks, men yelling, cursing. Not a man among us would swap places with these lard asses. As we passed I asked Fantino:

'How we looking back there?' His reply: 'No stragglers Sir. Every swinging dick is with us.' As we made a column-right to the pickup point, I looked back at our crew. No outfit in the Army had ever rendered a route step any better than these men at this moment. We piled onto the Hueys without the usual loading instructions and skidded away into the fading gray light."

At 6:45 P.M. the first lift ships roared into the small Albany clearing and Captain Myron Diduryk's troopers bailed out into the tall grass. The cavalry had ridden to the rescue. But the killing and dying and terror continued unabated outside the American perimeter as the long night began.

Voices to America: Letters Home

Various

Sergeant John J. Woods, US Army

Yam-Ky, Vietnam
23 November 64

My dearest daughter,

This letter is just for you. I'm writing it because I don't want you to worry about me.

Over here many people are dying because there are people who think that they should rule the whole earth. There is a road – not one that you can see. This road is one that they are building. It's a road that is built on communism at the cost of many people's freedom. This country of Vietnam is in the way but the people don't want this road, so that is why they are fighting here.

Your daddy, just like other daddies, is trying to help them with this fight so we can stop this road. If we don't it may someday reach America. Freedom is something you should never take for granted. The freedom that you enjoy today cost many lives, and so will this country, too.

If for any reason Daddy goes away, remember I will not be sorry. Because Daddy believes in freedom for all people, and especially for you and Mommy.

I love you and miss you. I'm taking care to see that I do

come home and help Mommy raise you to be above all a good American.

Love,
Daddy

Joe Pais, USMC

August 30, 1965

Dear Mom,

. . . Mom, I know I will never be the same Joe. Last night I lost one of my best buddies. It wasn't Bob, but he used to run around with us. Somehow the V.C. got through our lines and threw a grenade into where my buddy was sleeping. One of my other buddies was wounded seriously and he's expected to die any time. You know, Mom, things didn't really bother me until we got out here in the bad part of Da-Nang. And now I lose two of my buddies. It's hard, Mom, to get over something like this, that's why I say it's gonna be different.

I can't even smile anymore, nothing seems funny to me, everything is serious now. Once I get out of here I never want to hear another word about Vietnam or wars. You read in the papers about demonstrators and all this other bull . . . they ask why we are over here. Well we're stopping communism over here instead of in the people's backyard back home in the U.S.A. And we're doing a damn good job over here and we'll keep on doing a good job. Our Marine Corps saying "Death Before Dishonor."

Well the rainy season has finally moved in. It rains just about every day now. Sometimes all day and all night.

I've moved to a new position now, I'm squad leader. I'm in charge of six men. Of course I'm still in heavy machine guns, our job is real dangerous, our life expectancy in combat is 7 seconds. I'll be home though, I won't let anything stop me.

I sure would like to see my family, especially my little niece. It's gonna be like a new world when I get home. Everything is gonna be so different. You know I haven't slept in a good old bed since Jan. 2. Out here we sleep on a shelter half or a poncho with one blanket. The hard ground doesn't even bother me anymore. Hot chow, we very seldom get that. We've been eating C rations ever since we got here. I'm gonna have a straight back and an iron stomach. No more food poison for me. It wouldn't even bother me . . .

Well, Mom, I'm gonna have to rush off now. I'll write more later. God bless you.

I love you,
Joe

Private John O'Halloran, United States Army

18 July 1965

Dear Dad:

. . . Well guess what, I am in *Vietnam*. Today is Sunday, July 18 and I've been here since Wed., 14 July. That makes a total of four days so far spent in hell. Since I've been here I've been in one killing, and almost killed myself. Last Friday, July 16, we went on a fire mission into war zone "D" (that's where there is nothing else but Viet Cong), and were under heavy mortar fire. Believe me, I was never so scared in all my life, seeing everything around me being blown up. Two guys were killed and seven more wounded. The Captain ordered a quick retreat, and those words sounded so good I could have kissed him.

Saturday was the worst day of all. I was one of the guys picked to go out on a patrol . . . That was the most sickening day of my life. We were walking down a road, and coming from the opposite direction was a woman and a little baby in her arms. The Sergeant told us to watch out for a trap, because the V.C. use women all the time. We were maybe fifteen feet from her and she started crying like a baby. I didn't know what was going on, and the next thing I knew the Sergeant shot the hell out of the both of them. She had a grenade under the baby's blanket which was noticeable, but she was afraid to sacrifice her kid to kill us, so she started crying. The Sergeant said it's a dirty war, but it's kill or be killed.

This coming Wed., we are going on a six-day field mission

into "D" war zone that should be a wild battle. I am in Bien-Hoa, five miles from the "D" zone. The temperature out here ranges from 100 to 133 degrees. Today the temperature is 117, and it's hot. I pull guard duty every night for two hours, so you don't get much sleep. The other night some V.C. tried to capture one of the Australians from their camp. They tried to drag him away but he blew the hell out of two of them and the others took off. We sleep in sandbag bunkers built next to our howitzers.

Well I guess that's about all for now, write soon ... I intend to buy a camera, so that I can take some pictures and show you what this jungle looks like. To prove to you how scared I am, I went to mass and confession today.

Hope to see you soon.
Love,
John

Kenneth W. Bagby, 1st Battalion, 7th Cavalry

Bagby writes to his parents describing the battle of Ia-Drang.

Plei-Ku, Vietnam
Nov. 17, 1965

Dear Folks,

I met a boy on the ship coming over to Vietnam. He was a good guy from the State of Missouri. He was my friend. We lived in the same tent together, went into An-Khe together, and spent most of our free time together. I got to know this boy well, and he was my best friend. His name was Dan Davis.

On Monday morning, the 15th of November, he died in my arms of two bullet wounds in the chest. He said, "Ken, I can't breathe." There was nothing I could do.

To the right of me another friend, whose last name was Balango, died of a wound in the throat. Up front Sergeant Brown, my squad leader, was hit in the chest and leg. To my left Sp-4 A. Learn was hit in the ankle.

We were crossing a field and were pinned down by automatic

weapons fire from the enemy. We were pinned down for about 45 minutes before the rest of the platoon could get to us, and save the rest of us.

So went the biggest and worst battle that any American force has had in Vietnam. We outdone the Marines and Airborne by a long shot. Estimated V.C. killed, 2,000. Our casualties, I cannot give the information out. The battle took place on the Cambodian border.

In another line of attack my platoon leader Lieutenant Marm was shot in the neck right beside me, about ten feet to my right. Me and Sp-4 Ahewan took him back through the lines to the aid station.

Another situation, me, Daily, and Sergeant Riley captured two V.C. and were bringing them back through the lines when we were pinned down again, as one of them spotted a buddy and tried to signal him. I was going to kill both of them but Sergeant Riley stopped me.

Our battalion, the 1st BN 7th Cav., is completely inactive due to the killed and wounded of its men. My squad which consists of nine men, three came out, myself, Sergeant Scott, and a boy named Stidell.

Folks, by all rights I should be dead. The good Lord evidently saw fit to spare me, for some reason. I prayed, and prayed and prayed some more, the three days we were in battle.

The many men that died, I will never forget. The odor of blood and decayed bodies, I will never forget. I am all right. I will never be the same though, never, never, never. If I have to go into battle again, if I am not killed, I will come out insane. I cannot see and go through it again. I know I can't. The friends I lost and the many bodies I carried back to the helicopters to be lifted out, I will never forget.

The pen that I am writing this letter with belongs to Stash Arrows, the boy that rode up to Winchester with me, on my emergency leave. Pop, remember him. He was hit three times in the back. I don't know if he is still alive or not. I hope and pray he is. God, I hope so.

Folks, don't let these men die in vain. Appreciate what they are doing over here in Vietnam. They died protecting you all, and all the people in the United States. We just cannot have the enemy get to the folks back home. We have got to stop them here, before that happens. If it is God's will, we will do it. Tell the people back home to pray for us, as we need their prayers . . .

We raised the American flag on the grounds. We were fighting on Tuesday, the 16th of November. It waved proudly for the Armed Forces and the people of America, as it did in so many battles won in World War II and Korea. I sat beside a tree and looked at it, and hoped I would never see the day it would be torn down and destroyed.

Folks, I am glad Eddy is not here and my son Kenny is not here. I hope they never have to see or experience the horrors of war. I will give my life to see that they don't . . .

As always,
Your son,
Kenneth

PFC Richard E. Marks, Company C, 1st Battalion, 3rd Regiment, 3rd Marine Division

Last Will & Testament of PFC Richard E. Marks
December 12, 1965

Dear Mom,

I am writing this in the event that I am killed during my remaining tour of duty in Vietnam.

First of all I want to say that I am here as a result of my own desire – I was offered the chance to go to 2nd Marine Division when I was first assigned to the 4th Marines, but I turned it down. I am here because I have always wanted to be a Marine and because I always wanted to see combat.

I don't like being over here, but I am doing a job that must be done – I am fighting an *inevitable* enemy that must be fought – now or later.

I am fighting to protect and maintain what I believe in and what I want to live in – a democratic society. If I am killed while carrying out this mission, I want no one to cry or mourn for me. I want people to hold their heads high and be proud of me for the job I did.

There are some details I want taken care of. First of all, any money that you receive as a result of my death I want distributed in the following fashion.

If you are single, I want you and Sue to split it down the middle. But if you are married and your husband can support you, I want Sue and Lennie to get 75% of the money, and I want you to keep only 25% – I feel Sue and Lennie will need the money a lot more.

I also want to be buried in my Marine Corps uniform with all the decorations, medals, and badges I rate. I also want Rabbi Hirschberg to officiate, and I want to be buried in the same cemetery as Dad and Gramps, but I do not want to be buried in the plot next to Dad that I bought in mind of you.

That is about all, except I hope I never have to use this letter – I love you, Mom, and Sue, and Nan, and I want you all to carry on and be very happy, and above all be proud—

Love & much more love,
Rick

Private Marks was killed on 14 February 1966. He was nineteen years old.

Staff Sergeant Nolan Drewry, United States Army

Drewry writes to his sister, Mary.

Vietnam, February 1966

I had to leave for Saigon at the drop of a hat. Some equipment came in and I had to fly down and bring it back. The 17th we lost men going out on convoy. Two of them were old buddies of mine I had known for some time. I try and not get too attached to my men as I feel bad more so than usual when one is lost. Not much to write about here except the usual unpleasant things, no more of that. I hope you can read this. My nerves are getting a little shaky. Write when you can.

Love, N.

Nolan Drewry was killed in action near Bon Long on 8 March, 1966.

Captain Rodney R. Chastant, 1st Marine Air Wing

Vietnam, 19 October 67

Mom and Dad—

Your oldest son is now a captain in the United States Marine Corps. I was promoted yesterday. Of all the men selected for captain, 1,640 men, only about 50 men have been promoted to date. I was one of the 50, to my surprise and pleasure. My effective date of rank is 1 July 1967, which means I have technically been a captain for 3½ months. I am thus due back pay for 3½ months. With this promotion, my annual income is $9,000.00 a year. I'm single, 24 years old, college-educated, a captain in the Marine Corps, and I have $11,000.00 worth of securities. That is not a bad start in life, is it?

As I understand, Dad, you were married about this point in life. There was a war going on then too. I really know very little about those years in my parents' lives. Sometime you will have to tell me about them – what you were doing, what you were thinking, what you were planning, what you were hoping.

Mom, I appreciate all your letters. I appreciate your concern that some of the things you write about are trivial, but they aren't trivial to me. I'm eager to read anything about what you are doing or the family is doing. You can't understand the importance these "trivial" events take on out here. It helps keep me civilized. For a while, as I read your letters, I am a normal person. I'm not killing people, or worried about being killed. While I read your letters, I'm not carrying guns and grenades. Instead I am going ice skating with David or walking through a department store to exchange a lamp shade. It is great to know your family's safe, living in a secure country; a country made secure by thousands upon thousands of men who have died for that country.

In the Philippines I took a bus ride along the infamous route of the death march in Bataan. I passed graveyards that were marked with row after row after row of plain white crosses. Thousands upon thousands. These were American graves – American graves in the Philippines. And I thought about the American graves in Okinawa, Korea, France, England, North Africa – around the world. And I was proud to be an American, proud to be a Marine, proud to be fighting in Asia. I have a commitment to the men who have gone before me, American men who made the sacrifices that were required to make the world safe for ice skating, department stores and lamp shades.

No, Mom, these things aren't trivial to me. They are vitally important to me. Those are the truly important things, not what I'm doing. I hope you will continue to write about those "trivial" things because that is what I enjoy learning about the most.

Your son,
Rod

Captain Chastant was killed in action on 22 October 1968.

"You're in Bad Shape, Boss"

Major Charlie A. Beckwith

The CO of DELTA Force was injured in the opening of Operation Masher, a combined US, ROKA and ARVN search-and-destroy mission which took place in January 1966 in the Binh Dinh province.

This is Operation Masher. The idea is to sweep the coastal plain, drive the Viet Cong back up to Bong Son and into the mountains, then trap them in the An Loa. Project DELTA's mission is to find the enemy units. Once they have done this, the 1st Cav will be called in.

January 27th and 28th we ran some reconnaissance flights, and then late in the afternoon of the 28th I put three teams on the ground. The An Loa Valley is surrounded by high rugged mountains covered with double canopy foliage. Everything is quiet that night and I get some sleep. At first light one team comes up on our communication net and tells us that they've not made contact but there are VC all around them. They think they should come out. I agree. Ten minutes later the other two teams come up and they're in contact. One man is hit. Both teams are taking heavy fire. It's now about 1000 hours and it's raining. I can't do anything but wait for the weather to clear. I sit in the communications tent. I can't fly. These teams out there are in serious trouble and I can't help them. Everyone is very worried.

Finally it stops raining and the clouds break up a little – not much, but a little. Major Murphy, the helicopter commander, runs over to me. He's quite emotional, "Charlie, I think we can get up there." What I have in mind is to get onto the ground with my teams. I'm going to take my sergeant major and two radio operators. I feel if I get on the ground, then my ops officer, Bo Baker, will have some leverage to get the Cav to react more quickly.

Before we leave, I hand one of the guys my GMT Rolex. It's new and I don't want to get it banged up. We take off at once. We're forced by the weather to fly at treetop level. As we get close to the teams, we start receiving fire. Almost at once a .51-caliber machine gun bullet comes through the helicopter. It goes in one side of my abdomen and comes out the other. I pass out.

The next thing I remember I'm lying on a stretcher back in Bong Son. A Green Beret medic gives me a shot of morphine. Some of the guys are standing around me. I ask. "Tell me how I am?" Lonnie Ledford says. "You're in bad shape, Boss." People are running around. The slick that brought me back can't take off. It's shot up too bad. As luck has it, a chopper comes in right then. The guys grab the pilot. "Major Beckwith's been hit and we need to get him to the hospital in Qui Nhon." Because of shock and the morphine, I don't yet know exactly where I've been hit, and I don't feel pain. I remember the helicopter ride, the litter, the hospital. I don't know its number. (I get it later, the 85th EVAC.) My brain clears for a while. Triage. A big red-headed nurse major comes up and looks me over. Then two doctors. One of them says, "He'll bleed to death before we can do anything for him." They agree, I'm not worth fooling with. I'm not going to make it. I grab the big nurse, she's closest, "Now let's get one thing straight here. I ain't the average bear, and I didn't come in here to pack it in." That gets the two doctors' attention. They begin to prepare me for surgery. This part's as clear as a bell. I become very violent and very profane. It's taking them too long. I know I'm dying. "Goddamn it, let's get on with it." The nurse starts fooling with my arm. I still have a scar where she cut me trying to type my blood. I curse her. "I have to find out what type blood you have." "Goddamn it," I yell, "I'm A-positive. Look at my dog tags." They aren't real happy with me. They keep farting around. "Goddamn, let's move. Let's go!" I'm rolled into surgery. I start counting down from 100 and get to 94.

In the recovery room when I came to I knew I was in bad shape. I had hoses running in and out of me all over. A doctor came in and told me he'd had to remove my gallbladder and twenty-one inches of my small intestine. They'd cut me from the top of my chest all the way down to just above my penis. They had sewn me up with what looked like piano wire. They'd also done a temporary colostomy. The doctor told me I was fortunate to be alive.

I was very thirsty, but the nurses couldn't give me any water. Every couple of hours I got an ice cube to suck.

That evening a Hawaiian boy, shot up worse than I, was rolled in from the operating room. The duty nurse came over to me and said, "Major, this boy next to you is in a bad way." He'd been gut shot as well as having been hit in the shoulder, the hip, and the leg. He lay on the cot next to me. I reached over and grabbed his hand. "It's up to you," I told him. "If you want to make it you can. It's all in your mind." I squeezed as hard as I could. "If you want to quit you'll be dead by morning. If you're strong you'll live. Goddamn, son, make up your mind." He barely squeezed my hand back. Just a little pressure. As it turned out, he was up and out of the hospital long before I was.

I stayed in the recovery ward for thirty days. Again, they thought I was going to die. Bullets are not clean and I was severely infected. At first no one knew what was wrong with me. I went way down. I had a terrible fever. They called the chaplain and I had a last little conference with him. The doctor came around in the morning. I told him, "I feel like shit. I ain't sure I'm gonna make it. I'm losing strength." He said, "We can't figure it out." I said, "You know, I got a lump over here." He put his hand under my right armpit. "That's all pus!" Within a half hour I was back in surgery.

February 1966. I was sort of in charge of the recovery room by right of being there the longest. I was also the senior officer. There weren't a lot of majors getting shot up at this time. The doctors would bring other doctors around and they'd show them my operations. I was sort of, I guess, a showpiece. One doctor came looking for me. He wanted to see himself this man who had gone through twenty-three pints of blood during surgery.

There were many people coming in and out of that hospital. You could tell there was a war going on. Being next to the operating room I often saw doctors just come in, find a cot, and fall asleep for an hour until it was time to go back to work. They worked around the clock. The nurses were good to me. At night, when I couldn't sleep, they'd bring me a small cup of Kool-Aid. Goddamn, I really appreciated that.

One day a boy, just out of the OR, came out of his anesthesia and began to howl. I tried to encourage him, but he just laid there and shouted and moaned. This went on all night. He began to drive everyone in recovery crazy. Finally, about four o'clock I said, "You're the noisiest sonovabitch I've ever heard." About six o'clock he stopped hollering – when he died.

Another time, the nurses and orderlies came around sweeping, washing and cleaning. "What the hell's going on," everyone wanted to know. No one knew. All they'd heard was a code 7 or something was coming up for a visit. They knew the code number was the highest they'd ever received. That afternoon General Westmoreland paid a visit. He sat by my bed for a while and asked if I needed anything. He talked to every soldier there.

My guys came around to see me. Lonnie Ledford returned my Rolex. I had known Lonnie a long time. He'd been my old ops sergeant back in Buzz Miley's B Company at Fort Bragg. I'd told the guys that if anything ever happened to me I wanted them to divide up the weapons I'd collected and stored in my footlocker. I'd picked up a couple of folding-stock carbines and bolt-action rifles – things like that.

"How about the weapons?" I asked Ledford.

"We've divided them up."

"Can I have my 9mm Browning?"

"Nope. Sorry, sir. They're all divided up."

Lonnie also told me what happened to the three recon teams after I was hit. The first team that had come up on the radio early, the one which was not engaged, got out O.K. The other two, the ones I tried to reach, were not as fortunate. The 1st Cav made no effort to help them after I went down. Seven men were killed. The others hid in the jungle and eventually made their way out.

Hal Moore, the CO of the Cav's 3rd Brigade, the guy that had said, "You find them. I'll kill them," came around once and visited with his soldiers. I knew damn well he knew I was in that hospital, but he never said a word to me. I was wounded while supporting his brigade.

Soon I was flown to the Philippines. Then, with a large batch of wounded. I was moved to Letterman General Hospital in San Francisco. The next morning, early, 4:00 A.M., they woke all of us who had come in the night before and moved us to the loading area outside the hospital. We began to wait for the ambulances. We lay on our stretchers and waited. I'll tell you, San Francisco in March is cold. I began to hear guys up and down the line: "You know, I'm freezing my ass off." I was too. Finally, I started hollering. A nurse came out after a while, "What's your problem?" I said, "My problem is I want to see who is in charge of this hospital and I damn want to see him now! If you don't get him, I'm going to raise more hell than you ever thought about." A lieutenant colonel came over to me. I reached up and got hold of him by the hand. "You're the dumbest sonovabitch I've known. We've been lying out here over an hour, freezing to death. You get some blankets out here." In less time than it takes to tell it, we had blankets.

I eventually arrived at my final destination, Great Lakes

Naval Hospital outside of Chicago. Katherine came over from Michigan, where she had taken an apartment near her parents, and was there to welcome me with her loving care.

Of course, all during this period I was really concerned about where I was going next. I requested that I be sent to the 10th Special Forces Group in Germany. Then, one day while I was sitting in bed reading, the phone rang. I picked it up and heard, "Is this that snotty-nosed motor pool officer I sent to England?" It was Col. Boppy Edwards, who was now Director of the Ranger Department at Fort Benning. "Where you going to be reassigned?" I told him Germany. "I don't think you want to do that. I think you want to come on down to Benning and run one of the Ranger camps for me. Charlie, do you object if I sort of put my oar in the water and get your assignment changed?" Within a few days I was ordered to report to Fort Benning, Georgia.

In early May 1966, the doctors finally cleared and released me. After some more rest I went over to Detroit and bought a black Harley Sprint motorcycle. I planned on riding it from Michigan to Fort Benning. I like to feel the wind in my hair.

The General Goes Zapping Charlie Cong

Nicholas Tomalin

Tomalin was a reporter for the London *Sunday Times*. His article "The General Goes Zapping Charlie Cong' is one of the sources for Coppola's *Apocalypse Now*, with the real-life General James F. Hollingsworth transmogrified into Lt-Col Bill "Charlie Don't Surf" Kilgore.

Tomalin was killed in 1973 reporting the Yom Kippur War.

Sunday Times, 5 June 1966

After a light lunch last Wednesday, General James F. Hollingsworth, of Big Red One, took off in his personal helicopter and killed more Vietnamese than all the troops he commanded.

The story of the General's feat begins in the divisional office, at Ki-Na, twenty miles north of Saigon, where a Medical Corps colonel is telling me that when they collect enemy casualties they find themselves with more than four injured civilians for every wounded Viet Cong – unavoidable in this kind of war.

The General strides in and pins two medals for outstanding gallantry to the chest of one of the colonel's combat doctors. Then he strides off again to his helicopter, and spreads out a polythene-covered map to explain our afternoon's trip.

The General has a big, real American face, reminiscent of every movie general you have seen. He comes from Texas, and is forty-eight. His present rank is Brigadier General, Assistant Division Commander, 1st Infantry Division, United States Army (which is what the big red figure one on his shoulder flash means).

"Our mission today," says the General, "is to push those goddam VCs right off Routes Thirteen and Sixteen. Now you see Routes Thirteen and Sixteen running north from Saigon toward the town of Phuoc Vinh, where we keep our artillery. When we got here first we prettied up those roads, and cleared Charlie Cong right out so we could run supplies up.

"I guess we've been hither and thither with all our operations since, an' the ol' VC he's reckoned he could creep back. He's been puttin' out propaganda he's goin' to interdict our right of passage along those routes. So this day we aim to zapp him, and zapp him, and zapp him again till we've zapped him right back where he came from. Yes, sir. Let's go."

The General's UH 18 helicopter carries two pilots, two 60-calibre machine-gunners, and his aide, Dennis Gillman, an apple-cheeked subaltern from California. It also carries the General's own M-16 carbine (hanging on a strut), two dozen smoke-bombs, and a couple of CS anti-personnel gas-bombs, each as big as a small dustbin. Just beside the General is a radio console where he can tune in on orders issued by battalion commanders flying helicopters just beneath him, and company commanders in helicopters just below them.

Under this interlacing of helicopters lies the apparently peaceful landscape beside Routes Thirteen and Sixteen, filled with farmhouses and peasants hoeing rice and paddy fields.

So far today things haven't gone too well. Companies Alpha, Bravo and Charlie have assaulted a suspected Viet Cong HQ, found a few tunnels but no enemy.

The General sits at the helicopter's open door, knees apart, his shiny black toecaps jutting out into space, rolls a filtertip cigarette to-and-fro in his teeth, and thinks.

"Put me down at Battalion HQ," he calls to the pilot.

"There's sniper fire reported on choppers in that area, General."

"Goddam the snipers, just put me down."

Battalion HQ at the moment is a defoliated area of four acres packed with tents, personnel carriers, helicopters and milling GIs. We settle into the smell of crushed grass. The General leaps out and strides through his troops.

"Why, General, excuse us, we didn't expect you here," says a sweating major.

"You killed any 'Cong yet?"

"Well no, General, I guess he's just too scared of us today. Down the road a piece we've hit trouble, a bulldozer's fallen through a bridge, and trucks coming through a village knocked the canopy off a Buddhist pagoda. Saigon radioed us to repair that temple before proceeding – in the way of civic action, General. That put us back an hour . . ."

"Yeah. Well, Major, you spread out your perimeter here a bit, then get to killin' VCs, will you?"

Back through the crushed grass to the helicopter.

"I don't know how you think about war. The way I see it, I'm just like any other company boss, gingering up the boys all the time, except I don't make money. I just kill people, and save lives."

In the air the General chews two more filtertips and looks increasingly forlorn. No action on Route Sixteen, and another Big Red One general has got his helicopter in to inspect the collapsed bridge before ours.

"Swing us back along again," says the General.

"Reports of fire on choppers ahead, sir. Smoke flare near spot. Strike coming in."

"Go find that smoke."

A plume of white rises in the midst of dense tropical forest, with a Bird Dog spotter plane in attendance. Route

Sixteen is to the right, beyond it a large settlement of red-tiled houses.

"Strike coming in, sir."

Two F-105 jets appear over the horizon in formation, split, then one passes over the smoke, dropping a trail of silver, fish-shaped canisters. After four seconds' silence, light orange fire explodes in patches along an area fifty yards wide by three-quarters of a mile long. Napalm.

The trees and bushes burn, pouring dark oily smoke into the sky. The second plane dives and fire covers the entire strip of dense forest.

"Aaaaah," cries the General. "Nice. Nice. Very neat. Come on low, let's see who's left down there."

"How do you know for sure the Viet Cong snipers were in that strip you burned?"

"We don't. The smoke position was a guess. That's why we zapp the whole forest."

"But what if there was someone, a civilian, walking through there?"

"Aw come on, you think there's folks just sniffing flowers in tropical vegetation like that? With a big operation on hereabouts? Anyone left down there, he's Charlie Cong all right."

I point at a paddy field full of peasants less than half a mile away.

"That's different, son. We know they're genuine."

The pilot shouts, "General, half right, two running for that bush."

"I see them. Down, down, goddam you."

In one movement he yanks his M-16 off the hanger, slams in a clip of cartridges and leans right out of the door, hanging on his seatbelt to fire one long burst in the general direction of the bush.

"General, there's a hole, maybe a bunker, down there."

"Smoke-bomb, circle, shift it."

"But General, how do you know those aren't just frightened peasants?"

"Running? Like that? Don't give me a pain. The clips, the clips, where in hell are the cartridges in this ship?"

The aide drops a smoke canister, the General finds his ammunition and the starboard machine-gunner fires rapid bursts into the bush, his tracers bouncing up off the ground round it.

We turn clockwise in ever tighter, lower circles, everyone firing. A shower of spent cartridge cases leaps from the General's carbine to drop, lukewarm, on my arm.

"I . . . WANT . . . YOU . . . TO . . . SHOOT . . . RIGHT . . . UP . . . THE . . . ASS . . . OF . . . THAT . . . HOLE . . . GUNNER."

Fourth time round the tracers flow right inside the tiny sand-bagged opening, tearing the bags, filling it with sand and smoke.

The General falls back off his seatbelt into his chair, suddenly relaxed, and lets out an oddly feminine, gentle laugh. "That's it," he says, and turns to me, squeezing his thumb and finger into the sign of a French chef's ecstasy.

We circle now above a single-storey building made of dried reeds. The first burst of fire tears the roof open, shatters one wall into fragments of scattered straw, and blasts the farmyard full of chickens into dismembered feathers.

"Zapp, zapp, zapp," cries the General. He is now using semi-automatic fire, the carbine bucking in his hands.

Pow, pow, pow, sounds the gun. All the noises of this war have an unaccountably Texan ring.

"Gas bomb."

Lieutenant Gillman leans his canister out of the door. As the pilot calls, he drops it. An explosion of white vapour spreads across the wood a full hundred yards downwind.

"Jesus wept, lootenant, that's no good."

Lieutenant Gillman immediately clambers across me to get the second gas bomb, pushing me sideways into his own port-side seat. In considerable panic I fumble with an unfamiliar seatbelt as the helicopter banks round at an angle of fifty degrees. The second gas bomb explodes perfectly, beside the house, covering it with vapour.

"There's nothing alive in there," says the General. "Or they'd be skedaddling. Yes there is, by golly."

For the first time I see the running figure, bobbing and sprinting across the farmyards towards a clump of trees dressed in black pyjamas. No hat. No shoes.

"Now hit the tree."

We circle five times. Branches drop off the tree, leaves fly, its trunk is enveloped with dust and tracer flares. Gillman and the General are now firing carbines side by side in the doorway. Gillman offers me his gun: No thanks.

Then a man runs from the tree, in each hand a bright red flag which he waves desperately above his head.

"Stop, stop, he's quit," shouts the General, knocking the machine-gun so tracers erupt into the sky.

"I'm going to take him. Now watch it everyone, keep firing round-about, this may be an ambush."

We sink swiftly into the field beside the tree, each gunner firing cautionary bursts into the bushes. The figure walks towards us.

"That's a Cong for sure," cries the General in triumph and with one deft movement grabs the man's short black hair and yanks him off his feet, inboard. The prisoner falls across Lieutenant Gillman and into the seat beside me.

The red flags I spotted from the air are his hands, bathed solidly in blood. Further blood is pouring from under his shirt, over his trousers.

Now we are safely in the air again. Our captive cannot be more than sixteen years old, his head comes just about up to the white name patch – Hollingsworth – on the General's chest. He is dazed, in shock. His eyes calmly look first at the General, then at the Lieutenant, then at me. He resembles a tiny, fine-boned wild animal. I have to keep my hand firmly pressed against his shoulder to hold him upright. He is quivering. Sometimes his left foot, from some nervous impulse, bangs hard against the helicopter wall. The Lieutenant applies a tourniquet to his right arm.

"Radio base for an ambulance. Get the information officer

with a camera. I want this Commie bastard alive till we get back . . . just stay with us till we talk to you, baby."

The General pokes with his carbine first at the prisoner's cheek to keep his head upright, then at the base of his shirt.

"Look at that now," he says, turning to me. "You still thinking about innocent peasants? Look at the weaponry."

Around the prisoner's waist is a webbing belt, with four clips of ammunition, a water bottle (without stopper), a tiny roll of bandages, and a propaganda leaflet which later turns out to be a set of Viet Cong songs, with a twenty piastre note (about one shilling and six pence) folded in it.

Lieutenant Gillman looks concerned. "It's OK, you're OK," he mouths at the prisoner, who at that moment turns to me and with a surprisingly vigorous gesture waves his arm at my seat. He wants to lie down.

By the time I have fastened myself into yet another seat we are back at the landing pad. Ambulance orderlies come aboard, administer morphine, and rip open his shirt. Obviously a burst of fire has shattered his right arm up at the shoulder. The cut shirt now allows a large bulge of blue-red tissue to fall forward, its surface streaked with white nerve fibres and chips of bone (how did he ever manage to wave that arm in surrender?).

When the ambulance has driven off the General gets us all posed round the nose of the chopper for a group photograph like a gang of successful fishermen, then clambers up into the cabin again, at my request, for a picture to show just how he zapped those VCs. He is euphoric.

"Jeez I'm so glad you was along, that worked out just dandy. I've been written up time and time again back in the States for shootin' up VCs, but no one's been along with me like you before."

We even find a bullet hole in one of the helicopter rotor blades. "That's proof positive they was firin' at us all the time. An' firin' on us first, boy. So much for your fellers smellin' flowers."

He gives me the Viet Cong's water bottle as souvenir and

proof. "That's a Chicom bottle, that one. All the way from Peking."

Later that evening the General calls me to his office to tell me the prisoner had to have his arm amputated, and is now in the hands of the Vietnamese authorities, as regulations dictate. Before he went under, he told the General's interpreters that he was part of a hardcore regular VC company whose mission was to mine Route Sixteen, cut it up, and fire at helicopters.

The General is magnanimous in his victory over my squeamish civilian worries.

"You see, son, I saw rifles on that first pair of running men. Didn't tell you at the time. And, by the way you mustn't imagine there could have been ordinary farm folk in that house, when you're as old a veteran as I am you get to know about those things by instinct. I agree there was chickens for food with them, strung up on a pole. You didn't see anything bigger, like a pig or a cow, did yuh? Well then."

The General wasn't certain whether further troops would go to the farmhouse that night to check who died, although patrols would be near there.

It wasn't safe moving along Route Sixteen at night, there was another big operation elsewhere the next day. Big Red One is always on the move.

"But when them VC come back harassin' that Route Sixteen why, we'll zapp them again. And when they come back after that we'll zapp them again."

"Wouldn't it be easier just to stay there all the time?"

"Why, son, we haven't enough troops as it is."

"The Koreans manage it."

"Yeah, but they've got a smaller area to protect. Why, Big Red One ranges right over – I mean up to the Cambodian Border. There ain't no place on that map we ain't been.

"I'll say perhaps your English generals wouldn't think my way of war is all that conventional, would they? Well, this is a new kind of war, flexible, quick moving. Us generals must be on the spot to direct our troops. The helicopter adds a new dimension to battle.

"There's no better way to fight than goin' out to shoot VCs. An' there's nothing I love better than killin' 'Cong. No, sir."

Hanoi:
The Museum of the Revolution

Harrison E. Salisbury

A report from "behind the lines" in North Vietnam by Salisbury, veteran reporter for the *New York Times*. Dateline: 23 December 1966.

No one without a strong stomach should visit the Museum of the Revolution in Hanoi. Particularly not at 6 A.M. of a chilly December morning. It is a chamber of horrors – horrors of life in colonial Indochina, horrors of warfare against the French, horrors of warfare against the Americans. And passing from one exhibit to another I had the feeling that to the North Vietnamese the horrors blended together until it was difficult for them to distinguish between those which had occurred in 1885 and those which were occurring today, between the atrocities in the jungle warfare of the nineteen-hundreds and the atrocities in the jungle warfare of 1966, between the enemy who wore a French uniform and the enemy who wore an American one. The name "Museum of the Revolution" was a misnomer. This was a Museum of the Revolution, to be sure. It was filled with faded photographs of street demonstrations in the nineteen-twenties, of the hangings and torturings of revolutionary strike leaders in the rubber plantations, of manifestoes, leaflets and proclamations, proudly posed pictures of young men and women who composed the revolutionary committee, or the plenum, or the working cadre of one movement or another. It was all that. But basically it was a Museum of Vietnamese History, of Vietnamese nationalism, of the Vietnam nation, its ancient origins, its centuries of struggle for identity, for existence against one external threat after another.

First I was shown a detail map of Vietnam – all of Vietnam, North and South, with the minority nationalities picked out in mother of pearl. There were sixty of these minorities and they spattered the face of Vietnam like a case of measles. Then I was shown the prehistoric origins of the Vietnamese people – stone artifacts from Thanhhoa Province dating back, it was said, 300,000 years – axes and arrowheads.

"Notice how the arrowheads were fashioned in those times," said Director Ky. "You see how the head tapers and there is a strong indentation, then the arrowhead flares again. You know what that means? When the arrow goes in it can't be pulled out. Not unless you rip the flesh away. Our people in the mountains, the Montagnards, still use arrows made in this fashion. They cannot be pulled out once they pierce the flesh. A very useful weapon."

It was indeed. A useful, deadly weapon. I could see a man struggling to extract the head. It simply could not be done. Only a surgical operation would remove it. Each backward tug would only tear and lacerate the flesh and make a terrible wound more terrible.

He showed me another arrowhead – this one of copper, dating back to 208 B.C. It was fashioned on the same principle – a continuity in fighting technique which extended back almost three thousand centuries. A very long time. No wonder, I thought, this is so stubborn a war and fought with such frightful weapons. There was more – much more – of this kind of thing to be seen. There was a display of sharply pointed spikes set into wooden platforms. These had been buried along the trails followed by the barefooted French troops in the eighteen-seventies and eighties. In another room was a ghastly device – a kind of bird cage with movable cross-wires to which were fitted a set of jagged fishhooks. The bird cage was buried on a trail and covered with a light scattering of leaves. When a man came down the trail his leg would thrust down into the cage and the fishhooks would dig in. If he tried to lift his limb or struggle out, each pull would drive them deeper, more cruelly into the flesh. The barbs could not be removed except by a surgeon's knife. This was not a weapon of the past. This was a deadly device being set out that very day and every day in the jungle trails of the South where the Americans were seeking to flush out the Vietcong strongholds.

There were pictures of beheadings, of disembowelments, of stockades, of the "water cure," of men being buried alive and women being sliced to bits. Only by looking at the dates could one be certain whether an exhibit was historical or contemporary. The history of Vietnam was presented as one long record of torture, atrocity, killing, suffering and vengeance, and the longer I looked at the cruel parade, the stronger became my feeling that to a Vietnamese it must be almost impossible to distinguish one historic epoch from another – each blended into the other, each was equally cruel, equally ferocious.

But this was not the only impression that came through from the Museum of the Revolution.

The museum began with prehistory. But it quickly moved to the recorded wars and triumphs of Vietnam. The first heroes in the lengthy roll were Trung-Trac and Trung-Nhi – the legendary Trung sisters. Not mere folk heroes. Gods in the Vietnam iconography, twin Asian Joans of Arc. The Trung sisters lived just after the start of the Christian era – A.D. 40 is the generally accepted date. Vietnam then was under Chinese domination. The husband of Trung-Trac, a local lord, was killed by the Chinese. Trung-Trac and her sister, Trung-Nhi, rallied the populace and sallied forth against the Chinese. They drove them from the land and ascended the throne as queens. But the Chinese came back with a powerful punitive expedition. They defeated the Vietnamese, and the Trung sisters committed suicide. They entered the Vietnamese legends as gods. To this day they are worshiped. But by a curious anomaly – or perhaps not so curious – their worship was now stronger in the North than in the South. For the cult of the Trung sisters had been a special preoccupation of Madame Ngo Dinh Nhu, sister-in-law of the ill-fated Ngo Dinh Diem. She attempted to rally the Southern populace around the Trung sisters. Indeed, she seemed to act as though their spirit had been reincarnated in herself. She raised a great monument to the Trung sisters in the heart of Saigon. With her brother-in-law's death and her own precipitate fall from power, the cult of the Trungs fell into disfavor in the South. The monument was toppled from its pedestal in a symbolic act of reprisal against Madame Nhu and to this day it remained vacant. Rare was the word of the Trung sisters now heard in South Vietnam. But in the North they were venerated and held an honorable place in the Museum of the Revolution.

The next hero to whom I was introduced was Than Hung Dao, a great commander of the thirteenth century. He was celebrated for defeating a horde of 300,000 Mongols who entered the country in 1288. Three times, so I was told, the Mongols drove south. Three times they were defeated and thrust back north by the powerful generals of the Tran dynasty.

In these times the Chinese maintained nominal suzerainty over Indochina, but it was loosely exercised. Vietnam was virtually independent under its own powerful dynasties. Finally, in the fifteenth century a new challenge arose from the Ming dynasty of China. This, too, was thrust back by a Viet hero, Nguyen Trai.

As they told the story of the battles against the Mongols and the Mings, they made it seem almost like a contemporary story. The Mings, for example, had entered the country with powerful forces to re-establish Chinese power. For ten years the struggle raged. Then finally the Mings confessed defeat. Graciously the victorious Vietnamese provided their defeated enemy with horses and supplies to enable them to return to China.

"We would do the same for the Americans," the director said suddenly, underlining the thought which had arisen in my mind.

From that time on, according to the museum's version, the Vietnamese people ruled themselves. True, tribute was paid to the Forbidden City every three years. But for practical purposes the Vietnamese ran their own affairs. Peking was far away. The Nguyen dynasty reigned on its own, governing a powerful, aggressive substate which extended its domination over the now-vanished Champa Kingdom and the Khmer, or Cambodian, people and finally pushed to the shores of the Gulf of Siam.

So matters stood until the middle of the nineteenth century. For two hundred years Indochina had had extensive trade with the British, the French and the Dutch. Missionaries from the West entered the region early. The Jesuits appeared in the sixteenth century, and decade after decade a steady progress of conversion to Christianity occurred which laid the foundation for today's strong Vietnam Catholic community.

Then in the mid-nineteenth century French power began to impinge on Vietnam. French naval vessels attacked Vietnam ports in the eighteen-forties. By 1859 the French had seized Saigon. The occupation of Cochin China (the south) was completed in 1867. Hanoi was captured in 1873, but the French relinquished it only to return and seize Hanoi and Haiphong in 1883 with a handful of men. By the treaty of August 25, 1883, the Nguyen dynasty submitted to French overlordship. A protectorate was established over Tonkin (the north) and Annam (the central region). So ended Vietnam's independence.

And so began Vietnam's struggle for independence. Guerrilla warfare started almost immediately.

Indeed, whatever the actual historical record might show, the version presented by the Museum of the Revolution dated the start of today's catastrophe from the French accession in 1883. The war began on August 25 of that year. It was still in progress. It had gone through many forms. For decades the enemy was the French. Then with World War II it became the Japanese. Then the French again and now the Americans. These were distinctions of nationality with little difference of principle so far as the museum was concerned. I was to find as I spoke later with the North Vietnamese that they found it extremely hard to tell where the war against the French ended and that against the Americans began.

Now the museum brought the story swiftly down to more modern times.

It capsulized the past with a cartoon showing the French colonists sitting with their moneybags atop a pyramid formed of the backs of the suffering Vietnamese people. The cartoon interested me. It interested me enormously. I had first seen it – or its counterpart – in Bukhara, in Soviet Central Asia, where the old Emir was shown sitting on the backs of his people in precisely this manner. Then, later, I had seen it in Ulan Bator, where the Mongol rulers were shown sitting on the backs of the Mongol people in the same pyramid. Now I found it here in Indochina. I wondered how many other colonial peoples used this cartoon to simplify and epitomize for their people the story of the past.

The pattern of the story changed. It began to narrow and focus on Ho Chi Minh. He was shown early in his career. The exhibits did not quite go back to Paris at the time of World War I when Ho, as he himself has described it, was making a living as a photographer's retoucher and as a painter of freshly manufactured "Chinese antiquities." In those times, as Ho has recalled, he was a rather ignorant and naïve member of the French Socialist party, striving to gain some comprehension of the nature of the great issues which were shaking the world – Communism, Socialism, colonialism. His interests, of course, as he later was to recall, centered strongly and basically on colonialism. The attraction of Lenin was for him Lenin's understanding of the colonial problem. It was this which moved him onto the path that led to Communism and to his joining the French Communist party with its founding in 1920.

Ho, son of a minor mandarin, was born Nguyen That Than in northern Annam in 1890. The name by which the world knows him, Ho Chi Minh, means "He Who Enlightens." He chose it in adulthood, a not uncommon Vietnamese custom. Ho's father was a nationalist, and Ho, too, was a nationalist from boyhood. He made his way to Europe before World War I, working at a variety of jobs. Once he was a pastry cook in London's Carlton Hotel. For a time he worked on a French ship. He visited the United States. He appeared at the Versailles Conference and tried without success to get the statesmen of the world to grant Vietnam its independence.

The career of Ho and the struggle for Vietnam's independence became intertwined in the Revolution Museum with the early nineteen-twenties. Here he was pictured attending the Fifth Congress of the Comintern in 1924 and having his picture taken with Georgi Dimitriev, the famous Bulgarian revolutionary. Here he was shown founding the Indochinese Communist party on February 18, 1930. And here was the party's declaration of purpose:

To overthrow French imperialism, feudalism and the reactionary Vietnamese capitalist class.

To make Indochina completely independent.

To establish a worker-peasant and soldier government.

To confiscate all banks and other enterprises belonging to the imperialists and put them under the control of the worker-peasant and soldier government.

To confiscate all the plantations and property belonging to the imperialists and the Vietnamese reactionary capitalist class and distribute them to the poor peasants.

And all the rest. Signed with the name Ho was then using: Nguyen Ai Quoc.

Not all of Ho Chi Minh's history was spelled out in the wall displays and glass cases of the museum. Probably not even he could remember every twist and turn of the story. He had been a member of the French Communist party, a member of the Comintern in its great revolutionary days, a student of revolutionary techniques and tactics in Moscow; then he had gone to China, and there he had been a member of the Chinese Communist party. He had worked with Chiang Kai-shek before Chiang broke with the Communists. He had gone underground and devoted himself to revolution in his native Indochina. He had been sentenced to death by the French but found refuge in Hong Kong. He had been in a dozen prisons. Much of World War II he spent in Chinese prisons, in Liuchow and Kweilin, suspected of being a French spy. He had returned to his own land in 1945. Here under glass was the very handful of earth which he had kissed.

And here was the Declaration of Independence of the Democratic Republic of Vietnam.

This was the document of which Ho himself was author, proclaimed on September 2, 1945, when the Vietminh, the nationalist-oriented, Communist-led Vietnamese independence movement, took over power from the defeated Japanese (the French were virtually nonexistent in the north). Here was the document as it was proclaimed by Ho:

All men are created equal. They are endowed by their Creator with certain inalienable rights, among these are Life, Liberty and the pursuit of Happiness.

This immortal statement was made in the Declaration of Independence of the United States of America in 1776. In a broader sense this means all the peoples on the earth are equal from birth, all the peoples have a right to live, to be happy and free. . . .

So the document read, opening with a paraphrase – virtually an exact quotation – from our own historic proclamation.

What, I wondered, could have happened to turn history so awry? Here was a country and leader which had, for whatever reason, clearly drawn in its founding hour upon the very best of the American heritage. Yet here was a country in which I was now an enemy behind the lines, a country engaged in deep and deadly warfare with the United States, a country in arms against American power.

What had gone wrong?

Here, embedded in the Vietnamese Declaration of Independence, was another passage:

> *We are convinced that the allied nations which at Teheran and San Francisco have acknowledged the principles of self-determination and equality of nations will not refuse to acknowledge the independence of Vietnam.*
>
> *A people who have courageously opposed French domination for more than eighty years, a people who have fought side by side with the Allies against the Fascists during these last years, such a people must be free and independent.*

Within this declaration there were echoes of many things – of Ho's futile effort at Versailles to win recognition and independence for his people, of the World War II collaboration of Ho and his organization with the O.S.S. and with the Americans in the Indochinese underground, of the fierce nationalism which constantly seemed to temper and color Ho's Communism – to such an extent that not a few Americans who knew him well during and after the war were convinced that in a choice between Communism and nationalism Ho would choose nationalism – reluctantly, no doubt, and with full hopes that Communism might succeed, but nonetheless decisively.

Ho had negotiated with the French after the proclamation of Vietnam's independence in that curious document with its overtones of Thomas Jefferson and Woodrow Wilson. And an agreement had been signed on March 6, 1946, whereby France recognized Ho and his regime. It was a valid document. Ho had every reason to suppose that the long struggle – the eighty-year battle which his Declaration of Independence mentioned – had ended in success. But that went glimmering. The agreement proved to be nothing more than a piece of paper. It was never really accepted by the French, and before the year was out France and Ho's regime had slithered into violent combat. The French attacked Ho's new republic, bombarding Haiphong and killing thousands of Vietnamese in November of 1946, and a month later the Vietnamese attacked the French in Hanoi.

The deadly, dangerous drift of Vietnam into civil war and combat had begun, the slippery path that was to lead to one disaster after another, ending in the disaster of disasters at Dien Bien Phu.

Of all the events celebrated in the Museum of the Revolution this was the centerpiece – the crowning glory of Vietnam's resistance against France, the event which, I was soon to feel, had colored the Vietnamese psychology more than any other event in recent history.

Nothing equaled Dien Bien Phu and its victorious end on May 7, 1954 – the day the Vietminh, Ho's rebel movement, and its brilliant General Vo Nguyen Giap crushed the massive strongpoint which had been painstakingly built up by the French in northern Vietnam, in the valley of Dien Bien Phu, obliterating the surviving 15,094 men in the surrounded, contracting and desperately defended *place d'armes*.

The annihilation of Dien Bien Phu led directly to France's signature on July 21, 1954, of the Geneva accords, bringing to an end the Vietnam war. It was this triumph of Vietnam arms and Vietnam strategy and Vietnam tactics over Western arms and power which had etched itself into the minds of North Vietnam's leaders and which had been, through their propaganda, etched into the minds of even the lowliest of North Vietnamese peasants.

What had been done once could be done again. Patience and fortitude. If we wait long enough the Americans will follow the same path as the French and Dien Bien Phu will repeat itself. So ran the philosophy, so ran the thinking. I was to hear it again and again, either explicitly or implicitly. It lay behind every call to sacrifice, every hardship, every defeat. North Vietnam could suffer through them. It could suffer the destruction of Hanoi. Of Haiphong. The devastation of its cities and villages and fields. Because at the end like a glittering rainbow lay the promise of a new Dien Bien Phu.

I was not convinced that this psychology was valid. I did not think the parallel between France and the United States ran true. Missing from the museum was any accurate exposition of how and why the United States had become involved in Indochina. It was a chapter which I knew was missing from the background of most Americans.

The United States had stood aloof from Vietnam during the postwar struggle between Ho and the French. It was not until the outbreak of the Korean War that American interest was suddenly triggered in Southeast Asia. Vietnam then began to be seen as the "southern front" against China. It was thought to be part of the same struggle against world Communism to which we were so deeply committed in Korea. We did not commit troops, but we began to provide the French with matériel and supplies. We began to pick up more and more of the check for the costly war. Korea gradually began to yield to American pressure, but in Vietnam the French were pressed harder and harder. In the final weeks before the Dien Bien Phu disaster the French urgently called for American aid. Some American military men wanted to mount an air strike to save the French, but President Eisenhower refused.

Reluctantly the United States acquiesced in the 1954 Geneva agreement but did not sign it. With partition of the country U.S. support swiftly began to flow to the Saigon government of Diem. The gradual process of deeper and deeper American involvement had begun. But even today it was not like that of the French. The Americans fought not to stay in Vietnam but to establish a stability there which would permit them to get out.

I thought that Hanoi's reasoning, which held that the United States was a mere continuation of France, was dangerous and delusive. And as the days went by, I told this to many North Vietnamese officials. I did not believe they should deceive themselves. History sometimes repeats itself. But France was not the United States. Dien Bien Phu was not likely to happen again, and they should not count on it.

Another lesson had been ingrained in North Vietnamese minds – the lesson of distrust. This was born of North Vietnam's experience with France in 1946 and, however different our motives had been, with the United States in 1954. The Hanoi leaders felt that they had negotiated a valid end to their struggle with the French in 1946 and that Paris welshed on the agreement and utilized its terms to continue the war by other means. They thought the same thing had happened with the Geneva agreement in 1954. It had been signed, but the United States, not a signatory but now a stand-in for France, sought to overthrow its results and restore the *status quo ante.* From this stemmed a deep and constant stain of suspicion. Above all the North Vietnamese were wary of any negotiations, of any new agreement which might, in their view, turn out to be a new betrayal.

As my stay in Hanoi lengthened I came to feel, more and more, that nothing was more important in North Vietnamese minds than these two impressions born of the past – the feeling of self-confidence arising from Dien Bien Phu and that of distrust stemming from 1946 and 1954. Before any end could be brought to the war these twin barriers in Hanoi's psychology had to be overcome. Not an easy task.

Killed

Lieutenant-Commander John McCain III USN

> McCain was shot down flying a Navy A4E-Skyhawk on a
> bombing run over Hanoi in October 1967. He later became a
> US senator and presidential candidate.

We flew out to the west of Hanoi, turned, and headed in to
make our run. We came in from the west so that once we had
rolled in on the target, released our bombs, and pulled out we
would be flying directly toward the Tonkin Gulf. We had electronic countermeasure devices in our planes. In 1966, A-4s
had been equipped with radar detection. A flashing light and
different tone signals would warn us of imminent danger
from enemy SAMs. One tone sounded when a missile's radar
was tracking you, another when it had locked onto you. A
third tone signaled a real emergency, that a launched SAM
was headed your way. As soon as we hit land and approached
the three concentric rings of SAMs that surrounded Hanoi,
the tone indicating that missile radar was tracking sounded. It
tracked us for miles.

We flew in fairly large separations, unlike the tight formations flown in World War II bombing raids. At about nine
thousand feet, as we turned inbound on the target, our warning lights flashed, and the tone for enemy radar started
sounding so loudly I had to turn down the volume. I could
see huge clouds of smoke and dust erupt on the ground as
SAMs were fired at us. The closer we came to the target the
fiercer were the defenses. For the first time in combat I saw

thick black clouds of antiaircraft flak everywhere, images familiar to me only from World War II movies.

A SAM appears as a flying telephone pole, moving at great speed. We were now maneuvering through a nearly impassible obstacle course of antiaircraft fire and flying telephone poles. They scared the hell out of me. We normally kept pretty good radio discipline throughout a run, but there was a lot of chatter that day as pilots called out SAMs. Twenty-two missiles were fired at us that day. One of the F-8s on the strike was hit. The pilot, Charlie Rice, managed to eject safely.

I recognized the target sitting next to the small lake from the intelligence photographs I had studied. I dove in on it just as the tone went off signaling that a SAM was flying toward me. I knew I should roll out and fly evasive maneuvers, "jinking," in fliers' parlance, when I heard the tone. The A-4 is a small, fast, highly maneuverable aircraft, a lot of fun to fly, and it can take a beating. Many an A-4 returned safely to its carrier after being badly shot up by enemy fire. An A-4 can outmaneuver a tracking SAM, pulling more G's than the missile can take. But I was just about to release my bombs when the tone sounded, and had I started jinking I would never have had the time nor, probably, the nerve, to go back in once I had lost the SAM. So, at about 3,500 feet, I released my bombs, then pulled back the stick to begin a steep climb to a safer altitude. In the instant before my plane reacted, a SAM blew my right wing off. I was killed.

I knew I was hit. My A-4, traveling at about 550 miles an hour, was violently spiraling to earth. In this predicament, a pilot's training takes over. I didn't feel fear or any more excitement than I had already experienced during the run, my adrenaline surging as I dodged SAMs and flak to reach the target. I didn't think, "Gee, I'm hit – what now?" I reacted automatically the moment I took the hit and saw that my wing was gone. I radioed, "I'm hit," reached up, and pulled the ejection seat handle.

I struck part of the airplane, breaking my left arm, my

right arm in three places, and my right knee, and I was briefly knocked unconscious by the force of the ejection. Witnesses said my chute had barely opened before I plunged into the shallow water of Truc Bach Lake. I landed in the middle of the lake, in the middle of the city, in the middle of the day. An escape attempt would have been challenging.

I came to when I hit the water. Wearing about fifty pounds of gear, I touched the bottom of the shallow lake and kicked off with my good leg. I did not feel any pain as I broke the surface, and I didn't understand why I couldn't move my arms to pull the toggle on my life vest. I sank to the bottom again. When I broke the surface the second time I managed to inflate my life vest by pulling the toggle with my teeth. Then I blacked out again.

When I came to the second time, I was being hauled ashore on two bamboo poles by a group of about twenty angry Vietnamese. A crowd of several hundred Vietnamese gathered around me as I lay dazed before them, shouting wildly at me, stripping my clothes off, spitting on me, kicking and striking me repeatedly. When they had finished removing my gear and clothes, I felt a sharp pain in my right knee. I looked down and saw that my right foot was resting next to my left knee, at a ninety-degree angle. I cried out, "My God, my leg." Someone smashed a rifle butt into my shoulder, breaking it. Someone else stuck a bayonet in my ankle and groin. A woman, who may have been a nurse, began yelling at the crowd, and managed to dissuade them from further harming me. She then applied bamboo splints to my leg and right arm.

It was with some relief that I noticed an army truck arrive on the scene to take me away from this group of aggrieved citizens who seemed intent on killing me. Before they put me in the truck, the woman who had stopped the crowd from killing me held a cup of tea to my lips while photographers recorded the act. The soldiers then placed me on a stretcher, loaded me into the truck, and drove me a few blocks to an ocher-colored, trapezoid-shaped stone structure that occupied two city blocks in the center of downtown Hanoi.

I was brought in through enormous steel gates, above which was painted the legend "Maison Centrale." I had been shot down a short walk's distance from the French-built prison, Hoa Lo, which the POWs had named "the Hanoi Hilton." As the massive steel doors loudly clanked shut behind me, I felt a deeper dread than I have ever felt since.

They took me into an empty cell, in a part of the prison we called the Desert Inn, set me down on the floor still in the stretcher, stripped to my underwear, and placed a blanket over me. For the next few days I drifted in and out of consciousness. When awake, I was periodically taken to another room for interrogation. My interrogators accused me of being a war criminal and demanded military information, what kind of aircraft I had flown, future targets, and other particulars of that sort. In exchange I would receive medical treatment.

I thought they were bluffing, and refused to provide any information beyond my name, rank, serial number, and date of birth. They knocked me around a little to force my cooperation, and I began to feel sharp pains in my fractured limbs. I blacked out after the first few blows. I thought if I could hold out like this for a few days, they would relent and take me to a hospital.

For four days I was taken back and forth to different rooms. Unable to use my arms, I was fed twice a day by a guard. I vomited after the meals, unable to hold down anything but a little tea. I remember being desperately thirsty all the time, but I could drink only when the guard was present for my twice-daily feedings.

On about the fourth day, I realized my condition had become more serious. I was feverish, and was losing consciousness more often and for longer periods. I was lying in my own vomit, as well as my other bodily wastes. Two guards entered my cell and pulled the blanket down to examine my leg. I saw that my knee had become grossly swollen and discolored. I remembered a fellow pilot at Meridian who had broken his femur ejecting from his plane. His blood had pooled in his leg, and he had gone into shock and died. I realized the same thing was happening to me, and I pleaded for a doctor.

The two guards left to find the camp officer, who spoke some English. He was short and fat, with a strangely wandering right eye that was clouded white by a cataract. The POWs called him "Bug." He was a mean son of a bitch.

Desperate, I tried to bargain with him. "Take me to the hospital and I'll give you the information you want." I didn't intend to keep my word, reasoning that after my injuries had been treated, I would be strong enough to deal with the consequences of not holding up my end of the bargain.

Bug left without replying, but returned a short while later with a medic, a man the POWs called Zorba. Zorba squatted down and took my pulse. He turned to Bug, shook his head, and uttered a few words.

"Are you going to take me to the hospital?" I asked.

"No," he replied. "It's too late."

I appealed, "Take me to the hospital and I'll get well."

"It's too late," he repeated.

He and the doctor left my cell, and panic that my death was approaching briefly overtook me.

There were few amputees among the POWs who survived their imprisonment. The Vietnamese usually refused treatment to the seriously injured. I don't know whether they were negligent for purposes of cost efficiency, reasoning that Americans, unused to unsanitary conditions, were likely to develop fatal infections following an amputation, or if they refused us treatment simply because they hated us. Whatever the reason, a lot of men died who shouldn't have, the victims of genuine war crimes.

I lapsed into unconsciousness a few minutes after Bug and Zorba left me to my fate, a condition that blessedly relieved me of the terrible dread I was feeling. I was awakened a short while later when an excited Bug rushed into my cell and shouted, "Your father is a big admiral. Now we take you to the hospital."

God bless my father.

My parents were in London when I was shot down. They were dressing for a dinner party when my father received a telephone call saying that my plane had been shot down over Hanoi. My father informed my mother what had happened. They kept their dinner engagement, never mentioning to any of the other guests the distressing news they had just learned.

When they returned home, my father got a call from his boss, Admiral Tom Moorer, Chief of Naval Operations. Admiral Moorer was a friend and had decided to break the sad news to my father himself. "Jack, we don't think he survived."

My parents then called Carol, who had already been notified of my shootdown by the Navy. My mother told her to prepare for the worst: that I was dead, and they would have to find a way to accept that. My father, very matter-of-factly, said, "I don't think we have to."

After speaking with Carol, my parents placed calls to my sister and brother to break the bad news to them. Joe was working as a reporter for the *San Diego Tribune* at the time. He knew something was wrong when he answered the phone and both our parents were on the line.

Without any preliminaries, my mother said: "Honey, Johnny's been shot down."

"What happened?"

"He was hit by a missile and went down."

My brother's question hung in the air unanswered for a moment until my father explained: "His wingman saw his plane explode. They don't think he got out."

Joe began to cry, and then asked my father, "What do we do now?" He recalled my father answering in a soft, sad voice, "Pray for him, my boy."

The next day, October 28, Johnny Apple wrote a story that appeared on the front page of the *New York Times:* ADM. MCCAIN'S SON, *FORRESTAL* SURVIVOR, IS MISSING IN RAID.

I was moved by stretcher to a hospital in central Hanoi. As I was being moved, I again lapsed into unconsciousness. I came to a couple of days later and found myself lying in a filthy room, about twenty by twenty feet, lousy with mosquitoes and rats. Every time it rained, an inch of mud and water would pool on the floor. I was given blood and glucose, and several shots. After several more days passed, during which I was frequently unconscious, I began to recover my wits. Other than the transfusion and shots, I received no treatment for my injuries. No one had even bothered to wash the grime off me.

Once my condition had stabilized, my interrogators resumed their work. Demands for military information were accompanied by threats to terminate my medical treatment if I did not cooperate. Eventually, I gave them my ship's name and squadron number, and confirmed that my target had been the power plant. Pressed for more useful information, I gave the names of the Green Bay Packers' offensive line, and said they were members of my squadron. When asked to identify future targets, I simply recited the names of a number of North Vietnamese cities that had already been bombed.

I was occasionally beaten when I declined to give any more information. The beatings were of short duration, because I let out a hair-raising scream whenever they occurred. My interrogators appeared concerned that hospital personnel might object. I also suspected that my treatment was less harsh than might be accorded other prisoners. This I attributed to my father's position, and the propaganda value the Vietnamese placed on possessing me, injured but alive. Later, my suspicion was confirmed when I heard accounts of other POWs' experiences during their first interrogations. They had endured far worse than I had, and had withstood the cruelest torture imaginable.

Although I rarely saw a doctor or a nurse, I did have a constant companion, a teenage boy who was assigned to guard me. He had a book that he read at my bedside every day. In the book was a picture of an old man with a rifle sitting on the fuselage of a downed F-105. He would show me the picture, point to himself, and then slap me.

I still could not feed myself, so the boy would spoon-feed me a bowl of noodles with some gristle in it. The gristle was hard to chew. He would jam three of four spoonfuls in my mouth before I could chew and swallow any of it. Unable to force any more into my mouth, he would finish the bowl himself. I got three or four spoonfuls of food twice a day. After a while I really didn't give a damn, although I tried to eat as much as I could before the boy took his share.

After about a week in the hospital, a Vietnamese officer we called Chihuahua informed me that a visiting Frenchman had asked to look in on me, and had volunteered to carry a message back to my family. I was willing to see him, assuming at the time that my family probably believed I was dead.

As I later learned, the Vietnamese, always delighted when a propaganda opportunity presented itself, had already announced my capture, and helpfully supplied quotes from the repentant war criminal commending the Vietnamese people's strong morale and observing that the war was turning against the United States. And in an English-language commentary broadcast over the Voice of Vietnam, entitled "From the Pacific to Truc Bach Lake," Hanoi accused Lyndon Johnson and me of staining my family's honor.

Adding to the ever longer list of American pilots captured over North Vietnam was a series of newcomers. John Sidney McCain was one of them. Who is he? A U.S. carrier navy lieutenant commander. Last Thursday, 26 October, he took off from the carrier *Oriskany* for a raiding mission against Hanoi City. Unfortunately for him, the jet plane he piloted was one of ten knocked out of Hanoi's sky. He tried in vain to evade the deadly accurate barrage of fire of this city. A surface-to-air missile shot down his jet on the spot. He bailed out and was captured on the surface of Truc Bach Lake right in the heart of the DRV capital.

What were the feats of arms which McCain achieved? Foreign correspondents in Hanoi saw with their own eyes civilian dwelling houses destroyed and Hanoi's women, old folks and children killed by steel-pellet bombs dropped from McCain's aircraft and those of his colleagues.

Lt. Com. John Sidney McCain nearly perished in the conflagration that swept the flight deck of the U.S. carrier *Forrestal* last July. He also narrowly escaped death in Haiphong the Sunday before last but this time what must happen has happened. There is no future in it.

McCain was married in 1965 and has a ten-month-old daughter. Surely he also loves his wife and child. Then why did he fly here dropping bombs on the necks of the Vietnamese women and children?

The killing he was ordered to do in Vietnam has aroused indignation among the world's peoples. What glory had he brought by his job to his father, Admiral John S. McCain Jr., commander in chief of U.S. Naval Forces in Europe? His grandfather, Admiral John S. McCain, commander of all aircraft carriers in the Pacific in World War II, participated in a just war against the Japanese forces. But nowadays, Lt. Com. McCain is participating in an unjust war, the most unpopular one in U.S. history and mankind's history, too. This is Johnson's war to enslave the Vietnamese people.

From the Pacific to Truc Bach Lake, McCain has brought no reputation for his family in the United States. The one who is smearing McCain's family honor is also smearing the honor of Washington's United States of America. He is Lyndon B. Johnson.

Prior to the Frenchman's arrival, I was rolled into a treatment room, where a doctor tried to set my broken right arm. For what seemed like an eternity, he manipulated my arm, without benefit of anesthesia, trying to set the three fractures. Blessedly, the pain at its most acute rendered me unconscious. Finally abandoning the effort, he slapped a large and heavy chest cast on me, an act I can hardly credit as considerate on the part of my captors. The cast did not have a cotton lining, and the rough plaster painfully rubbed against my skin. Over time, it wore two holes in the back of my arm down to the bone. My other arm was left untreated.

Exhausted and encased from my waist to my neck in a wet plaster cast, I was rolled into a large, clean room and placed in a nice white bed. The room contained six beds, each protected by a mosquito net. I asked if this was to be my new room, and was told that it was.

A few minutes later, a Vietnamese officer, a Major Nguyen Bai, paid me a visit, accompanied by Chihuahua. He was the commandant of the entire prison system, a dapper, educated man whom the POWs had nicknamed "the Cat." The Cat informed me that the Frenchman who would arrive shortly was a television journalist, and that I should tell him everything I had told my interrogators. Surprised, I told the Cat I didn't want to be filmed.

"You need two operations on your leg, and if you don't talk to him, then we will take your cast off and you won't get any operations," he threatened. "You will say you are grateful to the Vietnamese people, and that you are sorry for your crimes, or we will send you back to the camp."

I assured him that I would say nothing of the kind, but believing that the Cat would send me back to Hoa Lo, and worrying that I could not endure the truck ride back, I agreed to see the Frenchman.

A few minutes later, François Chalais entered the room with two cameramen. He questioned me for several minutes, asking about my shootdown, my squadron, the nature of my injuries, and my father. I repeated the same information about my ship and squadron and told him I was being treated well by the doctors, who had promised to operate on my leg. Off camera, the Cat and Chihuahua were visibly displeased with my answers. Chihuahua demanded that I say more.

"I have no more to say about it," I replied.

Both Vietnamese insisted that I express gratitude for the lenient and humane treatment I had received. I refused, and when they pressed me, Chalais said, "I think what he told me is sufficient."

Chalais then inquired about the quality of the food I was getting, and I responded, "It's not like Paris, but I eat it." Finally, Chalais asked if I had a message for my family.

"I would just like to tell my wife that I'm going to get well. I love her, and hope to see her soon. I'd appreciate it if you'd tell her that. That's all I have to say."

Chihuahua told me to say that I could receive letters and pictures from home. "No," I replied. A visibly agitated Cat demanded that I say on camera how much I wanted the war to end so I could go home. Again, Chalais stepped in to help me, saying very firmly that he was satisfied with my answer, and that the interview was over. I appreciated his help.

Although I had resisted giving my interrogators any useful information and had greatly irritated the Cat by refusing his demands during the interview, I should not have given out information about my ship and squadron, and I regret very much having done so. The information was of no real use to the Vietnamese, but the Code of Conduct for American Prisoners of War orders us to refrain from providing any information beyond our name, rank, and serial number.

When Chalais had left, the Cat admonished me for my "bad attitude" and told me I wouldn't receive any more operations. I was taken back to my old room.

Carol went to see Chalais after he returned to Paris, and he gave her a copy of the film, which was shown in the States on the CBS evening news a short time later.

My parents saw it before it was broadcast nationally. A public affairs officer, Herbert Hetu, who worked for my father when my father was the Navy chief in Europe, had a friend who was a producer at CBS. His friend informed him that CBS had the film of my interview, and he offered to screen it for my parents. Hetu and my parents were in New York at the time. My father was scheduled to give a speech on the emerging strength of the Soviet Navy to the prestigious Overseas Press Club. It was an important and much-anticipated speech that he had been preparing for weeks.

Hetu viewed the film and decided not to show it to my father before he delivered his speech, fearing it would "uncork him." Instead, he persuaded his friend at CBS to hold the film until the morning, when my parents could view it. He then contacted my father's personal aide and told him: "After the speech, get with the admiral and tell him about this film. They're going to hold it and we'll take him over to CBS tomorrow. I'm sure he'll want to see it."

Hetu accompanied my parents to CBS the next day. He remembered my father reacting very emotionally to the film. "We took him over with Mrs. McCain, and I think I said to the admiral, 'I think you and Mrs. McCain ought to see this by yourselves. You don't want anybody else in there.' So that's the way they watched it, and it was a very emotional piece of film. . . . I think Admiral McCain and his wife looked at the film twice. His reaction afterward was very emotional, but he never talked to us about it. Some things are just too painful for words."

It was hard not to see how pleased the Vietnamese were to have captured an admiral's son, and I knew that my father's identity was directly related to my survival. Often during my hospital stay I received visits from high-ranking officials. Some observed me for a few minutes and then left without asking any questions. Others would converse idly with me, asking only a few innocuous questions. During one visit, I was told to meet with a visiting Cuban delegation. When I refused, they did not force the issue, either out of concern for my condition or because they were worried about what I might say. One evening, General Vo Nguyen Giap, minister of defense and hero of Dien Bien Phu, paid me a visit. He stared at me wordlessly for a minute, then left.

Bug arrived one day and had me listen to a tape of a POW denouncing America's involvement in the war. The POW was a Marine, a veteran who had flown in the Korean War. The vigor with which he criticized the United States surprised me. His language did not seem stilted, nor did his tone sound forced.

Bug told me he wanted me to make a similar statement. I told him I didn't want to say such things.

He told me I shouldn't be afraid to speak openly about the war, that there was nothing to be ashamed of or to fear.

"I don't feel that way about the war," I replied, and was threatened for what seemed like the hundredth time with a warning that I would be denied an operation because of my "bad attitude."

In early December, they operated on my leg. The Vietnamese filmed the operation. I haven't a clue why. Regrettably, the operation wasn't much of a success. The doctors severed all the ligaments on one side of my knee, which has never fully recovered. After the war, thanks to the work of a kind and talented physical therapist, my knee regained much of its mobility – enough, anyway, for me to return to flight status for a time. But today, when I am tired or when the weather is inclement, my knee stiffens in pain, and I pick up a trace of my old limp.

They decided to discharge me later that December. I had been in the hospital about six weeks. I was in bad shape. I had a high fever and suffered from dysentery. I had lost about fifty pounds and weighed barely a hundred. I was still in my chest cast, and my leg hurt like hell.

On the brighter side, at my request, the Vietnamese were taking me to another prison camp. Bug had entered my room one day and abruptly announced, "The doctors say you are not getting better."

The accusatory tone he used to relay this all too obvious diagnosis implied that I was somehow responsible for my condition and had deliberately tried to embarrass the Vietnamese medical establishment by refusing to recover.

"Put me with other Americans," I responded, "and I'll get better."

Bug said nothing in reply. He just looked at me briefly with the expression he used to convey his disdain for an inferior enemy, then withdrew from the room.

That evening I was blindfolded, placed in the back of a truck, and driven to a truck repair facility that had been converted into a prison a few years earlier. It was situated in what had once been the gardens of the mayor of Hanoi's official residence. The Americans held there called it "the Plantation."

To my great relief, I was placed in a cell in a building we called "the Gun Shed" with two other prisoners, both Air Force majors, George "Bud" Day and Norris Overly. I could have asked for no better companions. There has never been a doubt in my mind that Bud Day and Norris Overly saved my life.

Bud and Norris later told me that their first impression of me, emaciated, bug-eyed, and bright with fever, was of a man at the threshold of death. They thought the Vietnamese expected me to die and had placed me in their care to escape the blame when I failed to recover.

Despite my poor condition, I was overjoyed to be in the company of Americans. I had by this time been a prisoner of war for two months, and I hadn't even caught a glimpse of another American.

Hill 875

Peter Arnett

Arnett served as a correspondent for AP in Vietnam from 1962 to the fall of Saigon.

Associated Press, 22 November 1967

Hill 875, Vietnam AP – Hour after hour of battle gave the living and the dead the same gray pallor on Hill 875. At times the only way to tell them apart was to watch when the enemy mortars crashed in on the exhausted American paratroopers.

The living rushed unashamedly to the tiny bunkers dug into the red clay.

The wounded squirmed toward the shelter of trees blasted to the ground.

The dead – propped up in bunkers or face down in the dust – didn't move.

Since Sunday the most brutal fighting of the Vietnam war has ebbed and flowed across this remote hill in the western sector of the Dak To battleground. The 2nd Battalion of the 173rd Airborne Brigade went up 875 first. It nearly died.

Of the 16 officers who led the men across the ridgeline Sunday, eight were killed and the other eight wounded. Eleven of the 13 medics died.

The battalion took its first casualties at midday Sunday as it crested Hill 875, one of the hundreds of knolls that dot the

ridges in the Dak To fighting region near the Cambodi-
an-Laotian border.

All weekend as the paratroopers moved along the jungle
hills enemy base camps were uncovered. The biggest was on
875 and D Company lost several men in the first encounter
with the bunkers.

A Company moved back down the hill to cut a landing
zone and was chopped to pieces by a North Vietnamese
flanking attack.

The remnants fled back to the crest of the hill while a
paratrooper propped his gun on the trail and kept firing at
the advancing enemy, ignoring orders to retreat with the
others.

"You can keep gunning them down, but sooner or later
when there is enough of them they'll get to you," said Pfc.
James Kelly of Fort Myers, Fla, who saw the machine gunner
go down after killing about 17 North Vietnamese.

D Company, hearing the roar of battle below it, returned
to the crest of the hill and established a 50-yard perimeter
"because we figure we were surrounded by a regiment", one
officer said.

As the battalion was regrouping late in the afternoon for
another crack at the bunker system, one of the American
planes striking at the nearby enemy dropped a 500-pound
bomb too soon. About 30 of the paratroopers were killed.

"A foul play of war," said one survivor bitterly.

From then until a reinforcing battalion arrived the following night, the paratroopers on the hill dug in desperately.
Only one medic was able to work on the many wounded, and
the enemy kept driving off the rescue helicopters.

The relief battalion made it into the tiny perimeter on 875
Monday night. In the moonlight bodies of the dead lay
spread-eagled across the ground. The wounded whimpered.

The survivors, hungry and thirsty, rushed up eagerly to
get food and water, only to learn that the relief battalion had
brought enough supplies for one day only and had already
consumed them.

Monday night was sleepless but uneventful. On Tuesday the North Vietnamese struck with renewed fury.

From positions just 100 yards away, they pounded the American perimeter with 82mm mortars. The first rounds slapped in at daybreak, killing three paratroopers in a foxhole and wounding 17 others on the line.

For the rest of the day, the Communists methodically worked over the hill, pumping rounds in five or six at a time, giving new wounds to those who lay bleeding in the open and tearing through bunkers. The plop of the rounds as they left the enemy tubes gave the paratroopers a second or two to dash for cover.

The foxholes got deeper as the day wore on. Foxhole after foxhole took hits. A dog handler and his German shepherd died together. Men joking with you and offering cigarettes writhed on the ground wounded and pleading for water minutes later. There was no water for anyone.

Crouched in one bunker, Pfc. Angel Flores, 20, of New York City said: "If we were dead like those out there we wouldn't have to worry about this stuff coming in."

He fingered a plastic rosary around his neck and kissed it reverently as the rounds blasted on the ground outside.

"Does that do you any good?" a buddy asked him.

"Well, I'm still alive," Flores replied.

"Don't you know that the chaplain who gave you that was killed on Sunday?" said his buddy.

The day's pounding steadily reduced the platoon commanded by 1st Lt. Bryan Macdonough, 25, of Fort Lee, Va. He had started out Sunday with 27 men. He had nine left by noon Tuesday.

"If the Viets keep this up, there'll be none left by evening," he said.

The enemy positions seemed impervious to constant American air strikes. Napalm fireballs exploded on the bunkers 30 yards away. The earth shook with heavy bombs.

"We've tried 750 pounders, napalm and everything else, but air can't do it. It's going to take manpower to get those positions," Macdonough said.

By late afternoon a new landing zone was cut below the hill. The enemy mortars searched for it but the helicopters came in anyway. A line of wounded trudged down the hill and by evening 140 of them had been evacuated.

The arrival of the helicopters with food, water and ammunition seemed to put new life into the paratroopers. They talked eagerly of a final assault on the enemy bunkers.

As darkness fell flame throwers were brought up. The first stubborn bunker yielded, and the paratroopers were at last started on their way to gain the ridgeline which they had set out to take three days earlier.

And a Hard Rain Fell

Pfc John Ketwig

Ketwig entered the army in 1966, and in 1967 was sent to "The
Nam". He completed his tour of duty the following year. His
memoir of service was published in 1985 as *And a Hard Rain
Fell*.

Life went on at home, and time dragged on in The Nam. I
had arrived in early September. It was now mid-November.
Over sixty days had passed, and my calendar showed fewer
than three hundred Vietnamese sunrises remaining. Things
were heating up, especially a hundred miles north near an
outpost called Dak To. We had a small shop at Dak To. The
surrounding hills were supposedly a staging area for North
Vietnamese infiltrators coming off the Ho Chi Minh Trail;
and Dak To was a base camp for the Fourth Infantry Division's search-and-destroy operations. In November of 1967,
things went wrong for the Fourth Division. All around Dak
To, Charley had sprung coordinated ambushes with surprising numbers of well-equipped troops. It became the largest
battle of the war up to that point, and the tiny compound of
Dak To came under siege. Mortars and rockets crashed in
from the surrounding heights, disabling the airstrip. Before it
was over, it would become impossible for a helicopter to land
in the compound. Supplies had to be trucked in from Kontum
and Pleiku.

One morning in late November, our first sergeant asked
for volunteers to drive to Dak To. The cardinal rule of a

soldier is, Don't ever volunteer, but I did. It was an impulse, not a considered decision; but I was relieved to have stepped forward. For two months I had been holding my breath as the war swirled around me. I knew it would inevitably swallow me. I couldn't be this close to such a mammoth event and expect it to avoid me; it had a kinetic energy that was crushing the life out of kids like myself throughout this Godforsaken land. Once, long ago, I had believed I might escape the draft, the army, and the war. Now, deep in my gut, I knew there would be no escape. In my comfortable youth, I had never been forced to face a situation of such awesome importance. The tension had grown unbearable. I had to know how I would act under fire; and the convoy offered the opportunity to find out. Today. In a few hours. The opportunity to end the agonizing waiting, and to face both Charley and myself, out on the road to Dak To, away from my friends. If I failed, I would not directly threaten the guys.

As I gathered my equipment, I was almost giddy. Archie was incredulous. I felt an exhilaration, a sense of adventure. I had a lot of confidence in my driving ability. In my mind, I was a Grand Prix racing driver at Watkins Glen, or Monza, or the Nurburgring. The Targa Florio. Mille Miglia. No speed limits, no radar traps. High-speed adventure on narrow overseas roads; sneering drivers defying death with scarves dancing merrily on the wind. Nuvolari. Ascari and Stirling Moss. I trembled with excitement. If I had to meet the Viet Cong, let it be at the steering wheel.

The great confrontation would come at the wheel of a dented deuce-and-a-half, or two-and-a-half-ton stake-body truck. It looked tired, sagging beneath too many wooden cases of high explosive. In my mind's eye the faded olive-drab paint resembled British racing green, a color I had come to love as I had overlooked the pit straight at Watkins Glen. The interior was cramped and uncomfortable, like a Formula I Cooper or Porsche. A layer of sandbags on the floor was protection against shrapnel from mines, but I saw the interior of Surtees' Ferrari. I had seen Jimmy Clark,

Graham Hill, Richie Ginther, Von Tripps, Bandini, and Gendebein before a race. Cool. Calculating. Contemplative. I stayed to myself until my shotgun introduced himself. He had been volunteered and was too short for this crap – under a hundred days, and he didn't relish riding with some green recruit.

"Gentlemen, start your engines!" They probably used other words, but those were the words I heard. The diesel engine responded slowly; the throw of the shifter was far too long. I practiced "split-shifting," simultaneously shifting the four-speed and the high-low range levers, double clutching to keep the rpms up. Like a parade lap, the column crawled out of the compound for the start of the Grand Prix of Vietnam. Soon we were on the open road, churning and grinding, sliding and crawling over a rutted dirt trail that was Highway One, Vietnam's finest highway. Through the torrents of rain and inadequate wipers I strained my eyes to watch the truck ahead, a tractor-trailer flatbed of ammo. Damned governor; I needed power. Shotgun sucked bourbon and pronounced me "fuckin' crazy."

I was getting the hang of the ponderous truck, making it work, feeling it become one with me and I with it. We passed ragged Vietnamese with crude carts pulled by water buffalo, a column of nearly naked Montagnards with their strange cylindrical baskets, the broken hulk of a bus. We roared through Kontum and beyond, across a pontoon bridge, past a devastated American armored personnel carrier. The army acronym for these boxes on tracks was APC, but we called them PCs. This one had taken a B-40 rocket in the side and was settled dejectedly into the mud, its rear hatch hanging open.

We were on a straight stretch with heavy jungle on both sides threatening to engulf the road. The engine roared. Clumps of mud clattered against the undercarriage, and the canvas top clattered against the wind. Shotgun was telling me about ice fishing in Minnesota, when everything disappeared. There was a giant confusion up ahead, a curtain of mud, a blinding flash, a roar unlike anything I had ever heard. I couldn't see. I couldn't hear. I existed in a slow-motion world turned upside down. The great barrier grew, fire and mud and smoke and noise, and the earth heaved, and I thought I had been shot in the head and what I was experiencing was the final spasm of torn and shattered brain tissue. The wiper cut through the wash of mud, and I glimpsed a dark hole and went for it. We plunged in, and we came out, and I was out of control, and there was a giant dark green truck stopped dead in the road. Nothing to do, nowhere to go, a dead-end tunnel; then limbs and leaves pounding against the windshield, popping, scraping, tearing; and I can't see; and ... we were stopped. I sat, deflated and baffled. Frozen. I became aware of a frantic activity and confusion. I became aware that I was alive. Like a surreal movie, a face appeared to my right; a distorted, anguished face, obviously screaming, but I couldn't hear what it was saying. Where was Shotgun? I didn't remember him leaving. I couldn't hear! My hands went to my head, to my ears, and I realized I was hearing the most enormous, crushing, howling, roaring noise of my life. Little noise among the great noise. Crackling. My eyes were okay, I could see the seat, the dash, Shotgun's door hanging open. Where had he gone?

I lay across the seat to look out the door, to see where Shotgun had gone. There was a guy, lying in the mud, with a stick or ... and an abstract swarm of golden insects flew away from his head, and I concentrated on the crackling sound because it must be a clue; the stick was his rifle, and he was shooting, and the insects were shell casings, and the roar was a lot of explosive, and we were hit. I was alive, and everybody was down there, and I was up here, where the hell was Shotgun, and what should I do now? Where was my rifle? On the sandbags, muddy. Gotta get down with those guys, gotta shoot. Can't see anything but muddy splotches on dark green leaves, and vines, and grass. What the fuck is going on? I don't see anybody. The noise. God damn the noise. My head aches. Won't somebody please be quiet? I don't see anybody to shoot at. Big, dark, noisy shadows overhead, the roar again, the mud is shaking and none of this makes sense.

Suddenly, it was quiet. Bodies stirred around me. I rolled over, lay on my back looking up into the gray rain. My head hurt. I felt it, felt wet mud in my hair, and checked my hand. Mud, not blood. Back to my head. There! My ears! There was that roaring sound that wouldn't go away. That's how it had started. What was that? What had happened? A face leaned over, smiled, held out a hand. Pulled me to my feet, and my knees didn't want to hold me up, and the hand held out my rifle. It tugged at my arm, but I'd lost Shotgun, and I didn't know how, so I staggered off to look for him. I had to ask him what that noise was. I'd never heard a noise like that before. I stumbled past the dark form of a truck, and guys were gathered, looking at something, so I should probably look too. There was a crater, a huge bowl-shaped hole, right square in the middle of the road. Wider than the road, stretching the jungle walls back. Twisted, shredded, dark forms, probably metal, a set of wheels, a grotesque steel ladder. Fireworks, or gunpowder. I smelled gunpowder. What was going on? Why hadn't I seen that great big hole? How could I have missed it? What had happened? Must be a clue there somewhere. All those guys, all strangers, all so quiet. Were they keeping a secret from me? No. Most of them looked bewildered too.

Suddenly Shotgun was there, screaming, hugging me, slapping my back, raving at the top of his lungs. ". . . motherfucker had our name on it, and you fuckin' drove that fuckin' truck and we fuckin' made it, and . . . and . . . Fuckin' A! Fuckin' Christ, man, you fuckin' did it, you fuckin'-A did it, man, and . . ." I grabbed him, begged him to tell me what had happened. I felt very tired, very confused, and I just wanted to get this all sorted out and get on with it, get home. I didn't like this convoy shit, didn't understand it. What happened? Why were we stopped? What was that noise?

Shotgun stopped jabbering and looked at me. I guess, because he had been in The Nam so long, he realized that I had no idea what had happened. He lit two wrinkled cigarettes, put one in my lips, and explained. The flatbed just ahead of us had hit a mine. The whole load of ammo went off. Somebody said we went through it on two wheels, just from the force of the concussion. Blew that big fuckin' hole in the road. Dented the jungle. The guys in the truck? They were looking for them, for something to send home.

My knees gave out, and I knelt in the road. All the air had rushed out of me, as if some giant had squeezed me. My rifle lay beside me, in the goo. I saw it, but I had no control of my arms to reach over and pick it up. I was numb; everything was numb except my head, and it hurt so bad. I felt the cigarette fall from my lips, saw it land on the stinking mud. I started to tremble, then I started to shake, then I started to cry and to shake, and I almost fell over. Somebody put a bottle to my lips, and the fiery liquid seemed to cut through some of it, but I couldn't control the shaking. There was another cigarette, and they forced me to my feet, but I didn't want to walk. I didn't want to go anywhere, or do anything. Just think. Figure this out. They were screaming at me, and it wasn't my fault. "Go on." I didn't want to go on. "Got to. Got to."

Somehow, I went on. Choppers beat the air overhead. The truck was banged up bad. Shotgun's side of the windshield was gone, mine was starred and cracked. The canvas top hung low. The hood and left fender were buckled back. There were leaves and twigs and mud everywhere. I moved mechanically, stumbling without emotion. My blood had been drained; I was empty inside. The road cleared, the engine fired, and we rolled. Sheets of rain ripped in through Shotgun's broken windshield. He offered the bourbon, and it helped. I was thinking about driving over the torn road. Thought was returning. I went on. I'll never know how, but I went on.

I drove through a dream world. My head hurt, and I kept replaying those few moments. They didn't make sense, wouldn't make sense. My actions were mechanical. I saw my hands but didn't feel them. Just follow the truck ahead. I was shaking real bad, didn't know if I could breathe. Confused. It was happening all around me, and it was more than my mind could accept. Follow the truck ahead. Choppers overhead. Shotgun's booze. Confusion, and the headache. Wrestling the wheel.

We arrived at Dak To late in the afternoon. The noise was enormous, and it escalated as we got close. Chaos. Mud. There had been tanks, and PCs, and choppers. I could see a lot of activity, and I was driving into it, picking up momentum, a sense of urgency. Adrenaline flowing. Frantic, chaotic action. Noise, confusion, the smell of powder. Artillery roared. Incoming mortars whomped into the mud. There were squat, dark tents sinking into the goo, and men. Stooped, disheveled, frantic men. On the perimeter, firing with unbelievable ferocity. There was an emotion, a need, an intensity that seemed to grip me, as if the world had gone off its axis, and to do anything out of the ordinary might explode it all. It wasn't ordinary, just all-consuming, and you had to be a part of it because it was so enormous, so awesome. The endless rain seemed to beat against the place, driving it, and everyone in it, deeper into the depressing goo. The valley was sliced into horizontal thirds by a layer of blue-gray smoke accumulating fifty feet above the mud, and a huge, dark green hill loomed above the smoke. This was Hill 875, the focus of today's attention.

A muddied and rumpled man, his rank or unit unintelligible, leaped onto Shotgun's running board and screamed orders. In the roar and commotion most of what he said was lost, but Shotgun leaned over to yell, "No more than ten cases to each gun. I'll be working in graves registration. For Chrissake, don't leave without me." He punched my arm, hollered, "Keep your head down," and clambered out of the truck. After my cargo was unloaded, I would be on my own until the convoy formed up for the return trip in the morning. A nearby mortar round erupted in a huge geyser of mud and thunder, and I kicked the truck into motion.

Frantic men, distorted by wet and mud and fear, waved

me toward the perimeter. Figures seemed to loom up out of the sound and fury, then disappear as if consumed by it. The roar never quieted. It banged inside my head in waves, drowning out my thoughts, and I lost all sense of where I was or where I was going. It didn't matter; it all looked the same. I managed to coax the tired truck through the slime to a gun emplacement. As the gun roared, steam rose, and brown, half-naked men struggled to load another shell. I hesitated, not knowing what to do. Two of the men clambered up onto the truck and hefted the ammo down to their buddies. I pulled the lever out of gear and went back to help. "Only ten cases!" They ignored me, tossing the heavy wooden crates into the soft goo. There was no stopping them. These weren't men; one look at their eyes told me that. These were frightened animals desperate to survive. A slap to my helmet startled me. A face, distorted by clods of wet mud, shouted and pointed at a round erupting about a hundred yards away. "Go! Go! Get out of here!" The clear white of the eyes seemed incongruous against the dull brown mask. "They're walkin' 'em in on ya!" Another round, closer this time, threw swamp into the air. It was closer, and it was on a direct line toward us. Charley was adjusting his aim round by round, closer and closer to me. I had to get out of there. Sweat and debris seemed to cloud my eyes. I couldn't really see where I was headed, but I made the truck lurch forward. Behind me, I heard bumping and swearing as the gunners dived off. God, the noise was awful! There was so much noise, so much action, but it was a kind of action I had never seen, confusing, and I wished Shotgun had been there to offer advice. I saw another gun crew, figured they could use ammunition, and forced the truck toward them. It bogged, refused to move. I pulled levers, screamed at it, and it ground forward again. I lost sight of the gun when a sea of brown swill washed over the broken windshield. The wipers cut through, and I bounced toward my goal. I ground the tired truck to a halt and burst out the door in such a hurry I went facefirst into the slime. I pulled myself up and clambered onto the truck, fighting the weight the mud had added to my loose-fitting jungle fatigues. The ammo cases were heavy, bulky, slippery. I managed to get a couple over the side before the guys arrived. Mud-soaked forms rose to help, only their eyes and teeth showing color against the brown. I'm not sure why, but I heard myself shouting, "Only ten! Only ten cases!" again and again. Then the truck was empty and the men were back at the gun. Smack! A blow to the side of my head knocked me off my feet and out into space. I hit the mud on my back, and something heavy landed on top of me, threatened to smother me. I fought.

"Get down, asshole! Get down!" One of the guys had knocked me off the back of the truck, lost his footing, and tumbled on top of me. He put his face inches from mine and screamed. "You okay? You okay?" I said I was. "You were standing straight up in the back of that truck." He needed a shave and a bath.

I was ashamed of my stupidity. "I'm okay. I thought I was shot. Next time, just ask, or give me a shove."

He was grinning. His teeth were stained, and the wet pink of his mouth stood out in striking contrast to the muddy face. His eyes were red, tired. "I'd send ya a letter," he grinned, "but the mail hasn't been dependable lately! You liked to got yourself killed. Where ya from?"

"New York. Rochester, New York."

He motioned toward the frantic bedlam at the wire. "Hell of a show, ain't it? Fuckin' Charley don't give up. Four fuckin' days this been goin' on. Hell of a show!"

A personnel carrier slithered across the slime, tracks rattling. "Do us a favor," my new friend shouted against the noise. It wasn't so much a question as a statement of fact. "Get that truck outta here. Charley likes to drop mortars on trucks. Stick it over near those hootches, nobody gonna be sleeping in a hootch. Just get it away from here, then come back." I didn't want to move. I didn't want to get back in that truck. Every time I got in that truck, all hell broke loose. "C'mon!" he hollered, slapped the side of my helmet again, but with less force. "C'mon, get outta here. You gonna bring a whole buncha shit down on us!" There was a crazy, desperate look in his eyes. I struggled to the running board, then turned.

"You didn't say where you're from?"

"Ohio! Near Cleveland! Now get your young ass outta here, New York, and c'mon back so we can show ya how to fuck Charley's head up!" I pushed the lever into low and heard the tires growl.

I wrestled the truck into the little community of tents and struggled toward Ohio. Time after time I tripped or slipped, fighting to lift my sodden legs over ruts and out of puddles. It seemed I was moving in slow motion. The noise, that eternal, indistinguishable roar, seemed to be a wall. I felt the weight of the canteen on my hip, the cartridge clips in canvas pouches pulling the web belt lower. The pant legs seemed glued to my legs, stiff and heavy. I saw my rifle in my right hand, its familiar shape distorted by clods of mud. I felt grit in my mouth, sweat stinging my eyes. I tripped again. God damn it! An incoming round crashed on my right, a dull *whumpoom* threw up a cone of brown spray. I struggled forward, trying to keep my head down and still lift my legs high. My glasses were covered with filth, and I couldn't make out much of the scenario ahead. It all seemed to be closing in, swallowing me. I felt my right foot slip out from under me, the slow diving toward the muck. I watched the water splash away as I hit. I struggled to get my footing. I was straining, hurting, beginning to panic. Was there no escape. "C'mon, New York! C'mon! You're almost here. C'mon!" I saw the muddy barrel chest rise, the outstretched hand, the white teeth. I fell into the hole, disoriented. He held out that hand, helped me to my feet.

I didn't want to see. I didn't want to know what was going on around me. I wanted to crouch in the mud and slop, sink away, get away from all this. The noise was crushing me, squeezing in on my chest and my head. The weight of my limbs made me wonder if I had been shot, if the life was flowing out of me. Everything hurt, I couldn't pick out a specific pain. There was a glimpse of white, a flash near my head. I ducked so violently I smacked my head. Ohio was tugging me again, laughing. "Clean your glasses." He held out the white rag. It was damp and gritty, but I absentmindedly rubbed at the lenses. Ohio stuck a cigarette in my lips. They were quivering so badly it fell into the mud. "C'mon, New York! The fuckin' PX is closed. Get your shit together." He laughed, but there was a note of hurt in his voice. He held out another smoke. I held it carefully, pulled hard at it. God, it was good. My hands were shaking. Ohio held out a bottle. I swallowed, and my eyes cleared as my throat burned. I choked a little, then swallowed again. I could feel the heat in my gut now. Ohio had pushed gobs of mud off my rifle, wiping it with the rag. He lifted it over the sandbags, pointed it away, and squeezed off a few rounds without looking to see where they were going. I tipped the bottle again, leaned back against the sandbags. I struggled to control the shaking, lost it, felt heat on my thighs and belly, smelled urine. The bottle again. "Hey, that shit's harder to come by than cigarettes," and Ohio reached for it. "C'mon, meet the guys." The cigarette was soggy, but I sucked at it once more before I threw it away. We met the guys; most had naked torsos stained to the color of the mud. Everyone's hair seemed blond and wet. Stubble sparkled on their chins. I wasn't enthusiastic. They assigned me a post on the sandbags, looking out and downhill across the wire and mud to a dark line of trees. The noise had died somewhat, and the rain slowed to a drizzle. The blue layer of smoke seemed a canopy, pressing down, making it seem we were overlooking the entrance to a huge tunnel. It was nearly dark, but I thought I saw a human form.

"Ohio!"

He was a few feet to my left. "Yeah?"

"Is that a body out there?"

"On the wire? Yeah, patrol got hit last night. Shit got heavy, and that kid tried to make it back. There's about six of 'em right on the edge of that tree line. Probably a few gooks, too."

"You mean that's a GI?" I felt a chill.

"Yeah." Silence.

"How many were there?"

"Gooks? Or the patrol?"

"The patrol? How many American guys are out there?"

"Twelve. Maybe fifteen. I dunno. Poor fuckers got fucked up bad!"

"Hey, Ohio!"

"Yeah?"

"Got another cigarette? Mine got kinda wet."

A voice came out of the darkness behind us. "They're bad for your health!"

The darkness came fast. The incredible noise had died away, grown more distant. Occasionally a flare would pop and swing down on its silken parachute. The golden glow emphasized shadows. As soon as the dark returned, they seemed to move. I tried to make my eyes avoid that dark form by the wire, but they wouldn't obey. Somewhere, up above the smoky gray ceiling, a distant battle raged. Someone offered a box of C rations. Ham and lima beans. Shit! I lifted the dog tag chain over my head and set about opening a can of pears with my P-38 folding can opener. It was cold and damp now, the drizzle was getting heavier. Someone brought me a cup of coffee, two packages of C-ration Lucky Strikes, and a poncho. I wrapped the plastic poncho around me and swallowed the hot coffee, wondering how long eight cigarettes might last. I shivered and lit one. My mind struggled to comprehend the enormous events of the day. The explosion on the road seemed long ago. The sounds of distant firing and chopper blades seemed to set a mood, like music for dinner. The chaos of this place was overwhelming. Thousands of guys like myself, torn away from home and family, crouched in the mud, wishing they weren't here. How could all this happen? I pulled at the cigarette and finished the coffee. I moved two steps to the right and peed. What difference would it make? I pulled the poncho closer.

"Ohio?"

"Yeah?"

"You drafted?"

He moved toward me, dug into a thigh pocket and offered the bottle again. "Nightcap?" I needed the warmth. "I enlisted. My wife's brother was wasted last year, down in the delta somewhere. I wasn't doing much and wanted to get even. At the time, it seemed like a decent thing to do. She's stayin' with her folks, and I thought I was doing the right thing. Shit!" He swallowed from the bottle. "I was in-country six days and saw half my company get it. Three weeks later they send us here. I got three hundred 'n' seventeen days to go in this motherfucker, and I oughtta write to my wife, but I don't know what to say. She thinks her brother was a big fuckin' hero, ya know, and I'm gonna tell her about this?"

Did he really want an answer? Before I decided what to say, a voice from the darkness got me off the hook.

"Ho!"

Ohio looked up. Someone was splashing toward us. One of the guys hollered back, and a form dropped into the trench. There was excited whispering, then he moved to Ohio and me. Ohio nodded a greeting. "Lieutenant."

"How ya doin'?"

"All right, sir. Cold, wet, and hungry. What's up?"

"PC's going out after the patrol." He whispered, but belched loudly. "They want to get them in before they swell up and burst. Got some more near the gate. It's beehives at point-blank, right?"

"Got it."

The lieutenant splashed on down the trench. I realized how quiet it had become. Ohio shrugged. "Back to work."

"What's going on? What's a beehive?"

Ohio grinned. "Shit, New York, your education's been sadly neglected. C'mon, I'll show ya." We crept through the darkness to the gun. Ohio turned around to face me, holding something my mind interpreted as a watermelon. My eyes had tricked me. It was an artillery shell, about four inches in diameter and eighteen inches long, to be fired from a

105-millimeter Howitzer. "This is a beehive. Inside there are a couple thousand little steel arrows, about an inch long. Each one as sharp as a tack, and has four little steel quills. We use 'em for human waves. This sucker'll pin gooks to a tree forty deep. None of 'em'll be more than an inch thick. They're goin' out in a PC; try to bring that patrol in. The shit's apt to get pretty thick. If Charley gets pissed and comes at us, it's gonna be for real. There's a whole North Vietnamese division out there, shootin' up and gettin' half crazy. Somebody shouts, 'Go!' and there ain't no stopping them." He patted the dark cylinder. "This'll stop 'em."

I was chilled and shivering. My bones ached. I was bone-weary, and wet and dirty. Mostly, I was scared. Human waves? Visions of an army of drug-crazed Orientals in black pajamas, of John Wayne playing Davy Crockett at the Alamo, of hand-to-hand combat all ravaged my imagination. I was getting the shakes again, feeling the cold deep in my gut. In all my nineteen years, I had never seen anything like this. Hell, I had never imagined this might happen. Maybe it was a nightmare, and I would wake up and go to work. This couldn't be happening. I fought to remember my hand-to-hand combat training at Fort Dix. I had never paid that much attention, never dreamed I might have to rely on that training to stay alive. I wished I had a cup of coffee, a shower, or a few hours' sleep. I wanted to tuck into clean sheets, pull the pillow over my head to make the noise go away, and wake up in the morning to find myself home. As if to answer my thoughts, a flare popped and lit the slope in a golden glow. I saw the muddy hill, devoid of plants, streaming away toward the tangled wire. The tree line was a black wall now, an impenetrable black pit that led to the depths of hell. The sounds of war were distant now, but all around us. Surely, as they approached, we would be caught in the middle till Charley squeezed the life out of us. There was no place to go, no place to hide. Thousands of guys were kneeling in the mud, peering into the shadows and awaiting death, and none of them wanted to be here. What power could put so many American kids into a position like this? Why hadn't they told us about this while we were growing up? To my left a voice cut through the damp fog. "Holy Mary, Mother of God . . ." Were the others as scared as I? They were such a disheveled bunch, brawny and tough, it was hard to think of them as scared.

"Ohio?"

"Yeah?"

"You scared?"

"Fuckin' A I'm scared. I've been scared since I got off the plane at Cam Ranh Bay. Anybody that ain't scared shitless in a place like this is crazy as hell. You want a belt?"

I moved closer to him, thankful for the bottle. "Where the hell do you get this stuff? We been hittin' this bottle all day, and it never goes dry. You making your own or something?"

"Walker swapped some ammo to some Green Beanies, got us a whole case of it. At the time, we didn't think we'd need the ammo."

"Somebody coulda got killed."

"Yeah, but anything you do in this fuckin' place can get somebody killed. The Beanies must've really needed it, to give up a case of booze. So maybe we saved a life; who knows? Ain't it funny how little you know about what's goin' on around ya here? I mean, there's some heavy shit comin' down. Just listen. And what's it all about? No-fuckin'-body knows! It's fuckin' crazy. If somebody would just tell me what the fuck is going on around here, what they hope to gain, or what they stand to lose, or something . . . but, no! You see guys all blown to shit, and you don't know why." He tipped the bottle up and drank hard and long. "Hardest thing's gonna be goin' home, and seeing the wife and her family, and her kid brother got blown away over here, and I don't know what to tell them about it. I mean, how the fuck can you describe this to somebody's sister?"

"Yeah, but you're married to her. It'll come." For such a big man, he seemed very vulnerable. I tried to lift him up but didn't know how.

Ohio lit a cigarette. "Supposing we die tonight. What happens then? They put what's left in a body bag and ship you home, and some lifer in a dress uniform tells your wife you died for your country. They have a funeral, and they fold up a flag and present it to her, and they draft the kid next door!"

I hadn't thought about it. If I went home in a box, I didn't want the army involved in my funeral. Fuck 'em. I hadn't asked for any of this. I wasn't a hero. I would have to write to the folks, tell them not to allow a military funeral. Ohio flipped away the cigarette.

"How old are you, New York?"

"Nineteen."

"I was twenty, four days before I left home. The lieutenant's twenty-three, and he's the only guy older than I am. There's nineteen guys, and I'm the oldest. Only three of us are married. Can you imagine? My wife went to the recruiting office with me, and I enlisted to go to The Nam, and she just sat there and listened to the whole thing, and it was almost like she didn't have any emotion. So it's my birthday, right, and we're at her folks', and she brings out this cake with all the candles and says, 'Make a wish.' I wished, just once before I had to leave, that she would say she didn't want me to go. I blew out the candles, but I never got my wish. Look at this fuckin' place, would ya? My wife wanted me here! She thinks I'm doin' some kind of patriotic duty, and it's wonderful. What the fuck am I ever gonna have to say to her? She wanted me to come over here! I've been here a little over a month, and I'm not sure I love her anymore. I can't tell her what it's like, and I can't forgive her for wanting me to be here. Haven't written her a letter in weeks. How the fuck you gonna describe this? Shit! I don't know if I want to see her again. She'd tell her friends I was some kind of fuckin' hero, and I'd have to just tell her to shut the fuck up. I just hope if Charley fucks my shit up he does it right, 'cause I don't want to spend the rest of my life with her pushing me around in a wheelchair, telling people I did what I had to do. If she had asked me not to go, I would have stayed home. I don't need this shit! I don't need to hear what a fuckin' hero I am. I just need a bath, and a drink, and some good pussy. She can keep her mouth shut and her legs open, and we'll get along fine. I mean, I feel bad about her brother, but what fuckin' good am I doin' for him? He's dead, and I'm about to be, too, and I ain't seen anything getting a bit better because of it!"

My thoughts drifted away. There wasn't anything I could say to make it better. I thought about Jimmy Rollins, and my family. How would I talk to them? I heard an engine growl behind us, the clatter of tracks. Too much booze on an empty stomach. I had to pull my shit together. Thinking could get in the way. One more cigarette while the PC was going out; then I'd better have my shit together. God damn the rain!

The personnel carrier hung close to the trees, moving parallel to us. The sound of its engine, its General Motors three-speed automatic transmission seemed too loud, as if it were inviting the Cong to try something. Suddenly there was small-arms fire, then an explosion of firing. The PC zigzagged, bouncing and churning a haphazard dance from shadow to shadow. It accelerated, slowed, turned 180 degrees, stopped, accelerated again. The machine gun on top was hurling red tracers into the tree line. Ohio touched my arm, leaned close to whisper. "They find a body, and drive over it. Some poor bastard opens the back door a crack and leans out with a rope; ties it around a wrist or an ankle. They play out about ten feet of rope and slam the door, and go looking for the next one. Drag the whole string around; sometimes run over them with the tracks. They'll be all beat to shit, but you can't leave 'em out there. Charley'll crawl in, cut off their heads and stick 'em on poles with their balls in their mouth. In the morning the sun comes up and they're lookin' at ya all day long. Just be glad you aren't in graves registration tonight. They gotta bag 'em up to be shipped home; identify them and everything. Those guys are up to their ass in puke and guts and shit. I'd rather be here." I remembered Shotgun. That's where they had sent him.

A tremendous explosion erupted near the PC. "Mine." Ohio said it without emotion. "They pull a string to trigger it.

Charley's timing sucks!" The armored carrier moved to the right, became obscured by rain and fog. The firing died down, and the sound of the grinding tracks was washed out by the clatter of a chopper overhead. A flare popped. Occasional rifle fire made sleep impossible. About three in the morning a heavy mortar barrage fell behind us. It was amazing. You could actually hear the rounds sizzling overhead. I hadn't expected the explosions to be so loud. In the cold and wet, I was shaking again. I had to pee. I unbuttoned my fly and let go against the sandbags, never taking my eyes off the misty slope. Dawn brought a few more mortar rounds, again over our heads. Ohio suggested breakfast. I was a guest here. There was no question; I got ham and lima beans again. The lieutenant got the beans and franks. A short-timer got the fruit cocktail. We built a small fire and heated coffee in canteen cups, added a shot of booze and a little sugar. Breakfast was the best meal of the day. It meant you had survived the night, you were one day shorter. Two F-4 Phantom jets screamed across the sky, pulled up sharply. We heard a muffled *whuuumppff*. Dak To was open for business.

The sounds of fighting on Hill 875 were intensifying as we got the word to saddle up. I shook Ohio's muddy hand. I was searching for words when he spoke first. "You keep your head down, New York, and thanks for the ammo." I wasn't eager to go back out onto Highway One. "C'mon, asshole." Ohio was grinning. "You don't want to stay here, do ya? Shit, in a few hours you'll be taking a hot shower back in Pleiku. In a few days you'll be eating Thanksgiving turkey and all this'll seem unreal. You're over the hard part. Shit, you're a battle-scarred veteran. Now get down that fuckin' road, 'fore ya smoke up all our cigarettes. We'll see ya again." He held out the bottle, and I tipped the neck his way before I drank.

"Hey, Ohio?"

"Yeah?"

"Hell of a party! You take care. Thanks, man."

I ran across the morass to the truck. Shotgun was already

in his seat, and he started when I opened the door. His eyes were wild.

He looked away. I pushed the starter button. "Ready?"

He spoke out the open window, softly. "Just get us the fuck outta here!"

"You all right?"

"I don't think I'll ever be all right again, but get us the fuck outta here." He was crying. If graves registration did this to an experienced, hardened short-timer, I resolved to avoid it at all costs.

We ground up out of that stinking valley, leaving the sounds of battle behind us. Helicopters clattered overhead, and I kept a big distance between us and the truck ahead. Shotgun stared straight ahead, tears streaking his cheeks. We were rolling hard when he leaned out the window and puked. He was silent all the way back to Pleiku. It was an uneventful trip, if five hours of utter terror can be uneventful. No mines or ambushes, you had to feel fortunate. We ground to a halt at Camp Holloway. Shotgun punched my shoulder and spoke softly. "Good job. Hope ya make it." Then he just walked away, and I looked for a ride back to my compound.

I was in the shower when the shaking started. I thought about Ohio, how he had said I was over the hard part. Suddenly thirty hours of terror exploded in my stomach, and I started bawling like a baby. I rushed outside, stark naked, and threw up, on my knees in the mud. It all unwound out of me, like a coil spring. Unraveled. Came apart. I saw the explosion on the road again, the crater, the personnel carrier bouncing around in the dark, the disjointed body hanging on the wire. I heard the sound, that crushing roar that squeezed your ears till your brain went blank. I smelled the powder and the diesel fuel and the rot and the death. I went back into the shower, and I scrubbed till my skin was red, but it wouldn't come clean. Back at the hootch, I drank too much Scotch and fell on the bunk. When I closed my eyes I saw the road explode. I put the pillow over my head, tucked it tight against my ears, but the roar wouldn't go away. I felt very cold, got the uncontrollable shivers, pulled the heavy wool blanket tight around me. I saw the dump trucks loaded with bodies, the dark shadows trailing behind the PC. Christ, they must have hauled them right in to Shotgun. Never did know his name, or Ohio's. They never asked mine. Imagine experiencing something like that two feet from another guy, and you don't even know his name. You'll never see him again. Either of them. Wouldn't volunteer for another convoy if it was going to San Francisco! My volunteering days are over.

The guys burst into the tent, waving mail and laughing. I made believe I was sleeping. Archie shook me. "Jawn. Jawn." Damned Boston accent, leave me alone. "C'mawn, you gotta eat. Got a meal fit for a king." He whistled for an imaginary dog. "Here, King. Here, boy." How the hell could I ignore that? I sat up.

Archie looked at me kind of funny. "You look like hell. Pretty bad, huh?" I nodded. "Know what you need? Powdered potatoes! Stick to your ribs, give you intestinal fortitude to face the adversities of life in The Nam. Powdered potatoes'll fix anything. Half the bricks in Saigon are glued together with the army's powdered potatoes. C'mon, get dressed." He screwed up his face, made that handlebar mustache twist into a ridiculous caricature of a silent movie star. I had to laugh.

"Anybody ever tell you you're fuckin' crazy?"

He stepped back in mock horror, his eyebrows arched. "Sorry, fella, you got the wrong guy. Just 'cause I enlisted, you don't have to make disparaging remarks."

We ate, and I felt better. We talked about Dak To. I didn't go into detail, no need to get him upset. Every time I thought I was going to lose it. Archie clowned and got me over it. We smoked and drank too much, and went to bed early. The next day I would be back at the old grind.

Recon

Frank Camper

Frank Camper was a "Lurp", a member of a Long-Range
Reconnaissance Patrol; below he recounts his first mission,
operating out of a US firebase close to the Cambodian border
in February 1967.

THE DAWN ARRIVED cold and foggy. Mott gave the signal and
we came to our feet and entered the ghostly forest, the mist
smothering our footfalls.

For an hour there was no noise to disturb the unreal quality of the morning as we trod softly through the dew-soaked
bushes. My trouser legs and boots became as chilly and damp
as if we'd forded a stream.

You move with care and caution when your life depends
on it. We lifted our feet high as we walked, setting them down
slowly, toeing twigs and roots out of the way, pausing every
few meters to kneel and listen.

When blue sky finally shone through the treetops, and we
stopped to rest, we found a trail and made radio contact with
the firebase. I had counted a thousand meters we'd traveled,
a third of the way to our objective.

No small infantry patrols had been sent into this area, for
fear of losing them. Three companies operating out of the
firebase were working east from us, in hopes they might drive
the NVA this way, west toward Cambodia.

I covered tailgun, Steffens watched the flanks, and Payne
and Mott held the center. Mott had a long conversation with

the firebase over the radio, his map before him, weapon and hat laid aside.

Mott marked the location of the trail on the map, while the rest of us guarded both approaches. "We'll go north as long as this trail holds out," he said. "You take point."

I resolved to shoot first and ask questions later, switching to full automatic and proceeding up the path. This was baiting the tiger and we all knew it. One of the laws of jungle warfare is that if you want enemy contact, get on a trail.

I began to sweat from nervous tension, finding myself frequently holding my breath rather than risk the noise of inhaling or exhaling.

The team followed me, imitating my every move, watching my reactions, stepping where I stepped. The suspense was numbing.

In many places the overhead was so dense the sunlight couldn't penetrate. The trail was dim, beset by shadows, the rightful province of the ambusher.

The trail had a destination. I spied the first bunker far enough in advance so that I could blend down into the shrubbery gracefully. The team behind me went to earth so quickly it seemed a breeze had blown and, like smoke, they had disappeared.

Something was wrong. We were too close to the bunkers not to be dead already if the NVA were alert. I took a good look around. The bunkers seemed to be deserted. Soil had sunk between the logs and the firing ports were covered with withered camouflage.

I signaled for the team to stay down, and I checked out the nearest hole by creeping over to it. I was right. These were all old fortifications. I gave an all-clear whistle, and the team came out.

"Looks like a company or more dug in here," Mott said, surveying the positions. He took out his notebook and began to make a diagram of the bunkers.

We began to recover from the exertion of the day, muscles unknotting, fatigues drying out, stomachs growling for food.

I pulled a chicken-and-rice from my rucksack, boiling a canteen cup of water to reconstitute it, and sat back to wait.

I hadn't eaten all day, and I was starving. The ration slowly absorbed the water, swelling the packet. I had twenty minutes to wait for the dehydrated ration to reconstitute, but it seemed like an hour to my empty stomach.

To top off a hard day, a plague of sweat bees descended on us. They buzzed and lit everywhere, coming right back after being swatted off, trying to crawl into the corners of my eyes and into my mouth. I draped a handkerchief over my face.

I made a mistake then. My attention wandered for just an instant. I heard a slight sound near where I sat, and looked swiftly around to see what it was.

I found myself looking straight into the eyes of an NVA. He had come out of nowhere! I was sitting nearly out of his line of vision as he glanced in my direction. He acted as if he had not seen me. I was too stunned to move. He continued to look around, seemingly oblivious to my presence.

Then he casually turned to my left and walked out of sight. I couldn't function. Had he seen me? We had looked each other in the eye! I snap-rolled into a depression in the earth against some roots, flicking the safety off my CAR. I detected no sound. He had to be still out there. Probably just a short distance away, crouched in the underbrush.

I looked back and saw Payne as he repacked the radio equipment. I waved at him. He didn't look up. I motioned frantically, Payne totally not noticing me for what seemed to be one eternity.

When Payne finally saw me, he reacted by tapping Mott and going down into the thicket. We waited. Disaster on the first day? Maybe not. My heart knocked against my ribs so loudly I wasn't sure I could hear anything else.

Payne inched up to me. I indicated. *One dink, moving that way*, in a sign language. Payne pointed to himself, and to the right flank, then to me and to the left, motioning we should go out and get our visitor.

We tried the impromptu pincers movement, but only

found each other and the trail on which the man had made his escape. "This is how he got up on me without making any noise," I whispered to Payne. The trail was well used and wide.

We crawled back to the old bunkers to wait and listen.

I reached over and pulled my ration package to me, still hungry despite the circumstances. I found I was shaking so badly trying to eat, I was spilling half the rice off my spoon. When we had finished trying to eat, Mott told us to prepare to move, pointing to the trail.

The trail passed on through the bunkers and went for higher ground. I walked forward a few meters and found another trail branching off ours.

"We'll go north as long as the trails do," Mott said. "I believe they'll take us right to the Red Warrior LZ. And start looking for a good place to spend the night. I want to find a good one before it gets too late."

I agreed. This place was too damn active for us to be stumbling around in the dark. I searched carefully as we advanced, turning down any place that didn't afford maximum protection. It was easy to stay on our compass course. All I had to do was move from one trail to another. We were in a network.

It was hours before I came across some good high ground, and I led us up into it. It was so steep it was hard for us to climb. That was fine. Anyone trying to do it at night would make a hell of a lot of noise.

I pulled up from tree to tree, resting in place occasionally. I reached the top dripping with sweat and bleeding from thorn pricks and grass slices, but I didn't just barge in. I hugged the hillside below the crest, listening, calculating how fast I could jump backward and get away if the hill was already claimed for the night.

I peeked over a fallen log and scanned the hilltop. Safe so far. Loping in a crouch, I covered the distance across the small knoll and took cover behind a tree, looking down the opposite slope.

It wasn't as steep on the far side, being part of a ridge. I waved the team up, and we secured the hill for the night, spreading out. I chose the lower part of the slope, the team assuming its usual defensive position: team leader and RTO in the center, point and tailgun at the far ends.

A stick thrown by Mott hit me in the back while I waited. I turned and felt my heart sink as he gave me the *Be quiet* sign. Payne had his M-16 ready, his attention on something near us.

I picked up my weapon, moving nothing but my arm, believing we were about to be attacked. Mott and Payne sneaked into the foliage, moving with absolute silence. Then I heard it for myself.

A short distance away people were walking by, the scuffing of sandals on packed dirt very clear, voices in Vietnamese conversing without fear of detection.

They walked away. I had edged downward until I was absolutely flat against the ground. I realized we'd camped right beside another trail. Mott looked up at me, the whites of his eyes showing all around his pupils.

We dared not try to leave the hill – they would catch us for sure – but if we stayed here, all it would take was for one of them to get lucky and step off the trail, and zap, instant catastrophe.

When it became fully dark, we pulled in together. Payne made the last radio report of the day by only keying the handset and saying nothing aloud. We just couldn't afford it. We didn't unpack anything, lying with our rucksacks beside us.

Later, lights began to flash in the sky toward the firebase we had left. No one was asleep, so we raised our heads, hearing the sound of gunfire drift in on the wind. They were getting hit again.

The firebase responded with its artillery, firing out rounds in all directions and ranges. Flares went up, and tracers arced over the jungle, red for ours, green for theirs. A burning parachute flare fell into the treetops near us and took away our night, until it sputtered out.

Several stray artillery shells sailed in and hit our ridge-line, sounding much louder at night, the blasts echoing into the valley. Even a marker-round canister or two came whistling down and smashed into the trees; all too near for us.

And we soon had company again. A North Vietnamese squad rushed by us on the hidden trail, equipment bumping, heading for the action.

The night and the battle progressed. More NVA went past us, all involved in their own problems, none even guessing we were in pissing distance.

Then a roar greater than the fight below us vibrated through the valley. I glanced up and saw what appeared to be a million red tracers plunging out of the night sky.

Puff! The old C-47 cargo plane with the electric Gatling guns! Puff belched another terrific volley, an unbelievable column of pure bullets that soaked the forest below like a deadly rain.

That was the end to the fighting. No army could stand up to Puff. The dragonship's engines droned lazily overhead, occasionally spraying around the firebase with a breath more deadly than anything imagined in King Arthur's day.

Then it started coming our way! We had no arrangement for radioing anybody to get Puff away from us, the miniguns drowned out everything, and I expected the fire to nail us to the hill. I had heard of men being killed accidentally by Puff, hundreds of meters from the "beaten zone."

All things considered, it was a long night. The NVA retreated on our trail until dawn, trickling by, disorganized, carrying their wounded and dragging heavy loads.

As soon as it was light enough to see, we were ready to leave. Payne made the radio report, having to repeat himself to be understood, he spoke so low into the mike.

We needed speed, and got off the ridge the fast way, via last night's highway. It was a fresh trail, leading into the hills.

Once we were on low ground and headed for the old Red Warrior LZ, we ducked off the trail and took to the woods again. Evidence of enemy movement was everywhere we looked.

The layer of leaves on the ground had been trodden down in many places by men walking in single file. The dampness of the morning dew betrayed them. The untouched leaves glistened damply. The disturbed leaves were dull. It was easy to see the winding routes Vietnamese patrols had taken only hours before.

We covered the distance to the LZ before noon and without incident, being very careful. I had point again, and saw the first of the NVA fortifications that circled the old LZ.

We stealthily slipped into the old bunker line, the clearing visible ahead of us. The team lay back as I advanced to scout the LZ. I parted the high grass and peered into a vast open field. In the center, like a target, was the landing zone itself, the scars of the battle only now being reclaimed by nature. The pitifully shallow fighting holes had begun to vanish under patches of grass and shrubs.

The line of fire from the NVA position to the LZ was absolutely clear. No wonder they got their butts kicked, I thought dismally. It was so easy to imagine the horror out there, exposed from all sides, the helicopters being shot down, no place to run.

It took time, but we walked completely around the LZ, charting the positions and marveling at them. It was very slow work, checking for booby traps, pacing off yardage, guarding and watching.

Every bunker was firmly roofed over, the mortar pits looked like wells, and trenches connected all the heavy weapons positions. Anti-aircraft guns had been set in between the recoilless rifle and mortar emplacements, so a chopper flying across the LZ would be like a clay pigeon launched before a crowd of skeet shooters.

It was nearly dark when we had finished the reconnaissance job and had eaten. We sent a long radio report back, describing the patrol up to this point. But as Payne signed us off and packed his mike and antenna, Steffens reached down to his feet and pulled up a strand of buried wire.

"Commo wire!" he exclaimed in a loud whisper. It was

gray Chinese issue, not the black U.S. Army wire. "Follow it," Mott ordered.

Steffens ripped the line out of the earth until he came to a tree. It joined a terminal there, spliced into another line. Steffens held up the fistful of wire.

The splice was insulated by paper, and the paper was still fresh. We looked it over closely. They had recently wired this place, expecting to use it again. That answered all our questions for this mission.

Mott pointed to the slight rise toward the west. "Let's get into those thickets," he said, "and take cover for the night. Steve, lead out."

Steffens led us to an entanglement of dried bamboo and vines, and we crawled in like rabbits into a warren. After dark, we moved a hundred meters away on our hands and knees before we slept, to confuse any NVA that might have spotted us earlier.

The stars came out brilliantly and we rested, secure in the dense underbrush, wondering what the NVA were doing tonight. My apprehension was subdued, but it did not go away. We had enjoyed incredible luck so far. It could not continue.

We stayed late in our haven, eating our LRRP rations and making coffee, organizing our gear and watching the LZ through a hole in the foliage. The sun was high by the time Mott announced our next move.

"We're taking a straight 270 degrees west," he told me, "right to the border. We have enough rations to stay out two more days."

I was given the point again, and I kept a steady pace, pausing only long enough to examine a bit of evidence here or there that the enemy had also been this way.

It was as hot as two hells by noon. The forest had become lush jungle, enmeshed in swampy lowland and thick, green mossbeds along the streams. We ran out of energy pushing through the mass of it, sweat pouring off us, a direct sun cooking us unmercifully.

We found a slight clearing and fell into it, throwing our gear down and gasping for breath. Payne wiped the sweat from his neck with his flop hat. "Where the fuck are we?" he asked, his voice weak from the exertion.

Mott slipped his map from his thigh pocket. "About right here, I think," he said, indicating a place on the border. So this was Cambodia. It didn't look a bit different from Vietnam.

"We need to get an exact fix on where we are." Payne insisted. Steve looked around. All we could see was swamp and rain forest infested with vines. "Can't tell anything from here," he stated.

"I'll climb that tree," Payne volunteered, gazing at a tall stand of trees about a hundred meters away. Steve picked up his rifle. "I'll pull security for you," he said. Payne stripped off his shirt and boots, and slung a pair of binoculars over his neck.

He came back down skinned up a bit, but loaded with information. "I'd put us right on the border," he said as he dressed. "I could orient my map and get those mountains and these streams lined up just right."

Mott considered that briefly, then stood and pulled on his rucksack. "Okay. We're on our way home now. Camper, take the point. Back azimuth 90 degrees, let's go."

I aimed my compass, the arrow pointing our way back. We slopped through the swamp, trying to keep on the more solid ground as the humidity made the air itself dense and oppressive. Sweat ran in my eyes, and my uniform was chafing and binding, as wet after ten minutes' walking as if I'd dived into the stream.

As I walked through the grass and water, watching where I put my feet, I saw the footprint. It was a tire-tread sandal print, freshly made in the sandy soil alongside the water.

I felt a shock race straight up my spinal cord. They were here, close. Mott looked at the print. "Turn around, go the other way!" he whispered.

I hurried past the team and retraced our steps. The guy

who had made that print was only a few minutes ahead of us. I damned the circumstances that had put us here.

I was cautious, measuring my progress in minutes of life and not meters of ground. Mott whistled. I looked around and he motioned for me to hurry, by pumping his fist up and down like a drill instructor ordering double-time.

I signaled an unmistakable refusal. Mott waved me aside and took point himself. I let him go by and fell in behind. He began to move fast, without caring how much noise he made.

We got out of the swamp and climbed a bombed-out hillside, finding ourselves in a morass of dying elephant grass. Mott hadn't slowed down at all. I wondered if he was giving any thought to where he was taking us.

A semi-path through the grass attracted Mott. It had been pushed down before. We tromped on through the grass, chasing Mott, getting more lost by the meter.

Suddenly Mott seemed to fall in a most awkward way, his hat and rifle flying. I thought he'd tripped over a vine. I stopped, and sidestepped off the trail, squatting down, expecting Mott to get back to his feet.

Mott was scrambling to free his rifle from the vines. "Sarge," I whispered, "what's wrong?" Mott looked back at me, his face a mask of terror. Something was very wrong. "Dinks?" I asked. Mott could see something I couldn't.

"Shoot!" I said.

He did nothing. "Goddammit, if you're not going to fire, I am!" I threatened, unsure of the situation. I lifted my weapon and was flipping it off safe when a shot exploded from in front of me, blowing the grass back in my face. My ears rang.

I pulled the trigger instinctively, but my CAR fired just once. I almost had heart failure. I glanced down and saw the selector was only on semi.

I didn't take the time to flip it to full auto. I blasted out the whole magazine in a sweeping fan, my trigger finger moving like lightning.

The shit hit the fan for real then. A deafening cascade of small-arms fire erupted from in front of us. I saw Mott twitching, and thought he was being shot. Bullets hit all around him. I changed magazines, though I wouldn't realize I had done so until I found the empty mag in my shirt later.

Leaves flew off their branches around us and dirt hit my face as near misses bracketed me. I cringed, waiting for the impact of the rounds in my body.

I changed to automatic, somehow making my hand obey, as a Vietnamese jumped up surprisingly close, his AK-47 smoking from muzzle to magazine well, trying to see if he had hit Mott.

I was already pressing the trigger again as he exposed himself, and it was only by chance he was in my line of fire. He never saw me. I swung a burst across his chest and he disappeared, arms flung wide, his weapon spinning through the air.

Unhurt, Mott launched himself off the ground and passed me screaming, "*Go! Go! Go!*" I needed no urging. I was right behind Mott, running as I'd never run before.

It sounded like a firing range behind us. What had Mott done, stumbled into a platoon? I raced through the woods, dodging trees, breaking down vines, losing sight of Mott. My hat was knocked off. Where were Payne and Steffens? The NVA were shooting at me with every jump.

I ran into the clearing we'd passed earlier. It was six inches deep in napalm ashes, and I saw Mott ahead of me, leaving a wake of dust behind him like a whirlwind.

I caught up with him when he tried to leap through a forked tree stump and became stuck. I grabbed him by the seat of the pants and lifted as I passed, literally flipping him over the fork; he regained his feet and outran me.

The swamp was straight ahead, and I caught sight of Payne and Steffens waiting there for us. Mott and I dived into the swamp, totally out of breath. The gunfire had ceased.

Mott grabbed for the radio handset from Payne, getting me caught in the middle and tangled in the cord. I accidentally burned myself on my weapon, the short barrel and flash suppressor as hot as a furnace. "I got one, I got one . . ." I heard myself saying.

"My map, I think I lost it," Mott croaked. In my own semi-stupor of exhaustion I heard that statement. A map was gold to the NVA, especially one of ours marked with patrol routes and coordinate codes.

Steffens watched the grass. "We gotta get the hell out of here, I think they're coming after us!" he warned. Mott radioed battalion again. "Three-Three, I am changing to another location, wait out," he said, and began to slog out of the damp. "Let's go," Mott said nervously.

We trotted to higher ground, so tense an insect couldn't have moved without catching our eye. We found a break in the trees and laid out an aircraft marker panel; Payne hastily set up the radio and Steffens and I staked out the security.

Steffens cursed; his weapon was malfunctioning. He discovered it wouldn't change to automatic and had to be pried off safe with his knife. Payne swapped weapons with Steve while Mott called in our position.

We could see two helicopters in the air about five klicks away, and I hoped the firebase would relay our situation to them. But the minutes ticked past and the choppers flew on. "FAC's coming," Mott said excitedly, "get that panel out where he can see it!"

Talk about service. The small green spotter plane was on our radio frequency before Payne could move the panel. Mott keyed the handset and FAC rode the beam in. Payne stood and held the orange panel up like a big bedsheet – what a target.

"He's got us!" Mott said. Payne gratefully dropped the panel. "He says there's a bomb crater six hundred meters west of here, and to get to it!" Mott said.

The two helicopters had caught FAC's call and banked back toward us. Help at last! We ran to the crater, the drumming of the rotor blades getting closer.

I was the first man on the top. It must have been a hell of a bomb that had cleared this hill; it was as bare as a baby's butt. Only one tree was left standing, and it had no bark or limbs.

I saw the crater, the only cover anywhere, and made for it as fast as my rapidly expiring legs would take me. Two helicopters were approaching us in the sky from the east. We'd have transport in a matter of minutes.

But surprise! The NVA had beaten us to the hill. I saw one hiding in a bush, looking the other way. His khaki uniform gave him away.

"Steve, there's one!" I yelled to Steffens, who was close behind me, firing a full magazine at the bush. The man wasn't there anymore when I hit empty. Steffens saw another dink at the far end of the hilltop and blasted him at fifty meters, from the hip.

I saw the man scream and go down. I reached the bomb crater, and the team piled in on me. The NVA ambush was sprung, and its fire was unleashed on us, kicking dirt up all around our hole.

It was a small crater, and the whole team with rucksacks crowded it badly. The first helicopter came in low, trying to find a place to pick us up. Ground fire drove it away.

We threw red smoke toward the trees and Mott called the spotter plane for support. The second Huey was a gunship. He radioed Mott, asking for an azimuth to the enemy from the smoke. Mott quickly supplied that information.

The gunnie made a firing pass, quad M-60s stuttering, hot brass cartridge cases pelting us. The trees in the fire swayed in the onslaught, grass and brush disintegrating in billows of dust.

I crammed another magazine in my weapon and hammered it out in one pull of the trigger, putting out suppressive fire to our left flank. Steve emptied magazines off to the right, and Mott and Payne peppered the front.

"Get down! Rockets!" Mott shouted in the din, and we pressed into the soft earth of the bomb crater. The Huey barreled in like a fighter plane, rocket pods flaring, streaks of fire roaring over our hole, and the tree line exploded into a deafening storm of roots and flying splinters.

"He's coming back!" Mott said, his voice sounding distant

to my numb eardrums. The chopper cleared out his rocket racks, dumping everything. The projectiles went by just a few meters over our heads, but one caught our lone tree.

It was a white-phosphorus missile. It hit the very tip of the only standing obstruction on the hilltop and went off, showering us with a thousand arcing bits of incandescent particles. If there had been somewhere to go, we'd have unassed that crater then.

Incoming fire halted completely after the last rocket run. The gunship chose a new direction to rip up the trees from, and blazed down, machine guns running wild. We added as much of our fire at the tree line as we could, our hole filling with expended cartridge cases.

The smoke from the burning trees covered the hill thickly. We lost our visibility and had to stop shooting as Mott announced, "Slick coming in, cease fire!"

The rotor wash from the Huey blew the smoke down and outward as it hovered in carefully. I stepped on Payne's shoulder as I jumped out of the hole, and Mott scrambled out and outran me again as we dashed for the helicopter.

Mott had so much speed built up, he ran all the way around the ship and came in through the opposite door. Payne made it out of the hole and ran at the helicopter, but something was wrong with his balance. I didn't realize it then, but all during the firefight my CAR-15 muzzle had been inches from his ear, and the firing had temporarily upset his equilibrium. Payne slammed into the door gunner's machine-gun mount, and had to be pulled bodily into the helicopter.

I was third, as I had slowed down to cover Payne, raking the trees with one of my last magazines, and as I ran for the doorway, firing at the enemy with just one hand holding my CAR-15, my last two or three rounds punctured the tail boom of our own helicopter.

Now we were all in but Steve. He had remained in the crater and continued to fire, dutifully covering his team, performing his tailgun job to the last. He rose and made the dash, the strain showing on his face. His Starlight scope fell from under his rucksack flap.

He knew it fell. He stopped, his eyes still on us, and turned, going back after the instrument.

The rotors were spinning at takeoff speed, and our skids were off the ground. Payne was lying nearly unconscious on the deck, and the smoke was still obscuring the trees.

Steffens got to us just as the pilot propelled us upward. Mott and I desperately grappled at Steve's pack straps, hoisting him in, his feet dangling out during the fast, high climb.

I took one breath and collapsed against the bulkhead, watching the burning hill get smaller in the distance. My Lord, we were out of it.

R & R

Robert Mason

Mason flew over 1000 helicopter assault missions in Vietnam between August 1965 and July 1966.

By the time we landed in Taipei, I was feeling very good. Uncle Sam, in his great wisdom, provided all necessities for his warriors – just follow the line. In Saigon we had lined up for various cities: Taipei, Bangkok, Sydney, others. The attraction of each city was the same – drinking and fucking. Or fucking and drinking, depending on your morals.

As we deplaned, a smiling government employee directed us to a bus. The bus cruised the streets while a man gave us a rundown of various hotels, indicating prices and location. I elected to stay at the King's.

When the government dropped us off at the hotel, the Chinese-civilian half of the team swung into action. A kindly, knowledgeable Chinese man-about-town latched on to us as we stepped off the bus.

"Okay, boys. You have come to the right place." He smiled warmly. "Come right this way, I'll help you get your rooms, but we must hurry. There is so much to do in Taipei."

I tossed my bag into the room. A man named Chuck had the room across from mine. Chuck was in his mid-forties and was a captain back at work. In the hallway he wore a tourist costume much like mine – chinos, checked shirt, and loafers. We had just introduced ourselves when Danny, the guide, came rushing toward us.

"Come, come, gentlemen, we must hurry. There is much to do in Taipei."

Danny hurried us down the hall to the elevator. "Remember, gentlemen, you are here to enjoy yourselves, and I am here to help you. First, we must go across the street to a fine, high-class bar and have a drink to discuss our plans. You must tell me what you want to do and I will be your guide." Danny walked a little ahead of us, almost walking backward as he talked to us. He was so excited that you might have assumed that he, too, just got in from Vietnam.

Danny showed us through the door of the bar. I noticed thirty or forty women sitting along one wall, side by side. He herded Chuck and me toward the beginning of the line.

"Martha! So good to see you tonight," he said to the first girl. She nodded warmly to Danny and then to us.

"Hi," I said. "I'm Bob Mason." Martha looked very pleased to meet me.

We moved up the long line of girls, saying hello to almost everyone. At the end of the line we went up to the second floor and settled around a table where drinks were already being served by some of Danny's friends.

"So, gentlemen, which one do you want?"

"You mean, which one of those girls?" I asked.

"Of course. Tell me which one you prefer and she will be with you like that." He snapped his fingers.

"Well, I did see one girl I kinda liked, but I didn't get her name," I said.

"Where was she sitting?"

"I think she was about the tenth girl. She's wearing a violet dress."

"Ah, Sharon. You have very high-class taste, Bob."

"Thanks."

Chuck described the girl he remembered, and Danny got up and excused himself. "I will be right back, soon. Drink up!"

Immediately after Danny disappeared down the stairs, the girl in violet, Sharon, appeared and was escorted to a table at the other end of the room. She sat down across from her escort, facing me. How could I feel deceived by someone I didn't know? Of all the girls I had met in the lineup, she was the one whose eyes had locked on mine. As I sat there watching her, I realized that I absolutely loved her. There was something familiar about her. She was smiling gently as she met her escort, but her expression changed slightly when she looked up. She did not look away, and I knew she loved me, too.

Danny came back up behind two women. They were both dressed very nicely and carried evening bags. They sat down across from Chuck and me while Danny introduced them. "Linda, this is Bob. Vicki, this is Chuck." He stood back for a moment, grinning at the happy couples. "I must go see about your drinks." Before he left, though, he leaned over to me and whispered, "Sharon was already –" I nodded quickly.

Linda leaned across the table and whispered, "It is so sad that you could not get the one you loved. Do you wish me to leave?"

Yes, I did. That girl, Sharon, seemed to be an Oriental version of Patience. Patience looked at me the same way when we first met. But there wasn't enough whiskey in me to cause me to become callous. The fact that Linda was willing to leave, to be rejected, stirred what remained of my sensibilities, and I said, "No, of course not."

"She is more beautiful than I am," said Linda, fishing for compliments. In fact, Sharon was more beautiful than Linda, but I reminded myself that neither of them would be near me if I wasn't going to pay. In four days it would be over.

"Don't be foolish; you are more beautiful."

"Thank you for saying so." She smiled.

Sharon still looked at me occasionally. I wondered why.

I have dim memories of the insides of many different clubs, singing in the streets, and bright lights and taxis. I even woke up in a different hotel. My companion, for ten dollars a day, was Linda. She showed me the sights on the island in between servicing my desperate horniness. We ate at different clubs and restaurants every night, never visiting the same place twice. Occasionally, as we toured, I would see Sharon watching me familiarly.

In moments, the four days were spent.

Surprisingly, girls crowded outside the bus as we arrived at the airport. As we got off, reunions were formed by the departing soldiers and their Chinese girlfriends. The girls were actually crying. Why in the world? Perfect strangers five days ago were now sobbing tearful farewells. I climbed down out of the bus, but there was no Linda. I moved past the hugging couples, to follow a roped path to the terminal. Five steps away from the door, I heard my name called. I looked up and saw Sharon. She was smiling broadly, but tears flowed on her cheeks. She held her arms out and I instinctively hugged her. I could not understand why she was doing this.

"Please be careful," she said.

Part II

Home Front

The War in America Against the War in Vietnam

Little Duck Comes Home

John Fetterman

John Fetterman's story on the return home of the body of Pfc
James Gibson, known to his friends as "Little Duck", won him
a Pulitzer for local news reporting.

Louisville *Times*, July 1968

It was late on a Wednesday night and most of the people were
asleep in Hindman, the county seat of Knott County, when
the body of Private First Class James Thurman (Little Duck)
Gibson came home from Vietnam.

It was hot. But as the gray hearse arrived bearing the gray
Army coffin, a summer rain began to fall. The fat raindrops
glistened on the polished hearse and steamed on the street.
Hindman was dark and silent. In the distance down the
town's main street the red sign on the Square Deal Motor Co.
flashed on and off.

Private Gibson's body had been flown from Oakland,
California, to Cincinnati and was accompanied by Army
Staff Sgt Raymond A. Ritter, assigned to escort it home.
The body was picked up in Cincinnati by John Everage, a
partner in the local funeral home, and from that point on it
was in the care of people who had known the 24-year-old
soldier all his life.

At Hindman, the coffin was lifted out while Sgt Ritter,
who wore a black mourning band on his arm, snapped a

salute. One funeral home employee whispered to another: "It's Little Duck. They brought him back."

Most of his life he had been called Little Duck – for so long that many people who knew him well had to pause and reflect to recall his full name.

By Thursday morning there were few people who did not know that Little Duck was home – or almost home. During the morning the family came; his older brother, Herschel, whom they call Big Duck; his sister Betty Jo; and his wife Carolyn.

They stood over the glass-shielded body and let their tears fall upon the glass, and people spoke softly in the filling station next door and on the street outside.

The soldier's parents, Mr and Mrs Norman Gibson, waited at home, a neat white house up the hollow which shelters Flax Patch Creek, several miles away. Mrs Gibson had been ill for months, and the family did not let her take the trip to Hindman. Later in the morning, they took Little Duck home.

Sweltering heat choked the hills and valleys as Little Duck was placed back in the hearse and taken home. The cortege had been joined by Maj. Lyle Haldeman, a survival assistance officer, sent, like Sgt Ritter, to assist the family. It was a long, slow trip – over a high ridge to the south, along Irishman Creek and past the small community of Amburgey.

At Amburgey, the people stood in the sun, women wept and men removed their hats as the hearse went past. Mrs Nora Amburgey, the postmistress, lowered the flag of the tiny fourth-class post office to half-mast and said, "We all thought a lot of Little Duck."

At the point where Flax Patch Creek empties into Irishman Creek, the hearse turned, crossed a small wooden bridge and drove the final mile up Flax Patch Creek to the Gibson home. The parents and other relatives waited in a darkened, silent home.

As the coffin was lifted upon the front porch and through the door into the front living room, the silence was broken by cries of grief. The sounds of anguish swelled and rolled along the hollow. Little Duck was home.

All afternoon and all night they came, some walking, some driving up the dusty road in cars and trucks. They brought flowers and food until the living room was filled with floral tributes and the kitchen was crammed with food. The people filled the house and yard. They talked in small groups, and members of the family clasped to each other in grief.

They went, time and time again, to look down into the coffin and weep.

The mother, a sweet-faced mountain woman, her gray hair brushed back and fastened behind her head, forced back the pangs of her illness and moved, as in a trance, among the crowd as she said:

"His will will be done no matter what we say or do."

The father, a tall, tanned man, his eyes wide and red from weeping, said:

"He didn't want to go to the Army, but he knew it was the right thing to do; so he did his best. He gave all he had. I'm as proud of him as I can be. Now they bring him home like this."

Around midnight the rain returned and the mourners gathered in the house, on the porch and backed against the side of the house under the eaves.

The father talked softly of his son.

"I suppose you wonder why we called him Little Duck. Well, when the boys were little they would go over and play in the creek every chance they got. Somebody said they were like ducks.

"Ever since then Herschel was 'Big Duck' and James was 'Little Duck'.

"You worked hard all your life to raise your family. I worked in a 32-inch seam of coal, on my hands and knees, loading coal to give my family what I could.

"There was never a closer family. Little Duck was born here in this house and never wanted to leave."

Other mourners stepped up to volunteer tributes to Little Duck.

"He never was one to drink and run up and down the road at night."

"He took care of his family. He was a good boy."

Little Duck was a big boy. He was 6 feet 5½ inches tall and weighed 205 pounds. His size led him to the basketball team at Combs High School where he met and courted the girl he married last January.

Little Duck was home recently on furlough. Within a month after he went down Flax Patch Creek to return to the Army, he was back home to be buried. He had been married six months, a soldier for seven.

The Army said he was hit by mortar fragments near Saigon, but there were few details of his death.

The father, there in the stillness of the early morning, was remembering the day his son went back to the Army.

"He had walked around the place, looking at everything. He told me, 'Lord, it's good to be home.' "

"Then he went down the road. He said, 'Daddy, take care of yourself and don' work too hard.' "

"He said, 'I'll be seeing you.' But he can't see me now."

An elderly man, walking with great dignity, approached and said, "Nobody can ever say anything against Little Duck. He was as good a boy as you'll ever see."

Inside the living room, the air heavy with the scent of flowers, Little Duck's mother sat with her son and her grief.

Her hand went out gently, as to comfort a stranger, and she talked as though to herself:

"Why my boy? Why my baby?"

She looked toward the casket, draped in an American flag, and when she turned back she said:

"You'll never know what a flag means until you see one on your own boy."

Then she went back to weep over the casket.

On Friday afternoon Little Duck was taken over to the Providence Regular Baptist Church and placed behind the pulpit. All that night the church lights burned and the people stayed and prayed. The parents spent the night at the church.

"This is his last night," Little Duck's mother explained.

The funeral was at 10 o'clock Saturday morning, and the people began to arrive early. They came from the dozens of hollows and small communities in Letcher, Knot, and Perry counties. Some came back from other states. They filled the pews and then filled the aisle with folding chairs. Those who could not crowd inside gathered outside the door or listened beneath the windows.

The sermon was delivered by the Rev. Archie Everage, pastor at Montgomery Baptist Church, which is on Montgomery Creek near Hindman. On the last Sunday that he was home alive, Little Duck attended services there.

The service began with a solo, "Beneath the Sunset," sung by a young girl with a clear bell-like voice; then there were hymns from the church choir.

Mr Everage, who had been a friend of Little Duck, had difficulty in keeping his voice from breaking as he got into his final tribute. He spoke of the honor Little Duck had brought to his family, his courage and his dedication. He spoke of Little Duck "following the colors of his country". He said Little Duck died "for a cause for which many of our forefathers fought and died".

The phrase touched off a fresh wail of sobs to fill the church. Many mountain people take great pride in their men who "follow the colors". It is a tradition that goes back to October 1780, when a lightly regarded band of mountaineers handed disciplined British troops a historic defeat at Kings Mountain in South Carolina and turned the tide of the Revolutionary war.

Shortly before Little Duck was hit in Vietnam, he had written two letters intended for his wife. Actually the soldier was writing a part of his own funeral. Mr Everage read from one letter:

"Honey, they put me in a company right down on the

Delta. From what everybody says that is a rough place, but I've been praying hard for the Lord to help me and take care of me so really I'm not too scared or worried. I think if He wants it to be my time to go that I'm prepared for it. Honey, you don't know really when you are going to face something like this, but I want you to be a good girl and try to live a good life. For if I had things to do over I would have already been prepared for something like this. I guess you are wondering why I'm telling you this, but you don't know how hard it's been on me in just a short time. But listen here, if anything happens to me, all I want is for you to live right, and then I'll get to see you again."

And from another letter:

"Honey, listen, if anything happens to me I want you to know that I love you very very much and I want you to keep seeing my family the rest of their lives and I want you to know you are a wonderful wife and that I'm very proud of you. If anything happens I want Big Duck and Betty Jo to know I loved them very much. If anything happens also tell them not to worry, that I'm prepared for it."

The service lasted two hours and ended only after scores of people, of all ages, filed past the coffin.

Then they took Little Duck to Resthaven Cemetery up on a hill in Perry County. The Army provided six pallbearers, five of whom had served in Vietnam. There was a seven-man firing squad to fire the traditional three volleys over the grave and bugle to sound taps.

The pallbearers, crisp and polished in summer tans, folded the flag from the coffin and Sgt Ritter handed it to the young widow, who had wept so much, but spoken so little, during the past three days.

Then the soldier's widow knelt beside the casket and said softly, "Oh, Little Duck."

Then they buried Little Duck beneath a bit of the land he died for.

Police Break up Anti-War Protest

Studs Terkel

> More than ten thousand protestors, mostly students, went to Chicago in August 1968 to demonstrate against the Vietnam War. The city was hosting the Democratic Party convention. The journalist Studs Terkel reported on the second night of rioting, 27th August.

Last night, a gathering of the young in the park was broken up by Chicago police. Clubs were swung and heads were busted. Several young journalists were among those clobbered. The ministrations in the tent, a moment ago, brought to mind the wild night before. Would there be a repeat performance tonight? The indignant young, and a surprising number of the middle-aged, plan to gather once more in the park. Mayor Daley has ordered the police to disperse all at eleven o'clock. That is the park's official curfew. For years, it has been more honored in the breach than in the observance. For years, smelt fishermen have lingered and hoped all night long for a good catch. They have sat along the banks of the lake, in the area that is officially Lincoln Park, from nightfall to well past dawn. It has been a Chicago ritual ever since the Potawatamies. But tonight, Mayor Daley, with Nestor-like wisdom, has decreed that the curfew shall ring at the appointed hour.

Led by young clergymen of the North Side Ministry, a raggletaggle band is marching toward the park. A huge, rude wooden cross is borne at the head of the parade. James

Cameron [a British journalist] and I join the procession. It is a lovely midsummer evening. Thousands are seated upon the grass. Brief speeches are made. Familiar songs are sung. "Amen." "Down by the Riverside." "Come by Here." Even "We Shall Overcome." Cameron is "instantly transported back seven or eight years to Aldermaston." The feeling of déjà vu overcomes a number of others, too, including myself. The occasion is both tender and sad. Cameron notes that this ceremonial of what appears to be genuine dedication, touched by anxiety, anger, and some fear, is almost deliberately masked by outrageous costumes and fancy dress. A few youngbloods, hot out of Radcliffe and Amherst, protest the tranquil spirit. They are gently hooted down by the others. It is something of a religious occasion. Testimony is offered by one or another, caught in the spirit of the occasion. Even I.

A young clergyman recognizes me as one who talks a great deal, to others as well as to himself. At a microphone, one doesn't have to bear too much witness. "I am glad to be here, where life is," I intone preacherlike, "rather than at the Amphitheatre where life ain't." It doesn't really matter; the mike isn't working very well. I am certain, I let James Cameron know, that nothing will happen tonight. After all, last night's bloody encounter was chronicled by the world's press and television. The Whole World Is Watching. It was certainly a black eye for Chicago. Mayor Daley may not be Pericles, but he's not really so dumb as to stage an encore. He'll just let the kids say their say, shout their shouts, sing their songs, and wander off. . . .

James Cameron accepts my word, because I know such things. He and I shall soon wander off ourselves and toast a peaceful night with a martini or two. The era of good feeling is short-lived. About three minutes after my pronouncement, Cameron says, "Look out there." So does the young clergyman at the mike. All eyes peer into the semi-darkness across the green field. About two hundred yards away, in what appears to be a ghostly light, from lamps and headlights of cars speeding down Outer Drive, is gathered a Roman legion.

So it seems. We see helmets and shields, face shields of plastic. We see no faces. We are, all of us, transfixed. Have I seen this before on some wall tapestry? Or in some well-thumbed pictorial history of ancient times? Here, a band of raggletaggle Christians and all sorts of outcasts. There, a battalion of armed soldiers of the Empire. Or is it a summer festival of young pagans, about to be disrupted by figures out of some primordial myth? One thing is certain: we are dreaming awake.

Several police trucks are faintly visible. From one, a voice on the bullhorn is heard. It is impersonal in tone. "You are ordered to clear out of the park by eleven o'clock." We shall be allowed to go peacefully. Those who remain will be in violation of the law. The young clergyman suggests that those who wish to leave may do so now. We have about an hour to go. Hardly anyone moves. A band of young men uproot the huge cross from its original position, carry it some fifty yards forward, and implant it in the field. It stands between us and them. In the night vapors, it is awesome. Will it, as in medieval times, ward off the devil, wherever he may be? "I have never seen the crucifix more symbolically used," murmurs Cameron. . . . A young man says to Jim and me, "You two elderly people better go. We don't want you hurt. Tear gas is nasty." Cameron and I harrumph indignantly. Elderly, indeed! Yet, our indignation is muted by something deeply felt.

At first, there had been a gratitude expressed by a good number of the young that so many Over Thirty are here, to help them bear some sort of witness. Now, as Cameron observes, they are solicitous. Rather they be hurt than us. Advice is offered by young veterans to middle-aged rookies. When the gas comes, hold your nose. Breathe through your mouth. Moisten your handkerchief. We are waiting. Waiting. . . . It is nearly eleven o'clock. Now, the tension cannot be disguised. The helmeted figures across the field are motionless. So are the trucks. "They always have the advantage," observes Cameron. "The decision is theirs. They can keep us waiting as long as they want." "Eleven o'clock." A last warning from the voice on the bull-horn. Nobody moves. The faceless images come alive. They are coming toward us. So are the trucks. "I don't believe it," somebody says. A sound is heard. Another. And another.

Canisters of tear gas are being shot out from the tanklike trucks. Held noses and wet handkerchiefs do little good. We are coughing, hawking, crying, spitting, phlegming, cursing . . . We are helpless. And humiliated. The humiliating attributes of tear gas are astonishing. We are stumbling, helter-skelter, across the park, toward Clark Street. It is a retreat of stumblebums. James Cameron and I, among others whose presence we hardly sense, are two characters out of Samuel Beckett. We are Estragon and Vladimir. We are Hamm and Clov. We are Krapp. We cling to one another. We cough, we spit, we hawk, we curse. Like blind Pozzo, we stumble on. A canister falls at our feet. A tall young man, of flowing blond beard (I note, tearfully), immediately behind us, kicks the canister away, toward himself. "Are you all right? Are you all right?" he coughs at us, solicitously. "Grrrhhgg," we reply. "Are you sure?" "Grrrhhgg," we insist.

We are huddled, refugees, a good fifty of us, on the safety island in the middle of Clark Street. Sirens are sounding. The whole city, it seems, is possessed by the wailing of banshees. Nobody is in his right mind. Cars are racing past. We see the faces of the occupants. They are crazy with fear. Of us. One car deliberately swerves toward the island, on which we hover. I see the driver's face. It is distorted. Hate and terror. Of us. His hand is on the horn; stuck to it. Noise and confusion. We cry out. The car's fender scrapes against a young islander. It knocks him down. He howls, jumps up, and beats against the window. Others join him. Banging away at the car, they almost overturn it. Sirens. Horns. Rage. Madness.

The Chicago Seven Trial: The Testimony of Abbie Hoffman, Yippie.

Abbie Hoffman

Eight leaders of the Chicago 1968 anti-War protest were arrested and charged with conspiracy to incite rioting. One defendant, Black Panther Bobby Seale, was eventually tried separately. Some of the remaining "Chicago Seven", including Abbott "Abbie" Hoffman, the co-founder of the Youth International party, were convicted on lesser charges, but the convictions were overturned because of judicial bias in 1973. An investigation ("The Walker Report") by the national Commission on the Causes and Prevention of Violence concluded that the mayhem in Chicago had been "a police riot".

MR. WEINGLASS: Will you please identify yourself for the record?

THE WITNESS: My name is Abbie. I am an orphan of America.

MR. SCHULTZ: Your Honor, may the record show it is the defendant Hoffman who has taken the stand?

THE COURT: Oh, yes. It may so indicate. . . .

MR. WEINGLASS: Where do you reside?

THE WITNESS: I live in Woodstock Nation.

MR. WEINGLASS: Will you tell the Court and jury where it is?

THE WITNESS: Yes. It is a nation of alienated young people. We carry it around with us as a state of mind in the same way as the Sioux Indians carried the Sioux nation around with them. It is a nation dedicated to cooperation versus competition, to the idea that people should have better means of exchange than property or money, that there should be some other basis for human interaction. It is a nation dedicated to –

THE COURT: Just where it is, that is all.

THE WITNESS: It is in my mind and in the minds of my brothers and sisters. It does not consist of property or material but, rather, of ideas and certain values. We believe in a society –

THE COURT: No, we want the place of residence, if he has one, place of doing business, if you have a business. Nothing about philosophy or India, sir. Just where you live, if you have a place to live. Now you said Woodstock. In what state is Woodstock?

THE WITNESS: It is in the state of mind, in the mind of myself and my brothers and sisters. It is a conspiracy. Presently, the nation is held captive, in the penitentiaries of the institutions of a decaying system.

MR. WEINGLASS: Can you tell the Court and jury your present age?

THE WITNESS: My age is 33. I am a child of the 60s.

MR. WEINGLASS: When were you born?

THE WITNESS: Psychologically, 1960.

MR. SCHULTZ: Objection, if the Court please. I move to strike the answer.

MR. WEINGLASS: What is the actual date of your birth?

THE WITNESS: November 30, 1936.

MR. WEINGLASS: Between the date of your birth, November 30, 1936, and May 1, 1960, what if anything occurred in your life?

THE WITNESS: Nothing. I believe it is called an American education.

MR. SCHULTZ: Objection.

THE COURT: I sustain the objection.

THE WITNESS: Huh.

MR. WEINGLASS: Abbie, could you tell the Court and jury –

MR. SCHULTZ: His name isn't Abbie. I object to this informality.

MR. WEINGLASS: Can you tell the Court and jury what is your present occupation?

THE WITNESS: I am a cultural revolutionary. Well, I am really a defendant – full-time.

MR. WEINGLASS: What do you mean by the phrase "cultural revolutionary?"

THE WITNESS: Well, I suppose it is a person who tries to shape and participate in the values, and the mores, the customs and the style of living of new people who eventually become inhabitants of a new nation and a new society through art and poetry, theater, and music.

MR. WEINGLASS: What have you done yourself to participate in that revolution?

THE WITNESS: Well, I have been a rock and roll singer. I am a reporter with the Liberation News Service. I am a poet. I am a film maker. I made a movie called "Yippies Tour Chicago or How I Spent My Summer Vacation." Currently, I am negotiating with United Artists and MGM to do a movie in Hollywood.

I have written an extensive pamphlet on how to live free in the city of New York.

I have written two books, one called *Revolution for The Hell of It* under the pseudonym Free, and one called, *Woodstock Nation*.

MR. WEINGLASS: Taking you back to the spring of 1960, approximately May 1, 1960, will you tell the Court and jury where you were?

MR. SCHULTZ: 1960?

THE WITNESS: That's right.

MR. SCHULTZ: Objection.

THE COURT: I sustain the objection.

MR. WEINGLASS: Your Honor, that date has great relevance to the trial. May 1, 1960, was this witness' first public demonstration. I am going to bring him down through Chicago.

THE COURT: Not in my presence, you are not going to bring him down. I sustain the objection to the question.

THE WITNESS: My background has nothing to do with my state of mind?

THE COURT: Will you remain quiet while I am making a ruling? I know you have no respect for me.

MR. KUNSTLER: Your Honor, that is totally unwarranted. I think your remarks call for a motion for a mistrial.

THE COURT: And your motion calls for a denial of the motion. Mr. Weinglass, continue with your examination.

MR. KUNSTLER: You denied my motion? I hadn't even started to argue it.

THE COURT: I don't need any argument on that one. The witness turned his back on me while he was on the witness stand.

THE WITNESS: I was just looking at the pictures of the long hairs up on the wall. . . .

THE COURT: I will let the witness tell about this asserted conversation with Mr. Rubin on the occasion described.

MR. WEINGLASS: What was the conversation at that time?

THE WITNESS: Jerry Rubin told me that he had come to New York to be project director of a peace march in Washington that was going to march to the Pentagon in October, October 21. He said that the peace movement suffered from a certain kind of attitude, mainly that it was based solely on the issue of the Vietnam war. He said that the war in Vietnam was not just an accident but a direct by-product of the kind of system, a capitalist system in the country, and that we had to begin to put forth new kinds of values, especially to young people in the country, to make a kind of society in which a Vietnam war would not be possible.

And he felt that these attitudes and values were present

in the hippie movement and many of the techniques, the guerrilla theater techniques that had been used and many of these methods of communication would allow for people to participate and become involved in a new kind of democracy.

I said that the Pentagon was a five-sided evil symbol in most religions and that it might be possible to approach this from a religious point of view. If we got large numbers of people to surround the Pentagon, we could exorcize it of its evil spirits.

So I had agreed at that point to begin working on the exorcism of the Pentagon demonstration.

MR. WEINGLASS: Prior to the date of the demonstration which is October, did you go to the Pentagon?

THE WITNESS: Yes. I went about a week or two before with one of my close brothers, Martin Carey, a poster maker, and we measured the Pentagon, the two of us, to see how many people would fit around it. We only had to do one side because it is just multiplied by five.

We got arrested. It's illegal to measure the Pentagon. I didn't know it up to that point.

When we were arrested they asked us what we were doing. We said it was to measure the Pentagon and we wanted a permit to raise it 300 feet in the air, and they said "How about 10?" So we said "OK".

And they threw us out of the Pentagon and we went back to New York and had a press conference, told them what it was about.

We also introduced a drug called *lace*, which, when you squirted it at the policemen made them take their clothes off and make love, a very potent drug.

MR. WEINGLASS: Did you mean literally that the building was to rise up 300 feet off the ground?

MR. SCHULTZ: I can't cross-examine about his meaning literally.

THE COURT: I sustain the objection.

MR. SCHULTZ: I would ask Mr. Weinglass please get on

with the trial of this case and stop playing around with raising the Pentagon 10 feet or 300 feet off the ground.

MR. WEINGLASS: Your Honor, I am glad to see Mr. Schultz finally concedes that things like levitating the Pentagon building, putting LSD in the water, 10,000 people walking nude on Lake Michigan, and a $200,000 bribe attempt are all playing around. I am willing to concede that fact, that it was all playing around, it was a play idea of this witness, and if he is willing to concede it, we can all go home.

THE COURT: I sustain the objection.

MR. WEINGLASS: Did you intend that the people who surrounded the Pentagon should do anything of a violent nature whatever to cause the building to rise 300 feet in the air and be exercised of evil spirits?

MR. SCHULTZ: Objection.

THE COURT: I sustain the objection.

MR. WEINGLASS: Could you indicate to the Court and jury whether or not the Pentagon was, in fact, exersized of its evil spirits?

THE WITNESS: Yes, I believe it was. . . .

MR. WEINGLASS: Now, drawing your attention to the first week of December 1967, did you have occasion to meet with Jerry Rubin and the others?

THE WITNESS: Yes.

MR. WEINGLASS: Will you relate to the Court and jury what the conversation was?

THE WITNESS: Yes.

We talked about the possibility of having demonstrations at the Democratic Convention in Chicago, Illinois, that was going to be occurring that August. I am not sure that we knew at that point that it was in Chicago. Wherever it was, we were planning on going.

Jerry Rubin, I believe, said that it would be a good idea to call it the Festival of Life in contrast to the Convention of Death, and to have it in some kind of public area, like a park or something, in Chicago.

One thing that I was very particular about was that we didn't have any concept of leadership involved. There was a feeling of young people that they didn't want to listen to leaders. We had to create a kind of situation in which people would be allowed to participate and become in a real sense their own leaders.

I think it was then after this that Paul Krassner said the word "YIPPIE," and we felt that that expressed in a kind of slogan and advertising sense the spirit that we wanted to put forth in Chicago, and we adopted that as our password, really. . . .

Anita [Hoffman] said that "Yippie" would be understood by our generation, that straight newspapers like the *New York Times* and the U.S. Government and the courts and everything wouldn't take it seriously unless it had a formal name, so she came up with the name: "Youth International Party." She said we could play a lot of jokes on the concept of "party" because everybody would think that we were this huge international conspiracy, but that in actuality we were a party that you had fun at.

Nancy [Kursham] said that fun was an integral ingredient, that people in America, because they were being programmed like IBM cards, weren't having enough fun in life and that if you watched television, the only people that you saw having any fun were people who were buying lousy junk on television commercials, and that this would be a whole new attitude because you would see people, young people, having fun while they were protesting the system, and that young people all around this country and around the world would be turned on for that kind of an attitude.

I said that fun was very important, too, that it was a direct rebuttal of the kind of ethics and morals that were being put forth in the country to keep people working in a rat race which didn't make any sense because in a few years machines would do all the work anyway, that there was a whole system of values that people were taught to postpone their pleasure, to put all their money in the bank, to buy life insurance, a whole bunch of things that didn't make any sense to our generation at all, and that fun actually was becoming quite subversive.

Jerry said that because of our action at the Stock Exchange in throwing out the money, that within a few weeks the Wall Street brokers there had totally enclosed the whole stock exchange in bulletproof, shatterproof glass, that cost something like $20,000 because they were afraid we'd come back and throw money out again.

He said that for hundreds of years political cartoonists had always pictured corrupt politicians in the guise of a pig, and he said that it would be great theater if we ran a pig for President, and we all took that on as like a great idea and that's more or less – that was the founding.

MR. WEINGLASS: The document that is before you, D-222 for identification, what is that document?

THE WITNESS: It was our initial call to people to describe what Yippie was about and why we were coming to Chicago.

MR. WEINGLASS: Now, Abbie, could you read the entire document to the jury.

THE WITNESS: It says:

"A STATEMENT FROM YIP!

"Join us in Chicago in August for an international festival of youth, music, and theater. Rise up and abandon the creeping meatball! Come all you rebels, youth spirits, rock minstrels, truth-seekers, peacock-freaks, poets, barricade-jumpers, dancers, lovers and artists!

"It is summer. It is the last week in August, and the NATIONAL DEATH PARTY meets to bless Lyndon Johnson. We are there! There are 50,000 of us dancing in the streets, throbbing with amplifiers and harmony. We are making love in the parks. We are reading, singing, laughing, printing newspapers, groping, and making a mock convention, and celebrating the birth of FREE AMERICA in our own time.

"Everything will be free. Bring blankets, tents, draft-cards, body-paint, Mr. Leary's Cow, food to share, music, eager skin, and happiness. The threats of LBJ, Mayor Daley, and J. Edgar Freako will not stop us. We are coming! We are coming from all over the world!

"The life of the American spirit is being torn asunder by the forces of violence, decay, and the napalm-cancer fiend. We demand the Politics of Ecstasy! We are the delicate spores of the new fierceness that will change America. We will create our own reality, we are Free America! And we will not accept the false theater of the Death Convention.

"We will be in Chicago. Begin preparations now! Chicago is yours! Do it!"

"Do it!" was a slogan like "Yippie." We use that a lot and it meant that each person that came should take on the responsibility for being his own leader-that we should, in fact, have a leaderless society.

We shortly thereafter opened an office and people worked in the office on what we call movement salaries, subsistence, thirty dollars a week. We had what the straight world would call a staff and an office although we called it an energy center and regarded ourselves as a tribe or a family.

MR. WEINGLASS: Could you explain to the Court and jury, if you know, how this staff functioned in your office?

THE WITNESS: Well, I would describe it as anarchistic. People would pick up the phone and give information and people from all over the country were now becoming interested and they would ask for more information, whether we were going to get a permit, how the people in Chicago were relating, and we would bring flyers and banners and posters. We would have large general meetings that were open to anybody who wanted to come.

MR. WEINGLASS: How many people would attend these weekly meetings?

THE WITNESS: There were about two to three hundred people there that were attending the meetings. Eventually we had to move into Union Square and hold meetings out in the public. There would be maybe three to five hundred people attending meetings . . .

MR. WEINGLASS: Where did you go [March 23], if you can recall.

THE WITNESS: I flew to Chicago to observe a meeting being sponsored, I believe, by the National Mobilization Committee. It was held at a place called Lake Villa, I believe, about twenty miles outside of Chicago here.

MR. WEINGLASS: Do you recall how you were dressed for that meeting?

THE WITNESS: I was dressed as an Indian. I had gone to Grand Central Station as an Indian and so I just got on a plane and flew as an Indian.

MR. WEINGLASS: Now, when you flew to Chicago, were you alone?

THE WITNESS: No. Present were Jerry, myself, Paul Krassner, and Marshall Bloom, the head of this Liberation News Service.

MR. WEINGLASS: When you arrived at Lake Villa, did you have occasion to meet any of the defendants who are seated here at this table?

THE WITNESS: Yes, I met for the first time Rennie, Tom Hayden – who I had met before, and that's it, you know. . . .

MR. WEINGLASS: Was any decision reached at that meeting about coming to Chicago?

THE WITNESS: I believe that they debated for two days about whether they should come or not to Chicago. They decided to have more meetings. We said we had already made up our minds to come to Chicago and we passed out buttons and posters and said that if they were there, good, it would be a good time.

MR. WEINGLASS: Following the Lake Villa conference, do you recall where you went?

THE WITNESS: Yes. The next day, March 25, 1 went to the Aragon Ballroom. It was a benefit to raise money again for the Yippies but we had a meeting backstage in one of the dressing rooms with the Chicago Yippies.

MR. WEINGLASS: Do you recall what was discussed?

THE WITNESS: Yes. We drafted a permit application for the Festival to take place in Chicago. We agreed that Grant Park would be best.

MR. WEINGLASS: Directing your attention to the following morning, which was Monday morning, March 26, do you recall where you were at that morning?

THE WITNESS: We went to the Parks Department. Jerry was there, Paul, Helen Runningwater, Abe Peck, Reverend John Tuttle – there were a group of about twenty to thirty people, Yippies.

MR. WEINGLASS: Did you meet with anyone at the Park District at that time?

THE WITNESS: Yes. There were officials from the Parks Department to greet us, they took us into this office, and we presented a permit application.

MR. WEINGLASS: Did you ever receive a reply to this application?

THE WITNESS: Not to my knowledge.

MR. WEINGLASS: After your meeting with the Park District, where, if anywhere, did you go?

THE WITNESS: We held a brief press conference on the lawn in front of the Parks Department, and then we went to see Mayor Daley at City Hall. When we arrived, we were told that the mayor was indisposed and that Deputy Mayor David Stahl would see us.

MR. WEINGLASS: When you met with Deputy Mayor Stahl, what, if anything, occurred?

THE WITNESS: Helen Runningwater presented him with a copy of the permit application that we had submitted to the Parks Department. It was rolled up in the Playmate of the Month that said "To Dick with Love, the Yippies," on it. And we presented it to him and gave him a kiss and put a Yippie button on him, and when he opened it up, the Playmate was just there.

And he was very embarrassed by the whole thing, and he said that we had followed the right procedure, the city would give it proper attention and things like that. . . .

December 29, 1969

MR. WEINGLASS: I direct your attention now to August 5, 1968, and I ask you where you were on that day.

THE WITNESS: I was in my apartment, St. Marks Place, on the Lower East Side in New York City.

MR. WEINGLASS: Who was with you?

THE WITNESS: Jerry Rubin was there, Paul Krassner was there, and Nancy. Anita was there; five of us, I believe.

MR. WEINGLASS: Can you describe the conversation which occurred between you and Abe Peck on the telephone?

THE WITNESS: Mr. Peck and other people from Chicago, Yippies – had just returned from a meeting on Monday afternoon with David Stahl and other people from the City administration. He said that he was quite shocked because – they said that they didn't know that we wanted to sleep in the park.

Abe Peck said that it had been known all along that one of the key elements of this Festival was to let us sleep in the park, that it was impossible for people to sleep in hotels since the delegates were staying there and it would only be natural to sleep in the park.

He furthermore told me in his opinion the City was laying down certain threats to them in order to try and get them to withdraw their permit application, and that we should come immediately back to Chicago.

MR. WEINGLASS: After that phone conversation what occurred?

THE WITNESS: We subsequently went to Chicago on August 7 at night.

MR. WEINGLASS: Did a meeting occur on that evening?

THE WITNESS: Yes, in Mayor Daley's press conference room, where he holds his press conferences.

MR. WEINGLASS: Can you relate what occurred at this meeting?

THE WITNESS: It was more or less an informal kind of meeting. Mr. Stahl made clear that these were just exploratory talks, that the mayor didn't have it in his power to grant the permits. We said that that was absurd, that we had been negotiating now for a period of four or five months, that the City was acting like an ostrich, sticking its head in the sand, hoping that we would all go away like it was some bad dream.

I pointed out that it was in the best interests of the City to have us in Lincoln Park ten miles away from the Convention hall. I said we had no intention of marching on the Convention hall, that I didn't particularly think that politics in America could be changed by marches and rallies, that what we were presenting was an alternative life style, and we hoped that people of Chicago would come up, and mingle in Lincoln Park and see what we were about.

I said that the City ought to give us a hundred grand, a hundred thousand dollars to run the Festival. It would be so much in their best interests.

And then I said, "Why don't you just give two hundred grand, and I'll split town?"

It was a very informal meeting. We were just sitting around on metal chairs that they had.

All the time David Stahl had been insisting that they did not make decisions in the city, that he and the mayor did not make the decisions. We greeted this with a lot of laughter and said that it was generally understood all around the country that Daley was the boss of Chicago and made all the decisions.

I also said that I considered that our right to assemble in Lincoln Park and to present our society was a right that I was willing to die for, that this was a fundamental human right. . . .

MR. WEINGLASS: On August 14, approximately three days later, in the morning of that day, do you recall where you were?

THE WITNESS: I went to speak to Jay Miller, head of the American Civil Liberties Union. I asked if it was possible for them to work with us on an injunction in the Federal court to sue Mayor Daley and other city officials about the fact that they would not grant us a permit and were denying us our right to freedom of speech and assembly.

MR. WEINGLASS: Now, can you relate to the Court and jury what happened in court when you appeared at 10:00 A.M.?

THE WITNESS: It was heard before Judge Lynch.

There was a fantastic amount of guards all over the place.

We were searched, made to take off our shirts, empty our pockets—

MR. SCHULTZ. That is totally irrelevant. There happened to be threats at that time, your Honor—

THE WITNESS: He is right. There were threats. I had twenty that week.

THE COURT: The language, "There were a fantastic amount of guards," may go out and the jury is directed to disregard them.

MR. WEINGLASS: After the—

THE WITNESS: We came before the judge. It was a room similar to this, similar, kind of wall-to wall bourgeois, rugs and neon lights. Federal courts are all the same, I think.

The judge made a couple of references to us in the room, said that our dress was an affront to the Court.

It was pointed out by a lawyer that came by that Judge Lynch was Mayor Daley's ex-law partner. As a result of this conversation we went back into court about twenty, thirty minutes later.

MR. WEINGLASS: Did you speak to the Court?

THE WITNESS: I spoke to Judge Lynch. I said that we were withdrawing our suit, that we had as little faith in the judicial system in this country as we had in the political system.

He said, "Be careful, young man. I will find a place for you to sleep."

And I thanked him for that, said I had one, and left.

We withdrew our suit. Then we had a press conference downstairs to explain the reasons for that. We explained to the press that we were leaving in our permit application but withdrawing our Federal injunction to sue the city. We said it was a bit futile to end up before a judge, Judge Lynch, who was the ex-law partner of Mayor Daley, that the Federal judges were closely tied in with the Daley and Democratic political machine in Chicago and that we could have little recourse of grievance.

Furthermore, that we suspected that the judge would order us not to go into Lincoln Park at all and that if we did, that we would be in violation of contempt of court, and that it was a setup, and Judge Lynch planned to lynch us in the same way that Stahl was stalling us.

I pointed out that the names in this thing were getting really absurd, similarities. I also read a list of Yippie demands that I had written that morning – sort of Yippie philosophy.

MR. WEINGLASS: Now, will you read for the Court and jury the eighteen demands first, then the postscript.

THE WITNESS: I will read it in the order that I wrote it. "Revolution toward a free society, Yippie, by A. Yippie.

"This is a personal statement. There are no spokesmen for the Yippies. We are all our own leaders. We realize this list of demands is inconsistent. They are not really demands. For people to make demands of the Democratic Party is an exercise in wasted wish fulfillment. If we have a demand, it is simply and emphatically that they, along with their fellow inmates in the Republican Party, cease to exist. We demand a society built along the alternative community in Lincoln Park, a society based on humanitarian cooperation and equality, a society which allows and promotes the creativity present in all people and especially our youth.

"Number one. An immediate end to the war in Vietnam and a restructuring of our foreign policy which totally eliminates aspects of military, economic and cultural imperialism; the withdrawal of all foreign based troops and the abolition of military draft.

"Two. An immediate freedom for Huey Newton of the Black Panthers and all other black people; adoption of the community control concept in our ghetto areas; an end to the cultural and economic domination of minority groups.

"Three. The legalization of marijuana and all other psychedelic drugs; the freeing of all prisoners currently imprisoned on narcotics charges.

"Number four. A prison system based on the concept of rehabilitation rather than punishment.

"Five. A judicial system which works towards the abolition of all laws related to crimes without victims; that is, retention only of laws relating to crimes in which there is an unwilling injured party: i.e. murder, rape, or assault.

"Six. The total disarmament of all the people beginning with the police. This includes not only guns but such brutal vices as tear gas, Mace, electric prods, blackjacks, billy clubs, and the like.

"Seven. The abolition of money, the abolition of pay housing, pay media, pay transportation, pay food, pay education, pay clothing, pay medical health, and pay toilets.

"Eight. A society which works towards and actively promotes the concept of full unemployment, a society in which people are free from the drudgery of work, adoption of the concept 'Let the machines do it.'

"Number ten. A program of ecological development that would provide incentives for the decentralization of crowded cities and encourage rural living.

"Eleven. A program which provides not only free birth control information and devices, but also abortions when desired.

"Twelve. A restructured educational system which provides a student power to determine his course of study, student participation in over-all policy planning; an educational system which breaks down its barriers between school and community; a system which uses the surrounding community as a classroom so that students may learn directly the problems of the people.

"Number thirteen. The open and free use of the media; a program which actively supports and promotes cable television as a method of increasing the selection of channels available to the viewer.

"Fourteen. An end to all censorship. We are sick of a society that has no hesitation about showing people committing violence and refuses to show a couple fucking.

"Fifteen. We believe that people should fuck all the time, any time, wherever they wish. This is not a programmed demand but a simple recognition of the reality around us.

"Sixteen. A political system which is more streamlined and responsive to the needs of all the people regardless of age, sex, or race; perhaps a national referendum system conducted via television or a telephone voting system; perhaps a decentralization of power and authority with many varied tribal groups, groups in which people exist in a state of basic trust and are free to choose their tribe.

"Seventeen. A program that encourages and promotes the arts. However, we feel that if the free society we envision were to be sought for and achieved, all of us would actualize the creativity within us; in a very real sense we would have a society in which every man would be an artist."

And eighteen was left blank for anybody to fill in what they wanted. "It was for these reasons that we had come to Chicago, it was for these reasons that many of us may fight and die here. We recognize this as the vision of the founders of this nation. We recognize that we are America; we recognize that we are free men. The present-day politicians and their armies of automatons have selfishly robbed us of our birthright. The evilness they stand for will go unchallenged no longer. Political pigs, your days are numbered. We are the second American Revolution. We shall win.

"YIPPIE."

MR. WEINGLASS: When you used the words "fight and die here," in what context were you using those words?

THE WITNESS: It is a metaphor. That means that we felt strongly about our right to assemble in the park and that people should be willing to take risks for it. It doesn't spell it out because people were capable of fighting in their own way and making their own decisions and we never would tell anyone specifically that they should fight, fistfight.

MR. WEINGLASS: Did you during the week of the Convention and the period of time immediately before the Convention tell any person singly or in groups that they should fight in the park?

MR. SCHULTZ: Objection.

THE COURT: I sustain the objection.

MR. WEINGLASS: Directing your attention to the morning of August 19, 1968, did you attend a meeting on that day?

THE WITNESS: Yes. I went to the office of the Mobilization Committee.

MR. WEINGLASS: Was there a discussion?

THE WITNESS: I never stayed long at these meetings. I just went and made an announcement and maybe stayed ten or fifteen minutes. . . .

MR. WEINGLASS: Was there a course given in snake dancing on that day also?

THE WITNESS: Yes. Yes. People would have a pole and there would be about six people, and then about six people behind them, holding them around the waist, four or five lines of these people with men, women, and kids maybe eight years old in on this whole thing, and people would bounce from one foot to the other and yell "Wash oi, Wash oi," which is kind of Japanese for "Yippie," I guess.

And they would just march up and down the park like this, mostly laughing and giggling, because the newsmen were taking this quite seriously, and then at a certain point everybody would turn in and sort of just collapse and fall on the ground and laugh. I believe we lost about four or five Yippies during that great training.

The exciting part was when the police arrested two army intelligence officers in the trees.

MR. WEINGLASS: During the course of that day when you were in the park, did you notice that the police were hanging any signs in the park?

THE WITNESS: Late in the day, maybe four or five, I became aware that there were police nailing signs on the trees that said "11:00 p.m. curfew," maybe a few other words, but that was the gist of the signs.

MR. WEINGLASS: From Friday, August 23, on to the end of Convention week, did you ever discuss with any people the question of staying in the park after the curfew hours?

THE WITNESS: At a meeting on August 24, that subject came up, and there was lengthy discussion . . .

MR. WEINGLASS: Now, did you hear Jerry Rubin speak at that meeting?

THE WITNESS: Jerry said that the park wasn't worth fighting for; that we should leave at the eleven p.m. curfew. He said that we should put out a statement to that effect.

MR. WEINGLASS: And did you speak at that meeting?

THE WITNESS: I reported on a meeting that morning with Chief Lynskey. I had asked the Chicago cops who were tailing me to take me to Chief Lynskey who was in charge of the area of Lincoln Park. I went up to the chief and said, "Well, are you going to let us have the Festival?"

He said "No festival under any circumstances. If anybody breaks one city ordinance in that park, we clear the whole park."

He said, "You do any one thing wrong and I will arrest you on sight."

He said, "Why don't you try to kick me in the shins right now?"

And I said NBC wasn't there.

And he said, "Well, at least the kid's honest," and stuff like that.

Then I gave a speech to the police that were all assembled and I said, "Have a good time." I said, "The National Guard's coming in, they're probably going to whip you guys up, and I hope your walkie-talkies work better than ours," and stuff like that. And I just walked out.

Then we discussed what we were going to do. I said it was my feeling that Chicago was in a total state of anarchy as far as the police mentality worked. I said that we were going to have to fight for every single thing, we were going to have to fight for the electricity, we were going to have to fight to have the stage come in, we were going to have to fight for every rock musician to play, that the whole week was going to be like that.

I said that we should proceed with the festival as planned, we should try to do everything that we had come to Chicago to do, even though the police and the city officials were standing in our way.

MR. WEINGLASS: During the course of this Saturday and prior to this meeting, did you have occasion to meet Irv Bock in the park?

THE WITNESS: Oh, I met Irv Bock Saturday afternoon during some of the marshal training. Marshal training is a difficult phrase to use for Yippies. We always have a reluctance to marshals because they are telling people what to do and we were more anarchistic than that, more leaderless.

I sort of bumped into Irv Bock. I showed him a – it wasn't a gas mask but it was a thing with two plastic eyes and a little piece of leather that I got, I purchased in an army-navy store for about nineteen cents, and I said that these would be good protection against Mace.

He started running down to me all this complicated military jargon and I looked at him and said, "Irv, you're a cop, ain't you?"

He sort of smiled and said, "No, I'm not."

"Come on," I said, "We don't grow peaceniks that big. We are all quarterbacks. You've got to be a cop."

I said, "Show me your wallet."

So he said, "No, no. Don't you trust me?"

So I said, "Irv," I said, "last night there was a guy running around my house with a pistol trying to kill me," that I had twenty threats that week, and at that point I didn't trust Jerry Rubin. . . .

MR. WEINGLASS: Directing your attention to approximately two o'clock in the morning, which would now be Monday morning, do you recall what you were doing?

THE WITNESS: I made a telephone call to David Stahl, Deputy Mayor of Chicago at his home. I had his home number.

I said, "Hi, Dave. How's it going? Your police got to be the dumbest and the most brutal in the country," I said.

"The decision to drive people out of the park in order to protect the City was about the dumbest military tactic since the Trojans let the Trojan horse inside the gate and there was nothing to be compared with that stupidity."

I again pleaded with him to let people stay in the park the following night. "There will be more people coming Monday, Tuesday, and subsequently Wednesday night," I said, "and they should be allowed to sleep." I said that he ought to intercede with the Police Department. I said to him that the City officials, in particular his boss, Daley, were totally out of their minds.

I said, "I read in the paper the day before that they had 2,000 troops surrounding the reservoirs in order to protect against the Yippie plot to dump LSD in the drinking water. There isn't a kid in the country," I said, "never mind a Yippie, who thinks that such a thing could be done."

I told him to check with all the scientists at the University of Chicago – he owned them all.

He said that he knew it couldn't be done, but they weren't taking any chances anyway. . . .

MR. WEINGLASS: Can you tell the Court and jury where you were in Lincoln Park at approximately 11:30 Monday night?

THE WITNESS: I was walking through the barricade, my wife Anita and I.

MR. WEINGLASS: Did you see Allen Ginsberg at the barricade?

THE WITNESS: Yes. He was kneeling.

There was a crowd of people around. He was playing that instrument that he plays and people were chanting.

There was a police car that would come by and I believe it was making announcements and people would yell at the police car, you know, "Beat it. Get out. The parks belong to the people. Oink Oink. Pig Pig. Pigs are coming. Peace Now."

People were waving flags. People were running around being scared and people were running around sort of joyous. I mean, it was strange, different emotions. It was very dark in that place.

MR. SCHULTZ: The witness is not answering the question any more. He is giving another essay. I object.

MR. WEINGLASS: When the police finally came to the barricade, from what direction did they come?

THE WITNESS: They came in through the zoo.

They proceeded to climb and immediately started to club people.

They were throwing parts of the barricade, trashcans, at people.

MR. WEINGLASS: Now, at the time the police came to the barricade what did you do?

THE WITNESS: Well, I was coughing and spitting because there was tear gas totally flooding the air, cannisters were exploding all around me – I moved with the people out this way, out of the park trying to duck, picking up people that were being clubbed, getting off the ground myself a few times.

The police were just coming through in this wedge, solid wedge, clubbing people right and left, and I tried to get out of the park.

MR. WEINGLASS: Directing your attention to approximately six o'clock the following morning, do you recall where you were?

THE WITNESS: I got in the car of the police that were following me and asked them to take me to the beach – the beach part of Lincoln Park.

MR. WEINGLASS: What was occurring when you got there?

THE WITNESS: Allen Ginsberg and about – oh 150–200 people were kneeling, most of the people in lotus position which is a position with their legs crossed like this – chanting and praying and meditating.

There were five or six police cars on the boardwalk right in back, and there were police surrounding the group. Dawn was breaking. It was very cold, very chilly. People had a number of blankets wrapped around them, sitting in a circle. I went and sat next to Allen and chanted and prayed for about an hour. Then I talked to the group. People would give talks about their feelings of what was going on in Chicago. I said, "I am very sad about what has happened in Chicago.

"What is going on here is very beautiful, but it won't be in the evening news that night.

"The American mass media is a glutton for violence, and it would be only shots of what was happening in the streets of Chicago."

I said, "America can't be changed by people sitting and praying, and this is an unfortunate reality that we have to face."

I said that we were a community that had to learn how to survive, that we had seen what had happened the last few nights in Lincoln Park. We had seen the destruction of the Festival.

I said, "I will never again tell people to sit quietly and pray for change." . . .

MR. WEINGLASS: Now, directing your attention to approximately 6:00 A.M. the following morning, Wednesday, August 28, do you recall what you were doing?

THE WITNESS: I went to eat. I went with Paul Krassner, Beverly Baskinger, and Anita and four police officers – Paul also had two Chicago police officers following him, as well as the two that were following me. We walked and the four of them would drive along behind us.

MR. WEINGLASS: Could you describe for the jury and the Court what you were wearing at that time?

THE WITNESS: Well, I had cowboy boots, and brown pants and a shirt, and I had a grey felt ranger cowboy type hat down over my eyes, like this.

MR. WEINGLASS: What, if anything occurred while you were sitting there having breakfast?

THE WITNESS: Well, two policemen came in and said, "We have orders to arrest you. You have something under your hat."

So I asked them if they had a search warrant and I said "Did you check it out with Commander Braasch? Me and him got an agreement" – and they went to check it out with him, while we were eating breakfast.

MR. WEINGLASS: After a period of time, did they come back?

THE WITNESS: They came back with more police officers – there were about four or five patrol cars surrounding the restaurant. The Red Squad cops who had been following us came in the restaurant, four or five police, and they said, "We checked. Now will you take off your hat?" They were stern, more serious about it.

MR. WEINGLASS: What did you do?

THE WITNESS: Well, I lifted up the hat and I went "Bang! Bang!"

They grabbed me by the jacket and pulled me across the bacon and eggs and Anita over the table, threw me on the floor and out the door and threw me against the car, and they handcuffed me.

I was just eating the bacon and going "Oink Oink!"

MR. WEINGLASS: Did they tell you why you were being arrested?

THE WITNESS: They said they arrested me because I had the word "Fuck" on my forehead. I had put it on with this magic marker before we left the house. They called it an "obscenary."

I put it on for a couple of reasons, One was that I was tired of seeing my picture in the paper and having newsmen come around, and I know if you got that word on your forehead they ain't going to print your picture in the paper. Secondly, it sort of summed up my attitude about the whole thing – what was going on in Chicago.

I like that four letter word – I thought it was kind of holy, actually.

MR. WEINGLASS: Abbie Hoffman, prior to coming to Chicago, from April 1968 on to the week of the Convention, did you enter into an agreement with David Dellinger, John Froines, Tom Hayden, Jerry Rubin, Lee Weiner or Rennie Davis, to come to the city of Chicago for the purpose of encouraging and promoting violence during the Convention week?

THE WITNESS: An agreement?

MR. WEINGLASS: Yes.

THE WITNESS: We couldn't agree on lunch.

MR. WEINGLASS: I have no further questions.

THE COURT: Cross-examine.

MR. SCHULTZ: Thank you, your Honor. . . .

MR. SCHULTZ: Did you see numerous instances of people attacking the Guardsmen at the Pentagon, Mr. Hoffman?

THE WITNESS. I don not believe that I saw any instances of people attacking National Guardsmen. In fact, the attitude was one of comradeship. They would talk to the National Guardsmen continuously and tell them they were not the people that they had come to confront, that they were their brothers and you don't get people to oppose [their ways] by attacking them.

MR. SCHULTZ: Mr. Hoffman, the Guards and the troops were trying to keep the people from entering into the Pentagon for two days, isn't that right?

THE WITNESS: I assume that they were there to guard the Pentagon from rising in the air possibly. I mean, who knows what they are there for? Were you there? You probably watched it on television and got a different impression of what was happening. That is one aspect of myth-making – you can envisualize hordes and hordes of people when in reality that was not what happened.

MR SCHULTZ: Did you see some people urinate on the Pentagon?

THE WITNESS: On the Pentagon itself?

MR. SCHULTZ: Or at the Pentagon?

THE WITNESS: There were over 100,000 people. People have that biological habit, you know.

MR. SCHULTZ: Did you symbolically urinate on the Pentagon, Mr. Hoffman?

THE WITNESS: I symbolically urinate on the Pentagon?

MR. SCHULTZ: Yes.

THE WITNESS: I didn't get that close. Pee on the walls of

the Pentagon? You are getting to be out of sight, actually. You think there is a law against it?

MR. SCHULTZ: Are you done, Mr. Hoffman?

THE WITNESS: I am done when you are.

MR. SCHULTZ: Did you ever state that a sense of integration possesses you and comes from pissing on the Pentagon?

THE WITNESS: I said from combining political attitudes with biological necessity, there is a sense of integration, yes.

MR. SCHULTZ: You had a good time at the Pentagon, didn't you. Mr. Hoffman?

THE WITNESS: Yes I did. I'm having a good time now too. I feel that biological necessity now. Could I be excused for a slight recess?

THE COURT: Ladies and gentlemen of the jury, we will take a brief recess.

(brief recess)

MR. SCHULTZ: On the seventh of August, you told David Stahl that at your liberated area you—

THE WITNESS: What meeting was this, August 7?

MR. SCHULTZ: That's when you just flew in from New York.

THE WITNESS: Crossing state lines—

MR. SCHULTZ: At this meeting on the evening of August 7, you told Mr. Stahl that you were going to have nude-ins in your liberated zone, didn't you?

THE WITNESS: A nude-in? I don't believe I would use that phrase, no. I don't think it's very poetic, frankly.

I might have told him that ten thousand people were going to walk naked on the waters of Lake Michigan, something like that.

MR. SCHULTZ: You told him, did you not, Mr. Hoffman, that in your liberated zone, you would have—

THE WITNESS: I'm not even sure what it is, a nude-in.

MR. SCHULTZ: —public fornication.

THE WITNESS: If it means ten thousand people, naked people, walking on Lake Michigan, yes.

MR. KUNSTLER: I object to this because Mr. Schultz is acting like a dirty old man.

MR. SCHULTZ: We are not going into dirty old men. If they are going to have nude-ins and public fornication, the City officials react to that, and I am establishing through this witness that that's what be did.

THE COURT: Do you object?

MR. KUNSTLER: I am just remarking, your Honor, that a young man can be a dirty old man.

THE WITNESS: I don't mind talking about it.

THE COURT: I could make an observation. I have seen some exhibits here that are not exactly exemplary documents.

MR. KUNSTLER: But they are, your Honor, only from your point of view making a dirty word of something that can be beautiful and lovely, and—

MR. SCHULTZ: We are not litigating here, your Honor, whether sexual intercourse is beautiful or not. We are litigating whether or not the City could permit tens of thousands of people to come in and do in their parks what this man said they were going to do.

In getting people to Chicago you created your Yippie myth, isn't that right? And part of your myth was "We'll burn Chicago to the ground," isn't that right?

THE WITNESS: It was part of the myth that there were trainloads of dynamite headed for Chicago, it was part of the myth that they were going to form white vigilante groups and round up demonstrators. All these things were part of the myth. A myth is a process of telling stories, most of which ain't true.

MR. SCHULTZ: Mr. Hoffman—

Your Honor, Mr. Davis is having a very fine time here whispering at me. He has been doing it for the last twenty minutes. He moved up here when I started the examination so he could whisper in my ear. I would ask Mr. Davis, if he cannot be quiet, to move to another part of the table so that he will stop distracting me.

THE COURT: Try not to speak too loudly, Mr. Davis.

MR. DAVIS: Yes, sir.

THE COURT: Go ahead.

THE WITNESS: Go ahead, Dick.

MR. SCHULTZ: Didn't you state, Mr. Hoffman, that part of the myth that was being created to get people to come to Chicago was that "We will fuck on the beaches"?

THE WITNESS: Yes, me and Marshall McLuhan. Half of that quote was from Marshall McLuhan.

MR. SCHULTZ: "And there will be acid for all" – that was another one of your Yippie myths, isn't that right?

THE WITNESS: That was well known.

MR. SCHULTZ: By the way, was there any acid in Lincoln Park in Chicago?

THE WITNESS: In the reservoir, in the lake?

MR. SCHULTZ: No, among the people.

THE WITNESS: Well, there might have been, I don't know. It is colorless, odorless, tasteless. One can never tell. . . .

MR. SCHULTZ: The fact is, Mr. Hoffman, that what you were trying to do was to create a situation where the State and the United States Government would have to bring in the Army and bring in the National Guard during the Convention in order to protect the delegates so that it would appear that the Convention had to be held under military conditions, isn't that a fact, Mr. Hoffman?

THE WITNESS: You can do that with a yo-yo in this country. It's quite easy. You can see just from this courtroom. Look at all the troops around—

MR. SCHULTZ: Your Honor, may the answer be stricken?

THE COURT: Yes, it may go out. . . .

MR. SCHULTZ: Mr. Hoffman, in the afternoon on that Thursday you participated in a march, and then you laid down in front of an armored personnel carrier at the end of that march, at 16th or 19th on Michigan, laid down on the street?

THE WITNESS: Was that what it was? I thought it was a tank.

It looked like a tank.

Do you want me to show you how I did it? Laid down in front of the tank?

MR. SCHULTZ: All right, Mr. Hoffman. Did you make any gestures of any sort?

THE WITNESS: When I was laying down? See. I went like that, lying down in front of the tank.

I had seen Czechoslovakian students do it to Russian tanks.

MR. SCHULTZ: And then you saw a Chicago police officer who appeared to be in high command because of all the things he had on his shoulders come over to the group and start leading them back toward Grant Park, didn't you?

THE WITNESS: He came and then people left – and went back to the park, yes.

MR. SCHULTZ: Did you say to anybody, "Well, you see that cat?", pointing to Deputy Superintendent Rochford. "When we get to the top of the hill, if the cat doesn't talk right, we're going to hold him there, and then we can do whatever we want and the police won't bother us." Did you say that to anybody out there, Mr. Hoffman?

MR. WEINGLASS: That's the testimony of the intelligence officer, the intelligence police officer of the Chicago Police Department.

THE WITNESS: I asked the Chicago police officers to help me kidnap Deputy Superintendent Rochford? That's pretty weird.

MR. SCHULTZ: Isn't it a fact that you announced publicly a plan to kidnap the head pig—

THE WITNESS: Cheese, wasn't it?

MR. SCHULTZ: —and then snuff him—

THE WITNESS: I thought it was "cheese."

MR. SCHULTZ: —and then snuff him if other policemen touched you? Isn't that a fact, sir?

THE WITNESS: I do not believe that I used the reference of "pig" to any policemen in Chicago including some of the top cheeses. I did not use it during that week . . .

MR. SCHULTZ: You and Albert, Mr. Hoffman, were united in Chicago in your determination to smash the system by using any means at your disposal, isn't that right?

THE WITNESS: Did I write that?

MR. SCHULTZ: No, did you have that thought?

THE WITNESS: That thought? Is a thought like a dream? If I dreamed to smash the system, that's a thought. Yes, I had that thought.

THE COURT: Mr. Witness, you may not interrogate the lawyer who is examining you.

THE WITNESS: Judge, you have always told people to describe what they see or what they hear. I'm the only one that has to describe what I think.

MR. WEINGLASS: I object to any reference to what a person thought or his being tried for what he thought. He may be tried for his intent.

THE COURT: Overrule the objection.

THE WITNESS: Well, I had a lot of dreams at night. One of the dreams might have been that me and Stew were united.

MR. SCHULTZ: Mr. Hoffman, isn't it a fact that one of the reasons why you came to Chicago was simply to wreck American society?

THE WITNESS: My feeling at the time, and still is, that society is going to wreck itself. I said that on a number of occasions, that our role is to survive while the society comes tumbling down around us; our role is to survive.

We have to learn how to defend ourselves, given this type of society, because of the war in Vietnam, because of racism, because of the attack on the cultural revolution – in fact because of this trial.

MR. SCHULTZ: Mr. Hoffman, by Thursday, the twenty-ninth, the last day of the Convention, you knew you had smashed the Democrats' chances for victory, isn't that a fact?

THE WITNESS: No. My attitude was it was a type of psychic jujitsu where the people smash themselves – or the party wrecks themselves. The same way this trial is.

MR. SCHULTZ: By Thursday there was no doubt in your mind when you saw the acceptance speech that you had won, and there would be a pig in the White House in '69?

THE WITNESS: Well, that was our role in coming here, to nominate a pig. That pig did win. He didn't actually – which one did?

MR. SCHULTZ: And you went out for champagne, and you brought it back to Mobilization headquarters and toasted the revolution, you did just that, right?

THE WITNESS: We drank some champagne. It was warm, warm champagne.

MR. SCHULTZ: And toasted to your success, to your victory, isn't that right?

THE WITNESS: We toasted to the fact that we were still alive.

That was the miracle as far as I saw it, is still being alive by that last Thursday.

MR. SCHULTZ: That's all, your Honor.

THE WITNESSS: Right on!

THE COURT: Have you finished your cross-examination?

MR. SCHULTZ: Yes, I have.

THE WITNESS: Right on!

The Shootings at Kent State

John Kifner

On May 4 1970 four anti-War protestors were killed at Kent
State University, Ohio. Kifner reported for the *New York Times*.

Students here, angered by the expansion of the war into
Cambodia, have held demonstrations for the last three
nights. On Saturday night [May 2], the Army Reserve
Officers Training Corps building was burned to the ground
and the National Guard was called in and martial law was
declared.

Today's rally, called after a night in which the police and
guardsmen drove students into their dormitories and made
69 arrests, began as students rang the iron Victory Bell on the
Commons, normally used to herald football victories.

A National Guard jeep drove onto the Commons and an
officer ordered the crowd to disperse. Then several canisters
of tear gas were fired, and the students straggled up a hill that
borders the area and retreated into buildings.

A platoon of guardsmen, armed – as they have been since
they arrived here with loaded M-I rifles and gas equipment
– moved across the green and over the crest of the hill, chasing the main body of protesters.

The youths split into two groups, one heading farther
downhill toward a dormitory complex, the other eddying
around a parking lot and girls' dormitory just below Taylor
Hall, the architecture building.

The guardsmen moved into a grassy area just below the

parking lot and fired several canisters of tear gas from their short, stubby launchers.

Three or four youths ran to the smoking canisters and hurled them back. Most fell far short, but one landed near the troops and a cheer went up from the crowd, which was chanting "Pigs off campus" and cursing the war.

A few youths in the front of the crowd ran into the parking lot and hurled stones or small chunks of pavement in the direction of the guardsmen. Then the troops began moving back up the hill in the direction of the college.

The students in the parking lot area, numbering about 500, began to move towards the rear of the troops, cheering. Again, a few in front picked up stones from the edge of the parking lot and threw them at the guardsmen. Another group of several hundred students had gathered around the sides of Taylor Hall, watching.

As the guardsmen, moving up the hill in a single file, reached the crest, they suddenly turned, forming a skirmish line and opening fire.

The crackle of the rifle volley cut the suddenly still air. It appeared to go on, as a solid volley, for perhaps a full minute or a little longer.

Some of the students dived to the ground, crawling on the grass in terror. Others stood shocked or half-crouched, apparently believing the troops were firing into the air. Some of the rifle barrels were pointed upward.

Near the top of the hill at the corner of Taylor Hall, a student crumpled over, spun sideways and fell to the ground, shot in the head.

When the firing stopped, a slim girl, wearing a cowboy shirt and faded jeans, was lying face down on the road at the edge of the parking lot, blood pouring out onto the macadam, about 10 feet from this reporter.

The youths stood stunned, many of them clustered in small groups staring at the bodies. A young man cradled one of the bleeding forms in his arms. Several girls began to cry. But many of the students who rushed to the scene seemed almost too shocked to react. Several gathered around an abstract steel sculpture in front of the building and looked at a .30-caliber bullet hole drilled through one of the plates.

Winter Soldiers

Charles Stephens and Mike Misiaszek

The "Winter Soldier Investigation" was a three-day inquiry organized by Vietnam Veterans Against the War (VVAW) in Detroit, Michigan, beginning on January 31 1971. Some 109 veterans and 16 civilians testified about war crimes they had witnessed in Vietnam. A complete transcript of the Investigation was later entered into the Congressional Record. Stephens and Misiaszek were two "Winter Soldiers".

MODERATOR. Charles Stephens, former Pfc., medic with the 101st Airborne Division.

STEPHENS. I served with the 1st Brigade, 3/27, 101st Airborne Division as a medic. I went over in 1965, in December 1965, and I stayed until February '67. When I first got to Phan Rang, our base camp, our battalion commander said we were going to leave Phan Rang – going to Tui Hoa. And we'd be in Tui Hoa anywhere from three weeks to three months. And I believe we were gone about a year and seven days. But before we left he told us, he said, "Don't worry. I know you guys are impatient, but when you get to Tui Hoa there'll be enough VC to go around." Also, the chaplain added that it's better to give than to receive and do unto others before they do unto you. When we got to Tui Hoa the first battle we were in was in Happy Valley. And at Happy Valley we got quite a few of the people from our brigade killed. The very next operation I went on every village we went into we'd recon by fire and in one village, we wounded women and kids going into the village. When we got in there, this was in Tui Hoa, me and another guy were treating two unconscious babies – not babies but like five and six-year old kids and a woman lying in a hammock. I told the lieutenant that these people had to be evacuated because if not evacuated (this lady and these kids had shrapnel and they were unconscious) I said they're gonna die. And he said, "Well, forget it, Doc; we don't have time to stay and wait."

We went up on the hill right above this same village and we fired down on this village the next day while the people were trying to bury their dead, while they were doing their burial ceremony. And they killed another person in the village. The people, they didn't wait to see if the guy was dead or not. They just rolled him over and put him in the hole with the others and covered him up. We went down that same day to get some water and there were two little boys playing on a dike and one sergeant just took his M-16 and shot one boy at the dike. The other boy tried to run. He was almost out of sight when this other guy, a Spec. 4, shot this other little boy off the dike. The little boy was like lying on the ground kicking, so he shot him again to make sure he was dead. Then we went into the village and this papa-san, I don't know if he was a village chief or who he was, but he came up to us, he was telling us, he was making motions that a bird was flying over and the bird took a ____ and a thing went boom-boom. He was saying this was how a lot of the people in the village got hurt. I told the lieutenant and the lieutenant still wouldn't have the people evacuated. So, every operation we went on after that, after our Happy Valley, they didn't believe our body counts. So we had to cut off the right ear of everybody we killed to prove our body count. I guess it was company SOP, or battalion SOP, but nothing was ever said to you. Guys would cut off heads, put them on a stake and stick a guy's ____ in his mouth. At Nan Co. we were at the 95th, I think it was a base camp, a regiment base camp or

something, and they say the VC had just left there. We had
a guy with us, my senior aid man. He had about two weeks
left in country and because we couldn't get resupplied
(they didn't want to give away our position) we had to live
off the land. There were some chickens in this village and
my senior aid man was running through this elephant
grass to find the chickens. He tripped a land mine that the
VC had left behind. He blew his thighs and everything and
the back of his legs up. Well, his leg was just messed up. He
went into shock and died anyway because the doctors
wouldn't come in to take him out. They were afraid. They
had to stay with him that night, but they were afraid to
come down. It was cabled from the medivac. I have some
money here, this is North Vietnamese money. We took it
off a paymaster. It was on the Ho Chi Minh Trail but we
were supposed to be in Cambodia. We went ambush there
for about two weeks.

MODERATOR. You want to hold that money up and show
it to them?

STEPHENS. We had been on an ambush for about two
weeks. The first week that we were there we didn't fire at
any of the enemy. We just watched them come down, and
I guess further down the trail they were being knocked off.
I don't know.

But the second week we were told when anything came
down this trail, we were to shoot. About two-thirty one
morning this lady and a little boy and a dog came walking
down this trail (they did this every night) and the lady
made some kind of funny sign with a lantern. This particular night a guy met her on a bicycle. She went back to her
house alone, but this guy stayed on her trail and a few
minutes later some more guys came and joined him. As
they were coming down the trail, we knocked them off.
They said we were not supposed to use CS gas. We threw
CS gas and the whole business. That particular night the
password was "pussycat." There was like a big hill behind
us where we were supposed to all come up and meet after

the ambush. I was left with two Vietnamese ARVNs who were asleep during the ambush. There was an American machine gunner who couldn't get away from the ambush and on the way back up the hill the only thing we could do to keep from getting killed was to sing like "What's New, Pussycat." In Dak To, June '66, I think was the biggest battle fought by the 101st during the time I was over there. There was a captain who called in napalm on his own company and I think he got a big award for it. But he wasn't actually there. He was there when the fighting first started, but when he called in napalm he was in a helicopter with a megaphone telling us, "Get in there and mix it up. You're doing a good job."

When we went up to Dak To, all our companies were overstrength. But after the battle, I think our largest company had ninety-seven people in it. That was including officers and everyone. If you had wounded guys, you'd never leave wounded guys or dead Americans, you'd always take them with you or have them evacuated. But this time I was left with one round of .45 ammunition and I was left with three other guys. One guy had an M-79 with an HE round. Another guy had one magazine of M-16 ammo. We were told to follow a trail, and we had to create our own little war, to make the company commander come back and get us. Then he was going to court-martial us because he said we were cowards. That's about it.

MODERATOR. Charles, would you describe for us the policy of your unit with regard to the taking and the disposition of prisoners? I think you have something to say about the throwing of prisoners out of helicopters?

STEPHENS. Yes, In Tui Hoa, after Happy Valley, we didn't take any prisoners. If we were on an operation for one week and you caught a prisoner the last day of that operation, that meant you stayed out there a couple of more days because there were more people out there. So you took the guy to the woodside and you knocked him off. I saw on two different occasions these warrant officers come in in helicopters and take the prisoners. Like I was new over there then and I didn't know what they were going to do. I saw them take these prisoners, take them in the helicopter. I would see these guys sitting down watching the sky, laughing, you know, and here comes a guy waving down out of the sky. Then they bring the other two guys down and I guess they'd be saying something, so I imagine they'd be talking to them. I saw that on two different occasions.

MODERATOR. And they were actually pushed out of the helicopter?

STEPHENS. Yes.

MODERATOR. Thank you. Mike, Mike Misiaszek, former Spec. 4, also with the 101st Airborne Division.

MISIASZEK. Right, my name is Mike Misiaszek. I'm from Reading, Pennsylvania. I was with the 101st in the 1st Brigade, Support Element. We rigged up the choppers to fly supplies out to the troops and sometimes we'd go out and hand them out wherever they were. That was the last half. The first half, I was actually just a telephone answerer. I was in Vietnam from the first of December 1968 to the end of January 1970. This was at Camp Eagle and I was also down at Tam Ky after I got fired from my office job. My testimony concerns a whole bunch of things. Most of it's been heard before. I'd just like to elaborate on it for those who may not have been here before. The first thing I'd like to talk about is the destruction of a cemetery. The entire northeast corner of the 101st base camp, Camp Eagle, southwest of Hue, is built on a Vietnamese cemetery. They didn't plow under any graves; they didn't have to. They just built the compound on top of it, which means that there are still graves between some of the buildings. Some of the buildings are on top of old graves which had been plowed under and are all misshapen. I'd like to talk about harassment fire. Where we were sleeping was pretty close to a battery of 8-inch howitzers. These are big guns, man. They go off and they shake the ground. I think the round is as long as this table, maybe. And there's a lot of high explosives in there. They fired these things indiscriminately. They woke us up, they shook the whole place, and several of us got really ____ off. We wanted to find out why they were doing this all the time. This was every night. We talked to a specialist up in the battery, and he said they had orders to fire no less than thirty rounds nightly at a strip west of Camp Eagle. This strip was supposedly a free fire zone. Anybody could have been walking in there, like even some of our own people from other units, but they didn't really seem to care. They just shot this thing up! Another thing I'd like to talk about is the use of some chemical agents. On our perimeter we had CS gas, little canister with tear gas I guess, and what's known as Fugas. I don't know if anyone has brought this up. Fugas is a jelly-like substance. It's flammable, and they put it in barrels. What they do to it is they explode the barrel over an area and this flaming jelly-like substance lands on everything, if it's people or animals or whatever. And you can't get it off. It just burns, and you rub it and it sticks on. You just spread it all around. The only way to stop it is by suffocating it in mud or water. This was not around too often during the dry season, you know. When we were at Tam Ky, we convoyed in August back to Camp Eagle. They put a whole bunch of guys on a truck and we had C-rations. We made a pretty good game out of throwing C-rations at civilians as hard as we could. Then we tried to see if we could maybe get them through the grass huts. Like we would throw them at a grass hut. It would go through and we'd wait and see if someone comes out yelling or something. I'd also like to talk about mad minutes. This was mentioned before. Our mad minutes, for those of you who may not have heard it, were at the perimeter fence. Every once in a while at Camp Eagle, every two months or so, the order would just come down, "Okay guys, get to it." You got a mad minute. And everybody picks up a weapon with both hands, both feet, and they shoot. And they don't care what they shoot at, just as long as it's away from the base area. That's a lot of fun, too. All those sickees.

MODERATOR. Mike, is there the chance that into the areas where you were firing during these mad minutes there were unarmed persons?

MISIASZEK. Absolutely. Sometimes there were. There were maybe cows. I never saw any, but I've heard of some people who were shooting cows.

MODERATOR. Thank you.

Born on the Fourth of July?

Ron Kovic

Ronald Kovic (born on the 4th of July 1946) served on two tours of Vietnam with the USMC; on January 20, 1968, while participating on an attack on a village north of the Cua Viet River in the DMZ, he was shot. The injury sustained left him paralysed from the waist down. Repatriated, he became one of the leading veteran voices in the anti-War movement. He infiltrated the 1972 Republican National Convention that re-nominated Richard Nixon as presidential candidate. He described the scene in his memoir, later filmed by Oliver Stone, *Born on the Fourth of July*.

It was the night of Nixon's acceptance speech and now I was on my own deep in his territory, all alone in my wheelchair in a sweat-soaked marine utility jacket covered with medals from the war. A TV producer I knew from the Coast had gotten me past the guards at the entrance with his press pass. My eyes were still smarting from teargas. Outside the chain metal fence around the Convention Center my friends were being clubbed and arrested, herded into wagons. The crowds were thick all around me, people dressed as if they were going to a banquet, men in expensive summer suits and women in light elegant dresses. Every once in a while someone would look at me as if I didn't belong there. But I had come almost three thousand miles for this meeting with the president and nothing was going to prevent it from taking place.

I worked my way slowly and carefully into the huge hall,

moving down one of the side aisles. "Excuse me, excuse me," I said to delegates as I pushed past them farther and farther to the front of the hall toward the speakers' podium.

I had gotten only halfway toward where I wanted to be when I was stopped by one of the convention security marshals. "Where are you going?" he said. He grabbed hold of the back of my chair, I made believe I hadn't heard him and kept turning my wheels, but his grip on the chair was too tight and now two other security men had joined him.

"What's the matter?" I said. "Can't a disabled veteran who fought for his country sit up front?"

The three men looked at each other for a moment and one of them said, "I'm afraid not. You're not allowed up front with the delegates." I had gotten as far as I had on sheer bluff alone and now they were telling me I could go no farther. "You'll have to go to the back of the convention hall, son. Let's go," said the guard who was holding my chair.

In a move of desperation I swung around facing all three of them, shouting as loud as I could so Walter Cronkite and the CBS camera crew that was just above me could hear me and maybe even focus their cameras in for the six o'clock news. "I'm a Vietnam veteran and I fought in the war! Did you fight in the war?"

One of the guards looked away.

"Yeah, that's what I thought," I said. "I bet none of you fought in the war and you guys are trying to throw me out of the convention. I've got just as much right to be up front here as any of these delegates. I fought for that right and I was born on the Fourth of July."

I was really shouting now and another officer came over. I think he might have been in charge of the hall. He told me I could stay where I was if I was quiet and didn't move up any farther. I agreed with the compromise. I locked my brakes and looked for other veterans in the tremendous crowd. As far as I could tell, I was the only one who had made it in.

People had begun to sit down all around me. They all had Four More Years buttons and I was surprised to see how many of them were young. I began speaking to them, telling them about the Last Patrol and why veterans from all over the United States had taken the time and effort to travel thousands of miles to the Republican National Convention. "I'm a disabled veteran!" I shouted. "I served two tours of duty in Vietnam and while on my second tour of duty up in the DMZ I was wounded and paralyzed from the chest down." I told them I would be that way for the rest of my life. Then I began to talk about the hospitals and how they treated the returning veterans like animals, how I, many nights in the Bronx, had lain in my own shit for hours waiting for an aide. "And they never come," I said. "They never come because that man that's going to accept the nomination tonight has been lying to all of us and spending the money on war that should be spent on healing and helping the wounded. That's the biggest lie and hypocrisy of all – that we had to go over there and fight and get crippled and come home to a government and leaders who could care less about the same boys they sent over."

I kept shouting and speaking, looking for some kind of reaction from the crowd. No one seemed to want to even look at me.

"Is it too real for you to look at? Is this wheelchair too much for you to take? The man who will accept the nomination tonight is a liar!" I shouted again and again, until finally one of the security men came back and told me to be quiet or they would have to take me to the back of the hall.

I told him that if they tried to move me or touch my chair there would be a fight and hell to pay right there in front of Walter Cronkite and the national television networks. I told him if he wanted to wrestle me and beat me to the floor of the convention hall in front of all those cameras he could.

By then a couple of newsmen, including Roger Mudd from CBS, had worked their way through the security barricades and begun to ask me questions.

"Why are you here tonight?" Roger Mudd asked me. "But don't start talking until I get the camera here," he shouted.

It was too good to be true. In a few seconds Roger Mudd and I would be going on live all over the country. I would be doing what I had come here for, showing the whole nation what the war was all about. The camera began to roll, and I began to explain why I and the others had come, that the war was wrong and it had to stop immediately. "I'm a Vietnam veteran," I said. "I gave America my all and the leaders of this government threw me and the others away to rot in their V.A. hospitals. What's happening in Vietnam is a crime against humanity, and I just want the American people to know that we have come all the way across this country, sleeping on the ground and in the rain, to let the American people see for themselves the men who fought their war and have come to oppose it. If you can't believe the veteran who fought the war and was wounded in the war, who can you believe?"

"Thank you," said Roger Mudd, visibly moved by what I had said. "This is Roger Mudd," he said, "down on the convention floor with Ron Kovic, a disabled veteran protesting President Nixon's policy in Vietnam." . . .

Suddenly a roar went up in the convention hall, louder than anything I had ever heard in my life. It started off as a rumble, then gained in intensity until it sounded like a tremendous thunderbolt. "Four more years, four more years," the crowd roared over and over again. The fat woman next to me was jumping up and down and dancing in the aisle. It was the greatest ovation the president of the United States had ever received and he loved it. I held the sides of my wheelchair to keep my hands from shaking. After what seemed forever, the roar finally began to die down.

This was the moment I had come three thousand miles for, this was it, all the pain and the rage, all the trials and the death of the war and what had been done to me and a generation of Americans by all the men who had lied to us and tricked us, by the man who stood before us in the convention hall that night, while men who had fought for their country were being gassed and beaten in the street outside the hall. I thought of Bobby who sat next to me and the months we had spent in the hospital in the Bronx. It was all hitting me at once, all those years, all that destruction, all that sorrow.

President Nixon began to speak and all three of us took a deep breath and shouted at the top of our lungs, "Stop the bombing, stop the war, stop the bombing, stop the war," as loud and as hard as we could, looking directly at Nixon. The security agents immediately threw up their arms, trying to hide us from the cameras and the president. "Stop the bombing, stop the bombing," I screamed. For an instant Cronkite looked down, then turned his head away. They're not going to show it, I thought. They're going to try and hide us like they did in the hospitals. Hundreds of people around us began to clap and shout "Four more years," trying to drown out our protest. They all seemed very angry and shouted at us to stop. We continued shouting, interrupting Nixon again and again until Secret Service agents grabbed our chairs from behind and began pulling us backward as fast as they could out of the convention hall. "Take it easy," Bobby said to me. "Don't fight back."

I wanted to take a swing and fight right there in the middle of the convention hall in front of the president and the whole country. "So this is how they treat their wounded veterans!" I screamed.

A short guy with a big Four More Years button ran up to me and spat in my face. "Traitor!" he screamed, as he was yanked back by police. Pandemonium was breaking out all around us and the Secret Service men kept pulling us out backward.

"I served two tours of duty in Vietnam!" I screamed to one newsman. "I gave three-quarters of my body for America. And what do I get? Spit in the face!" I kept screaming until we hit the side entrance where the agents pushed us outside and shut the doors, locking them with chains and padlocks so reporters wouldn't be able to follow us out for interviews.

All three of us sat holding on to each other shaking. We had done it. It had been the biggest moment of our lives, we had shouted down the president of the United States and disrupted his acceptance speech. What more was there left to do but go home?

I sat in my chair still shaking and began to cry.

Fly Me, I'm Micki

Micki Voisard

Micki Voisard was a flight attendant with a civilian airline taking troops to and from Vietnam.

I took on the job as a flight attendant with a civilian airline flying into Vietnam because I heard the money was good. It was, and somewhere along the way I convinced myself that this would be a perfect opportunity to save some money to continue my education. This was in 1969. I knew there was a war going on and that I would be flying in and out of the war zone on a regular basis.

I went through six interviews in two weeks, going from one to another, and there was a process of elimination. I didn't know what that process was until we had completed the six weeks of training and some of the girls didn't make it. It was like going through your final vows in the convent or something; you had to complete all this training, get the shots and pass the tests, then you still might not make it. I found out only after graduation that we were actually selected through handwriting analysis! I remember writing several stupid little paragraphs on why I wanted to be a stewardess, and they were using these to find out your personality traits, to see if you could handle this kind of thing.

I was real good at what I did because I have been cheer-leading all of my life. I really was a cheerleader in high school, and it just seemed to carry on through; I still am at times. When we went through the training they didn't give us any beauty training, like they did in the other airlines. I would come across other crews and would talk about their training, and they would say, "Oh, we spent three weeks doing things on our hair." And I went, "God, we never spent three hours doing that." But, one thing about the company I worked for, they really were up on emergency procedures; I mean, that was essential. They were trying their hardest to prepare us for something that they themselves did not know was going to come about.

What they didn't prepare us for, and did very little work on, was how to work with 215 GIs on board the airplane, and I don't think anybody can prepare you for that. We would ask questions – you know, "What are they going to be like?" Their typical response would be "Boys will be boys; men will be men." That is the way it was left, and thinking back, what people are calling sexual abuse today was what went on all the time on those airplanes. I think it was up to you as an individual. When something happened to you, you reacted to it. The second time it happened, you had a choice of acting or reacting . . . and there is a big difference there. I learned that as a survival method. Whether anybody had any personal contact with you or not, you understood where you fit in. And it wasn't always in the best light; I never saw women as being in the best light with a lot of the men in the military.

Our headquarters was in Los Angeles, but the main stewardess headquarters was in San Francisco, and we had a contract with Travis AFB. We were connected with the Military Air Command (MAC), which is their airlift. During the war, the military needed their transports to fly equipment rather than troops, so this was contracted out to private companies like Continental, Flying Tigers, Pan Am, TIA, World, et cetera. My second home base was in Japan. The company had a hotel there and we had privileges at the Air Force bases.

Our trips lasted seven to fourteen days, during which time your whole life had to change. Your social life went with you like your suitcase did; you had to make it happen right there. And you couldn't wait until you got home because the company ended up screwing you, making sure that if you planned something, it wasn't going to happen: those two weeks skiing in Tahoe would suddenly become a turnaround flight back to Vietnam. It happened all the time.

We flew from Japan into Cam Ranh Bay, Bien Hoa, Da Nang, Tan Son Nhut, and generally they were seventeen-hour round trips. You flew in, waited for them to clean the plane and reload passengers, and then flew out. It was a long haul. That was if nothing happened. Sometimes you flew in and didn't come out until a couple of days later because of mechanical problems with the airplane or rocket attacks.

The very first flight into Vietnam I was in awe of what we were doing. I was walking around with my mouth open, going, "Wow!" A limousine came to take some dignitaries who were on the flight and then a school bus for the officers. The draftees were herded into this big, open cattle truck and were driven away, just like cattle going away to slaughter. There was no glory, no John Wayne stuff; this was war. . . . This is what people are so willing to do today, and it angers me, but if every mother could see her son going off like that they wouldn't accept it. It was a disgusting sight.

On the average trip you would see twelve hundred to fifteen hundred guys, and to this day, being the visual person that I am, my mind is filled with faces that I can bring back any time. I call them the faces of Vietnam. It was interesting to me when *Life* magazine came out with an issue called "The Faces of Vietnam." It became a turning point in my life as a flight attendant going into the war zone. We were flying from Yokota, Japan, to Travis AFB, taking a group of guys back from Vietnam. I had galley duty; it was real late at night, and I had nothing to do so I picked up a magazine, and on the cover was the face of a GI. *Life* was dedicating that issue to ending the war. So I started looking through page after page of faces until one of them was very familiar. A guy I had gone through school with. I looked at it and thought, "He can't be dead." I started reading all the captions under the photographs. Then it hit me that he was dead. . . . He was the hometown all-American boy. Every girl in my high school was in love with him; he was the special one. He was president of the student body and was the quarterback on the football team; he had a scholarship. The whole town gave him a send-off party . . . to Vietnam. . . . They sent him off to war. And when he was killed, it was amazing what happened. His father committed suicide; his mother had to be institutionalized. People just couldn't accept this. They mourned for weeks. When I saw his picture, it just hit me – so many of the guys on these flights who weren't going home, so many of those faces.

On one flight, we got caught in a B-52 bombing mission. It's interesting, I think if I had given it any more thought, I wouldn't be here today I'd be in an institution, I'm sure. We were just outside of Da Nang heading to Japan, filled up with troops going home. I was looking out of the porthole of the aft galley door, just admiring the view, and thought I saw something go by real fast. And when you are up in the air you feel a little uncomfortable about that; there is just not enough room up there for something that close going that fast. . . . Then I saw it again. I looked down the center aisle of the airplane, and all the people who were window-watching were pointing to something. Then the captain came on and said, "That was a B-52 bomber that just flew by us." It turned out that they were flying above us. They were in a bombing raid and were maintaining radio silence. One of them dropped down to see what this blip was on their radar, and it was us. So, it had to go through the chain of command for them to stop and let us through. (This is my interpretation of it – what we were picking up from the captain.) I remember going up front and seeing the looks on the passengers' faces. They had just gone through thirteen months of horror; they were going home in a civilian aircraft and are put under this stress . . . How could this happen?

Well, at first you couldn't see or hear them; then we got to this point where you could look out the window and see the bombs down there, hitting below us about thirty thousand feet. It was so silent – so clean – it was incredible. And for a good half an hour we sat there, strapped to our seats, waiting on pins and needles for our plane to clear the bombing area. We just wanted to do a right-hand turn and get the hell out of there! You felt like a mosquito in a shower: how are you not going to get wet?

In those years, I was three different people, three personalities. I had to be a cheerleader for the guys going over. Then on the way home, I had to tell them about things that I didn't want to tell them. The country was not welcoming heroes any more. They were so happy to be going home; you didn't want to break their hearts and say, "But, it's not going to be good. It's not going to be what Mom and your sisters have been writing. They are going to expect you to be the same guy that left."

I would go home, and my parents would say, "It's okay now, Micki. Why don't you forget it while you are on vacation?" Even if what I wanted to talk about was terrible, I still needed to do it, but nobody wanted to listen. One time – the first time I had ever been shelled, in Cam Ranh Bay – I came home twenty-four hours later, and my boyfriend had tickets to the play *Hair*. He called me up and said, "Can you be ready in half an hour?" I said, "You won't believe this – I just had a terrible experience. I don't think I want to go." And he said, "Every time you go on your trips all you do is talk about that stuff. . . . I spent twenty-five dollars on these tickets, and I hope you are going to be ready." I was stupid; you know, I put on my clothes and went. So, I'm sitting there looking around the room, thinking, "Just twenty-four hours ago, I was in a bunker, and here I am watching this antiwar play. . . . what am I doing? Am I crazy?" I walked out.

And I began wondering what the hell I was doing. I was flying over there, getting paid to be in the war. I'd come home and find myself going to Berkeley and marching in the antiwar demonstrations. And, after reading the *Stars and Stripes* newspaper, which I had to hand out to each seat on the return flights, I couldn't believe what they were passing off. I had to do that because it was my job, but I justified it by taking a whole bunch of those newspapers home and burning them at a demonstration. Everybody was burning their draft cards, I burned *Stars and Stripes* newspapers. That felt good to me. For three years I was playing so many different roles; it was so confusing. Why? How could anybody stay in there that long? And it was no longer the money. I mean, I wasn't even saving money. The guilt that I've had the last fifteen years is, Why in the hell *did* I stay for that long? Well, I was twenty-one. Who knows what you do when you are twenty-one years old. And if I look at my cultural background – I'm Catholic. I remember going into confession and making up my sins. I felt guilty that I didn't have all the sins down so I could give my penance, so I made them up as I went along. Then one day, I was talking to a couple of friends, and they said, "Well, who doesn't make up their sins?" Nobody believed in it, but they still went in there and did it. We didn't question those things. And I believed in the president ... believed that there was somebody in charge. That was a big slap in the face – as I went through the war, I discovered there was never anybody in charge of that war. . . .

Cam Ranh Bay was a target because it was a main artillery base, and Charlie figured that out in a short period of time. Every time we would bring ships in, they probably were sitting there with their binoculars, watching them hauling in all this ammunition and putting it in the warehouses and Quonset huts around Cam Ranh Bay. Then they would go, "Okay," and they would blow them up. On one particular flight Cam Ranh was under fire when we came in; we didn't have a choice because we were low on fuel and couldn't go to an alternative airport. It was take your chance while you have it. The captain told us that there was all kinds of junk on the runway; they didn't know what to expect.

He did a great job landing, and then we sat there. All the lights were off in the airplane, the air conditioning is off, everybody is sweating, and you couldn't see faces because it was so dark. . . . You can feel 215 people in there. . . . I had to wait for six rings from the captain and then pull the emergency door, and the emergency slide is supposed to inflate. I'm flying number two position, sitting in the front jump seat and straining to hear six rings through all this "pow, pow!" And the plane is shaking. . . . I'm going, "One, two . . . I think I hear . . ." Finally the six rings come, and as I jumped out of the seat, I got my leg caught in the seat springs somehow. I had this feeling like I had my dress stuck, and being in such a frantic situation, I just ripped myself out and grabbed for the door. The slide didn't open – it just fizzled out! I am panicking because I could see everybody else letting their guys out. I have about fifty guys just sitting there in this dark coffin, waiting. There were three officers in front of me, and one said, "Let's go hand over hand." So, they went down and made, like, a chain ladder, and about halfway through he said, "It's your turn." I said, "I'm supposed to be the last one off the airplane." He says, "Get down there, lady!" and they practically threw me down. Then on the tarmac, I'm going, "Where am I? Is this Cam Ranh Bay?" In training they had shown slides of where there were bunkers at the various air bases. We had that information, but the troops on the airplane didn't know there were bunkers. They are saying, "Where do we go now?" And you go, "Oh, I saw slides of them once . . ." I mean, I remember the slides, and they showed the blue coral reefs in the background, and you thought, "Oh, that should be easy to find." You didn't realize that none of this is going to happen during the day – it is going to be dark. . . . Who is going to be looking for blue coral reefs?

Then some guy pointed in one direction, and I remember looking back at the airplane and seeing reflections in it like the whole earth was blowing up . . . lights, explosions . . . I thought, "Oh, Micki, you blew it. You were supposed to be the last one off that airplane. . . . The rules said . . ." I was even going to go back; you know, I had seen too many God-damn John Wayne movies – "Oh, leave me here, you go ahead" – type stuff. I didn't know that I was hurt. I had cut my foot down to the muscle, and I ran on that foot through all the glass and debris on the tarmac. But the only thing I remember when we were running was the smell of sulfur everywhere. We got into the bunkers and stayed there for two hours – stood there, it was so tight. Then finally they moved us into a warehouse, and that's when I discovered my foot was hurt. Some guy said, "Eeew, you've got blood all over your pantyhose." Here we are, there are rockets going off outside, and the guy is still looking at my legs. I'm going, "Goddamn it! Some guys are . . ." But he was just trying to tell me that I was hurt. There was a medic right there, and he said, "Let me look at that. You do have blood on your panty-hose." I looked down at my foot and almost fainted!

After it was over, they refueled the airplane and got our crew on board. The medic had reported my injury to the senior stew, and she wrote it up. When we got to Yokote, I went into the hospital on Tachikawa air base and spent the night. Then the company flew us home, since our plane was damaged and was going to be worked on in Japan. We flew home thinking, "Oh, we'll probably get two weeks off, maybe a bonus. . . ." They gave us a turnaround! I was back in Viet-nam in forty-eight hours! I mean, any excuse you would give them was not good enough, or bad enough. I called them up and said, "God, last night we were shelled in Vietnam. I'm really not feeling very good." They would go. "When can you be back on the line?" It was amazing. It was nothing to them. . . . You meant nothing to them. So, that was gnawing at me: "Well, why the hell did you stay there then, Micki?" I lived with that for years. The reasons I came up with, in addition to my Catholic background, was I knew I was on to something. . . . Having a journalistic background, I was intrigued. It kept me going. I knew that the discrepancies were just too great, and that I had privileged information in my position. I could walk around as freely as can be, photographing and talking with people. I could ask any person what their side of the story was. . . . It was amazing . . . the stories, the confusion; nothing made sense, nothing.

The value was more than I could ever pay for, and the

time that I spent in Vietnam was a significant and valuable period in my life. It haunts me to this day. I would not have traded it for anything. I was not injured over there to an extent where I was incapacitated, I didn't see my best friend die – or a lot of things that people saw over there – but I had my life on the line every time I flew in there.

And I had to deal with sexual abuse. I saw men masturbating all the time on the airplanes. I remember when I was new, having one stewardess tell me, "Never take a blanket off a sleeping GI." Then, once in a while, someone in Los Angeles who had forgotten we were hauling troops would put sanitary napkins on board, so we had to check out the lavs to see if there were any sanitary napkins. But there were times when we forgot or the guys would bring them on themselves. They would put ketchup down the center of the napkin, lay it in the middle of the aisle, and wait for your reaction. The first time it happened to me I was real embarrassed. Then there was the guy who got stuck in his seat belt; you were to save the day, helping him with it while he sits there with a big smile on his face and everybody around him is laughing. So, you learn the art of seat belt deployment by verbal command. Or, the guy who asks for a pillow and, as you reach up to get one, he has his hand up your dress. . . . You learned to never do things impulsively. You won't believe this one: the guy who follows you to the john to see if you locked the door. They would wait until you got comfortable, then jerk the door open, and everybody down the aisle could see you! So, to me right now, thinking of those things, it seems incredible, but it got to be routine. There were a lot of bad apples, but there were also guys that would let you know that they didn't approve of what they saw going on. A lot of them would come up and say, "I'm real sorry that happened to you." They weren't all older guys either; some were just young kids. You saw where respect came from.

Even now I have a way with men that . . . Fortunately I came out of it not hating them. I knew a lot of girls that ended up that way. They were having difficulty dealing with the men on the flights. I was able to function and talk with the GIs the whole time; it's just that I found myself giving commands all the time. In order to survive, I had to challenge them. They would challenge you, and if you could speak louder and be more authoritarian, then they would buckle under to you. Just my sense of survival, I guess.

Then there is the story about the bomb on our airplane. It was a pressurized bomb which, they figured, was supposed to go off above twelve thousand feet. It had been planted by one of the Vietnamese who cleaned out the airplane. We used to just stroll off the airplane and go down to the beach while they worked. . . . Well, that stopped real fast! The military started coming on board and standing there with M-16s pointed at these guys while they cleaned the plane.

I was in the aft galley with another girl, whose jump seat was right in front of the coffee maker, and on takeoff, it came out and hit her in the back of the head. She was actually holding it in place with her head – this big, heavy thing. We started pushing and shoving on it, trying to get it back in place and asked a couple of guys who were sitting near there to help us. Finally, we called the flight engineer, and he came back to check it out. We were all milling around, getting things ready for meal service, and meanwhile the plane is climbing. The flight engineer looks in behind the coffee maker with his trusty flashlight and says, "Oh, my God, everybody get out of here, right now!" Here is this happy-go-lucky-type guy who suddenly goes into instant fear. He says, "There's a bomb here." I remember standing there with all this coming back to me. I had been pushing on it, hitting it! Now, all of a sudden, I can't move; I can't even walk past that thing.

The captain came back, they discussed it, then went forward and talked with somebody on the radio in Cam Ranh. They were pretty sure it was a pressurized bomb and told us to level off and stay at our altitude until they could get some kind of a bomb squad together down there. Then we had to return, and it was up to the captain to bring that baby in as light as can be . . . and not make any drastic changes in altitude . . . slowly bring it down. The captain left the door of the cockpit open, and everybody on board was included. He let us hear the communication of he and the ground crew. They were joking and discussing this openly. Everybody felt 100 percent better because they were able to participate in this. He let that thing just glide into Cam Ranh Bay and landed. Everybody cheered! There were a lot of different kinds of heroes in that war.

I was telling someone this story, and they said, "Oh, you mean the *North* Vietnamese planted the bomb." I said, "No, a South Vietnamese." They said, "But we were fighting *for* the South Vietnamese." It was just amazing how people thought the war was that black and white: "Here is the north; all the bad guys live over here. Here is the south, and all the good guys live there, and we are saving the good guys, keeping communism away."

Then you come home, and they give the body count each night at dinnertime. They say, "North Vietnam lost fifteen hundred and we lost thirty. Isn't that great!" You know, to me that's where we really lost it, on that body count. Because people would be sitting there watching the six o'clock news, saying, "That's not too bad, only thirty guys. . . . They lost fifteen hundred. We are doing a good job over there." Nobody thought of thirty individuals. . . . Those guys got lost in there, somehow. Fifty-eight thousand people got lost in that body count.

Spirit of the Bayonet

Gustav Hasford

Hasford served as combat correspondent with the 1st Marine Division in Vietnam. His best-selling novel about Nam, *The Short-Timers* (1979), was turned into the Hollywood movie, *Full Metal Jacket*, directed by Stanley Kubrick.

The below excerpt from *The Short-Timers* is set on Parris Island, the basic training facility for the US Marine Corps. The character of Private "Joker" is based on Hasford himself.

DURING OUR SIXTH WEEK, Sergeant Gerheim orders us to double-time around the squad bay with our penises in our left hands and our weapons in our right hands, singing: *This is my rifle, this is my gun: one is for fighting and one is for fun.* And: *I don't want no teen-aged queen; all I want is my M-14.*

Sergeant Gerheim orders us to name our rifles. This is the only pussy you people are going to get. Your days of finger-banging ol' Mary Jane Rottencrotch through her pretty pink panties are over. You're married to *this* piece, this weapon of iron and wood, and you *will* be faithful.

We run. And we sing:

> Well, I don't know
> But I been told
> Eskimo pussy
> Is mighty cold . . .

Before chow, Sergeant Gerheim tells us that during World War I Blackjack Pershing said, "The deadliest weapon in the world is a Marine and his rifle." At Belleau Wood the Marines were so vicious that the German infantry called them *Teufel-Hunden* – "devil dogs."

Sergeant Gerheim explains that it is important for us to understand that it is our killer instinct which must be harnessed if we expect to survive in combat. Our rifle is only a tool; it is a hard heart that kills.

Our will to kill must be focused the way our rifle focuses a firing pressure of fifty thousand pounds per square inch to propel a piece of lead. If our rifles are not properly cleaned the explosion will be improperly focused and our rifles will shatter. If our killer instincts are not clean and strong, we will hesitate at the moment of truth. We will not kill. We will become dead Marines. And then we will be in a world of shit because Marines are not allowed to die without permission; we are government property.

The Confidence Course: We go hand over hand down a rope strung at a forty-five-degree angle across a pond – the slide-for-life. We hang upside down like monkeys and crawl headfirst down the rope.

Leonard falls off the slide-for-life eighteen times. He almost drowns. He cries. He climbs the tower. He tries again. He falls off again. This time he sinks.

Cowboy and I dive into the pond. We pull Leonard out of the muddy water. He's unconscious. When he comes to, he cries.

Back at the squad bay Sergeant Gerheim fits a Trojan rubber over the mouth of a canteen and throws the canteen at Leonard. The canteen hits Leonard on the side of the head. Sergeant Gerheim bellows, "Marines *do not cry!*"

Leonard is ordered to nurse on the canteen every day after chow.

During bayonet training Sergeant Gerheim dances an aggressive ballet. He knocks us down with a pugil stick, a five-foot pole with heavy padding on both ends. We play war with the pugil sticks. We beat each other without mercy. Then Sergeant Gerheim orders us to fix bayonets.

Sergeant Gerheim demonstrates effective attack techniques to a recruit named Barnard, a soft-spoken farm boy from Maine. The beefy drill instructor knocks out two of Private Barnard's teeth with a rifle butt.

The purpose of bayonet training, Sergeant Gerheim explains, is to awaken our killer instincts. The killer instinct will make us fearless and aggressive, like animals. If the meek ever inherit the earth the strong will take it away from them. The weak exist to be devoured by the strong. Every Marine must pack his own gear. Every Marine must be the instrument of his own salvation. It's hard, but there it is.

Private Barnard, his jaw bleeding, his mouth a bloody hole, demonstrates that he has been paying attention. Private Barnard grabs his rifle and, sitting up, bayonets Sergeant Gerheim through the right thigh.

Sergeant Gerheim grunts. Then he responds with a vertical butt stroke, but misses. So he backhands Private Barnard across the face with his fist.

Whipping off his web belt, Sergeant Gerheim ties a crude tourniquet around his bloody thigh. Then he makes the unconscious Private Barnard a squad leader. "Goddamn it, there's one little maggot who knows that the spirit of the bayonet is to *kill*! He'll make a damn fine field Marine. He ought to be a fucking general."

On the last day of our sixth week I wake up and find my rifle in my rack. My rifle is under my blanket, beside me. I don't know how it got there.

My mind isn't on my responsibilities and I forget to remind Leonard to shave.

Inspection. Junk on the bunk. Sergeant Gerheim points out that Private Pyle did not stand close enough to his razor.

Sergeant Gerheim orders Leonard and the recruit squad leaders into the head.

In the head, Sergeant Gerheim orders us to piss into a toilet bowl. "LOCK THEM HEELS! YOU ARE AT ATTENTION! READDDDDY . . . WHIZZZZ . . ."

We whiz.

Sergeant Gerheim grabs the back of Leonard's neck and forces Leonard to his knees, pushes his head down into the yellow pool. Leonard struggles. Bubbles. Panic gives Leonard strength; Sergeant Gerheim holds him down.

After we're sure that Leonard has drowned, Sergeant Gerheim flushes the toilet. When the water stops flowing, Sergeant Gerheim releases his hold on Leonard's neck.

Sergeant Gerheim's imagination is both cruel and comprehensive, but nothing works. Leonard continues to fuck up. Now, whenever Leonard makes a mistake, Sergeant Gerheim does not punish Leonard. He punishes the whole platoon. He excludes Leonard from the punishment. While Leonard rests, we do squat-thrusts and side-straddle hops, many, many of them.

Leonard touches my arm as we move through the chow line with our metal trays. "I just can't do nothing right. I need some help. I don't want you boys to be in trouble. I—"

I move away.

The first night of our seventh week of training the platoon gives Leonard a blanket party.

Midnight.

The fire watch stands by. Private Philips, the House Mouse, Sergeant Gerheim's "go-fer", pads barefoot down the squad bay to watch for Sergeant Gerheim.

In the dark, one hundred recruits walk to Leonard's rack.

Leonard is grinning even in his sleep.

The squad leaders hold towels and bars of soap.

Four recruits throw a blanket over Leonard. They grip the corners of the blanket so that Leonard can't sit up and so that his screams will be muffled.

I hear the hard breathing of a hundred sweating bodies

and I hear the fump and thud as Cowboy and Private Barnard beat Leonard with bars of soap slung in towels.

Leonard's screams are like the braying of a sick mule, heard far away. He struggles.

The eyes of the platoon are on me. Eyes are aimed at me in the dark, eyes like rubies.

Leonard stops screaming.

I hesitate. The eyes are on me. I step back.

Cowboy punches me in the chest with his towel and a bar of soap.

I sling the towel, drop in the soap, and then I beat Leonard, who has stopped moving. He lies in silence, stunned, gagging for air. I beat him harder and harder and when I feel tears being flung from my eyes, I beat him harder for it.

The next day, on the parade deck, Leonard does not grin.

When Gunnery Sergeant Gerheim asks, "What do we do for a living, ladies?" and we reply, "KILL! KILL! KILL!," Leonard remains silent. When our junior drill instructors ask, "Do we love the Crotch, ladies? Do we love our beloved Corps?" and the platoon responds with one voice, "GUNG HO! GUNG HO! GUNG HO!," Leonard is silent.

On the third day of our seventh week we move to the rifle range and shoot holes in paper targets. Sergeant Gerheim brags about the marksmanship of ex-Marines Charles Whitman and Lee Harvey Oswald.

By the end of our seventh week Leonard has become a model recruit. We decide that Leonard's silence is a result of his new intense concentration. Day by day, Leonard is more motivated, more squared away. His manual of arms is flawless now, but his eyes are milk glass. Leonard cleans his weapon more than any recruit in the platoon. Every night after chow Leonard caresses the scarred oak stock with linseed oil the way hundreds of earlier recruits have caressed the same piece of wood. Leonard improves at everything, but remains silent. He does what he is told but he is no longer part of the platoon.

We can see that Sergeant Gerheim resents Leonard's attitude. He reminds Leonard that the motto of the Marine Corps is *Semper Fidelis* – "Always Faithful." Sergeant Gerheim reminds Leonard that "Gung ho" is Chinese for "working together."

It is a Marine Corps tradition, Sergeant Gerheim says, that Marines never abandon their dead or wounded. Sergeant Gerheim is careful not to come down too hard on Leonard as long as Leonard remains squared away. We have already lost seven recruits on Section Eight discharges. A Kentucky boy named Perkins stepped to the center of the squad bay and slashed his wrists with his bayonet. Sergeant Gerheim was not happy to see a recruit bleeding upon his nice clean squad bay. The recruit was ordered to police the area, mop up the blood, and replace the bayonet in its sheath. While Perkins mopped up the blood, Sergeant Gerheim called a school circle and poo-pooed the recruit's shallow slash across his wrists with a bayonet. The U.S.M.C.-approved method of recruit suicide is to get *alone* and take a razor blade and slash deep and vertical, from wrist to elbow, Sergeant Gerheim said. Then he allowed Perkins to double-time to sick bay.

Sergeant Gerheim leaves Leonard alone and concentrates on the rest of us.

Sunday.

Magic show. Religious services in the faith of your choice – and you *will* have a choice – because religious services are specified in the beautiful full-color brochures the Crotch distributes to Mom and Dad back in hometown America, even though Sergeant Gerheim assures us that the Marine Corps was here before God. "You can give your heart to Jesus but your ass belongs to the Corps."

After the "magic show" we eat chow. The squad leaders

read grace from cards set in holders on the tables. Then: "SEATS!"

We spread butter on slices of bread and then sprinkle sugar on the butter. We smuggle the sandwiches out of the mess hall, risking a beating for the novelty of unscheduled chow. We don't give a shit; we're salty. Now, when Sergeant Gerheim and his junior drill instructors stomp us we tell them that we love it and to do it some more. When Sergeant Gerheim commands: "Okay, ladies, give me fifty squat-thrusts. And some side-straddle hops. Many, many of them," we laugh and then do them.

The drill instructors are proud to see that we are growing beyond their control. The Marine Corps does not want robots. The Marine Corps wants killers. The Marine Corps wants to build indestructible men, men without fear. Civilians may choose to submit or to fight back. The drill instructors leave recruits no choice. Marines fight back or they do not survive. There it is. No slack.

Graduation is only a few days away and the salty recruits of Platoon 30–92 are ready to eat their own guts and then ask for seconds. The moment the Commandant of the Marine Corps gives us the word, we will grab the Viet Cong guerrillas and the battle-hardened North Vietnamese regulars by their scrawny throats and we'll punch their fucking heads off.

Sunday afternoon in the sun. We scrub our little green garments on a long concrete table.

For the hundredth time, I tell Cowboy that I want to slip my tube steak into his sister so what will he take in trade?

For the hundredth time, Cowboy replies, "What do you have?"

Sergeant Gerheim struts around the table. He is trying not to limp. He criticizes our utilization of the Marine Corps scrub brush.

We don't care; we're too salty.

Sergeant Gerheim won the Navy Cross on Iwo Jima, he says. He got it for teaching young Marines how to bleed, he says. Marines are supposed to bleed in tidy little pools because Marines are disciplined. Civilians and members of the lesser services bleed all over the place like bed wetters.

We don't listen. We swap scuttlebutt. Laundry day is the only time we are allowed to talk to each other.

Philips – Sergeant Gerheim's black, silver-tongued House Mouse – is telling everybody about the one thousand cherries he has busted.

I say, "Leonard talks to his rifle."

A dozen recruits look up. They hesitate. Some look sick. Others look scared. And some look shocked and angry, as though I'd just slapped a cripple.

I force myself to speak: "Leonard talks to his rifle." Nobody moves. Nobody says anything. "I don't think Leonard can hack it anymore. I think Leonard is a Section Eight."

Now guys all along the table are listening. They look confused. Their eyes seem fixed on some distant object as though they are trying to remember a bad dream.

Private Barnard nods. "I've been having this nightmare. My . . . rifle talks to me." He hesitates. "And I've been talking back to it . . ."

"There it is," says Philips. "Yeah. It's cold. It's a cold voice. I thought I was going plain fucking crazy. My rifle said—"

Sergeant Gerheim's big fist drives Philips's next word down his throat and out of his asshole. Philips is nailed to the deck. He's on his back. His lips are crushed. He groans.

The platoon freezes.

Sergeant Gerheim puts his fists on his hips. His eyes glare out from under the brim of his Smokey the Bear campaign cover like the barrels of a shotgun. "Private Pyle is a Section Eight. You hear me? If Private Pyle talks to his piece it is because he's plain fucking crazy. You maggots *will* belay all this scuttlebutt. Don't let Private Joker play with your imaginations. I don't want to hear another word. Do you hear me? Not one word."

Night at Parris Island. We stand by until Sergeant

Gerheim snaps out his last order of the day: "Prepare to mount
... Readddy ... MOUNT!" Then we're lying on our backs in
our skivvies, at attention, our weapons held at port arms.

We say our prayers:

I am a United States Marine Corps recruit. I serve in the
forces which guard my country and my way of life. I am
prepared to give my life in their defense, so help me God
... GUNG HO! GUNG HO! GUNG HO!

Then the Rifleman's Creed, by Marine Corps Major General W. H. Rupertus:

This is my rifle. There are many like it but this one is
mine. My rifle is my best friend. It is my life. I must
master it as I master my life.

My rifle, without me, is useless. I must fire my rifle true.
I must shoot straighter than my enemy who is trying to
kill me. I must shoot him before he shoots me.

I will.

Leonard is speaking for the first time in weeks. His voice
booms louder and louder. Heads turn. Bodies shift. The platoon voice fades. Leonard is about to explode. His words are
being coughed up from some deep, ugly place.

Sergeant Gerheim has the night duty. He struts to Leonard's rack and stands by, fists on hips.

Leonard doesn't see Sergeant Gerheim. The veins in
Leonard's neck are bulging as he bellows:

MY RIFLE IS HUMAN, EVEN AS I, BECAUSE IT IS
MY LIFE. THUS I WILL LEARN IT AS A BROTHER.
I WILL LEARN ITS ACCESSORIES, ITS SIGHTS,
ITS BARREL.
   I WILL KEEP MY RIFLE CLEAN AND READY,

EVEN AS I AM CLEAN AND READY. WE WILL BECOME PART OF EACH OTHER.

WE WILL . . .

BEFORE GOD I SWEAR THIS CREED. MY RIFLE AND MYSELF ARE THE MASTER OF OUR ENEMY. WE ARE THE SAVIORS OF MY LIFE.

SO BE IT, UNTIL VICTORY IS AMERICA'S AND THERE IS NO ENEMY BUT PEACE!

AMEN.

Sergeant Gerheim kicks Leonard's rack. "Hey – *you* – Private Pyle . . ."

"What? Yes? YES, SIR!" Leonard snaps to attention in his rack. "AYE-AYE, SIR!"

"What's that weapon's name, maggot?

"SIR, THE PRIVATE'S WEAPON'S NAME IS CHARLENE, SIR!"

"At ease, maggot." Sergeant Gerheim grins. "You are becoming one sharp recruit, Private Pyle. Most motivated prive in my herd. Why, I may even allow you to serve as a rifleman in my beloved Corps. I had you figured for a shitbird, but you'll make a good grunt."

"AYE-AYE, SIR!"

I look at the rifle slung on my rack. It's a beautiful instrument, gracefully designed, solid and symmetrical. My rifle is clean, oiled, and works perfectly. It's a fine tool. I touch it.

Sergeant Gerheim marches down the length of the squad bay. "THE REST OF YOU ANIMALS COULD TAKE LESSONS FROM PRIVATE PYLE. He's squared away. You are all squared away. Tomorrow you will be Marines. READDDY . . . SLEEP!"

Graduation day. A thousand new Marines stand tall on the parade deck, lean and tan in immaculate khaki, their clean weapons held at port arms.

Leonard is selected as the outstanding recruit from Platoon 30–92. He is awarded a free set of dress blues and is allowed to wear the colorful uniform when the graduating platoons pass in review. The Commanding General of Parris Island shakes Leonard's hand and gives him a "Well done." Our series commander pins a RIFLE EXPERT badge on Leonard's chest and our company commander awards Leonard a citation for shooting the highest score in the training battalion.

Because of a special commendation submitted by Sergeant Gerheim, I'm promoted to Private First Class. After our series commander pins on my EXPERT's badge, Sergeant Gerheim presents me with two red and green chevrons and explains that they're his old PFC stripes.

When we pass in review I walk right guide, tall and proud.

Cowboy receives an EXPERT's badge and is selected to carry the platoon guidon.

The Commanding General of Parris Island speaks into a microphone: "Have you seen the light? The white light? The great light? The guiding light? Do you have the vision?"

And we cheer, happy beyond belief.

The Commanding General sings. We sing too:

> Hey, Marine, have you heard?
> Hey, Marine . . .
> L. B. J. has passed the word.
> Hey, Marine . . .
> Say good-bye to Dad and Mom.
> Hey, Marine . . .
> You're gonna die in Viet Nam.
> Hey, Marine, yeah!

After the graduation ceremony our orders are distributed. Cowboy, Leonard, Private Barnard, Philips, and most of the other Marines in Platoon 30–92 are ordered to ITR – the Infantry Training Regiment – to be trained as grunts, infantrymen.

My orders instruct me to report to the Basic Military Journalism School at Fort Benjamin Harrison, Indiana, after I graduate from ITR. Sergeant Gerheim is disgusted by the fact that I am to be a combat correspondent and not a grunt. He calls me a poge, an office pinky. He says that shitbirds get all the slack.

Standing at ease on the parade deck, beneath the monument to the Iwo Jima flag raising, Sergeant Gerheim says, "The smoking lamp is lit. You people are no longer maggots. Today you are Marines. Once a Marine, always a Marine . . ."

Leonard laughs out loud.

Our last night on the island.

I draw fire watch.

I stand by in utility trousers, skivvy shirt, spitshined combat boots, and a helmet liner which has been painted silver.

Sergeant Gerheim gives me his wristwatch and a flashlight. "Good night, Marine."

I march up and down the squad bay between two perfectly aligned rows of racks.

One hundred young Marines breathe peacefully as they sleep – one hundred survivors from our original hundred and twenty.

Tomorrow at dawn we'll all board cattle-car buses for the ride to Camp Geiger in North Carolina. There, ITR – the infantry training regiment. All Marines are grunts, even though some of us will learn additional military skills. After advanced infantry training we'll be allowed pogey bait at the slop chute and we'll be given weekend liberty off the base and then we'll receive assignments to our permanent duty stations.

The squad bay is as quiet as a funeral parlor at mid-night. The silence is disturbed only by the soft *creak-creak* of bed-springs and an occasional cough.

It's almost time for me to wake my relief when I hear a voice. Some recruit is talking in his sleep.

I stop. I listen. A second voice. Two guys must be swapping scuttlebutt. If Sergeant Gerheim hears them it'll be my ass. I hurry toward the sound.

It's Leonard. Leonard is talking to his rifle. But there is also another voice A whisper. A cold, seductive moan. It's the voice of a woman.

Leonard's rifle is not slung on his rack. He's holding his rifle, hugging it. "Okay, okay. I *love* you!" Very softly: "I've given you the best months of my life. And now you—" I snap on my flashlight. Leonard ignores me. "I LOVE YOU! DON'T YOU UNDERSTAND? I CAN DO IT. I'LL DO ANYTHING!"

Leonards words reverberate down the squad bay. Racks squeak. Someone rolls over. One recruit sits up, rubs his eyes.

I watch the far end of the squad bay. I wait for the light to go on inside Sergeant Gerheim's palace.

I touch Leonard's shoulder. "Hey, shut your mouth, Leonard. Sergeant Gerheim will break my back."

Leonard sits up. He looks at me. He strips off his skivvy shirt and ties it around his face to blindfold himself. He begins to field-strip his weapon. "This is the first time I've ever seen her naked." He pulls off the blindfold. His fingers continue to break down the rifle into components. Then, gently, he fondles each piece. "Just look at that pretty trigger guard. Have you ever seen a more beautiful piece of metal?" He starts snapping the steel components back together. "Her connector assembly is so beautiful . . ."

Leonard continues to babble as his trained fingers reassemble the black metal hardware.

I think about Vanessa, my girl back home. We're on a river bank, wrapped in an old sleeping bag, and I'm fucking her eyes out. But my favorite fantasy has gone stale. Thinking about Vanessa's thighs, her dark nipples, her full lips doesn't give me a hard-on anymore. I guess it must be the saltpeter in our food, like they say.

Leonard reaches under his pillow and comes out with a loaded magazine. Gently, he inserts the metal magazine into his weapon, into Charlene.

"Leonard . . . where did you get those live rounds?"

Now a lot of guys are sitting up, whispering, "What's happening?" to each other.

Sergeant Gerheim's light floods the far end of the squad bay.

"OKAY, LEONARD, LET'S GO." I'm determined to save my own ass if I can, certain that Leonard's is forfeit in any case. The last time Sergeant Gerheim caught a recruit with a live round – just one round – he ordered the recruit to dig a grave ten feet long and ten feet deep. The whole platoon had to fall out for the "funeral." I say, "You're in a world of shit now, Leonard."

The overhead lights explode. The squad bay is washed with light. "WHAT'S THIS MICKEY MOUSE SHIT? JUST WHAT IN THE NAME OF JESUS H. CHRIST ARE YOU ANIMALS DOING IN MY SQUAD BAY?"

Sergeant Gerheim comes at me like a mad dog. His voice cuts the squad bay in half: "MY BEAUTY SLEEP HAS BEEN INTERRUPTED, LADIES. YOU *KNOW* WHAT THAT MEANS. YOU HEAR ME, HERD? IT MEANS THAT ONE RECRUIT HAS VOLUNTEERED HIS YOUNG HEART FOR A GODDAMN HUMAN SACRIFICE!"

Leonard pounces from his rack, confronts Sergeant Gerheim.

Now the whole platoon is awake. We all wait to see what Sergeant Gerheim will do, confident that it will be worth watching.

"Private Joker. You shitbird. Front and center."

I move my ass. "AYE-AYE, SIR!"

"Okay, you little maggot, *speak*. Why is Private Pyle out of his rack after lights out? Why is Private Pyle holding that weapon? Why ain't you stomping Private Pyle's guts out?"

"SIR, it is the private's duty to report to the drill instructor that Private . . . Pyle . . . has a full magazine and has locked and loaded, SIR."

Sergeant Gerheim looks at Leonard and nods. He sighs. Gunnery Sergeant Gerheim looks more than a little ridiculous in his pure white skivvies and red rubber flip-flop shower shoes and hairy legs and tattooed forearms and a beer gut and a face the color of raw beef, and, on his bald head, the green and brown Smokey the Bear campaign cover.

Our senior drill instructor focuses all of his considerable powers of intimidation into his best John-Wayne-on-Suribachi voice: "Listen to me, Private Pyle, You *will* place your weapon on your rack and—"

"NO! YOU CAN'T HAVE HER! SHE'S MINE! YOU HEAR ME? SHE'S MINE! I LOVE HER!"

Gunnery Sergeant Gerheim can't control himself any longer. "NOW YOU LISTEN TO ME, YOU FUCKING WORTHLESS LITTLE PIECE OF SHIT. YOU *WILL* GIVE ME THAT WEAPON OR I'M GOING TO TEAR YOUR BALLS OFF AND STUFF THEM DOWN YOUR SCRAWNY LITTLE THROAT! YOU HEAR ME, MARINE? I'M GOING TO PUNCH YOUR FUCKING HEART OUT!"

Leonard aims the weapon at Sergeant Gerheim's heart, caresses the trigger guard, then caresses the trigger . . .

Sergeant Gerheim is suddenly calm. His eyes, his manner are those of a wanderer who has found his home. He is a man in complete control of himself and of the world he lives in. His face is cold and beautiful as the dark side surfaces. He smiles. It is not a friendly smile, but an evil smile, as though Sergeant Gerheim were a werewolf baring its fangs. "Private Pyle, I'm proud—"

Bang.

The steel buttplate slams into Leonard's shoulder.

One 7.62-millimeter high-velocity copper-jacketed bullet punches Gunnery Sergeant Gerheim back.

He falls.

We all stare at Sergeant Gerheim. Nobody moves.

Sergeant Gerheim sits up as though nothing has happened. For one second, we relax. Leonard has missed. Then dark blood squirts from a little hole in Sergeant Gerheim's chest. The red blood blossoms into his white skivvy shirt like a beautiful flower. Sergeant Gerheim's bug eyes are focused upon the blood rose on his chest, fascinated. He looks up at Leonard. He squints. Then he relaxes. The werewolf smile is frozen on his lips.

My menial position of authority as the fire watch on duty forces me to act. "Now, uh, Leonard, we're all your bros, man, your brothers. I'm your bunkmate, right? I—"

"Sure," says Cowboy. "Go easy, Leonard. We don't want to hurt you."

"Affirmative," says Private Barnard.

Leonard doesn't hear. "Did you see the way he looked at her? Did you? I knew what he was thinking. I knew. That fat pig and his dirty—"

"Leonard . . ."

"We can kill you. You know that." Leonard caresses his rifle. "Don't you know that Charlene and I can kill you all?"

Leonard aims his rifle at my face.

I don't look at the rifle. I look into Leonard's eyes. I know that Leonard is too weak to control his instrument of death. It is a hard heart that kills, not the weapon. Leonard is a defective instrument for the power that is following through him. Sergeant Gerheim's mistake was in not seeing that Leonard was like a glass rifle which would shatter when fired. Leonard is not hard enough to harness the power of an interior explosion to propel the cold black bullet of his will.

Leonard is grinning at us, the final grin that is on the face of death, the terrible grin of the skull.

The grin changes to a look of surprise and then to confusion and then to terror as Leonard's weapon moves up and back and then Leonard takes the black metal barrel into his mouth. "NO! Not—"

Bang.

Leonard is dead on the deck. His head is now an awful lump of blood and facial bones and sinus fluids and uprooted teeth and jagged, torn flesh. The skin looks plastic and unreal.

The civilians will demand yet another investigation, of course. But during the investigation the recruits of Platoon

30–92 will testify that Private Pratt, while highly motivated, was a ten percenter who did not pack the gear to be a Marine in our beloved Corps.

Sergeant Gerheim is still smiling. He was a fine drill instructor. Dying, that's what we're here for, he would have said – blood makes the grass grow. If he could speak, Gunnery Sergeant Gerheim would explain to Leonard why the guns that we love don't love back. And he would say, "Well done."

I turn off the overhead lights.

Part III

The End

Vietnam 1967–75

Voices in America: Enlistment

Anonymous

I came from San Jose, California. I grew up in the suburbs and went to public school. I lived on the last block of a new development surrounded on three sides by apricot orchards and vineyards.

The high school was typically middle class. There were very few blacks. We had warm weather and cars. Most of the kids' dads were engineers at Lockheed or they worked at IBM. Most of my friends were preparing for a college degree.

From San Jose, people would go up to San Francisco for concerts. Smoking dope was just coming in at the time and psychedelic music. Some of the kids I knew were involved with that. They weren't pioneers. They were the ones who joined, who wanted to be the first to do this or that – the trendy group.

Then I was conservative. I hadn't experienced any inequality in the social system. Things looked pretty hunky-dory to me. Plus I had read all the war fiction. It never had a particular fascination for me, but it implanted this idea in my mind that war was a place for you to discover things.

I saw older people, World War II age, who weren't in that war. When they were asked about it and what they were doing then, they had to say, "Oh, well, I was in college." It was a major historical event that convulsed the world, and yet they missed it. I was the perfect age to participate in Vietnam and I didn't want to miss it, good or bad. I wanted to be part of it, to understand what it was.

Why should I take the God damn SATs and go off to college? Everybody was going to San Jose State College right there in town. And who wants to do what everybody else does anyway?

I joined the Army at the end of my senior year in high school with delayed induction. I would leave for basic training at the end of the summer when everybody else went away to college. I spent the last summer at home, playing a lot of basketball, riding around with my friends in an old '54 Ford. Nobody's picked up on their adult life. *American Graffiti*.

I come from a conservative Republican area. I was brought up in a strict, anonymous, nomadic suburban environment, where privilege was part of our legacy. We had our boats. We had our recreation. We had our stability. We had our fifteen-thousand-dollar-a-year jobs guaranteed to us as soon as we got out of college.

I never felt I belonged there, but I never imagined I'd end up in Vietnam. I was in undergraduate school and my deferment ran out. I'd spent some time in Brazil – my junior year abroad. I had thought I was going to get a full year of credits and I didn't get them. During the extra year of college I had to go through, my Draft Board advised me that they had changed my classification from 2S to 1A.

So I thought, I'll just go back to Brazil or I'll join the Peace Corps. But I really got hung up on finishing school. I had it in my head that if I went off then I'd never come back to school and get my degree. It was a real adolescent attitude. That degree was my working papers, my union card.

ROTC on campus had started a new crash programme for guys who had never taken ROTC, but who wanted to go into the service as officers. All I had to do was stick around for one more year and take nothing but ROTC courses, and I'd get a commission. I said to myself, "Fuck it, I don't want to go in and peel potatoes. I don't want to be some private. I'm basically antisocial and I hate authority. If I go in in that position, I'll just get in trouble and end up in jail. I might as well get myself a little autonomy, a little anonymity." I wanted to be left alone and to have my own way. So my last year in college I was an ROTC major.

I was a fuck-up. My hair was always too long, my uniform was always dirty. I wasn't consciously rebellious. I just couldn't take it seriously. I couldn't sit in class and talk about war the way they were talking about it. It wasn't that I was an intellectual or into politics. I had a strong moral upbringing with my Catholic background. I was very influenced by the lives of the saints, and by Christ, his example – more than I'd like to admit probably. I believed it in a way, you know? I'd talk about the Geneva Convention and how absurd it was to try to talk about the legality of war. I thought it was silly to try to reduce what was essentially an immoral experience into a question of legislation.

I remember having to go out to this athletic field and march around in a baggy uniform, feeling like a complete asshole. Older than the other guys, not taking it seriously, I was very aware of my expedient motives in the whole thing. I was afraid of the experience of being just an average grunt. I was doing what I had pretty much done all my life, using my wits to get over. I had this kind of contempt for the other guys going through all the military paces, who were seeking this power and leadership, who wanted to move other guys around like chess pieces on a board.

Out of the corner of my eye, I saw this small delegation of campus SDS outside the gate of the track field. I felt a tremendous affinity for them. That day, I had a very strong image of me literally slogging through the field, dragging my ass, going through the paces, but having a secret identification with those demonstrators. But they came from an entirely different world than me. For better or worse, I was part of the American experience and I thought there was no way I could bridge the gap. I guess I felt that I wouldn't be accepted, that I was a different species.

After I graduated, I went to the ROTC summer training camp. Essentially, I tried to be invisible most of the time. I failed the marksmanship requirement. I hated guns. I pledged to myself that no matter what position I was in, I would never use a gun, I would never kill anybody. I didn't try to fail, I was just uninterested.

Everybody else in my company was a junior in college. They had to be back and finish their last year and then they would get their commission at the graduation ceremony. I was going to get my commission after camp. I was able to use the officers' club which was a special privilege. A buddy of mine from college who was already a first lieutenant in the signal corps would come by after the day's training and pick me up in his Oldsmobile convertible – a big, fat luxury car, a real meat wagon. I used to feel real cocky. The other guys would be down there polishing the floors and doing all that shit. I'd put on my Madras blazer, my jeans, my tassel loafers and no socks, my buddy the lieutenant would pull up and there was nobody who would say me nay.

It was fucked in a way, it was really fucked. I was never aware until recently how lonely I was, disengaged from my life. How alienated I was from other people, from society and community. Some kind of weird Jesuit.

I graduated from college three days after Robert Kennedy was shot, two months and three days after Martin Luther King was assassinated, an incredible double whammy. The war was hanging there like a sword over everybody. I had been reclassified in the middle of my senior year from 2S to 1A and gone through about six solid months of really examining my feelings about the war. Chiefly, I read a lot of pacifist literature to determine whether or not I was a conscientious objector. I finally concluded that I wasn't, for reasons that I'm still not sure of.

The one clear decision I made in 1968 about me and the war was that if I was going to get out of it, I was going to get out in a legal way. I was not going to defraud the system in order to beat the system. I wasn't going to leave the country, because the odds of coming back looked real slim. I was unwilling to give up what I had as a home. Spending two years in jail was as dumb as going to war, even less productive. I wasn't going to shoot off a toe. I had friends who were starving themselves to be underweight for their physicals. I wasn't going to do it – probably because it was "too far to walk". I wasn't just stupidly righteous, there was a part of me that was real lazy at the same time. I wanted to be acted on, and it was real hard for me to make a choice of any kind. Making no choice was a choice.

With all my terror of going into the Army – because I figured that I was the least likely person I knew to survive – there was something seductive about it, too. I was seduced by World War II and John Wayne movies. When I was in high school, I dreamed of going to Annapolis. I was, on some silly level, really disturbed when the last battleship was decommissioned. One of my fantasies as a kid was to be in command of a battleship in a major sea battle, and having somewhere in my sea chest Great-uncle Arthur's naval dress sword from the eighteenth century.

One way or another in every generation when there was a war, some male in the family on my father's side went to it. I had never had it drilled into me, but there was a lot of attention paid to the past, a lot of not-so-subtle "This is what a man does with his life" stuff when I was growing up. I had been, as we all were, victimised by a romantic, truly uninformed view of war.

I got drafted at the end of the summer. I went into a state of total panic for days. What the fuck am I going to do? I went running off to recruiters to see if I could get into the Coast Guard or the Navy or the Air Force. No way.

There were probably some strings that I could have pulled. One of the things that is curious to me, as I look back on it, is that I had all the information, all the education and all the opportunity that a good, middle-class, college-educated person could have to get out of it . . . and I didn't make a single choice that put it anywhere but breathing down my neck. Even in the midst of the terror after the induction notice came, there was a part of me that would lie in bed at night and fantasise about what it would be like if I went.

The long and the short of the story is that at least half of my emotions were pulled to going. I couldn't get into any other branch of the service, so my final choice was to enlist in the Army. They had a delayed enlistment option. It was August when I got drafted and I figured, "Shit, I don't want to go until October." I took the option. I spent that time at a cottage in Maine, enjoying the wonderful weather, reading books and writing dramatic farewell letters.

This is War, Man

Donald Bodey

Don Bodey was born in Fort Wayne, Indiana; he went to college to avoid the draft, but after graduation in 1968, he was drafted anyway. He served as a mortarman in Vietnam. On his return to America he earned an MFA in the writing program at University of Oregon. In this excerpt from his novel *F.N.G.* (1979), Gabriel "Chieu Hoi" Sauer's squad has just ambushed a Viet Cong patrol. F.N.G. is Vietnam slang for "Fucking New Guy".

BLOOD.

Like cottage-red paint shot from a fire hydrant, blood everywhere: sprayed all over the leaves and rocks and running in the rainwater that trickles off the rocks. *Jesus-fuckinchrist.*

"Oh, muthafucker, they're dead."

"We musta got 'em all."

"Let's go. We're lucky this didn't draw a tiger last night."

As we came up, some rodents scampered away and as we are standing there I look away and meet two little eyes looking at us from under a rock. I feel like I hate the goddamn rodent. I hate everything. There are four dinks. Two of them were cut in half by our claymores. *How goddamn much blood is there in a person?* I might faint. It seems like everything should be still but there are flies by the hundreds and the birds in the canopy are squawking. There must be an animal in the matted grass behind the bodies because there is noise there too. At first I can't identify the other sound I hear; then I realize it is the static of the radio.

I have been breathing fast and I'm sweating, but I can't turn away. The rain is drizzle now, but it seems like it would have washed more blood away. I smell something besides wet jungle, but it doesn't smell dead. *Does blood have a smell of its own? Is that what the vultures smell?* I feel faint again: like my mind is swinging up there in the canopy, like *I'm a vulture seeing us look at the bodies. I see Pops break the silence.*

"Four of 'em. That's all we want to know. Let's go back to the top and call it in. I don't want to stand around here. Pick up the rifles." *And I can see me pick up a gun.* When I feel it my mind comes back to earth. We go back up where our rucks are.

The rifle is an AK. I can't forget the sound after the day Chickenfeed got hit. The rifle is beat to pieces. It only has half the original stock; the back half is a piece of wood with twig marks on it still, carved on the end to fit a shoulder. *Which of the four did it come from?*

"Greenleaf, this is Titbird. How's your copy?"

Pops has the radio up on a rock, and the way he is standing there talking makes me flash on a cop, *downtown Cincinnati*, calling in from a beat box. I feel fuckin' drugged. OK, *this is war, man. This ain't Cincinnati. You're part of this, Gabriel.* Everybody looks the same – empty. Muthafucker, *can this be?* I smell the rifle to see if it was fired last night but there isn't any smell but metal. This ain't the fuckin' movies; you ain't John Wayne. I wonder if it had shot any GIs. It's heavier than my rifle. The ammo clip is curved. The more I stare at the gun the more it looks unreal, toy-like. No, it actually looks more real than my plastic M-16 but there is something child-ish about it. *The fucking thing looks homemade. That carved butt piece, the way it's wired together. Homemade.*

Pops is scooting the radio up the rock now. It occurs to me that I haven't been watching the bush. Eltee gets up and goes to help Pops. He seems to have regained his composure but his face is tight-looking. Peacock is picking his nose with one hand and toothbrushing the feed mechanism of the Sixty with his other.

"We got four rabbits out here. Coming back to your position. Over."

"Titbird, Greenleaf."

"Stand by."

"Them dinks caught our claymores letters-high," Pea says, to nobody in particular.

"Think of how much dinky damage they musta done to the Z."

"Titbird, how's your copy? Over."

"Good copy. Go ahead, dammit."

"Titbird, Higher says cut a chimney, they'll be out. Over."

Prophet angrily slams his hat on his thigh and Pops bangs the microphone with his free hand.

"No way," Pops says to Eltee. "Fuck those lifers. You tell 'em, we can't cut a chimney through that canopy. All they want to do is make sure we counted right, and I ain't fuckin' doing it."

I can't imagine how we could cut a hole, big enough to let a Loach down, and I can't imagine why.

Pops reads my mind.

"They wanna bring a Chieu Hoi out here and see if he can tell what unit the dinks are from."

"There isn't enough left of the four dinks to tell anybody jack-shit."

"Eltee, tell the fuckers to walk out here. We did," Prophet says.

Lieutenant Williams is standing up with his arms folded across the radio. He is rocking back and forth on his heels and toes. He never looks our way. The radio is low-volume static. If I can read Eltee's mind, I know he is torn, tortured, confused. He's going to be caught in the middle.

"Well, do something, for chrissakes. We can't cut 'em a hole, and we sure as fuck don't want to stay here much longer. Charlie is gonna be looking for these guys."

"Greenleaf, Titbird. Code name William."

"Go, Titbird."

"Greenleaf, too much canopy, too high. We'll bring captured weapons to your papa. These rabbits are in parts. Repeat, in parts. Not enough left for ID. Copy?"

"Code name William, code name Beaver. Wait one."

Pops flips through the code book.

"It's that short red-haired fucker, Billingham."

I didn't know his name, but I figured that's who it was. He's some kind of aide to the colonel and he carries a Car-15. A few days ago I saw his radioman taking his picture. He had a flak jacket and helmet on then, and the asshole probably hasn't ever been to the Bush. This is beginning to get real shitty. I'm becoming afraid again. We blew these guys away and their pals must be around here somewhere. If we don't get going we'll be sitting ducks. I feel my anger and fear mount together. I have a quick fantasy of taking a swing at that fat little fucker.

"Titbird, Greenleaf."

Even the radio seems alive and against us. It must be my fear that makes me think that way all of a sudden. Unfuckin' fair to be out here in the middle of nowhere and scared, talking long-distance and visualizing Billingham sitting in a sandbagged conex telling us to do something we already told him we can't fuckin' do.

"Titbird, it is essential that you provide us a way of identifying your rabbits. Many lives may depend on it."

"Many lives! Our lives are the only ones relevant to them dead dinks; where does he get off giving us a lecture like we're still in The World? This ain't practice. There ain't enough of them dinks left to tell anything. Make the fucker understand they're using us for bait."

Peacock is standing beside Williams now, struggling to keep his voice under control. Eltee looks at him blankly, puts a hand on his back, then pushes his own helmet back on his head. Eltee looks five years older than he did yesterday, and he looks confused.

"Oh, fucker . . ." Callme moans.

Prophet has been sitting with his elbows on his knees,

looking away from us. Now he looks up at the canopy and shakes his head.

"Greenleaf, code name William, over."

"Go."

"I repeat. No can do."

"Titbird, that's affirm. Transport your rabbits to Checkpoint Bravo. Out."

No! *Bullshit*. I'm dreaming. Or is this a movie?

Peacock slumps down into the mud and begins stabbing at it with his knife. He is soon using both hands to stab with. He's nuts. I feel crazy too. Everybody else *looks* crazy. Eltee lets the microphone drop against the rock and stands staring at us. He looks like he's trying to get his mind to work.

"OK—" he starts.

"OK, so let's go to Bravo and they can fuckin' walk back up here without us. We'll tell 'em right where the ambush is."

"Listen up," Eltee says. "This is some real bullshit, but there's no alternative."

"No alternative? Let's just fuckin' refuse to do it."

"Pops, you're a short-timer. If we don't do it we're all guilty of disobeying a direct order and we're all going to get court-martialed. You know that. Not just me. They'd bust us, send us all to jail, then send us back out here, and that jail time is bad time. You won't rotate out of here until *next* year. Think about it."

Pops's face is stretched round with red anger. He looks like he's ready to explode. I expect an outburst, but instead he slumps down to his knees and turns his face upward to let the silent rain hit him. He sighs.

"Eltee is right," Peacock says.

"If we're gonna do it, let's do it. We'll get even with them fuckin' Higher-highers," Prophet says.

Lieutenant Williams looks at him and opens his mouth but doesn't say anything.

"You never heard me say that, Eltee, for your own good. We like you and I know what you're thinking, but just forget it. You're one of us, for now."

Jesus, this is escalating. I don't know for sure what Prophet is saying, but his tone is severe and he isn't about ready to back down from anything the Eltee can offer.

"I won't hump no dead guy," Callme says.

"Dinks don't weigh much," Pea says.

Callmeblack makes his big black hand into a big black fist and drives it into his wadded-up poncho. Then he half buries his face in the poncho and either sobs or sighs.

Dear Dad: You won't believe this. Dear Brother Bob: Go to Canada. Dear President Johnson: Could you do this? Dear God: For my mother's sake, numb me. (Fucking jail! . . . Everybody knows the horror stories about military prisons, especially in The Nam.) There's nothing fair about some Army officer three kilometers away telling us to obey this insane order or go to jail. But why should I expect fairness? I'm in the Army, and the Army is in a war. It's simple. I don't have any choice.

So I'm the first one to move. I stand up and unroll my poncho. I'm conscious of the rest of them watching me but I don't look at them.

"Are we supposed to call 'em when we get there?"

"Yeah," Prophet says, "call 'em and say send a taxi after we dragged the muthafuckin' corpses all the way through this damn jungle while they meanwhile sit back there getting dug in, then fly out to meet us."

He stands and is talking loud but not yelling.

"Then, goddammit, then they'll turn that helicopter around and we'll goddamn have to walk back too!"

"Those hardcore Shake-and-Bake officers don't even think about us killing these poor bastards, let alone have to haul around what's left. They probably can't think of it, just have wet dreams about being a hero when they get home."

We're psyching ourselves up. Everybody but Peacock is getting ready now. Eltee already has his ruck on. He goes over to Callme and squats alongside him. They don't even say anything but I can see Callme's courage – or whatever it is – coming back. I feel a little jealous of Eltee right now. I'm ready. My ruck doesn't feel so heavy and I'm not as tired as I was before it got light.

"Pray for luck," Peacock says. "If Charlie is around here close and sees this mess, you know he ain't gonna goddamn worry about big guns out here. He's gonna have our shit on a stick. He'll be hawking my goddamn watch in Hanoi if he knows what we're carrying and just happens to see us clod-hoppin' American boys here in his jungle. Them lifers think about the wrong things, that's all. They call the war by numbers. They're gonna say them four dinks only had one arm anyway, so we really blew eight away."

"Peacock," Pops says, "I never heard you be so right."

"Man, I'm just talking to keep from seeing, because seeing is believing."

"That's more like your old self, you asshole. That doesn't make any sense."

Jesus the flies.

We have two sets of ponchos snapped into pairs and are going to gather the bodies onto the ponchos, then split the weight up so four guys can carry the two slings. Even then, two guys will have to hump the radio, the machine gun, and the extra weapons, so really we'll be fuckin'-A useless if anything happens. Prophet goes to look for the best way by himself; we want to keep him as light as we can because he will be walking point. When he leaves, the rest of us go back to the site together. The flies are so loud I hear them from behind the first set of rocks, ten meters away.

We spread the ponchos out. Nobody talks. At first we all stand still. Then Callmeblack begins humming "Swing Low, Sweet Chariot" and Pops drags most of a body onto one of the ponchos. The guts drag along between the body's legs. The flies swarm in one extra-loud sound and land again when the body is on the poncho. Pops goes off from us a bit.

Right at my feet is an arm. It's short but it looks like what there is is almost all of what there ever was, like it came off at the shoulder. There are green flies around its bloody end. Callme is still humming and has tossed a couple pieces onto the poncho. I pick the arm up by the unbloody hand and it is like shaking hands with a snake. I'm careful not to touch the fingers. I fling the arm onto the pile that must be most of two guys now. Or women. Pops is back, white and old-looking.

Callmeblack sits down and spits a lot between his boots, but doesn't puke. The head that had been hanging by a thread of skin onto the body Pops carried is between Callmeblack and me and we both see it at the same time. It is most of a face, but half of it is turned into the muddy trail so it looks like a mask except for the flies. Callmeblack and I both look at it and then at each other and he looks back between his boots and half spits, half retches. I kick the head good; the face sails a foot off the ground and lands at the top of the pile, then rolls over the top. I'm glad it doesn't end up looking at me.

Eltee and Pops are about to fold the poncho over their pile and tie it shut.

"Let's be damn sure they're about the same weight."

"I pretended I was splitting a hundred pounds of Cambodian Red weed, man. I eyeballed it like I didn't know which half was mine, I—"

"OK, OK, OK. Shut up."

Peacock looks hurt. His tattoo is showing. I don't think it's raining. I think what is coming down is dripping off the canopy. Peacock's face is an eggshell color. In fact the light is all like that, the color of a dirty white dog.

I take as much air into my lungs as I can. I walk second, behind Prophet, who is carrying one of the captured rifles. Peacock has the other end of the poncho; then Pops and Callmeblack carrying the other sling, and Eltee is walking last. We tried slinging the weight on vines, in hopes that it would be easier carrying, but that didn't work because the trail is so sharp in places that the vines were too long to turn without the lead guy having to stop and turn around. So I twist the corners of the poncho together and use both hands to shoulder my end. Prophet helped me sling my rifle with shoelaces so it at least hangs in front of me and will be possible to get at, if it comes to that.

Eltee stays quite a ways back from the rest of us. Incredibly, he has the radio, the Sixty, and an extra rifle, and he has to pull rear security. I can't breathe normally – it's more like taking a gulp of air in and walking until it's used up, then gasping again, like I've swum too far away from shore. The going is slow and seems noisy. For a while we walk on a fairly level trail and our footing is solid, but the weight gets to us and we have to rest. When we set the poncho down the flies all seem to catch up and swirl into the holes between the snaps on the ponchos. The blood still isn't dried, so when I pick up the knot that makes my handle the blood squeezes out, and some runs down my arms.

After fifteen minutes my back begins to throb. Trying to walk mostly downhill now and still trying to keep the poncho fairly level to make it easier on Peacock strains my muscles and makes me aware of the spots I slept on last night. I'm constantly gasping for breath, and the bag keeps swinging, so I have to struggle to keep my balance. I come to the edge of my endurance. I want to cuss and throw something. I want to destroy. Finally, the slippery knot comes out of my grasp and the sling falls. Without looking back, because I am so goddamn out of touch, I keep walking, dragging the poncho behind me. It slides easily enough through the mud and makes a small sound like a brake rubbing against a bicycle tire. We don't go on like that very long before Prophet stops us and points at a swale below: Checkpoint Bravo. I simply fall down, gasping so hard I wonder if it's possible to catch up on the air I'm missing. I lie there with my eyes closed, listening to the others catching their breath and the buzzing of the flies.

It is almost as though I am asleep, momentarily, because the sound of the flies begins to sound like a song. Honest to God: song. I hear snatches of nursery rhymes, and church choirs and classical music, and the ditty that is the commercial for life insurance. . . . When my breathing gets closer to normal the smell of reality fights its way back, and once again the predominant sound is that of the bloodthirsty flies swarming. I could puke in my own lap and it wouldn't make any difference right now.

From a sitting position I can see cleanly through the foliage. Checkpoint Bravo is a small, almost round, hollow. It looks marshy. Instead of jungle it looks like tall grass. I wonder how deep the water is. My breath has come back now. I see that one of the arms has worked its way partly out from the bundled poncho. I'll be damned if I'm going to touch it again to shove it back in. I don't care if it gets lost.

Eltee is making radio contact; otherwise there isn't any sound except for the goddamn flies. It takes skill to use an Army PRC-25 radio so that it isn't like hearing a supermarket speaker, and Williams is good enough that I can barely hear the transmissions from five meters away. I semi-want to smoke a cigarette, but my hands smell like the blood that is drying black now. I try to think of what it resembles, having squeezed out of the poncho, but it doesn't look like anything but what it is. Thinking about carrying these pieces of dinks to a helicopter landing in a small clearing makes the fear come hard, but who is there to tell I'm scared, and what good would it do?

"Wait till we hear the birds coming," Eltee says. "Pass it on."

We whisper it ahead and Prophet nods. His face is rock-hard and dirty. The way the light is hitting his face I can see the rivulets of sweat running over the wax we use to camouflage our faces. He must have mostly used the stick of green. I used brown. The camo sticks are precious; it is one more thing the Army never has enough of. Prophet sits quietly looking around all 360 degrees, spitting silently between his teeth. I'm glad the rain has quit, at least for now; I'm still cold, or shivering from fear. It isn't long before we hear the helicopters coming. We don't want to give our position away any sooner than we absolutely have to, so we don't move until the birds are in sight. As high up as they stay, their sound is no louder than the noise of the flies. Everybody chambers a round, ready to pick up the ponchos for the last time.

"Pray, baby," Peacock whispers. I nod. I do. I breathe as deeply as I can.

The clearing is a shade different in color than everything else around, darker green. From this distance, it looks like briars, but I've never seen briars over here. I can tell the grass is too tall for a bird to come down in, that we'll have to hack some of it away. My question is what we're going to do with these fucking bodies in the meantime.

Eltee is working his way up the line, whispering to everybody as he goes by. It strikes me as absurd, although not stupid, for him to be whispering. I don't know, maybe he isn't whispering: it's as though all I can hear are the goddamn flies, like a radio station off the air for the night – a low *hummmzaat*. As Williams moves up he walks hunchback to carry the weight of the radio and his ruck. My ruck straps cut into me all the way down the trail but I didn't notice the ache much until now. Fuck it. All we have to do is get these slings another thirty meters, cut a hole, and catch a ride back to the LZ.

Before I know it Eltee is at my side.

"We're about ready to move," he says. His face is like a clock, so exact is the intensity of his expression. I notice his nose looks wider on one side than the other. I listen to what he says, and it seems to echo through my mind even after he's gone. We'll be up and move fast. We're dropping the ponchos on signal. Three of us go out for security and the other three hack a hole in the weeds, good enough for a bird to come down long enough to pick up the pieces; when that bird is gone another will come in to get us. I'm going to be one who cuts.

My mouth feels like I've been sucking a rubber band. The nylon pads in my shoulder straps look freshly painted, and I feel conscious of every one of the five hundred more seconds we sit there. Eltee is still up front with Prophet. I can see them both through a hole in the trees. Eltee is talking on the radio some of the time. First one of their faces shows in the hole, then the other – like watching TV.

We're up. I get the signal from Prophet and pass it on to Peacock, who passes it on. Now we pick up the sling. Heavy. This time I'm very conscious of my rifle swinging in front of me. I've gotten used to having it in my hand when I want it, and right now I want it.

We hustle. Everything hurts – my back, my head where the steel pot has bounced, my arms from having the sling behind me, my feet, my chafing asshole, even my goddamn eyes from sleeplessness. I hurt inside too. I feel like a piece of shit, like nobody. But on we go. In five minutes we're into the swamp. The water is quickly up to my shins, finally up to my balls. It doesn't feel warm or cold, not thick or clean, just wet and one more thing to fight against. We drop the poncho and it half sinks. The flies are there, like they're pissed off. They swirl in a wave like paint flung off a roller. I hate them. Air escapes from the poncho and comes to the surface, and the water turns the color of aged leather from the mud we stir up and the blood.

By pure luck, we stumble upon a hard bottom so we can stand up and hack away at the bushes exactly at water level. It's me, Prophet, and Peacock. We don't speak. We give it hell, our machetes swirling. The bushes are mostly easy to cut, and it doesn't take long to hack a ten-foot by ten-foot hole down to the waterline, and it isn't long after that that the bird arrives.

It comes over the tree line like a hotrod cresting some country hill, then settles over us with the motion that only helicopters have, a gliding sort of motion, with its tail swerving from side to side. The machine gunners give us a long peace sign. We half carry, half float the ponchos over. It takes four of us to get them out of the water and into the bird. As we're loading the second, trying to keep the chopped-up grass and water out of our eyes and struggling to keep our footing, rounds begin pelting the windshield of the helicopter and either the pilot or the copilot gets hit. I dive into the water and weeds and futilely try to keep my rifle up.

Rounds begin to ricochet all over hell. The gunners open up, firing directly over our heads into the tree line. The shell casings come off the gun in a perfect arc, and some of them land on the grass we have cut that floats on the water. I'm disoriented and afraid to fire because I don't know where anybody else is, but I get my safety off and try to be careful to keep the barrel pointed up while I work my way, staying oh-so-low, away from where the bird is. I glance quickly at it and I can see the gunner taking the vibration of his gun with exact concentration. There is scurrying behind him and either the other gunner or a crew chief is leaned into the cockpit, probably aiding the pilot. I catch sight of Peacock, who has his Sixty at shoulder height. He is pouring rounds out toward the tree line.

The helicopter gets up and hovers for only an instant before it banks slightly and takes off away from the tree line we're facing. It circles and comes back over, low, stirring up the water and cut weeds. It passes over the tree line and both gunners fire continually. Then it comes back again and keeps a steady stream of rounds slashing into the tree line.

Eltee is yelling and signaling to make a circle. He has the radio mike in his hand. His rifle is slung downward and the AK is strapped to the radio. Prophet and Callme come out of the weeds behind him and run as best they can through the water until they reach the edge of our cut. Pops and I begin making it toward the cleared spot from opposite sides. Pops's face is covered with blood. I can't tell if he has been hit or not. Just as I get to where I intend to stop there is an explosion a few meters on the other side of Peacock, then another one, then two more. Mortars. The bursts hit the swamp in tandems now. First, two beyond us; then two in front of us. Peacock is trying to move back to our position but he has to get down every time a mortar lands. They bracketed, and have the range on those tubes now, so I expect the next rounds to come right on top of us. The helicopter is still hanging above the tree line, blasting it.

Four more mortars. The first two are off target but the

second ones land almost right on top of Lieutenant Williams, maybe twenty meters away from me on the other side of the clearing. He screams. The wave of water from the mortar's concussion passes by me and there is still shit in the air. Pops slips out of his ruck and begins to work his way toward Eltee. Everybody else begins to pump rounds into the tree line. I fire about where the helicopter is working out because I thought I saw a muzzle flash come from somewhere near there. As I am looking I see one for sure, a few feet off the ground. I squeeze three or four rounds off at where I saw it, then have to change magazines and when I look up again, the spot is being torn apart by the bird's Sixties. I cheer to myself. *Kill the fuckers.* I expect more mortars any time.

Pops is coming back toward us. He has the radio in one hand and is dragging Eltee behind him in a sort of backward-walking fireman's carry. Eltee is no longer screaming. A second helicopter comes over the opposite tree line. Eltee is dead.

The first helicopter continues working on the tree line and the second one comes at us rapidly. We all make a break for it. I go to Pops to help him. Together, we manage to get to the bird with our gear and the body. He didn't live past the scream. More than half of that handsome black face has been ripped back toward his skull. As long as the body was in the water the blood didn't show much, but when we are loaded and drag the body in after us, a pool of blood the color of fire spreads across the floor. We're all in, we're up, we head away from the tree line, high above which the bird with the ponchos full of bodies now hovers. Exhaustion hits and my body feels like a wet paper bag.

Jesus, there's no way to describe the ride. We get up fast, over a set of mountains, then up again. Riding along on the vibration of the bird is like being wind-rocked in a hammock. The five of us are sitting toward the front. I am leaning against the aluminum wall that defines the cockpit; the machine gunner is between me and the open door; past him

I can see a patch of sky and beyond that mountains, mountains, mountains.

The sound of the rotor is steady: *rum thump thump rum thump thump*.

God, I stink. I've been sweating into these same clothes for at least ten days; I've been wallowing around in swamp water.

My mind just roams around like my eyes. The door gunner on my side is dark-complexioned and stocky. His mustache is trimmed and just a dab of black hair shows below the headset helmet. The back of his helmet has something painted on it but I can't read it. Across from me, against the wall on the other side of the doorway to the cockpit, Pops is slumped in a heap. He's filthy. There is a line of mud that runs from the top of his head, over his face and through his mustache, through the hair on his belly, and down to his pants. His shirt is unbuttoned and his flak jacket isn't hooked. Just a trace of a paunch hangs over the belt loops. He looks thinner now than he did just a month ago.

The others are leaning against whatever there is to lean against, and toward the back is Eltee's body. I stare at it, and it doesn't seem like he could be dead. I can't see his head that is half mincemeat now and I can't really believe he will never move again. Dead. Goddamn dead. It could've been anybody. He got a mortar; the dinks weren't going for the radio and they weren't going for him because he was an officer. They were just going for anybody and trying to disable the helicopters. I wonder who will have to write a report up on this mission, and I wonder what Lieutenant Williams's family will find out.

Thump rump kathump kathump. We are descending. I have to sit up straight to see the Z below us and I feel so tired. As we come down we scoot toward the door. It isn't easy because the bird isn't level and the ruck seems to weigh more than ever. I'm so tired. I just want to lie down. It seems like there should be more waiting for us than this goddamn hill full of holes. This, my man, is home for now. Eltee doesn't even have this.

Fifty feet up, then thirty. It's like working on a high, high ladder. The guys on the ground all move away from the pad and cover their eyes. Parts of C-ration cartons whirl up as high as we are and dive through the crazy air currents like bats going after insects in a porch light. All the dudes on the ground are wearing flak jackets, and a lot of them have helmets on. The landing pad is built out of sandbags, and from a few feet up it reminds me of a caned chair seat. We settle between two big slings of ammunition. After the bird shuts down to a low speed, guys start again at unloading the slings and carrying the ammo away. Most of it is for our mortars and artillery. The rounds come in wooden boxes about two feet long.

Over by the big guns are stacks of ammo crates, and guys are carrying these empties away to fill full of sand and build hooches.

The CO comes over to the bird with his face down. He is a stern-looking guy, maybe thirty years old. His expression isn't mean-looking but it sure as hell isn't joyful. He reaches up and helps us off the bird, just puts his hand under our rucks. When he helps me off he is already looking at whoever is behind me.

"There's coffee over there," he says to all of us. "I want to see the whole squad in a few minutes."

We all drop our rucks as soon as we're far enough away from the pad. Getting the ruck off is like taking a good shit. It's cloudy and there's dust in the air from something. Since we've been out, there has probably been a couple thousand sandbags filled. Some are laid into flat parapet walls and some of the hooches are getting to be deep enough for roofs. Ammo crates and full sandbags make squat, solid walls.

Most of three companies are on the Z now and it has spread out like a carnival parking lot. When we started to dig in, we were on the outside of the perimeter but now the perimeter has moved out in all directions.

There are two guys sitting near the coffeepot smoking and waiting for us. They have been humping ammo from the pad. "Hey, what is it."

"It is a muthafucker," Pops says. It seems like a long time since I have heard his voice.

"You guys the squad that got some dinks last night?"

"Yeah, four. How bad was it here?"

"Bad, man. Mostly incoming, but they almost broke through on the other side of the hill. Over there." The guy points to our right.

"Charlie put some shit in here last night," the other guy says. He emphasizes "put" by pounding his rifle's butt plate against the ammo crate he has his feet resting on.

"Eighty-twos?"

"Mostly."

"He was keying on that side of the hill. We were over there, the other side, and everything went over us, wounded one guy out on LP. Alpha Company got it the worst. I heard six KIAs and twenty wounded."

"Our Eltee ate an eighty-two round."

"Dead?"

"Fuckin'-A dead."

"Anybody else get hit?"

"Nope. Freaky. We were loading those goddamn dinks and Charlie walked about a dozen rounds in."

"Bravo Company is going to move out that direction."

"You guys from Bravo?"

"Yeah. We aren't even dug in, but they keep trying to stick us on ammo detail."

"Well, man, Charlie's out there. Even though it musta been bad here last night, I'd rather be here tonight."

"Dig it, but at least our whole company's going out."

I'm surprised the coffee tastes good. C-ration coffee sucks; this came from a big urn shaped like a fire hydrant. There are some shit-green food cans lined up behind the coffee, but it looks like the food must have come in sometime yesterday because some of the cans have shrapnel in them. After I get my coffee I sit down on a pile of sandbags that have been filled but not tied off yet. I can see the bad side of the Z, where there must be twenty shallow craters. The thing I didn't expect to see is the shrapnel holes everywhere and even a few pieces of shrap. There's none nearby but I can see it glint in the sun in a few paths.

Big guns sound somewhere. I wonder what time it is. The sun is still a little above the west ridge of mountains. I'd guess it will be dark in four hours. I wonder if these guys from Bravo are going to try to get dug in tonight. I look at them and try to see the fear that I know is somewhere in their faces.

One guy is Italian-looking. He is sitting on one of the melomite cans, sipping coffee from his canteen cup.

"Eltee didn't have a shot at it," Callme says.

I don't feel like saying anything. I helped float his body through the water. I flash on the body over there in the bird in a pool of blood. The CO is just starting back from the pad. Even though there isn't any dust flying now, he still walks with his face down. Somebody is leaning into the helicopter. Slowly, the rotor starts to turn, and when the CO gets to us the bird is starting off. We all have to shield ourselves from the shit that flies around. When I look up, the CO is looking at Peacock, who's still looking down. So the CO looks right at me.

"What's your name, soldier?"

"Gabriel Sauers, sir."

"Tell me about it."

"About the patrol?"

"Yeah, from the time you made contact."

"Well . . ." I don't know what to say. Talking to an officer always bothers me. Eltee was an officer though, too. "Well," I say again, "it all happened awful fast. We were set up on a trail, and me and Callme were pretty close together and the rest of them were spread out. Peacock was ahead of us with the Sixty. We heard them coming and somebody blew the claymores. I could see the explosion and action. I emptied a clip and reloaded. That's all I know."

"Did you hear anything afterwards?"

"Nothing, sir."

"Who's the squad leader?"

"I am," Pops says. He doesn't add "sir."

"What's your name, Sergeant?"

"Pops," he says. He has undone his pants and is standing there talking to the CO with his dick out, rubbing one finger all around the jungle rot on his balls. I notice the CO has rot too, on his neck.

"You have anything to add, Pops?"

"I don't think Eltee Williams should be dead."

"What are you saying, soldier?"

"I think somebody fucked up back here. Those dinks were in pieces no bigger than these damn sandbags and there was no reason to bring 'em back here, but we hadda goddamn carry 'em down the fuckin' hill and into that clearing. Any-fuckin'-body woulda known the dinks were gonna drop some shit in there, but if we coulda got right in and right out of the edge of it, then Eltee wouldn't have gotten fuckin' killed. They walked 'em right in on us."

"Sergeant, your squad killed four enemies who might be responsible for killing ten GIs. That's what you have to think of. And" – he puts his hand on Pops's hand, which is still on his nuts, and looks around at all of us – "I understand how you feel. There's nothing I can do about it. Echo Company didn't make the decision, you know that. Listen, I *know* how you feel."

The way he says it, the way he looks around at all of us with a tiny little frown, the way he gives Pops's ball-handling wrist an additional shake . . . something makes me think he *does* know how Pops feels, and probably how I feel even if I don't. I feel something in my throat. Prophet spits, Callme spits, Peacock spits. The CO turns to leave and spits. I spit.

Khe Sanh: Life in the V Ring

John T. Wheeler

Wheeler reported Vietnam for AP. The Viet Cong and North
Vietnamese Army 'Tet Offensive 'against South Vietnam began
on January 30 1968.

Associated Press, 12 February 1968

Khe Sanh, Vietnam (AP) – The first shell burst caught the
Marines outside the bunkers filling sandbags. More explod-
ing rockets sent showers of hot fragments zinging. The
Americans dove for cover.

"Corpsman! Corpsman!"

The shout came from off to the right.

"We've got wounded here!"

"Corpsman! Corpsman!" The shouts now came from the
distance. You could see the men dragging a bleeding buddy
toward cover.

Inside the bunkers the Marines hugged their legs and
bowed their heads, unconsciously trying to make themselves
as small as possible. The tempo of the shelling increased and
the small opening to the bunker seemed in their minds to
grow to the size of a barn door. The 5,000 sandbags around
and over the bunker seemed wafer thin.

Although it could increase their chances of survival only
minutely, men shifted their positions to get closer to the
ground.

Some measured the angle to the doorway and tried to wiggle a bit more behind those next to them.

There were no prayers uttered aloud. Two men growled a stream of profanity at the North Vietnamese gunners who might snuff out their lives at any moment.

Near misses rocked the bunker and sent dirt cascading down everyone's neck.

Outside the random explosions sent thousands of pounds of shrapnel tearing into sandbags and battering already damaged messhalls and tent areas long ago destroyed and abandoned for a life of fear and filth underground.

This is the life in the V Ring, a sharpshooter's term for the inner part of the bull's eye. At Khe Sanh the V Ring for the North Vietnamese gunners neatly covers the bunkers of Bravo Company, 3rd Reconnaissance Battalion. In three weeks, more than half the company had been killed or wounded. It was recon's bad luck to live in an area bordered by an ammunition dump, a flightline loading area, and the 26th Marine Regiment's command post.

Shrapnel and shell holes cover the area. The incoming rounds could hardly be noticed once the barrage stopped, such is the desolation.

And then the shells did stop. Silent men turned their faces from one to the other. Several men scrambled out of the bunker to see if more dead or wounded men from their unit were outside. Medics scurried through the area, crouching low.

Inside one bunker a Marine returned to his paperback book, a tale of Wild West adventure. Another man whose hand had stopped in the midst of strumming a guitar resumed playing. Two men in a card game began flipping the soggy pasteboards again.

The shelling wasn't worth discussing. It was too common-place and none from Bravo Company had been hit this time. Like jungle rot, snipers and rats, artillery fire was something to be hated and accepted at the same time.

But the shellfire had taken its toll. Minutes before the

barrage opened, Army Spec. 4 William Hankinson had drifted off from the other members of his communications team assigned to this Marine base.

When the first shell hit, he dived into a Marine bunker. After the explosions stopped, he talked with the Marines awhile before starting back to his bunker.

There were no prayers uttered aloud. Two men growled a stream of profanity at the North Vietnamese gunners who might snuff out their lives at any moment.

Near misses rocked the bunker and sent dirt cascading down everyone's neck.

Outside the random explosions sent thousands of pounds of shrapnel tearing into sandbags and battering already damaged messhalls and tent areas long ago destroyed and abandoned for a life of fear and filth underground.

A white-faced Leatherneck joined the group.

"You look kind of sick," a Marine buddy said. "What happened?"

"The whole Army bunker got wiped out," he replied. "Jesus, what a mess."

Hankinson started to run toward the smashed bunker where his friends' shattered bodies lay. Marines caught and blocked him. Then with a tenderness not at all out of place for hardened fighting men, they began to console the Army specialist, a man most had never spoken to before that day.

One dud mortar round was half-buried in the runway of the airstrip. Planes carrying priority supplies had to be waved off until the round could be removed.

Two demolition experts raced from shelter with fire axes and chopped it out of the aluminum sheet runway. Neither would give his name. Both had told their families they were safely out of the war zone.

"An awful lot of Marines are big liars on that point," one said.

The men of No. 2 gun, Charlie Battery, didn't think of cover when the shelling began. After what they had been through when the main ammunition dump 200 yards away exploded during an earlier barrage, "This is coasting," one gunner said.

And alone of the Marines at Khe Sanh, the artillery could fire back at the enemy. No. 2 gun, commanded by Cpl Anthony Albo, kept pouring out 105mm rounds even though a shell splinter had started a fire in the gun's ready ammo bunker.

At Charlie Med, the main casualty clearing station, wounded were coming in. Some were on stretchers, some hobbled by themselves, some were hauled in across the shoulder of a comrade.

One prayed, a few cried, some were unconscious. Many showed shock on their faces.

In between shellings, Lance Cpl Richard Noyes, 19, of Cincinnati, Ohio, roughhoused on the dirt floor of his bunker with a friend. Noyes lives with five buddies in the center of the V Ring. The war was pushed far into the background for a moment as ripples of laughter broke from the tangled, wrestling forms.

Then the first shell of a new barrage hit.

Both men recoiled as if a scorpion had been dropped between them. Even though they were underground in a bunker, everyone put on helmets. Across the front of his "brain pot", Noyes long ago had written in ink, "God walks with me."

A blank stare in the eyes of some is not uncommon at Khe Sanh where the Communists have fired up to 1,500 rounds of rockets, artillery and mortar shells in a single day.

It is called the 1,000-yard stare. It can be the sign of the beginning of combat fatigue.

For Noyes and thousands of others at this surrounded combat base, the anguish is bottled up within tolerable limits.

Noyes had had luck, lots of it. A rocket once drove through the bunker's sandbags and exploded, killing 4 and wounding 14 of the 20 men inside. Noyes was slightly wounded.

It was Noyes' second Purple Heart. One more and he automatically would be sent out of Vietnam under Marine regulations. Noyes doesn't want the third medal.

Despite heavy casualties, the survivors of the recon company are frightened but uncowed. When the call for stretcher bearers comes, the young Marines unhesitatingly begin wriggling through the opening in their bunker to help.

At night the men in Noyes' bunker sit and talk, sing, play cards, almost anything to keep from being alone with their thoughts. During a night when more than 1,000 rounds hit Khe Sanh, Noyes turned to a buddy and said:

"Man, it'll be really decent to go home and never hear words like incoming shells, mortars, rifles, and all that stuff. And the first guy who asks me how it feels to kill, I'll ..." A pause. Then: "You know, my brother wants me to go duck hunting when I get home. Man, I don't want to even see a slingshot when I get out of here."

Lt C.J. Slack of Carlsbad, Calif., said: "When I get back to California, I'm going to open a bar especially for the survivors of Khe Sanh. And any time it gets two deep at that bar, I'll know someone is lying."

Noyes smokes heavily and his hands never seem to be entirely still. Looking at the side of a cigarette pack, Noyes said with a wry smile, "Caution, Khe Sanh may be hazardous to your health. Oh, man, yeah."

Still later, he called out, "Okay, we're going to sing now. Anyone who can't sing has to hum. Because I said so. Okay, let's hear it."

Lance Cpl Richard Morris, 24, of North Hollywood, Calif., began playing a guitar. Two favorites that night were "Five Hundred Miles" and "Where Have All the Flowers Gone?"

A hard emphasis accompanied the verse that went: "Where have all the soldiers gone? To the graveyard every one. When will they ever learn? When will they ever learn?"

Finally the two small naked light bulbs were turned out and the Marines struggled toward sleep.

My Lai

Seymour Hersh

Hersh's investigation of the My Lai massacre on 16 March 1968 by US troops won him a Pulitzer Prize.

Nobody saw it all. Some, like Roy Wood, didn't even know the extent of the massacre until the next day. Others, like Charles Sledge, who served that day as Calley's radioman, saw more than they want to remember.

But they all remember the fear that morning as they climbed onto helicopters at LZ Dotti for the assault on Pinkville. They all remember the sure knowledge that they would meet face-to-face for the first time with the enemy.

Calley and his platoon were the first to board the large black Army assault helicopters. They were heavily armed, each man carrying twice the normal load of rifle and machine-gun ammunition. Leading the way was Calley, who had slung an extra belt of M16 rifle bullets over his shoulder. There were nine helicopters in the first lift-off, enough for the first platoon – about twenty-five men – and Captain Medina and his small headquarters unit of three radiomen, some liaison officers and a medic. It was sunny and already hot when the first helicopter started its noisy flight to My Lai 4. The time was 7:22 A.M.; it was logged by a tape recorder at brigade headquarters. A brief artillery barrage had already begun; the My Lai 4 area was being "prepped" in anticipation of that day's search-and-destroy mission. A few heavily armed helicopters were firing thousands of small-caliber bullets into the area by the time Calley and his men landed in a soggy rice paddy 150 meters west of the hamlet. It was harvest season; the green fields were thick with growth.

The first platoon's mission was to secure the landing zone and make sure no enemy troops were left to fire at the second wave of helicopters – by then already airborne from LZ Dotti. As the flight of helicopters hovered over the landing area, the door gunners began spraying protective fire to keep the enemy – if he were there – busy. One of the helicopter's pilots had reported that the LZ was "hot," that is, Viet Cong were waiting below. The first platoon came out firing. But after a moment some men noticed that there was no return fire. "I didn't hear any bullets going past me," recalled Charles Hall, a machine gunner that day. "If you want to consider an area hot, you got to be fired on."

The platoon quickly formed a perimeter and secured the landing zone. Sergeant Cowen spotted an old man. Sledge was a few yards to Cowen's right: "We came to a well and there was a VC. We thought it was a VC. He was standing and waving his arms. Cowen fell back and said, 'Shoot the so-and-so.' I fired once, and then my [rifle] magazine fell out." Paul Meadlo noted that "the gook was standing up shaking and waving his arms and then he was shot." Allen Boyce saw it a little differently: "Some guy was in a rice field, doing something to a rice plant. He looked up and he got it. That was the most confused operation I ever went on. Just everything was screwed up."

By this time those Viet Cong who were in the area had slipped away. Some local supporters of the guerrillas also left, but they did not go too far. They watched as Charlie Company went through My Lai 4.

After about twenty minutes the second flight of helicopters landed, and the fifty men of the second and third platoons jumped off. Gary Garfolo heard the helicopter blades make sharp crackling sounds as they changed pitch for the landing. "It was a 'pop, pop, pop' sound like a rifle. Lots of us never even heard a hot LZ before. We knew we were going into a hot place. This got their adrenalin going." The men were quickly assembled. Calley's first platoon and Lieutenant Stephen Brooks' second platoon would lead the sweep into the hamlet – Calley to the south, and Brooks to the north. The third platoon, headed by Lieutenant Jeffrey La Crosse, would be held in reserve and move in on the heels of the other men. Captain Medina and his headquarters unit would move with the third platoon and then set up a command post (CP) inside to monitor the operation and stay in touch with other units. Charlie Company was not alone in its assault; the other two companies of Task Force Barker set up blocking positions to the north and south. They were there to prevent the expected Viet Cong troops from fleeing.

The My Lai 4 assault was the biggest thing going in the American Division that day. To get enough airlift, Task Force Barker had to borrow helicopters from other units throughout the division. The air lanes above the action were carefully allotted to high-ranking officers for observation. Barker monitored the battle from the 1,000-foot level. Major General Samuel Koster, commanding general of the division, was allotted the air space at 2,000 feet. His helicopter was permanently stationed outside his door at division headquarters twenty-one miles to the north, waiting to fly him to the scene of any action within minutes. Oran K. Henderson, commander of the 11th Brigade, was given the top spot – at 2,500 feet. All of the helicopters were to circle counterclockwise over the battle area. Flying low, beneath the 1,000-foot level, would be the gunships, heavily armed helicopters whose mission was to shoot down any Viet Cong soldiers attempting to escape.

Brigade headquarters, sure that there would be a major battle, sent along two men from the Army's 31st Public Information Detachment to record the event for history. Jay Roberts of Arlington, Virginia, a reporter, and photographer Ronald L. Haeberle of Cleveland, Ohio, arrived with the second wave of helicopters and immediately attached themselves to the third platoon, which was bringing up the rear.

The hamlet itself had a population of about 700 people, living either in flimsy thatch-covered huts – "hootches," as the GIs called them – or in solidly made red-brick homes, many with small porches in front. There was an east-west footpath just south of the main cluster of homes; a few yards further south was a loose surface road that marked a hamlet boundary. A deep drainage ditch and then a rice paddy marked the eastern boundary. To the south of My Lai 4 was a large center, or plaza area – clearly the main spot for mass meetings. The foliage was dense: there were high bamboo trees, hedges and plant life everywhere. Medina couldn't see thirty feet into the hamlet from the landing zone.

The first and second platoons lined up carefully to begin the hundred-meter advance into My Lai 4. Walking in line is an important military concept; if one group of men gets too far in front, it could be hit by bullets from behind – those fired by colleagues. Yet even this went wrong. Ron Grzesik was in charge of a small first-platoon fire team of riflemen and a machine gunner; he took his job seriously. His unit was supposed to be on the right flank, protecting Calley and his men. But Grzesik's group ended up on Calley's left.

As Brooks' second platoon cautiously approached the hamlet, a few Vietnamese began running across a field several hundred meters on the left. They may have been Viet Cong, or they may have been civilians fleeing the artillery shelling or the bombardment from the helicopter gunships. Vernado Simpson, Jr., of Jackson, Mississippi, saw a man he identified as a Viet Cong soldier running with what seemed to be a weapon. A woman and a small child were running with him. Simpson fired . . . again and again. He killed the woman and the baby. The man got away. Reporter Roberts saw a squad of GIs jump off a helicopter and begin firing at a group of people running on a nearby road. One was a woman with her children. Then he saw them "shoot two guys who popped up from a rice field. They looked like military-age men . . . when certain guys pop up from rice fields, you shoot them." This was the young reporter's most dangerous assignment. He had never been in combat before. "You're scared to death out there. We just wanted to go home."

The first two platoons of Charlie Company, still unfired upon, entered the hamlet. Behind them, still in the rice paddy, were the third platoon and Captain Medina's command post. Calley and some of his men walked into the plaza area in the southern part of the hamlet. None of the people was running away; they knew that U.S. soldiers would assume that anyone running was a Viet Cong and would shoot to kill. There was no immediate sense of panic. The time was about 8 A.M. Grzesik and his fire team were a few meters north of Calley; they couldn't see each other because of the dense vegetation. Grzesik and his men began their usual job of pulling people from their homes, interrogating them, and searching for Viet Cong. The villagers were gathered up, and Grzesik sent Meadlo, who was in his unit, to take them to Calley for further questioning. Grzesik didn't see Meadlo again for more than an hour.

Some of Calley's men thought it was breakfast time as they walked in; a few families were gathered in front of their homes cooking rice over a small fire. Without a direct order, the first platoon also began rounding up the villagers. There still was no sniper fire, no sign of a large enemy unit. Sledge remembered thinking that "if there were VC around, they had plenty of time to leave before we came in. We didn't tiptoe in there."

The killings began without warning. Harry Stanley told the C.I.D. that one young member of Calley's platoon took a civilian into custody and then "pushed the man up to where we were standing and then stabbed the man in the back with his bayonet . . . The man fell to the ground and was gasping for breath." The GI then "killed him with another bayonet thrust or by shooting him with a rifle . . . There was so many people killed that day it is hard for me to recall exactly how some of the people died." The youth next "turned to where some soldiers were holding another forty- or fifty-year-old man in custody." He "picked this man up and threw him down a well. Then [he] pulled the pin from a M26 grenade and threw it in after the man." Moments later Stanley saw "some old women and some little children – fifteen or twenty of them – in a group around a temple where some incense was burning. They were kneeling and crying and praying, and various soldiers . . . walked by and executed these women and children by shooting them in the head with their rifles. The soldiers killed all fifteen or twenty of them . . ."

There were few physical protests from the people; about eighty of them were taken quietly from their homes and herded together in the plaza area. A few hollered out, "No VC, No VC." But that was hardly unexpected. Calley left Meadlo, Boyce and a few others with the responsibility of guarding the group. "You know what I want you to do with them," he told Meadlo. Ten minutes later – about 8:15 A.M. – he returned and asked, "Haven't you got rid of them yet? I want them dead." Radioman Sledge, who was trailing Calley, heard the officer tell Meadlo to "waste them." Meadlo followed orders: "We stood about ten to fifteen feet away from them and then he [Calley] started shooting them. Then he told me to start shooting them. I started to shoot them. So we went ahead and killed them. I used more than a whole clip – used four or five clips." There are seventeen M16 bullets in each clip. Boyce slipped away, to the northern side of the hamlet, glad he hadn't been asked to shoot. Women were huddled against their children, vainly trying to save them. Some continued to chant, "No VC." Others simply said, "No. No. No."

Do Chuc is a gnarled forty-eight-year-old Vietnamese peasant whose two daughters and an aunt were killed by the GIs in My Lai 4 that day. He and his family were eating breakfast when the GIs entered the hamlet and ordered them out of their homes. Together with other villagers, they were marched a few hundred meters into the plaza, where they were told to squat. "Still we had no reason to be afraid," Chuc recalled. "Everyone was calm." He watched as the GIs set up a machine gun. The calm ended. The people began crying and begging. One monk showed his identification papers to a soldier, but the American simply said, "Sorry." Then the shooting started. Chuc was wounded in the leg, but he was covered by dead bodies and thus spared. After waiting an hour, he fled the hamlet.

Nguyen Bat, a Viet Cong hamlet chief who later defected, said that many of the villagers who were eating breakfast outdoors when the GIs marched in greeted them without fear. They were gathered together and shot. Other villagers who were breakfasting indoors were killed inside their homes.

The few Viet Cong who had stayed near the hamlet were safely hidden. Nguyen Ngo, a former deputy commander of a Viet Cong guerrilla platoon operating in the My Lai area, ran to his hiding place 300 meters away when the GIs came in shooting, but he could see that "they shot everything in sight." His mother and sister hid in ditches and survived because bodies fell on top of them. Pham Lai, a former hamlet security guard, climbed into a bunker with a bamboo top and heard but did not see the shootings. His wife, hidden under a body, survived the massacre.

By this time, there was shooting everywhere. Dennis I. Conti, a GI from Providence, Rhode Island, later explained to C.I.D. investigators what he thought had happened: "We were all psyched up, and as a result, when we got there the shooting started, almost as a chain reaction. The majority of us had expected to meet VC combat troops, but this did not turn out to be so. First we saw a few men running . . . and the next thing I knew we were shooting at everything. Everybody was just firing. After they got in the village, I guess you could say that the men were out of control."

Brooks and his men in the second platoon to the north had begun to systematically ransack the hamlet and slaughter the people, kill the livestock and destroy the crops. Men poured rifle and machine-gun fire into huts without knowing – or seemingly caring – who was inside.

Roy Wood, one of Calley's men who was working next to

Brooks' platoon, stormed into a hut, saw an elderly man hiding inside along with his wife and two young daughters: "I hit him with my rifle and pushed him out." A GI from Brooks' platoon, standing by with an M79 grenade launcher, asked to borrow his gun. Wood refused, and the soldier asked another platoon mate. He got the weapon, said, "Don't let none of them live," and shot the Vietnamese in the head. "These mothers are crazy," Wood remembered thinking. "Stand right in front of us and blow a man's brains out." Later he vomited when he saw more of the dead residents of My Lai 4.

The second platoon went into My Lai 4 with guns blazing. Gary Crossley said that some GIs, after seeing nothing but women and children in the hamlet, hesitated: "We phoned Medina and told him what the circumstances were, and he said just keep going. It wasn't anything we wanted to do. You can only kill so many women and children. The fact was that you can't go through and wipe out all of South Vietnam."

Once the first two platoons had disappeared into the hamlet, Medina ordered the third platoon to start moving. He and his men followed. Gary Garfolo was caught up in the confusion: "I could hear heavy shooting all the time. Medina was running back and forth everywhere. This wasn't no organized deal." So Garfolo did what most GIs did when they could get away with it. "I took off on my own." He ran south; others joined him. Terrified villagers, many carrying personal belongings in wicker baskets, were running everywhere to avoid the carnage. In most cases it didn't help. The helicopter gunships circling above cut them down, or else an unfortunate group ran into the third platoon. Charles West sighted and shot six Vietnamese, some with baskets, on the edge of My Lai 4: "These people were running into us, away from us, running every which way. It's hard to distinguish a mama-san from a papa-san when everybody has on black pajamas."

West and his men may have thought that these Vietnamese were Viet Cong. Later they knew better. West's first impression upon reaching My Lai 4: "There were no people in the first part . . . I seen bodies everywhere. I knew that everyone was being killed." His group quickly joined in.

Medina – as any combat officer would do during his unit's first major engagement – decided to move his CP from the rice paddy. John Paul, one of Medina's radiomen, figured that the time was about 8:15 A.M. West remembered that "Medina was right behind us" as his platoon moved inside the hamlet. There are serious contradictions about what happened next. Medina later said that he did not enter the hamlet proper until well after 10 A.M. and did not see anyone kill a civilian. John Paul didn't think that Medina ever entered the hamlet. But Herbert Carter told the C.I.D. that Medina did some of the shooting of civilians as he moved into My Lai 4.

Carter testified that soon after the third platoon moved in, a woman was sighted. Somebody knocked her down, and then, Carter said, "Medina shot her with his M16 rifle. I was fifty or sixty feet away and saw this. There was no reason to shoot this girl." The men continued on, making sure no one was escaping. "We came to where the soldiers had collected fifteen or more Vietnamese men, women and children in a group. Medina said, 'Kill every one. Leave no one standing.' " A machine gunner began firing into the group. Moments later one of Medina's radio operators slowly "passed among them and finished them off." Medina did not personally shoot any of them, according to Carter, but moments later the captain "stopped a seventeen- or eighteen-year-old man with a water buffalo. Medina told the boy to make a run for it," Carter told the C.I.D. "He tried to get him to run but the boy wouldn't run, so Medina shot him with his M16 rifle and killed him . . . I was seventy-five or eighty meters away at the time and I saw it plainly." At this point in Carter's interrogation, the investigator warned him that he was making very serious charges against his commanding officer. "What I'm telling is the truth," Carter replied, "and I'll face Medina in court and swear to it."

If Carter was correct, Medina walked first into the north side of My Lai 4, then moved south with the CP to the hamlet plaza and arrived there at about the same time Paul Meadlo and Lieutenant Calley were executing the first group of villagers. Meadlo still wonders why Medina didn't stop the shooting, "if it was wrong." Medina and Calley "passed each other quite a few times that morning, but didn't say anything. I don't know if the CO gave the order to kill or not, but he was right there when it happened ... Medina just kept marching around."

Roberts and Haeberle also moved in just behind the third platoon. Haeberle watched a group of ten to fifteen GIs methodically pump bullets into a cow until it keeled over. A woman then poked her head out from behind some brush; she may have been hiding in a bunker. The GIs turned their fire from the cow to the woman. "They just kept shooting at her. You could see the bones flying in the air chip by chip." No one had attempted to question her; GIs inside the hamlet also were asking no questions. Before moving on, the photographer took a picture of the dead woman. Haeberle took many more pictures that day; he saw about thirty GIs kill at least a hundred Vietnamese civilians.

When the two correspondents entered My Lai 4, they saw dead animals, dead people, burning huts and houses. A few GIs were going through victims' clothing, looking for piasters. Another GI was chasing a duck with a knife; others stood around watching a GI slaughter a cow with a bayonet.

Haeberle noticed a man and two small children walking toward a group of GIs: "They just kept walking toward us ... you could hear the little girl saying, 'No, no ...' All of a sudden the GIs opened up and cut them down." Later he watched a machine gunner suddenly open fire on a group of civilians – women, children and babies – who had been collected in a big circle: "They were trying to run. I don't know how many got out." He saw a GI with an M16 rifle fire at two young boys walking along a road. The older of the two – about seven or eight years old – fell over the first to protect him. The GI kept on firing until both were dead.

As Haeberle and Roberts walked further into the hamlet,

Medina came up to them. Eighty-five Viet Cong had been killed in action thus far, the captain told them, and twenty suspects had been captured. Roberts carefully jotted down the captain's statistics in his notepad.

The company's other Vietnamese interpreter, Sergeant Duong Minh, saw Medina for the first time about then. Minh had arrived on a later helicopter assault, along with Lieutenant Dennis H. Johnson, Charlie Company's intelligence officer. When he saw the bodies of civilians, he asked Medina what happened. Medina, obviously angry at Minh for asking the question, stalked away.

Now it was nearly nine o'clock and all of Charlie Company was in My Lai 4. Most families were being shot inside their homes, or just outside the doorways. Those who had tried to flee were crammed by GIs into the many bunkers built throughout the hamlet for protection – once the bunkers became filled, hand grenades were lobbed in. Everything became a target. Gary Garfolo borrowed someone's M79 grenade launcher and fired it point-blank at a water buffalo: "I hit that sucker right in the head; went down like a shot. You don't get to shoot water buffalo with an M79 every day." Others fired the weapon into the bunkers full of people.

Jay Roberts insisted that he saw Medina in My Lai 4 most of the morning: "He was directing the operations in the village. He was in the village the whole time I was – from nine o'clock to eleven o'clock."

Carter recalled that some GIs were shouting and yelling during the massacre: "The boys enjoyed it. When someone laughs and jokes about what they're doing, they have to be enjoying it." A GI said, "Hey, I got me another one." Another said, "Chalk up one for me." Even Captain Medina was having a good time, Carter thought: "You can tell when someone enjoys their work." Few members of Charlie Company protested that day. For the most part, those who didn't like what was going on kept their thoughts to themselves.

Herbert Carter also remembered seeing Medina inside the hamlet well after the third platoon began its advance: "I saw all those dead people laying there. Medina came right behind me." At one point in the morning one of the members of Medina's CP joined in the shooting. "A woman came out of a hut with a baby in her arms and she was crying," Carter told the C.I.D. "She was crying because her little boy had been in front of their hut and . . . someone had killed the child by shooting it." When the mother came into view, one of Medina's men "shot her with an M16 and she fell. When she fell, she dropped the baby." The GI next "opened up on the baby with his M16." The infant was also killed. Carter also saw an officer grab a woman by the hair and shoot her with a .45-caliber pistol: "He held her by the hair for a minute and then let go and she fell to the ground. Some enlisted man standing there said, 'Well, she'll be in the big rice paddy in the sky.'"

In the midst of the carnage, Michael Bernhardt got his first good look at My Lai 4. Bernhardt had been delayed when Medina asked him to check out a suspicious wood box at the landing zone. After discovering that it wasn't a booby trap, Bernhardt hurried to catch up with his mates in the third platoon. He went into the hamlet, where he saw Charlie Company "doing strange things. One: They were setting fire to the hootches and huts and waiting for people to come out and then shooting them. Two: they were going into the hootches and shooting them up. Three: they were gathering people in groups and shooting them. The whole thing was so deliberate. It was point-blank murder and I was standing there watching it. It's kind of made me wonder if I could trust people any more."

Grzesik and his men, meanwhile, had been slowly working their way through the hamlet. The young GI was having problems controlling his men; he was anxious to move on to the rice paddy in the east. About three quarters of the way through, he suddenly saw Meadlo again. The time was now after nine. Meadlo was crouched, head in his hands, sobbing like a bewildered child. "I sat down and asked him what happened." Grzesik felt responsible; after all, he was supposed to be a team leader. Meadlo told him Calley had made him shoot people. "I tried to calm him down," Grzesik said, but the fire-team leader couldn't stay long. His men still hadn't completed their sweep of My Lai 4.

Those Vietnamese who were not killed on the spot were being shepherded by the first platoon to a large drainage ditch at the eastern end of the hamlet. After Grzesik left, Meadlo and a few others gathered seven or eight villagers in one hut and were preparing to toss in a hand grenade when an order came to take them to the ditch. There he found Calley, along with a dozen other first platoon members, and perhaps seventy-five Vietnamese, mostly women, old men and children.

Not far away, invisible in the brush and trees, the second and third platoons were continuing their search-and-destroy operations in the northern half of My Lai 4. Ron Grzesik and his fire team had completed a swing through the hamlet and were getting ready to turn around and walk back to see what was going on. And just south of the plaza, Michael Bernhardt had attached himself to Medina and his command post. Shots were still being fired, the helicopters were still whirring overhead, and the enemy was still nowhere in sight.

One of the helicopters was piloted by Chief Warrant Officer Hugh C. Thompson of Decatur, Georgia. For him, the mission had begun routinely enough. He and his two-man crew, in a small observation helicopter from the 123rd Aviation Battalion, had arrived at the area around 9 A.M. and immediately reported what appeared to be a Viet Cong soldier armed with a weapon and heading south. Although his mission was simply reconnaissance, Thompson directed his men to fire at and attempt to kill the Viet Cong as he wheeled the helicopter after him. They missed. Thompson flew back to My Lai 4, and it was then, as he told the Army Inspector General's office in June, 1969, that he began seeing wounded and dead Vietnamese civilians all over the hamlet, with no sign of an enemy force.

The pilot thought that the best thing he could do would be to mark the location of wounded civilians with smoke so that the GIs on the ground could move over and begin treating some of them. "The first one that I marked was a girl that was wounded," Thompson testified, "and they came over and walked up to her, put their weapon on automatic and let her have it." The man who did the shooting was a captain, Thompson said. Later he identified the officer as Ernest Medina.

Flying with Thompson that day was Lawrence M. Colburn, of Mount Vernon, Washington, who remembered that the girl was about twenty years old and was lying on the edge of a dyke outside the hamlet with part of her body in a rice paddy. "She had been wounded in the stomach, I think, or the chest," Colburn told the Inspector General (IG). "This captain was coming down the dyke and he had men behind him. They were sweeping through and we were hovering a matter of feet away from them. I could see this clearly, and he emptied a clip into her."

Medina and his men immediately began moving south toward the Viet Cong sighted by Thompson. En route they saw the young girl in the rice paddy who had been marked by the smoke. Bernhardt had a ground view of what happened next: "He [Medina] was just going alone . . . he shot the woman. She seemed to be busy picking rice, but rice was out of season. What she really was doing was trying to pretend that she was picking rice. She was a hundred meters away with a basket . . . if she had a hand grenade, she would have to have a better arm than me to get us . . . Medina lifted the rifle to his shoulder, looked down the barrel and pulled the trigger. I saw the woman drop. He just took a potshot . . . he wasn't a bad shot. Then he walked up. He got up real close, about three or six feet, and shot at her a couple times and finished her off. She was a real clean corpse . . . she wasn't all over the place, and I could see her clothing move when the bullets hit . . . I could see her twitch, but I couldn't see any holes . . . he didn't shoot her in the head." A second later,

Bernhardt remembered, the captain "gave me a look, a dumb shit-eating grin."

By now it was past 9:30 A.M. and the men of Charlie Company had been at work for more than two hours. A few of them flung off their helmets, stripped off their heavy gear, flopped down and took a smoke break.

THE DAY – PART II

Hugh Thompson's nightmare had only begun with the shooting of the girl. He flew north back over the hamlet and saw a small boy bleeding along a trench. Again he marked the spot so that the GIs below could provide some medical aid. Instead, he saw a lieutenant casually walk up and empty a clip into the child. He saw yet another wounded youngster; again he marked it, and this time it was a sergeant who came up and fired his M16 at the child.

Larry Colburn, who was just eighteen years old at the time, noticed that "the infantrymen were killing everything in the village. The people didn't really know what was happening. Some of them began walking out of there and the GIs just started going up to them and shooting them all in the back of the head." He added, "We saw this one woman hiding there. She was alive and squatting; she looked up when we flew over. We dropped a smoke marker. When we came back she was in the same position – only she was dead. The back of her head was blown off. It had to be point-blank."

Thompson was furious. He tried unsuccessfully to radio the troops on the ground to find out what was going on. He then reported the wild firings and unnecessary shootings to brigade headquarters. All the command helicopters flying overhead had multi-channel radios and could monitor most conversations. Lieutenant Colonel Barker apparently intercepted the message and called down to Medina at the CP just south of the plaza. John Kinch of the mortar platoon heard Medina answer that he "had a body count of 310." The captain added, "I don't know what they're doing. The first platoon's in the lead. I am trying to stop it." A moment later, Kinch said, Medina called Calley and ordered, "That's enough for today."

Harry Stanley was standing a few feet away from Calley near some huts at the drainage ditch when the call came from Medina. He had a different recollection: "Medina called Calley and said, 'What the fuck is going on?' Calley said he got some VC, or some people that needed to be checked out." At this point Medina cautioned Calley to tell his men to save their ammunition because the operation still had a few more days to run.

It is not clear how soon or to whom Medina's order was given, but Stanley told the C.I.D. what Calley did next: "There was an old lady in a bed and I believe there was a priest in white praying over her . . . Calley told me to ask about the VC and NVA and where the weapons were. The priest denied being a VC or NVA." Charles Sledge watched with horror as Calley pulled the old man outside: "He said a few more words to the monk. It looked like the monk was pleading for his life. Lieutenant Calley then took his rifle and pushed the monk into a rice paddy and shot him point-blank."

Calley then turned his attention back to the crowd of Vietnamese and issued an order: "Push all those people in the ditch." Three or four GIs complied. Calley struck a woman with a rifle as he pushed her down. Stanley remembered that some of the civilians "kept trying to get out. Some made it to the top . . ." Calley began the shooting and ordered Meadlo to join in. Meadlo told about it later: "So we pushed our seven to eight people in with the big bunch of them. And so I began shooting them all. So did Mitchell, Calley . . . I guess I shot maybe twenty-five or twenty people in the ditch . . . men, women and children. And babies." Some of the GIs switched from automatic fire to single-shot to conserve ammunition. Herbert Carter watched the mothers "grabbing their kids and the kids grabbing their mothers. I didn't know what to do."

Calley then turned again to Meadlo and said, "Meadlo, we've got another job to do." Meadlo didn't want any more jobs. He began to argue with Calley. Sledge watched Meadlo once more start to sob. Calley turned next to Robert Maples and said, "Maples, load your machine gun and shoot these people." Maples replied, as he told the C.I.D., "I'm not going to do that." He remembered that "the people firing into the ditch kept reloading magazines into their rifles and kept firing into the ditch and then killed or at least shot everyone in the ditch." William C. Lloyd of Tampa, Florida, told the C.I.D. that some grenades were also thrown into the ditch. Dennis Conti noticed that "a lot of women had thrown themselves on top of the children to protect them, and the children were alive at first. Then the children who were old enough to walk got up and Calley began to shoot the children."

One further incident stood out in many GIs' minds: seconds after the shooting stopped, a bloodied but unhurt two-year-old boy miraculously crawled out of the ditch, crying. He began running toward the hamlet. Someone hollered, "There's a kid." There was a long pause. Then Calley ran back, grabbed the child, threw him back in the ditch and shot him.

Moments later Thompson, still in his helicopter, flew by. He told the IG what happened next: "I kept flying around and across a ditch . . . and it . . . had a bunch of bodies in it and I don't know how they got in the ditch. But I saw some of them were still alive." Captain Brian W. Livingston was piloting a large helicopter gunship a few hundred feet above. He had been monitoring Thompson's agonized complaints and went down to take a look for himself. He told a military hearing: "There were bodies lying in the trenches . . . I remember that we remarked at the time about the old Biblical story of Jesus turning water into wine. The trench had a grey color to it, with the red blood of the individuals lying in it."

By now Thompson was almost frantic. He landed his small helicopter near the ditch, and asked a soldier there if he could help the people out: "He said the only way he could help them was to help them out of their misery." Thompson took off again and noticed a group of mostly women and children huddled together in a bunker near the drainage ditch. He landed a second time. "I don't know," he explained, "maybe it was just my belief, but I hadn't been shot at the whole time I had been there and the gunships following hadn't . . ." He then saw Calley and the first platoon, the same group that had shot the wounded civilians he had earlier marked with smoke. "I asked him if he could get the women and kids out of there before they tore it [the bunker] up, and he said the only way he could get them out was to use hand grenades. 'You just hold your men right here,' " the angry Thompson told the equally angry Calley, " 'and I will get the women and kids out.' "

Before climbing out of his aircraft, Thompson ordered Colburn and his crew chief to stay alert. "He told us that if any of the Americans opened up on the Vietnamese, we should open up on the Americans," Colburn said. Thompson walked back to the ship and called in two helicopter gunships to rescue the civilians. While waiting for them to land, Colburn said, "he stood between our troops and the bunker. He was shielding the people with his body. He just wanted to get those people out of there." Colburn wasn't sure whether he would have followed orders if the GIs had opened fire at the bunker: "I wasn't pointing my guns right at them, but more or less toward the ground. But I was looking their way." He remembered that most of the soldiers were gathered alongside a nearby dyke "just watching. Some were lying down; some of them were sitting up, and some were standing." The helicopters landed, with Thompson still standing between the GIs and the Vietnamese, and quickly rescued nine persons – two old men, two women and five children. One of the children later died en route to the hospital. Calley did nothing to stop Thompson, but later stormed up to Sledge, his radioman, and complained that the pilot "doesn't like the way I'm running the show, but I'm the boss."

Gregory Olsen, who had watched the encounter from his

machine-gun position a few dozen meters away, said that "the next thing I knew Mitchell was just shooting into the ditch." At this point Grzesik and his fire team came strolling into the area; they had gone completely through the hamlet, had a break, and were now returning. It was about ten o'-clock. Grzesik saw bodies all over the northeastern quarter of My Lai 4. He glanced at the ditch. Suddenly Mitchell yelled, "Grzesik, come here." He walked over. Calley then ordered him to go to the ditch and "finish off the people." Grzesik had seen the helicopter carrying some wounded Vietnamese take off from the area a moment earlier; much later he concluded that Calley – furious with Thompson's intervention – wanted to make sure there were no more survivors in the ditch. Calley told Grzesik to gather his team to do the job. "I really believe he expected me to do it," Grzesik said later, with some amazement. Calley asked him again, and Grzesik again refused. The lieutenant then angrily ordered him to take his team and help burn the hootches. Grzesik headed for the hamlet plaza.

Thompson continued to fly over the ditch and noticed that some of the children's bodies had no heads. He landed a third time after his crew chief told him that he had seen some movement in the mass of bodies and blood below. The crew chief and Colburn began walking toward the ditch. "Nobody said anything," Colburn said. "We just got out." They found a young child still alive. No GIs were in the immediate area, but Colburn was carrying a rifle. The crew chief climbed into the ditch. "He was knee-deep in people and blood," Colburn recalled. The child was quiet, buried under many bodies. "He was still holding onto his mother. But she was dead." The boy, clinging desperately, was pried loose. He still did not cry. Thompson later told the IG, "I don't think this child was even wounded at all, just down there among all the other bodies, and he was terrified." Thompson and his men flew the baby to safety.

In other parts of My Lai 4, GIs were taking a break, or loafing. Others were systematically burning those remaining houses and huts and destroying food. Some villagers – still alive – were able to leave their hiding places and walk away. Charles West recalled that one member of his squad who simply wasn't able to slaughter a group of children asked for and received permission from an officer to let them go.

West's third platoon went ahead, nonetheless, with the killing. They gathered a group of about ten women and children, who huddled together in fear a few feet from the plaza, where dozens of villagers already had been slain. West and the squad had finished their mission in the north and west of the hamlet, and were looking for new targets. They drifted south toward the CP. Jay Roberts and Ron Haeberle, who had spent the past hour watching the slaughter in other parts of the hamlet, stood by – pencil and cameras at the ready. A few men now singled out a slender Vietnamese girl of about fifteen. They tore her from the group and started to pull at her blouse. They attempted to fondle her breasts. The old women and children were screaming and crying. One GI yelled, "Let's see what she's made of." Another said, "VC Boom, Boom," meaning she was a Viet Cong whore. Jay Roberts thought that the girl was good-looking. An old lady began fighting with fanatical fury, trying to protect the girl. Roberts said, "She was fighting off two or three guys at once. She was fantastic. Usually they're pretty passive . . . They hadn't even gotten that chick's blouse off when Haeberle came along." One of the GIs finally smacked the old woman with his rifle butt; another booted her in the rear.

Grzesik and his fire team watched the fight develop as they walked down from the ditch to the hamlet center. Grzesik was surprised: "I thought the village was cleared . . . I didn't know there were that many people left." He knew trouble was brewing, and his main thought was to keep his team out of it. He helped break up the fight. Some of the children were desperately hanging onto the old lady as she struggled. Grzesik was worried about the cameraman. He may have yelled, "Hey, there's a photographer." He remembered thinking, "Here's a guy standing there with a camera that you've never seen before." Then somebody said, "What do we do with them?" The answer was, "Waste them." Suddenly there was a burst of automatic fire from many guns. Only a small child survived. Somebody then carefully shot him, too. A photograph of the woman and child, with the young Vietnamese girl tucking in her blouse, was later published in *Life* magazine. Roberts tried to explain later: "It's just that they didn't know what they were supposed to do; killing them seemed like a good idea, so they did it. The old lady who fought so hard was probably a VC." He thought a moment and added, "Maybe it was just her daughter."

West was annoyed at the photographer: "I thought it was wrong for him to stand up and take pictures of this thing. Even though we had to do it, I thought, we didn't have to take pictures of it." Later he complained personally to Haeberle about it.

By now it was nearly 10:30 A.M. and most of the company began drifting aimlessly toward the plaza and the command post a few yards to the south. Their work was largely over; a good part of the hamlet was in flames. The villagers "were laying around like ants," William Wyatt remembered. "It was just like somebody had poisoned the water and everybody took a drink and started falling out."

Herb Carter and Harry Stanley had shed their gear and were taking a short break at the CP. Near them was a young Vietnamese boy, crying, with a bullet wound in his stomach. Stanley watched one of Captain Medina's three radio operators walk along a trail toward them; he was without his radio gear. As Stanley told the C.I.D., the radio operator went up to Carter and said, "Let me see your pistol." Carter gave it to him. The radio operator "then stepped within two feet of the boy and shot him in the neck with a pistol. Blood gushed from the child's neck. He then tried to walk off, but he could only take two or three steps. Then he fell onto the ground. He lay there and took four or five deep breaths and then he stopped breathing." The radio operator turned to Stanley and said, "Did you see how I shot that son of a bitch?" Stanley told him, "I don't see how anyone could just kill a kid." Carter got his pistol back; he told Stanley, "I can't take this no more . . ." Moments later Stanley heard a gun go off and Carter yell. "I went to Carter and saw he had shot himself in the foot. I think Carter shot himself on purpose."

Other children were also last-minute targets. After the scene with the women and children, West noticed a small boy, about seven years old, staring dazedly beside a footpath. He had been shot in the leg. "He was just standing there staring; I don't think he was crying. Somebody asked, 'What do we do with him?' " At this point West had remembered there had been an order from Captain Medina to stop the shooting. "I just shrugged my shoulders," West recalled, "and said, 'I don't know,' and just kept walking." Seconds later he heard some shots, turned around and saw the boy no longer standing on the trail.

Haeberle and Roberts were walking together on the edge of the hamlet when they also noticed the wounded child with the vacant stare. In seconds, Roberts said, "Haeberle, envisioning the war-torn-wounded-waif picture of the year, got within five feet of the kid for a close-up. He was focusing when some guy, just walking along, leveled his rifle, fired three times and walked away." Haeberle saw the shooting through the lens of his camera. "He looked up in shock," Roberts added. "He just turned around and stared. I think that was the thing that stayed in our mind. It was so close, so real, we just saw some kid blown away."

By then a helicopter, called in by Medina, had landed near the command post to fly out the wounded Carter. Sergeant Duong Minh, the interpreter who had angered Medina with his questions about the dead civilians, was also put aboard.

One of Haeberle's photographs shows the company medic, Nicholas Capezza of Queens, New York, bandaging Carter, with Medina and a radio operator, Rodger Murray of Waukegan, Illinois, in the background near a partially destroyed red-brick house. Medina was on the radio. William Wyatt remembered the scene; that was the first time he'd seen Medina that morning. Roy Wood also saw him then for the first time. Others recalled, however, that the captain had left his CP south of the plaza many times during the late morning to tour the northern and western sections, urging the men to stop the shooting and get on with the job of burning down the buildings. Some GIs from the second platoon, under Lieutenant Brooks, found three men still alive. Gary Crossley heard the GIs ask Brooks, "What do we do now?" The lieutenant relayed the question by radio to Medina. "Don't kill them," the captain said. "There's been too much of that already." Gary Garfolo remembered that Medina seemed frantic at times, literally dashing about the hamlet. "He was telling everybody, 'Let's start getting out – let's move out of here.' "

Roberts also thought that Medina "was all over." He and Haeberle had crossed from the south to the north side of the hamlet to look around, and saw the captain there. "Then Carter shot himself and Medina went back," Roberts said. At some point earlier in the morning, Roberts had watched some GIs interrogate an old man. He didn't know anything, and somebody asked the captain what to do with him. Medina "indicated he didn't care," Roberts said, "that the guy wasn't of any use to him, and walked away." The GIs shot the man. Sergeant Mitchell may have witnessed the same scene. He saw both Calley and Medina interrogating an old man; Mitchell thought he was a monk. "Four or five of us weren't far away. We were watching. The old monk mumbled something and Medina walked off. I looked away for a second, and when I looked back the old man had been shot and Calley was standing over him."

Richard Pendleton remembered Medina himself shooting a civilian that day. Pendleton was standing about fifty feet away from the captain sometime that morning – Pendleton isn't sure exactly when. Pendleton hadn't seen the captain earlier and he wondered what Medina thought about what was going on. "Medina was standing there with the rest of the

CP. It was right there in the open. I was watching." There was a small Vietnamese child, "the only one alive among a lot of dead people." He said he watched Medina carefully aim his M16 rifle at the child. "He shot him in the head, and he went down."

Pendleton may have been mistaken. There was a child shot near the command post that day, after Carter shot himself. Charles Gruver of Tulsa, Oklahoma, remembered vividly how it happened: he saw a small boy, about three or four years old, standing by a trail with a wound in his arm. "He just stood there with big eyes staring like he didn't believe what was happening. Then the captain's RTO [radio operator] put a burst of 16 [M16 rifle fire] into him." Ronald Grzesik also saw it. He was just watching the child when he heard a rifle shot; he looked back and saw that the radio operator was still in braced firing position. But Medina, Grzesik recalled, "was around the corner" in the command post at the time. Roberts also witnessed the shooting; he thought the toddler was searching through the pile of dead bodies for his mother or father, or a sister. He was wearing only a shirt. The impact of the M16 flung the small body backward onto the pile.

After that incident Grzesik said he went up to John Paul, one of Medina's radiomen, and told him what had been going on inside My Lai 5. Paul promptly asked him to tell the captain. Grzesik declined, thinking that Medina "was going to find out anyway if he walked up a few feet."

There were some small acts of mercy. A GI placed a blanket over the body of a mutilated child. An elderly woman was spared when some GIs hollered at a soldier just as he was about to shoot her. Grzesik remembered watching a GI seem to wrestle with his conscience while holding a bayonet over a wounded old man. "He wants to stab somebody with a bayonet," Grzesik thought. The GI hesitated . . . and finally passed on, leaving the old man to die.

Some GIs, however, didn't hesitate to use their bayonets. Nineteen-year-old Nguyen Thi Ngoc Tuyet watched a baby trying to open her slain mother's blouse to nurse. A soldier shot the infant while it was struggling with the blouse, and then slashed at it with his bayonet. Tuyet also said she saw another baby hacked to death by GIs wielding their bayonets.

Le Tong, a twenty-eight-year-old rice farmer, reported seeing one woman raped after GIs killed her children. Nguyen Khoa, a thirty-seven-year-old peasant, told of a thirteen-year-old girl who was raped before being killed. GIs then attacked Khoa's wife, tearing off her clothes. Before they could rape her, however, Khoa said, their six-year-old son, riddled with bullets, fell and saturated her with blood. The GIs left her alone.

There were "degrees" of murder that day. Some were conducted out of sympathy. Michael Terry, the Mormon who was a squad leader in the third platoon, had ordered his men to take their lunch break by the bloody ditch in the rear of the hamlet. He noticed that there were no men in the ditch, only women and children. He had watched Calley and the others shoot into that ditch. Calley seemed just like a kid, Terry thought. He also remembered thinking it was "just like a Nazi-type thing." When one soldier couldn't fire any more and threw down his weapon, "Calley picked it up." Later, during lunch, Terry and his men saw that some of the victims were still breathing. "They were pretty badly shot up. They weren't going to get any medical help, and so we shot them. Shot maybe five of them."

James Bergthold saw an old man who had been shot in both legs: "He was going to die anyway, so I figured I might as well kill him." He took his .45-caliber pistol (as a machine-gun ammunition carrier, he was entitled to one), carefully placed the barrel against the upper part of the old man's forehead and blew off the top of his head. Carter had watched the scene and remembered thinking that Bergthold had done the old man a favor. "If me and you were together and you got wounded bad," Carter later told an interviewer, "and I couldn't get you to a doctor, I'd shoot you, too."

Most of the shooting was over by the time Medina called a

break for lunch, shortly after eleven o'clock. By then Roberts
and Haeberle had grabbed a helicopter and cleared out of the
area, their story for the day far bigger than they wanted.
Calley, Mitchell, Sledge, Grzesik and a few others went back
to the command post west of My Lai 4 to take lunch with
Captain Medina and the rest of his headquarter's crew.
Grzesik recalled that at that point he'd thought there couldn't
be a survivor left in the hamlet. But two little girls showed up,
about ten and eleven years old. John Paul said they came in
from one of the paddies, where they apparently had waited
out the siege. "We sat them down with us [at the command
post]," Paul recounted, "and gave them some cookies and
crackers to eat." When a C.I.D. interrogator later asked
Charles Sledge how many civilians he thought had survived,
he answered, "Only two small children who had lunch with
us."

In the early afternoon the men of Charlie Company
mopped up to make sure all the houses and goods in My Lai
4 were destroyed. Medina ordered the underground tunnels
in the hamlet blown up; most of them already had been
blocked. Within another hour My Lai 4 was no more: its red-
brick buildings demolished by explosives, its huts burned to
the ground, its people dead or dying.

Michael Bernhardt later summarized the day: "We met no
resistance and I only saw three captured weapons. We had no
casualties. It was just like any other Vietnamese village – old
papa-sans, women and kids. As a matter of fact, I don't
remember seeing one military-age male in the entire place,
dead or alive. The only prisoner I saw was in his fifties."

The platoons pulled out shortly after noon, rendezvousing
in the rice paddies east of My Lai 4. Lieutenant Brooks' platoon had about eighty-five villagers in tow; it kept those of
military age with them and told the rest to begin moving
south. Following orders, Medina then marched the GIs
northeast through the nearly deserted hamlets of My Lai 5
and My Lai 6, ransacking and burning as they went. In one
of the hamlets, Medina ordered the residents gathered, and

then told Sergeant Phu, the regular company interpreter, to tell them, as Phu later recalled, that "they were to go away or something will happen to them – just like what happened at My Lai 4."

By nightfall the Viet Cong were back in My Lai 4, helping the survivors bury the dead. It took five days. Most of the funeral speeches were made by the Communist guerrillas. Nguyen Bat was not a Communist at the time of the massacre, but the incident changed his mind. "After the shooting," he said, "all the villagers became Communists."

When Army investigators reached the barren area in November, 1969, in connection with the My Lai probe in the United States, they found mass graves at three sites, as well as a ditch full of bodies. It was estimated that between 450 and 500 people – most of them women, children and old men – had been slain and buried there.

On December 1, one week after Paul Meadlo's startling television confession, the *Wall Street Journal* published an informal poll on My Lai 4 that its reporters had taken in cities across the nation. The results were interesting. Many of those interviewed refused to believe that the mass killings had taken place; others wondered why the incident was attracting so much attention.

"It was good," exclaimed a fifty-five-year-old elevator starter in Boston. "What do they give soldiers bullets for – to put in their pockets?" In Cleveland a woman defended the shooting of children: "It sounds terrible to say we ought to kill kids, but many of our boys being killed over there are just kids, too." A Los Angeles salesman said, "I don't believe it actually happened. The story was planted by Viet Cong sympathizers and people inside this country who are trying to get us out of Vietnam sooner." A teletype inspector in Philadelphia also said he didn't think it happened: "I can't believe our boys' hearts are that rotten." Not all of the 200 persons interviewed had such extreme attitudes, but only a handful said that what happened at My Lai 4 had changed their minds on the war.

Much of America's anger at the disclosures was directed toward the newspapers and television stations publicizing them. The *Cleveland Plain Dealer*, on the morning it published Ron Haeberle's shocking photographs of My Lai 4, received more than 250 telephone calls. About 85 percent of them said that the photographs should not have been published. "Your paper is rotten and anti-American," one woman said. Another asked, "How can I explain these pictures to my children?" When one of the photographs, depicting about twenty slain women and children in a ditch, was later published on the front page of the *Washington Star*, that paper received calls complaining that the photograph was obscene. The callers were alluding to the fact that some of the dead victims were unclothed. After his interview with Meadlo, CBS correspondent Mike Wallace received 110 telephone calls, all but two of them abusive. One viewer fired off a telegram saying: "Wallace is pimping for the protesters." A *New York Times* survey of some GIs serving in the Quang Ngai area near My Lai 4 found wholesale resistance to the idea that Charlie Company had massacred some civilians. "There's gotta be something missing," one GI complained. Another said, "The company must have been hit hard before the action."

In early December, American Legion members in Columbus, Georgia, home of Fort Benning, took a four-column newspaper advertisement in the local newspaper proclaiming support for Calley and Captain Medina. The advertisement accused newspapers and television of trying to "tear down America and its armed forces." A week later a group of former servicemen in Atlanta, Georgia, began a petition movement to get the Army to drop its charges against Calley. During a rally on December 14, James A. Smith, chief spokesman for the group, said that "no American would ever kill 109 people like that" and suggested that the Haeberle photographs were fake. About fifty to seventy-five persons attended the rally, far less than the two hundred expected, but Smith said his group had collected 3,000 signatures on the petition. A few days later Calley personally opened a bank account with the Fourth National Bank of Columbus to handle contributions to his defense. Within a month the bank received several hundred letters, and more than $1,200 was on deposit. Calley had by then reached the status of a celebrity in Columbus. Most of the citizens openly supported him; some used-car salesmen even put his name in lights in front of their lots, urging contributions to the Calley Defense Fund.

A statewide poll published shortly before Christmas by the *Minneapolis Tribune* showed that 49 percent of 600 persons interviewed there believed that the reports of mass murder at My Lai 4 were false. To another query, 43 percent said they were horrified when they first heard the story and decided that it wasn't true. A later *Time* magazine poll of 1,600 households indicated that 65 percent of the American public believed such incidents were bound to happen in any war; and an even greater percent of the public, asked about news media coverage, complained that the press and TV should not have reported statements by GIs prior to a court-martial. The Pentagon even produced a poll. Deputy Secretary of Defense David Packard showed a group of newsmen a public-opinion study which he said had been conducted in the upper half of South Vietnam, an area that includes Quang Ngai Province. It showed, Packard said, that "only 2.8 percent of the people disapprove of the behavior of American troops in their country."

By mid-January six American Legion posts in Jacksonville, Florida, announced plans to raise a $200,000 defense fund for Calley. The lieutenant was granted permission to leave Fort Benning and fly to Jacksonville for a fund-raising party. He was greeted like a hero. A few fellow passengers recognized him, tapped him on the shoulder as they climbed off the airliner and said, "Good luck, son." A newspaper poll of the citizens in Duval County (Jacksonville) showed that more than 71 percent thought the Army should drop its charges against Calley. Robert C. Lenten, commander of one of the local Legion posts, told newsmen, "We are not saying he is guilty or not guilty. We feel Lieutenant Calley has been condemned and vilified for performance of his duties in combat without benefit of the opportunity to defend himself." In February former Governor George Wallace of Alabama endorsed Calley publicly. They met for more than one hour in Montgomery, Alabama, on February 20, and then came out together to face a battery of reporters. Wallace said he was "proud" to meet Calley and added, "I'm sorry to see the man tried. They ought to spend the time trying folks who are trying to destroy this country instead of trying those who are serving their country." The 1968 Presidential aspirant said, "I've been shot at myself and there's nothing like it." Calley said little.

At Fort Benning, many of Calley's fellow officers were outraged by the murder charges. "They're using this as a goddamned example," one officer said. "He's a good soldier. He followed orders." Another said, "It could happen to any of us. He's killed and seen a lot of killing ... killing becomes nothing in Vietnam. He knew that there were civilians there, but he also knew that there were VC among them." A third officer, a West Point graduate, added, "There's this question – I think anyone who goes to Nam asks it. What's a civilian? Someone who works for us at day and puts on Viet Cong pajamas at night?"

One veteran of Vietnam told his local newspaper, in the aftermath of the My Lai 4 controversy, how he had witnessed Viet Cong prisoners being thrown out of helicopters during interrogation by U.S. GIs. He was quickly subjected to a barrage of abusive telephone calls. "You ought to take a helicopter ride with me," one man said. "I know just exactly what to do with guys like you. You should be the one taken up and dropped out." Another caller said, "Someone should burn your house down, and maybe they just will."

Protests were voiced also by the Hawks in Congress. Senator Allen Ellender, Louisiana Democrat, told a television interviewer that the Vietnamese who had been slain "got just what they deserved." Senator Ernest Hollings, South Carolina Democrat, publicly wondered if all soldiers who made "a mistake in judgment" were going to be tried "as common criminals, as murderers."

Senator Peter H. Dominick, Colorado Republican, led a number of legislators in attacks on the reporters who disseminated the news about My Lai 4, repeatedly accusing the news media of sensationalism and trial by press. In doing so, he singled out the interview with Meadlo and the publication in *Life* magazine of Haeberle's photographs. "They go too far," Dominick told the Senate on December 2, "when interviews of potential witnesses are carried on nationwide TV, when these interviews are republished in newspapers all across the country over and over, and when a nationwide magazine publishes photographs of a highly inflammatory, and, I might add, revolting nature . . ." He argued that the public's right to know was met in full by the Army's public release of the charges against Calley on September 6.

"Burning Flesh": The Memoir of a Naval Nurse

Maureen Walsh

In August of 1966 I took my oath in the new Federal Building in down-town Boston. After women's officer school, I went to Quonset Point, Rhode Island, to the naval air station there and spent two years, which was a varied experience, being around the planes and the ships as well as the naval station hospital. I had a lot of experience flying in the planes and went through the low pressure chambers so I could fly in jets. I got to spend a lot of time on the ships, especially the carriers. I was head nurse in the dependents' units and also the emergency room there, and then, because we were near Groton, Connecticut, got involved with submarine medicine as well.

At that point I was rather addicted to military nursing, and of course, the social life wasn't any small part of it as well. Vietnam was starting to become prominent in the military picture, and I decided that I would volunteer to go over, much to my mother's dismay. My chief nurse discouraged me. She said, "You know, you're very young. They're only taking people who are very experienced, and you shouldn't go near Vietnam unless you've had a lot of experience." I decided after I got to Vietnam that there was nothing in the United States that could ever prepare me for that, absolutely nothing. But I was adventuresome, and I decided, what the heck, might as well go. So, I entreatied the chief nurse to endorse my request. She did, and said, "I do it with a lot of reservation. I know that you can do the work, but I really worry about your lack of experience." Sure enough, three months later, I received orders. She was more surprised than anybody, but I wasn't; I said I knew I'd be going anyway, because that was my intent. Ever since I was a little kid I wanted to be a Navy nurse and be stationed at the naval academy – of course, I had all of this glamour idea. The other thing, I wanted to be in a war zone or someplace where I could really experience my skills, et cetera . . . .

Well, that bubble burst after I got over there. It was September of '68. The memory is very vivid. I remember coming in to the airport at Da Nang, and it was raining of course – we were coming into the monsoon season. We got off the plane and really went through a culture shock. Everybody had guns; people were lining up; there were people in the airport sleeping all over the place. There was nothing but artillery from one end of the airport to the next. There were a lot of Vietnamese people walking around very, very depressed-looking. Off in the distance we could hear the guns exploding, and I thought to myself, "My God, this is like a John Wayne movie." You could actually see the explosions going off in the hills. But the eerie thing about it was, people were walking around like automatons. The explosions were going on, but nobody was paying any attention. Every time something would explode, I could just feel my heart skip a beat; it was both exciting and very frightening.

We unloaded at what seemed to be an old courthouse. It was dusty but it was the only place where the inside was dry. We sat down to write out the endless papers that you have to fill out when you go from one place to another in the military. As the explosions were going on, the desks or the tables that we were writing on would raise up off the floor. And the guy who was talking to us was talking nonstop like this was just ordinary traffic going by outside.

Anyway, we got to our quarters, which was in the east end of Da Nang, right along the South China Sea. It was a beautiful place, paradoxically, very beautiful and very hostile at the same time. We were right off the beach, where Seabees were on one end of the compound and the Marine engineers on the other. Across the street there were helicopters and the Marine airfield, and then beyond that was the beach. Marble Mountain was to the left as we were looking out to sea and to the right was Monkey Mountain. Behind us there was a Vietnamese village, and probably about ten miles out there was another mountain range, Hivan Pass. The hospital was made up of Quonset huts. It was the largest combat casualty unit in the world at the time. I don't remember how many personnel were there. There were hundreds; it was like a little city in itself. We lived in a Quonset hut and, according to the standards of Vietnam, lived rather luxuriously. I mean, we had our own toilets – we even had a washing machine! We each had an individual room with the metal military beds and a desk, but at least we had privacy. The Marines and Seabees had made a patio out in the back with a fence surrounding it. We would often pull up a chair, grab a beer, and watch the war as we could see it going on in the mountains north and south of us. Our chief nurse let us rest for about twenty-four hours to go through the jet lag, and then we were hustled onto the wards.

Each unit, which was one Quonset hut, had five corpsmen, with about thirty to sixty patients. And each of the huts would be divided into orthopedics, surgery, medicine, intensive care, or whatever. There were several of these huts lined up, and each had a walkway entrance to it so we could get from one to the next. The walkways had bunkers along them. The Navy nurses, because we had so many corpsmen in each ward, would be responsible for like three hundred to three hundred fifty patients, and what we'd have to do is go from one building to the next, get the report from the corpsmen, and take care of the sickest patients.

The first two nights I was there we didn't have any incoming or anything, though we could hear it in the peripheral areas. But my introduction to Vietnam nursing was on the third night as I was walking outside, going from one building to the next, checking the patients – and I was feeling overwhelmed as it was. From the mountains behind us, the Viet Cong were sending in mortars and rockets, and I heard this tremendous roar go over my head. I never heard a rocket in my life. I didn't know whether it was a plane, or a helicopter – I couldn't imagine what it was. Phew! This red, flaming thing came flying over, and I thought, "Oh, my God, that thing's from outer space." Well, when I heard that whoosh I went into one of the bunkers, and I know that I did not reach the bottom, because I felt all this stuff crawling around down there. I think I hit bottom and bounced right back out. I knew they were rats; they had to be rats! I said to myself, "Dear God, am I going to get bit by a rat and have to go home, or am I going to get hit by the shrapnel up here?" I decided it would be more honorable to be hit by the shrapnel, such a choice! So I just kind of buried into the sidewalk, and as I was kissing the concrete I looked up to watch all of this action. As I turned my head to the right – we were sort of on a hill on a sand dune – I could see the Marine base receiving rockets. As they went in I could see the planes explode. Oh, my God, this was like a movie! I couldn't conceive that I was really there. I was a participant, but I still didn't feel like I was going to get hit, because I really wasn't there; it was total denial.

Finally, everything stopped and I didn't know whether to get up. Navy nurses wore white uniforms over there, and we were walking targets. The Vietnamese village – we called it "the vill" – the Viet Cong vill was right behind us. Often times our people would take sniper fire at night. I didn't know about the sniper fire – that came a few days later – but I took my white hat off. If I had had something to put around me I would've, because I knew instinctively I was a sitting duck out there. So I just got up and said, "Well, I guess I'm in Vietnam, and I've got to do the best I can," looked down to make sure I hadn't wet my pants, went on to the next building, and walked into the ward. Some of my corpsmen had been there six or seven months, and this was a routine night to them. I must've looked as white as my uniform, and they started laughing as I came into the unit. They started teasing me about getting into a little action already. I could've clobbered them. So I guess I got my initiation; that was it. I was frightened as hell, and I was excited, yet on the other hand, if I let the emotions run away with me, I would've been totally incapacitated.

As it was, I was fighting inexperience; my former chief nurse was right. I was really flying by the seat of my pants as far as going into these units and checking the patients. To make up for my inexperience, I'd read the chart, check all the IVs, dressings, and casts several times for each patient. Each person had enough "plumbing" to make the average plumber marvel. I mean, there were machines on every person – suction, respirators, monitors of all sorts – everybody had multiple intravenous fluids infusing, catheters, and all sorts of sundry tubes and drains. By the time you weed through that to find the poor individual under it all, you couldn't really make him out. It was incredible!

I really had to stifle the emotions in order to be able to focus in on what was happening to each and every one of those patients and to keep all of that data in mind, write everything down, as well as talk to all of the corpsmen. I didn't even know all of the corpsmen at that point; I didn't know all of the patients. I would hope and pray every time I would leave a unit to go to the next one that I wouldn't find so much devastation, because already I was overwhelmed from the other wards. But I found similar situations on every ward. I think I had five wards that were my responsibility. And that's what we did when we worked the night shift. I had so much responsibility and so much to do on each of the units that I couldn't worry about the extraneous goings on outside.

Nights were especially difficult because this was the time when people who were wounded would be very frightened – moaning and groaning and calling out. Marines were incredibly stoic. It was surprising that they didn't cry out more than they did. There were a lot of times when they died on us at night. I mean, I would go from one unit to the next and have three, four, five Marines die maybe in the period of one night. Some of them in my arms. I'd be holding them, and they'd be hanging on – "Oh, I don't want to die!" You have to say, "Well, God, I can't get involved, I can't get involved," but it's pretty damn hard not getting involved when you see a nineteen- or twenty-year-old blond kid from the Midwest or California or the East Coast screaming and dying. A piece of my heart would go with each! You knew that their families would be getting a visit from the Marine Corps two days later. It was all I could do to hold back the tears, and we did hold back a lot, which I think was very unhealthy. It started very early; we had no way to really let loose with each other. One of the things we found is that we were all so extremely busy that we didn't have *time* to let loose with each other. The other aspect was that there was some sort of a feeling with nurses at the time that we were all volunteers that went over there. Since we were volunteers, we had to take what we got and not complain about it. The "shut up and do your work" mentality.

We also had to put up with the hostile environment as well. Besides the incoming, there were the rats, there were the snakes, there were the monsoons. We would often go down to a ward that was flooded from the monsoons. We were taking care of patients . . . There'd be rats in the water; sometimes there'd be snakes there. That bothered me more than any-thing . . . We also took care of the Viet Cong and the NVA. This brought us down to the realities of war – there were young men there from the opposite side. They were the same age as our own fellas; most of them were even younger. They didn't want to be there any more than we did.

It took me about two days to realize that it was such a mis-take being over there. We were so pumped up when we went to Vietnam, so patriotic, so full of American idealism, and when we got over there, it was nothing but a sham. The war was going on – there was no sense to it, there was no sense of "Okay, we're going into a battle. We're going to take over some of the geography; we're going to hold it, then we'll go on to the next part; we'll take over that. Then there will be peace." Our guys would go in to a hill or a village, get the hell beat out of them, and then we would receive the casualties. The next day they would be pulled out of there. Then they'd go back another week; we'd take more casualties. It was like that for the entire time we were over there. Marines were getting shot, they were getting mutilated, and there was no purpose; there was no rhyme nor reason to it.

So besides dealing with our own emotions and then dealing with that, We were in conflict between anger and grief constantly. There was just no resolution to any of that. Even when we went into town there was evidence of the Vietnamese taking advantage of us. The black markets were set up all over the place; they were milking us from every single angle that you could imagine. But we took care of *them*, we took care of them well. I remember the Viet Cong were like jungle rats, surviving in the jungles. Their skin was scarred like leather. They were very unsocialized. The average twenty-year-old looked like he was forty, fifty, sixty years old. Some of them I became quite attached to. The NVA were more educated, and a lot of their officers were very fluent in English; some of them had studied in the States. God, they didn't want to be there any more than we did. What we found was that the women, the NVA and VC women, were very, very vicious in behavior. I remember one night I brought a dinner tray to one of them, and she was on a bed with two casts on her legs, having had abdominal and eye surgery and all of the usual plumbing. I gave the woman a tray and turned around to get a sheet, and she had picked up a fork and was going right into my back. I just turned around in time and knocked it out of her hand. That was typical of the female behavior – they never gave up; they tenaciously fought to escape.

I want to talk about the intensive care unit. The other units were nothing compared with what the intensive care units were like. Many times when we were on duty and there were a lot of casualties coming in, the doctors would necessarily be taken to the triage area. That left the nurses and the corpsmen to do the best we could on the units. We couldn't call the doctors to do some of the things that were physician-related. For instance, patients would pop bleeders on the ward; they would start bleeding under their dressings. What we would have to do is make decisions about . . . We'd have to go in and clamp off bleeders. And it was rather a touchy situation because, you know, it looks pretty clear when you're in the laboratory or the operating room, but if you're not a surgeon, it's pretty hard to tell one artery from a ureter. It was anxiety-producing, to say the least.

Several times when we would have incoming, the mortars would blow out our regular and emergency generators. Of about twenty patients in the ICU, there were usually ten to fifteen on respirators, with chest tubes, and when the electricity went off, you can just imagine what chaos ensued. We often had to do mouth-to-mouth or trach-to-trach breathing for these people until the emergency power came on. We would have a few ambubags. We'd be throwing them around like footballs from one end of the unit to the other. So we lost people that way too. It was so frustrating, and a lot of times we'd have to give up breathing because we were so exhausted we would have passed out. That happened four or five times when I was on duty.

One night I was walking through one of the units that was right off the helicopter pad, when a mortar came in and exploded. Shrapnel came in the door – went right by me, under my legs. Another piece came in as I was counting narcotics for one of the corpsmen at the medicine cabinet near the door. The shrapnel went through his eye and through his head, went through the medicine cabinet, exited through the unit on the other side, and lodged in the wall. God, that was awful, that was awful to see that.

Another night that we had some incoming, we were walking along the walkway and I saw one of the mortars hit smack-dead on one of our units; it exploded. There was not a lot of screaming and yelling, but mostly what really hit me was the stench, the burning flesh. The Marines never screamed, which is incredible, their training is incredible. I remember going into the ward. The lights were all out, so I couldn't see a thing, but we knew there was a lot of activity. I'm not so sure I would've been prepared to see immediately what was happening. I had a flashlight with me . . . opened the flashlight and there was just chunks of flesh and blood all over the wall. Wounded men had been wounded again in the unit. Four of our corpsmen were killed that night. One of our nurses that was out going from one unit to another got down just in time. The way the shrapnel came it would've decapitated her had she not been down. I don't know how any of our nurses missed getting hit – by some miracle.

There were times when, as I say, the doctors weren't immediately available, and we had to make major life-saving decisions. One night as a typical example, I was on a neurosurgery unit. We had a lot of casualties, and the doctors were all tied up in triage. I had a young man that was put on the unit, and the doctor said, "You've got to do the best you can with him." As soon as the doctor left, he went into respiratory distress, and I had to do a tracheostomy on him, and God, there was no equipment on the unit to do something like that – most of our patients went to the operating room to have something like that done. I just had to put a slit in his throat, and all I had was a ball-point pen; I had to unscrew that and put the tube of the pen into the trachea, which is a common thing actually – it's the only thing you had on you. There were a lot of those kinds of things going on that we had to do, things that we were never taught.

I'll never forget this one night. I was sitting next to this bed, and a young corpsman came in . . . and I looked at his name, of course. I had known him in the States. He was one of the fellows that was at the naval air station with me, but when I had seen him, I didn't recognize him because his wounds were so severe and numerous. There's no way you can save somebody like that, but the most incredible thing is that he was clear – he was talking with me; he knew who I was. I was holding the one hand that he had left, and as I was talking with him he said, "I know I'm not going to live." . . . I remember him telling me to contact his mother, and he was telling me how much he enjoyed our friendship, and he said, "Please don't leave me." This young man was losing blood at a tremendously quick rate, and what amazed me is that he was still so clear. He grabbed my hand and I talked to him for as long as possible, and I just felt that grip loosening and loosening and loosening. The only thing I could do was sit there and pray with him. I knew he was going to leave this holocaust; he was lucky. I just told him good-bye.

Many times I'd have fellows that would come in the ward – especially the Navy corpsmen, some of whom I had trained – and some of them had been stationed with me at the units back at Quonset Point. That was horrible, seeing those men come in wounded. They were just like brothers to us, because the Navy nurses and the Navy corpsmen and the Corps WAVES had a very close bond. We worked very very closely and went through a great deal together. You knew their families, where they came from – you knew everything about them. And to see them come in – they were just like having your own family, own brothers, get killed. Those are some of the memories in the intensive care unit.

It sounds like there was a lot of gore over there, but there were good times as well, in between. We used to have lulls in the war. When we had time, we played. When we were not too tired we used to go over to the officers' club. Once in a while, in the one day we had off a week – if we did have the day off – we would go over on the beach.

We did a lot of things, also, in the community. I volunteered to go on the civil action patrols. We went out a number of times with some of the corpsmen, Marines and physicians that used to volunteer to go into the villages to see patients. And my eyes were opened out there too – people living in these slovenly, dirty huts – dirt floors – with the chickens and the ducks. We'd go in there and deliver babies in the filth and the crap. We went to the orphanages, played with the kids, and took them to the beaches every now and then.

Some of us got in to town; it was more or less off limits – you know, we had to deal with the sniper fire and everything else. Most of the time we didn't tell the chief nurse we were going in. I had a friend who was a Korean; he would pick me up on his motorcycle, and we would go to the different restaurants downtown. It was a dead giveaway that I had been there, because of all the garlic and kim chee and everything else that they used – it was awful-smelling.

The saddest thing that happened for me over there too, among all those other things, was I lost my fiancé. He was a Marine pilot, and I was with him the night that he died; he was going on a mission. I was sitting in the officers' club, and I knew he wasn't coming back. I practically begged him not to go, but there's no way he couldn't go. It was his job, he had to go. And he was shot down. The worst thing was that I was not allowed to grieve for the whole time that I was there. . . . I don't know if any of the other nurses really knew about it. I told them, but it was just one of those things that you didn't – you couldn't share because everybody else had their own little world of grief. Quite frankly, each of my friends, each of the nurses out there, was just totally saturated with their problems, with their own fatigue. . . . And again, the stiff upper lip-type martyr syndrome of nursing didn't allow for that to happen. I think I was more able to talk to the other Navy and Marine friends that I had out there. We had quite a relationship with the Marines that were around us, they were always in our club or took us out. They were more or less our confidants. I think my Marine friends knew more about me than the people that I actually worked with. They used to pick us up with their jeeps. I remember going out on a date with somebody riding shotgun . . . rather a lot of fun. I'll never forget, one night I was going out to the officers' club with one of my friends, and it was kind of a strange sensation having somebody go on a date with a .45 around his waist and a rifle on the dash of the jeep. We went through this village and somebody took a potshot at us, and I remember the bullet coming in and over my head and behind his and out through the other end of the jeep. The attitude that we had: we looked at each other and laughed. What else could you do?

Well, what I can say is, I did come back from the holocaust, from the horrific experience over there, with a very peaceful philosophy, a changed value system about life and death. We came into California and when I saw that Golden Gate Bridge I wanted to reach down and hug it. And by God, when we got to Travis Air Force Base I got down on the ground and kissed it. I remember having to stop there overnight and going to this swimming pool where all the officers' wives and everybody were chitchatting about the day's events. I thought to myself, "My God, I have been in hell. These women are sitting around talking, and they have no concept of what is going on over there." I was extremely depressed. But I knew I was coming home the next day. I was met in Boston by my folks. It was great to see them. I had requested to come to Annapolis to fulfill my dream, but it was for a different reason this time – it was to come back here for peace and quiet. I didn't want to go back to one of these huge hospitals. I didn't want to see any more carnage. There's nothing more pastoral and more quiet and soothing than this water around here.

I had injured my back when I was about three weeks away from coming home. I didn't tell anybody. What had happened is that the rockets came in and I belly flopped on the floor and really tore up the back. It gave me a lot of trouble when I came here to the States, shortly after I started working on the units. The horrible part about it was that I had a lot of pain and problems that I was going through, and I couldn't get anybody to believe me. You know, they were essentially saying, "Well, you're just a baby" or "It's all in your head." For about three years I went through all this pain. I had gotten orders from Annapolis to Bethesda Naval Hospital, and I finally went through surgery. They found a lot of damage in the back, so at least that vindicated me, but still I decided right then and there I was going to get out of the service.

I really didn't know what I wanted to do. I had reached the epitome of what it was to be a nurse. There was nothing I could possibly do in the United States that would equal that experience. My fellow nurses that had been over there, incredibly, never asked me what I went through. We went through an ignominious kind of a situation where, a couple times in Annapolis and in Bethesda, I did some things on the units that were not considered nursing responsibilities – but out of reaction, you know, gut-level reactions – and got chastised for it. There was no level of understanding that maybe I knew what I was doing, maybe it was okay for me to do what I was doing even though it wasn't accepted protocol. It was clear to me that I could never go back to being the kind of nurse I was before I left for Vietnam.

When I had my back surgery, I was temporarily retired from the service, and I went back to school at the University of Maryland to get my degree in nursing. It just so happened that one of my professors had had acupuncture, and she had suggested that I go through it, because even after surgery, I still had a lot of pain. The Navy kind of wrote me off and said, "You know, it's a degenerative process. It's just going to get worse. You have a choice – you can retire; we'll separate you from the service – you have a choice." I accepted the fact that I wanted to be separated from the service, because I couldn't see a future in the Navy anymore. Somehow all the, as I call it, "poop and circumstance" didn't mean anything anymore. It was a lot of . . . bullshit as far as I was concerned.

I started having the acupuncture treatments, and pretty soon things started coming together for me – and things started unraveling at the same time. A lot of the old stuff had started coming back – from the war zone, you know, as it often does. Things clear out when you start taking a natural therapy such as that. I was getting better and better, and finally I realized that, "Hey, I went through my hell, went through my training and education; all of the experiences were for me to do something like this." I went back to school to study acupuncture. I went to England to study at the

College for Traditional Acupuncture in Oxford. Then I came back and did some clinical work in acupuncture and decided that I needed to deal with the spiritual role in healing as well. I went to Loyola College and got my master's degree in pastoral psych counseling to add to my bachelor's degree in nursing and the degrees I was getting in England for acupuncture.

I am now in my own private practice – doing nursing as well, but the kind of nursing that I know and feel ought to be done. I'm doing acupuncture and I'm doing counseling. I have one patient now who is a World War II veteran. He's gone through a lot of hell; he was a Navy man on a ship and had seen a lot of killing and wounding around him. This man is in his sixties, and he was still having these horrible, horrible dreams about the war. I sat down with him and listened to him and said, "Look, I know where you are; I know what you're feeling. I've been there." He looks at me as if saying, "I can't believe this is a woman who understands." Since he started treatments, he hasn't had any more of those dreams – after thirty, forty years. But it's because of my own feelings of where I need to deal with him – the holocaust he has been through – I can put myself in that position.

It really hurts every Veterans Day, when I see the Vietnam veterans rising up and getting so upset about not getting benefits and so forth. It starts opening wounds. You never forget what you've gone through. When the prisoners from Iran came back, I was shattered. It seems every time I get to a point where things have healed, or I think they have healed, something comes up in the news, and all the wounds start opening like Pandora's box. My question is, when is it all going to end? How much do you keep? I don't think you ever get rid of it. From all experiences, one can either become shattered or take the experience and incorporate it, learn from it, and make a positive thing from it. As a nurse, I really feel for the Vietnam veteran that came back to nothing. Most of us nurses were able to come back to professions; we weren't ostracized by bosses. We were just ignored, but we weren't ostracized by the fact that we were Vietnam veterans and therefore second-class citizens. I don't know, I have not really talked to any of my compatriots out there – surprisingly. I don't know what they're feeling or what they've done with their lives.

I was just thinking that my formative years in nursing have all been spent in the Navy. Whatever I've learned and gained and experienced, whether good, bad, or indifferent, I've learned in the Navy. That's what I took out into civilian life. A lot of my philosophy and the way I deal with problems is based on what I learned in the Navy. I may get upset at little things, but major crises – I'm just right there, cool, calm, collected. The ironic part is that when I came back I was supposed to forget the skills and the responsibility that had become second nature, so ingrained in me. I don't feel any regrets; I feel like I've pulled myself up. I've gone through school, I'm doing what I want to do, and I'm using the experiences probably with a deeper understanding than I ever would have, had I not gone over there.

With each person who goes out of my office from the acupuncture treatments in harmony, if they feel more peaceful, then somehow I've vindicated the war. I guess what I'm doing vicariously through them is coming to peace, coming to terms in a creative way. I certainly haven't prolonged the agony, I haven't prolonged the war, I haven't prolonged the chaos, but in fact have chosen something that is creating harmony, and I guess that's the testimony to my life now.

Fortunate Son

Lieutenant Lewis B. Puller, Jr.

Puller was the son of General "Chesty" Puller, the most decorated US Marine in history. Severely injured during a tour as a platoon leader in Vietnam, Puller Jr later developed an addiction to painkilling drugs and alcohol. He died by his own hand in 1994. This account comes from his autobiography, *Fortunate Son*.

Captain [Clyde] Woods devised an ambitious operation. . . . As Woods outlined the plan, in effect a cordon and search operation, for his platoon leaders and platoon sergeants a few days after our earlier conversation, I could see several of the men nod their heads and murmur approvingly. We could not be certain of engaging any of our enemies, of course, but our own risk was minimal. If our timing was right, the operation could turn out to be a turkey shoot.

. . . The word came down that the choppers were on their way, and I smoked one last cigarette before assembling the men by squads in their staging area.

As soon as our chopper alighted, the men raced to its yawning tailgate and piled aboard. I made certain we all were accounted for before taking a seat beside the door gunner and giving the crew chief the thumbs-up. As we lifted off, I felt the familiar pull in the pit of my stomach caused by our rapid ascent, and when we leveled off, I relaxed my hold on the side of the craft and watched the blur of foliage passing just beneath us. The sky was streaked with the red of the rising sun, and I realized, as I watched its reflection on the glassy surface of the South China Sea, that at least for today the rain was finished. The pilot nosed down in a clearing between the beach and Viem Dong after only a few minutes aloft, and we scrambled down the gangway and fanned out to take up our positions as he reversed his direction and banked up into the sky.

I concentrated as best I could on making certain that the two squads to my left were on line and in position to hook up with the platoon adjacent to them, but in the confusion and noise from the other helicopter around us, control was almost impossible. . . . After I had gotten my men on line, my next assignment was to connect with his location. Watson followed closely in my tracks with the radio, but the two nearest men to us were at least twenty meters away on either side and for all intents and purposes out of hearing range. As we maneuvered, I scanned the area to my immediate front, which I had been neglecting in my effort to maintain platoon integrity.

Suddenly I saw a squad of green-uniformed North Vietnamese soldiers begin running out of the village and in my direction. They had apparently panicked when the helicopters began landing and were now probing for a way out of the noose we were drawing around them. As they advanced toward me, I was unable to get the attention of the marines near me, and it dawned on me, to my horror, that I was the only obstacle between them and freedom. I raised my rifle to my shoulder and attempted to draw a bead on the lead soldier; but my first bullet was off the mark, and when I pulled the trigger the second time, my rifle jammed. By now the North Vietnamese soldiers had spotted me, and several of them fired wildly in my direction until they abruptly altered their advance and veered off to my left. Standing alone with a malfunctioning weapon and seven enemy soldiers bearing down on me, I was at once seized by a fear that was palpable and all-encompassing. My throat became as dry as parchment, and beads of perspiration popped out on my forehead before coursing down my face. I turned abruptly, with Watson in tow, and ran as fast as I could toward the safety of the bluffs above Viem Dong, where the company headquarters party was to be located.

A narrow trail led up the hill to the headquarters group, and as I approached, it never occurred to me that the thirty meters between my course and the commanders' position had not been secured. I knew only that the firepower advantage of the NVA squad I had just encountered would be neutralized if I could reach the men milling at the crest of the hill. With only a few meters left to cover in my flight, a thunderous boom suddenly rent the air, and I was propelled upward with the acrid smell of cordite in my nostrils.

When I landed a few feet up the trail from the booby-trapped howitzer round that I had detonated, I felt as if I had been airborne forever. Colors and sound became muted, and although there was now a beehive of activity around me, all movement seemed to me to be in slow motion. I thought initially that the loss of my glasses in the explosion accounted for my blurred vision, and I had no idea that the pink mist that engulfed me had been caused by the vaporization of most of my right and left legs. As shock began to numb my body, I could see through a haze of pain that my right thumb and little finger were missing, as was most of my left hand, and I could smell the charred flesh, which extended from my right wrist upward to the elbow. I knew that I had finished serving my time in the hell of Vietnam.

As I drifted in and out of consciousness, I felt elated at the prospect of relinquishing my command and going home to my wife and unborn child. I did not understand why Watson, who was the first man to reach me, kept screaming, "Pray, Lieutenant, for God's sake, pray." I could not see the jagged shards of flesh and bone that had only moments before been my legs, and I did not realize until much later that I had been forever set apart from the rest of humanity.

For the next hour a frantic group of marines awaited the medevac chopper that was my only hope of deliverance and worked at keeping me alive. Doc Ellis knelt beside my broken body and with his thumbs kept my life from pouring out into the sand, until a tourniquet fashioned from a web belt was tied around my left stump and a towel was pressed tightly into the hole where my right thigh had joined my torso. My watch and rifle were destroyed by the blast, and my flak jacket was in tatters; but I did manage to turn my undamaged maps and command of the platoon over to Corporal Turner during one of my lucid intervals. I also gave explicit orders to all the marines and corpsmen hovering around me that my wife was not to be told of my injuries until after the baby was born. There was, of course, no possibility of compliance with my command, but the marines ministering to me assured me that my wishes would be honored.

Because we were on a company-size operation, there were six corpsmen in the immediate area around Viem Dong, and each of them carried a supply of blood expanders, which were designed to stabilize blood pressure until whole blood could be administered. As word spread of my injuries, each of the company's corpsmen passed his expanders to Doc Ellis, who used up the last of them while my men slapped at my face, tried to get me to drink water, and held cigarettes to my lips in an attempt to keep me awake. When the chopper finally arrived, I was placed on a stretcher and gently carried to its entrance, where a helmeted crew chief and medevac surgeon helped me aboard. Someone had located my left boot which still contained its bloody foot and that, too, was placed on the stretcher with me.

As the chopper began its race toward the triage of the naval support hospital in Da Nang, I was only moments from death, but I remember thinking clearly before losing consciousness that I was going to make it. I never again saw the third platoon of Golf Company, a remarkable group of young men with whom I had had the most intense male relationships of my life, and I felt guilty for years that I had abandoned them before our work was finished. I was to feel even worse that I was glad to be leaving them and that, in my mind, I had spent my last healthy moments in Vietnam running from the enemy. I came to feel that I had failed to prove myself worthy of my father's name, and broken in spirit as well as body, I was going to have to run a different gauntlet.

. . . When I regained consciousness, I was in a clean bed with white sheets. An assortment of tubes carried liquids to and from my body, and when I reached up to remove the annoying one affixed to my nose, I found that I could not do so because both my hands were wrapped in bandages the size of boxing gloves. I understood the reason for my bandaged hands because I had seen my right hand with its missing thumb and little finger earlier, and I also knew that my left hand now retained only a thumb and half a forefinger. The word prehensile no longer applied to me. I did not yet know or knew only vaguely that I had lost my right leg at the torso and that only a six-inch stump remained of my left thigh. In addition to the damage to my extremities, I had lost massive portions of both buttocks, my scrotum had been split, I had sustained a dislocated shoulder and a ruptured eardrum, and smaller wounds from shell fragments peppered the remainder of my body. Only my face had been spared. It remarkably contained only one small blue line across my nose from a powder burn.

Voices from Vietnam, 1968–70

Various

Lieutenant James Simmen, 5th Battalion,
60th Infantry (Mechanized)

Simmen writes to his brother.

13 March [1968]

Hi Vern,

The shit has been hitting the fan, but I've managed to miss the spray. One guy was shooting at my ambush last night. I reported it as heavy contact and got eight barrels of artillery to shoot white phosphorus and high explosives in the wood line. We found a body this morning so the colonel was happy.

A company ambushed my platoon, and I only lost one man. A rocket ricocheted off my truck, and the VC charged it. Your prayers must have been talking up a storm to God then. No kidding. I believe!

You'd be surprised how similar killing is to hunting. I know I'm after souls, but I get all excited when I see a VC, just like when I see a deer. I go ape firing at him. It isn't that I'm so crazy. I think a man who freezes killing a man would freeze killing a deer. I'm not perverted, crazy, or anything else. Civilians think such thinking is crazy, but it's no big deal. He runs, you fire. You hunt so I think you'd feel the same way. It isn't all that horrifying.

When you see a man laughing about it, remember he talks the same about killing a deer. Of course, revenge has a part in wanting him just like you want a deer for a trophy and meat. I know I'm not nuts. If I killed a man in the U.S., everyone would stare. Last night I killed and everyone has been patting me on the back, including the battalion commander. What do you think?

A friend got killed on an ambush last week. [The colonel] told him to move in the middle of the night. As he drew in all his claymores, Charlie hit. Last night they told me to move twice. It'll be a cold day in hell when I move. Thirty minutes later I reported "Moved." The colonel isn't about to come out to see where I am. I'm chicken but not stupid!

It isn't all that horrifying. It's rough living in the field, but big deal. They sell mohair tailored sports coats for $35 here and sharkskin suits for $60. I'll buy a few before I leave. What a deal! . . .

Lieutenant Joseph Abodeely, 2nd Battalion,
7th Cavalry, 1st Air Cavalry Division

Abodeely maintained a regular correspondence with his family throughout his entire tour of Vietnam, and in addition kept a diary detailing events. In the letter and diary extract below, Abodeely describes his part in the relief of the Khe Sanh firebase, besieged by the North Vietnamese during their Tet Offensive.

Vietnam 21 March 1968 (1440)

Dear Mom and Dad,

This time it is a legitimate greeting as I received both leters [sic] (from both of you) yesterday. Thank you both for writing. Today is the first day of Spring and it's very hot. It's been getting hotter (both day and night) and we still get occasional [sic] showers in the evenings. I'm sitting on an air mattress on the ground. I rigged up a little sun shelter composed of 4 stakes in the ground to which I tied my poncho liner [quilt-like cover]. At night 6 of us (my headquarters) sleep in a 3-sided sand bag fortification because the VC frequently rocket and mortar Camp Evans. In case you're wondering what Camp Evans is

– it's going to be the 1st Cav's HQ up north as An Khe used to be. My back is to the perimeter wire now so I'm looking into the center where there are many tent structures. There are loads of trucks and jeeps and, of course, choppers. There are underground fueling points where the choppers refuel and can be airborne immediately. My company, D company, is manning the southern sector of the Camp's perimeter. If we go to the field on an operation [sweep of villages or search and destroy], then other units are substituted to cover the perimeter. So far we've been here a few days now. Each night and sometimes during the day, the company sends out patrols. Last night, my platoon went one way and 3d platoon went another. We've been receiving our missions pretty late in the evening so last night we moved out just before dark. We moved about 1000 meters to a hill where I put my platoon in a perimeter defense. Because it was dark and I could not see the surrounding hills to shoot an asimuth on my compass, I called for artillery to shoot two air bursts of white phosphorus from which I took readings in the dark and knew exactly where my platoon was located on the map. When we set up night "goats" [ambushes], we dig in [usually on trails or well traveled paths] and set up trip flares and claymore mines to give warning of enemy approaching. Last night nothing happened and we walked back to this perimeter this morning.

One night when we were sweeping villages along the coast, my platoon set up right on a river to catch any escaping VC moving down the river. I was sitting in my foxhole with baboo [*sic*] thickets between the river and me when I heard a lot of automatic weapons fire about 30 meters away. I jumped down and got my weapon and then I checked the situation out as I discovered I wasn't being shot at. One of my positions, about 30 meters away along the river, opened up on people getting out of a san pan [boat]. They were VC. One man got away; we captured one man and woman, and killed two women. I had no remorse about seeing the wounded man and woman or the two dead women as we found a Chineese [*sic*] Communist grenade and 2 rifles in the boat. One of the dead women had a VC insignia on her clothing. As I stared at her head split open by an M-16 bullet and saw her brains hanging out, I felt no remorse at all. Five of my men were wounded on 27 Feb and my men and I have been shot at too damn many times for me to feel sorry if a young boy or woman dies who sides with or personally participates with those trying to kill my men. This incident is just to give some insight into the horror of this war, but none the less, it is war. I read the articles you both sent me and I want the war to end, too; but, I believe we have commitments – to ourselves and to others. We are fighting a worthwhile war but we're not going all out. I believe the government (U.S.) and the people should go all out – send troops – gear the economy, etc. to win the war rather than prolong it. People who want to pull out or stay half-ass either don't realize the military and political repercussions which are bad or they have other interests which they are putting first. No one is brain washing me on this stuff; I just hate to see these times exist.

I must admit though, there are some light moments and good times. I have a good platoon as you would expect because I constantly check on them. There is a water hole right outside the perimeter where the camp purifies its water, and some of my men and I went swimming bare-assed in the water hole. We also washed out fatigues there as there is no laundry set up yet. I wear the same clothes weeks at a time. I haven't had a good bath in months except in water holes or even some murky water holes filled with leaches [*sic*].

Yesterday, my platoon was on a wire laying detail on the other side of the perimeter. It was hot and the men were tired. Because I'm the platoon leader, I didn't lay wire so I bummed a truck and went to the PX. Beer and coke can only be bought at batallion [*sic*] level, but I talked a sergeant into selling me 4 cases of beer for my platoon. I took it back to the perimeter where they were laying wire and we drank beer until we had to come back to our sector of the perimeter. We've been getting a lot of replacements lately so now I have 38 people in my platoon. I was down to 27 at one time.

I don't know how long I'll be here at Evans (between Quang Tri and Hue). We may just work out of Camp Evans for a while and conduct patrols nearby or maybe they'll send us back along the coast to sweep villages there. There is rumor that we may go to Khe Sanh where the marines are getting rocketed and mortared just about every day. I suspect that if we don't go there, we'll stay here just in case the VC and NVA make another bid for Hue. We're close enough that we can support a defense there.

Ma, I believe I told you before that I got the radio and flashlight batteries. Thanks. I use both. I have my radio in this bunker. We listen to it at night when reception is best. Dad, thanks for the letter and the statistics money-wise, etc. I'm not worried about my money. Don't you worry about me – hang on to what you get through liquidation. I'll have the GI Bill when I get out. I still want to finish law school but I'm seriously considering extending in the Army for 6 months *only* if I get the job I want. That way I'd make captain, get the money, and enjoy myself if I get a job like officer in charge of an R&R center. I'll have to wait and see what happens. Meanwhile, I live day to day hoping I get through it to the next day. I just hope everything turns out all right. I'm glad to hear Bob is doing well in school. I think he'll like teaching. It'll give him the time he needs for extra curricular activities such as hunting and scuba-diving. Tell Bob I can show if [*sic*] a few tricks about living in the boonies under *very* adverse conditions.

Well, I'll close for now. All is well. Give my regards to everyone – Aunt T, Aunt Emily, Grandma, Uncle Kenny, Rose G., and anyone else who asks about me.

Diary: Friday, March 22 1968. 1507. It's hot. I'm sitting under a poncho liner tied to four stakes for a sun shelter. Tonight my platoon is to go out to set up a goat on Highway I to catch any VC setting up mines on the road. We're supposed to be air assaulted but we could go by truck or walk. We turned in one of our M-60 MGs today to get a new one. Rumor still is that we'll go to Khe Sanh. During the evenings, it's been raining.

Saturday, March 23. 0637. My platoon and I are sitting on top of a hill overlooking Highway I. It's dawn now and I just went to my positions to check if the men were awake. As we moved in last night, three of my men saw two people across the highway on the other side. I thought for sure we'd be sniped at, but we weren't. Today, we'll probably act as a blocking force.

2310. We hit some NVA today. Several of 1st plt. got wounded; one medic killed. My plt. and I moved under fire to get the wounded out. Tomorrow we go back to recover the dead body.

Sunday, March 24. 1635. We air assaulted to find the body. The medic had been shot in the eye. Tonight we go out on a goat here from Camp Evans.

Monday, March 25. 1700. Last night on our goat, it rained. VC started mortaring Camp Evans, but I called artillery in on the mortar positions in the dark. Today, my platoon found the mortar site and brought back mortar rounds and other equipment. The battalion commander and CO were pleased. Now we are at a bridge in an old French bunker. An ARVN Sgt. is in here; we made friends as I talked to him from my translation book.

Tuesday, March 26. 1655. Today I coordinated with a Major at the ARVN compound down the road. On the way back, Sgt. Blank, Pvt. Osman and I stopped and had a beer in the village. We got in trouble with some MPs who passed by and said we were "off limits." A "mamason" who sells stuff nearby came to the bunker. I got "laid" today. My men are filling sandbags now. Some ARVNs are helping them. We are setting claymores and trip flares all around our positions – more than usual. Last night, a VC turned two claymores around. It was good we did not set them off.

Wednesday, March 27. 1115. Last night we spotted some VC

moving around and shot at them. I called some artillery illuminations. The "mamason" came today and we bought fourteen more hats. She left some "pot" with me for safe keeping because the ARVNs will kill her if they find out she has it. Since I don't even smoke cigarettes, much less pot, I buried the marijuana by the bunker just in case "mamason" was trying to set me up.

Thursday, March 28. 1130. Some of my men and I are here at the river. I'm sitting here nude on the grassy bank. Some Vietnamese children are washing my pants and socks. We got the word yesterday – we move north. Some of the children are sitting next to me. My men are swimming. We will probably leave the bridge today or tomorrow.

Friday, March 29. 0940. The sun is getting bright now. I'm in the tower bunker. There are a lot of flies. The ARVNs got in a firefight this morning to our south. We could hear the shooting. I've been practicing speaking Vietnamese and I can get by O.K. now. One of the ARVNs told me this morning that four VC slept in the village last night and left in the early morning. My company will probably go back to Camp Evans today.

Saturday, March 30. 1435. My half of the platoon moved to the company site along the road between the bridges. It was relaxing being at the bridge. The kids who sold the cokes and beer were cute. Now, we'll go to Camp Evans to move north near Khe Sanh.

Tuesday, April 2. 0645. We air assaulted to the top of this mountain surrounded by a river on three sides. It's jungle and grassy. I jumped from the chopper and hurt my arm. I could see bomb strikes off in the distance as the sky lit up and the ground shook.

1000. The sun is out. We're on a high mountain top. Today my company is to air assault to a new location to set up there.

We just got a log ship with food and water. It was nice sleeping last night.

1720. D Company led the air assault to where we are now. My platoon led a ground movement. We found an NVA site for a 50-caliber anti-aircraft gun. Also some of my plt. found some ammo and grenades. Now we are waiting to see where we'll set up. We're hot and tired.

Wednesday, April 3. 0953. We are sitting in the jungle right now. 3d plt. hit some NVA a little while ago. They got one of their men KIA. The S-3 carried him back on his shoulders and then three of my men took the KIA to the rear. We're waiting for artillery to come in. There are huge bomb craters all around. I can hear the choppers circling the area now. There are trees, high grass, and ferns all around.

1808. We moved to Hill 242. The NVA mortared us; we had ten or eleven wounded. NVA have us surrounded now. One platoon from another company tried to bring us food and water, but got pinned down. I hope we make it through the night. We dug in and made overhead cover.

Thursday, April 4. 1540. Last night we received more mortar and artillery fire. We are now back at the guns. I have my platoon in position on the perimeter. As we came back today, we picked up a couple of the dead and wounded who tried to get us supplies yesterday. When we got back here we saw more dead and wounded. The 2d plt. ldr. of C Company was killed. One medevac chopper was shot up. The NVA here are dangerous. I don't like this area. I hope we all get out alive. I got a card from Colleen today which cheered me up. We didn't have any food or water all day yesterday and for most of today. Everyone is tired.

Friday, April 5. 1550. I got the word today that our battalion may walk to Khe Sanh tomorrow. This could be disastrous. We've incurred a lot of dead and wounded since we've been here. I hope to God we make it alive. I've had a lot of close calls and I'm getting scared again. Everyone is scared of this area. The NVA are near us and good fighters. We're digging in again for tonight.

Jets keep circling the hill. There are also a lot of choppers in the air. Artillery keeps pounding the surrounding areas also. I hope the NVA move out. They ambush a lot here.

Saturday, April 6. 1400. Well, we tried to walk from this LZ to Khe Sanh, but we had to come back as the two forward companies received effective fire. Now our company is supposed to air assault to five hundred meters east of Khe Sanh. I hope we make it; we have many reporters with us.

Sunday, April 7. 1045. We air assaulted to an open area on a mountain top and received light sniper fire. We found an NVA complex with rockets, mortar-tubes and ammo, AK-47s, and all sorts of material. I have a sharp AK-47 which I hope to keep. We are to go to Khe Sanh.

1700. We are at Khe Sanh camped outside the east entrance on Highway 9.

Monday, April 8. 1130. Today, D Company was the first to walk into Khe Sanh on Highway 9 in over two months. The marines had been pinned in, but now they can move. My platoon was the first in. This place is bunkers and trenches. The incoming artillery is deadly. I sent my AK-47 in with Sp. 4 Sanders who I hope will take care of it for me. My men sent in their captured weapons yesterday and they've been distributed out as trading material. This pisses me off, but I talked to the CO and maybe we can do something about it.

2345. I'm writing by moonlight. I'm sitting on guard at a bunker. I can see to the west (Laos) where flares are shot over the mountains. A plane is shooting red streams of tracer bullets into the mountains.

Tuesday, April 9. 1055. Our company is waiting along the air strips to get air lifted back to LZ Mark (named after CO's son – also called LZ Thor) to the fire base there. I've still got a VC bugle that I blow for the company. I blew it when we came to Khe Sanh. There is rumor we'll go back to Evans soon. I hope so.

Thursday, April 11. 0730. Yesterday afternoon my plt. took a bulldozer west down Highway 9 to fill in bomb holes and clear away trees. We found two dead NVA. They smelled and flies and maggots covered the distorted bodies.

Today we moved from LZ Thor to a mountain top overlooking a bridge below. The rest of the company is at another bridge. I'm pissed off because we didn't get food and water because we weren't on the right radio frequency to call the log ship in. The CO didn't even act concerned.

Friday, April 12. 1405. Today my plt. hitched a ride with a Marine convoy (trucks and tanks) to LZ Thor. We're waiting here to go to Khe Sanh and later to Camp Evans. It appears that our work is done here. I hope so. Last night it was cold on the mountain top. The sky looks like rain.

Tim Driscoll, United States Army

Vietnam, March 4, 1968

Well Mom,

There really is a war going on over here. We made contact in daylight yesterday for the first time since I've been here. You know how they say war is not like the movies show it. Well, they're wrong. It's exactly like the movies.

We were on a Company-size patrol when they hit us. 1st plt was in the front, we were next, and 2nd plt was in the rear. Wayne was working with the 2nd plt on the machine guns.

They hit the first plt, and everyone got down. Then first moved up 50 meters, and we moved out to the left. As soon as we moved behind a hedgeline, an automatic weapon opened on us. We just kept moving.

We finally got out of range about 100 meters down the trail.

Then we got on line and assaulted a hedgeline 50 meters in front of us. We didn't meet any resistance; so, after we got on the other side, we got down and waited. Then we got the word the 1st plt was in bad shape and needed us. So, we were going to move out on line about 50 meters and then swing to our right and get the gooks in the middle of us and 1st.

We started out on line, keeping low and moving slow. It was a clear, open field we were going across. We were halfway across when fire opened up from our right. Everyone got down, and the St/Sgt started yelling at us to keep moving; so, we being young, brave Marines got back on line and kept moving.

But then the bullets started zipping around our legs and raising dust. We knew for sure they were shooting at us then. We weren't about to stay on line after that. We bolted to the right, ran about 25 meters, and took cover behind dirt piled up all along this road.

We waited there, just the 1st squad (2nd and 3rd squad were behind us), for about five minutes. They weren't shooting anymore; so, we start sticking our fool necks up to see what was happening. And they started shooting again. Now we knew where they were, tho. They were dug in right behind a thick bamboo patch, about 2 squads. At least now we could shoot back. We were doing pretty good – holding our own. Four of them started to run, and we cut them down.

THEN! we started receiving fire from our rear. I started getting scared, then, because we had no protection to the rear. They had us pinned down for ½ hour. We couldn't even raise our heads to see where they were. Finally the 2nd and 3rd squads moved up and cleared up our rear. We continued the fire fight to our front.

By this time, we had taken a few casualties, including our St/Sgt – shot through the neck close to the collarbone. A medevac chopper landed right behind us as we set up a hard base of fire, turning our M-16s on automatic. Our St/Sgt wouldn't leave tho; and he kept running around yelling orders, his neck all patched up. (He thinks he's John Wayne.)

After a while, we thought we had wiped them out because they kept running and we kept cutting them down. After a while, the fire stopped; and the St/Sgt wanted a frontal assault on the positions. We didn't like that idea because, if there was one automatic weapon left, it could tear our whole squad to pieces.

We finally made him see the light. We threw a few grenades; and, sure enough, they started shooting again. We just exchanged fire for another hour, and then the TANKS!!! came. Three tanks with the 2nd plt swept through the position from our right. I saw Wayne with the M-60. There were 3 gooks left. The tanks opened fire when they saw them. Killed two and took one prisoner.

All that took a little over five hours. One of our Corpsmen was put up for a medal.

Wayne told me later that he was feeding the machine gun, and the A gunner was shooting, when a chicom landed right next to the A gunner. He toppled over Wayne, and Wayne had to take charge of the gun. That plt had one killed.

Mike sent me a letter and told me not to tell you he is coming to Nam. I'll write him and tell him how lousy everything is around here. We got mail three times last week, and I got a whole mess of letters from you. I got a letter from Sonny, and he says Dan will be OK. I hope so.

Where do you think I should go for R&R (in 5 months)? Tokyo, Hong Kong, Bangkok, Taipei, Australia, Hawaii, P.I. or Oki?

I'll write soon . . . Tim

Second-Lieutenant Robert ("Mike") Ransom Jr, 4th
Battalion, 3rd Infantry

April 1968

Dear Mom and Dad,

Well, I've had my baptism by fire, and it's changed me I think. Two days ago my platoon was on a mission to clear three suspected minefields. We were working with a mechanized platoon with four tracks, and our tactic was to put the tracks on line and just roar through the minefields, hoping to blow them. Since the majority of the VC mines are antipersonnel, the tracks could absorb the explosions with no damage done to them or the people inside. My platoon rode along just as security in case we were attacked. We spent the whole day clearing the three fields and came up with a big zero.

The tracks were then returning us to where we would stay overnight. When we reached our spot we jumped off the tracks, and one of my men jumped right onto a mine. Both his feet were blown off, both legs were torn to shreds – his entire groin area was completely blown away. It was the most horrible sight I've ever seen. Fortunately he never knew what hit him. I tried to revive him with mouth-to-mouth resuscitation, but it was hopeless to begin with.

In addition, the explosion wounded seven other people (four seriously) who were dusted off by medevac, and three others lightly, who were not dusted off. Of the four seriously wounded, one received a piece of shrapnel in the heart and may not survive. The other three were almost completely riddled with shrapnel, and while they will be completely all right, it will be a slow and painful recovery.

I was one of the slightly wounded. I got three pieces in my left arm, one in my right knee, and about twenty in both legs. I am completely all right. In fact I thought I had only gotten one in the arm and one in the knee. It was not until last night when I took off my clothes to take a shower that I noticed the other spots where I had been hit.

I came back to Chu Lai yesterday because my knee is now quite stiff and swollen, and will probably be here a couple of days, what with x-rays and what not. Believe it or not, I am extremely anxious to get back to platoon. Having been through this, I am now a bonafide member of the platoon. They have always followed my orders, but I was an outsider. Now I'm a member of the team, and it feels good.

I want to assure you that I am perfectly all right. You will probably get some sort of notification that I was lightly wounded, and I just don't want you to worry about it at all. I will receive a Purple Heart for it. People over here talk about the Million-Dollar Wound. It is one which is serious enough to warrant evacuation to the States but which will heal entirely. Therefore, you might call mine a Half-Million-Dollar Wound. My RTO, who was on my track sitting right next to me, caught a piece of shrapnel in his tail, and since he had caught a piece in his arm about two months ago, he'll get out of the field with wounds about as serious as a couple of mosquito bites.

I said earlier that the incident changed me. I am now filled with both respect and hate for the VC and the Vietnamese. Respect because the enemy knows that he can't stand up to us in a fire fight due to our superior training, equipment and our vast arsenal of weapons. Yet he is able. Via his mines and booby traps, he can whittle our ranks down piecemeal until we cannot muster an effective fighting force.

In the month that I have been with the company, we have lost 4 killed and about 30 wounded. We have not seen a single verified dink the whole time, nor have we even shot a single round at anything. I've developed hate for the Vietnamese because they come around selling Cokes and beer to us and then run back and tell the VC how many we are, where our positions are, and where the leaders position themselves. In the place where we got hit, we discovered four other mines, all of them placed in the spots where I, my platoon sergeant, and two squad leaders had been sitting. I talked to the mechanized platoon leader who is with us and he said that as he left the area to return to his fire base, the people in the village he went through were laughing at him because they knew we had been hit. I felt like turning my machine guns on the village to kill every man, woman and child in it.

Sorry this has been an unpleasant letter, but I'm in a rather unpleasant mood.

All love,
Mike

Ransom died of wounds on 11 May 1968.

PFC David Bowman, Company B, 1st Battalion, 8th Cavalry

n.d. [1968]

Dear Civilians, Friends, Draft Dodgers, etc:

In the very near future, the undersigned will once more be in your midst, dehydrated and demoralized, to take his place again as a human being with the well-known forms of freedom and justice for all; engage in life, liberty and the somewhat delayed pursuit of happiness. In making your joyous preparations to welcome him back into organized society you might take certain steps to make allowances for the past twelve months. In other words, he might be a little Asiatic from Vietnamesitis and Overseasitis, and should be handled with care. Don't be alarmed if he is infected with all forms of rare tropical disease. A little time in the "Land of the Big PX" will cure this malady.

Therefore, show no alarm if he insists on carrying a weapon to the dinner table, looks around for his steel pot when offered a chair, or wakes you up in the middle of the night for guard duty. Keep cool when he pours gravy on his dessert at dinner of mixed peaches with his Seagrams VO. Pretend not to notice if he acts dazed, eats with his fingers instead of silverware and prefers C-rations to steak. Take it with a smile when he insists on digging up the garden to fill sandbags for the bunker he is building. Be tolerant when he takes his blanket and sheet off the bed and puts them on the floor to sleep on.

Abstain from saying anything about powdered eggs, dehydrated potatoes, fried rice, fresh milk or ice cream. Do not be alarmed if he should jump up from the dinner table and rush to the garbage can to wash his dish with a toilet brush. After all, this has been his standard. Also, if it should start raining, pay no attention to him if he pulls off his clothes, grabs a bar of soap and a towel and runs outdoors for a shower.

When in his daily conversation he utters such things as "Xin loi" and "Choi oi" just be patient, and simply leave quickly and calmly if by some chance he utters "didi" with an irritated look on his face because it means no less than "Get the h – out of here." Do not let it shake you up if he picks up the phone and yells "Sky King forward, Sir" or says "Roger out" for good-bye or simply shouts "Working."

Never ask why the Jones' son held a higher rank than he did, and by no means mention the word "extend." Pretend not to notice if at a restaurant he calls the waitress "Numbuh I girl" and uses his hat as an ashtray. He will probably keep listening for "Homeward Bound" to sound off over AFRS. If he does, comfort him, for he is still reminiscing. Be especially watchful when he is in the presence of women – *especially* a beautiful woman.

Above all, keep in mind that beneath that tanned and rugged exterior there is a heart of gold (the only thing of value he has left). Treat him with kindness, tolerance, and an occasional fifth of good liquor and you will be able to rehabilitate that which was once (and now a hollow shell) the happy-go-lucky guy you once knew and loved.

Last, but not least, send no more mail to the APO, fill the ice box with beer, get the civvies out of mothballs, fill the car with gas, and get the women and children off the streets – BECAUSE THE KID IS COMING HOME!!!!!

Love,
Dave

Sergeant Stanley Homiski, 3/4 Cavalry, 25th Infantry Division

Homiski writes to his wife.

Vietnam, 25 May, 1968

Dear Roberta,

Today is probably the worst day I have ever lived in my entire, short life. Once again we were in contact with Charlie, and once again we suffered losses. The losses we had today hit home, as my best friend in this shit hole was killed. He was only 22 years old and was going on R&R on the first of June to meet his wife in Hawaii. I feel that if I was only a half second sooner in pulling the trigger, he would still be alive.

Strange how short a time a half of a second is – the difference between life and death. This morning we were talking about how we were only two years different in age and how we both had gotten married before coming to this place. You know, I can still feel his presence as I write this letter and hope that I am able to survive and leave this far behind me.

If there is a place called Hell this surely must be it, and we must be the Devil's disciples doing all his dirty work. I keep asking myself if there is a God, then how the hell come young men with so much to live for have to die. I just hope that his death is not in vain.

I look forward to the day when I will take my R&R. If I play my cards right, I should be able to get it for Hawaii so our anniversary will be in that time frame. The reason I say this is by Sept., I will have more than enough time in country to get my pick of places and dates. I promise I will do everything necessary to insure that I make that date, and I hope that tomorrow is quiet.

We will be going into base camp soon for our three-day stand down. I will try to write you a longer letter at that time. Please don't worry too much about me, as if you won't, for I will take care of myself and look forward to the day I am able to be with you again.

Love,
Stan

Larry Jackson, 129 AHC

Vietnam, 11 September 1969

Dear Mom and Dad,

Getting short, Mom, coming home pretty soon. Going to quit flying soon, too much for me now. I went in front of a board for sp/5 will know soon if I made it. I have now 20 oak leaf clusters and some more paper for you. I have flown 1500 hours now, and in those hours I could tell you a lifetime story. I have been put in for a medal again, but this time I have seen far beyond of what ever you will see. That is why I'm going to quit flying. I dream of Valerie's hand touching mine telling me to come home; but I wake up, and it's some sergeant telling me I have to fly. Today I am 21, far away but coming home older.

    Love,
    Larry

This was Jackson's last letter home. He was killed in action on the following day.

Sergeant Joseph Morrissey, Company C, 1st Battalion, 12th Cavalry, 1st Cavalry Division (Airmobile)

Oct. 1969

Hello Brother,

How are you treating life these days? Have you gotten a grip on those Merrimack students yet? . . .

This place is sort of getting to me. I've been seeing too many guys getting messed up, and I still can't understand it. It's not that I can't understand this war. It's just that I can't understand *war* period.

If you do not get to go to that big peace demonstration [on] October 15th I hope you do protest against war or sing for peace – I would. I just can't believe half of the shit I've seen over here so far . . .

Do you know if there's anything wrong at home? I haven't heard from anyone in about two weeks, and normally I get 10 letters a week. You mentioned in your last letters that you haven't heard from them for a while either. I couldn't take sitting over [in] this place if I thought there was anything wrong at home.

Well, brother, I hope you can get to your students and start them thinking about life. Have you tried any marijuana lectures lately? I know they dig that current stuff.

I gotta go now. Stay loose, Paul, sing a simple song of freedom and I'll be seeing you come summer.

Feb. 9, 1970

Hello Brother,

How is America acting these days? Are the youth still planning new ways to change our world? I think the 70s will see a lot of things changed for the better.

I'm still trying to survive over here but the NVA aren't making it too easy lately. We've just been in contact with them for three days and things aren't looking too bright. When you have bullets cracking right over your head for a couple days in a row, your nerves begin to fizzle. When you're getting shot at, all you can think about is – try to stay alive, keep your head down and keep shooting back.

When the shooting stops, though, you sort of sit back and ask yourself, Why? What the hell is this going to prove? And man, I'm still looking for the answer. It's a real bitch.

Thanks for that *Playboy* you sent me. I sort of forgot what girls looked like. I think the real personality of Jesus has been sort of hidden from us. Either that or no one's wanted to look for it before. If he were alive today he'd probably be living in Haight-Ashbury and getting followed by the FBI who'd have him labeled as a communist revolutionary. He'd definitely be shaking some people up . . .

Well, it's time to make my delicious C-ration lunch. Stay loose and stay young . . .

The beat goes on,
Joe

Thomas Pellaton, 101st Ambulance Division

6 September '70

Dear John,

. . . Saigon [is] completely different from I Corps – almost luxurious. The MACV [Military Assistance Command/ Vietnam] complex, where so many of my friends work, has a golf course, Olympic-size swimming pool, etc. But with all the surface glitter and bustle of Saigon, I came away with a very gloomy feeling. The people are frantically trying to make every last cent they can from the Americans before [the soldiers] leave. The war has brought out all the venality imaginable in these people . . .

My friends are somewhat depressed. It now seems they have to rewrite all their reports because the truth they are putting out is too pessimistic. The higher echelons, for their career's sake and the plans of Nixon's Vietnamization, will not allow a bad situation to exist – no matter how true it may be! I saw myself some of the different drafts of some reports that were to go to [General Creighton] Abrams [commander of American forces in Vietnam] – and how they had to be changed to get to him. What a disgrace – and still people are dying every day!

To top this all off, we got hit again last week – twice in one night. The second phase was while we were all watching a Korean floor show. It was mass hysteria when those rockets started coming in! Chairs flying, people running to bunkers! Boy, do I hate those things. I'm going to be a nervous wreck when I get out of here! Then, there has begun a witch hunt for pot smokers. We have a group of self-appointed vigilantes (most of whom are Southern beer-drinking, obnoxious alcoholics! You can see my prejudices in that statement!) who go around spreading untrue rumors about those they do not like. It's at such a point that open warfare might break out in the company. I'm so worked up now because one of the vigilantes is my own boss. It just makes me sick! My own impressions are that the supposed "pot heads" are much easier to work with, more pleasant, never bothersome, and more intelligent than the redneck faction of boozers! Yet that counts for nothing in the Army . . .

John, Peace – my warmest regards – and thanks for letting me ramble on and take out my frustrations.

Tom

Phoenix Rising

Mike Beamon, US Navy SEALs

Beamon was a scout with the US Navy SEALs in the Mekong Delta from August 1968 to February 1969

The Phoenix Program was a very carefully designed program to disrupt the infrastructure of the Viet Cong village systems. And apparently on some occasions the plan was to come in and assassinate a village chief and make it look like the Viet Cong did it. It was a really difficult program for me because I didn't totally understand it when I was in Vietnam. I was just a scout, and my responsibility was to scout in and get us to a village, get us to a particular spot, go in there and get the person out that we wanted, and then they would be handled. It was my understanding that these people were wanted for questioning, that they were high-level Viet Cong. What I have come to understand since then, and what I really feel was going on at the time, was that we were just going in there to make it look like the Viet Cong came through and killed this person. Now, understand that we are going into areas that have not been touched by Americans. They were Viet Cong strongholds.

There were booby traps all over the place. I was barefoot. We didn't want to make any boot prints. We were walking along barefoot, and Americans don't go into jungles barefoot. I had no identification on me except for a morphine syringe around my neck. If I was hit, I'd shoot morphine. My number was 50, it was on all my clothes. My face was completely painted out black. Often I would wear a black pajama top. I learned how to walk like a Viet Cong, move like a Viet Cong, think like a Viet Cong.

I'm a tall person. I had to learn how to walk small and slump over. There's a certain way you walk through the jungle when you're comfortable with it and I got very comfortable in that style of walking. It's more of an experience . . . it's like a cat who walks and knows where he's going and what he's doing. Most Americans didn't know where they were going or what they were doing in Vietnam. They were kind of tromping around out there. I was moving slowly, hesitating, blending in with my environment, moving up to a structure, getting close to it, trying to blend in all the time. I had, on one occasion, a Viet Cong call to me and talk to me. That's how good I was at moving in this fashion. That was the only way I was going to survive out there, to look and be like a Viet Cong.

We would walk in, and we wouldn't be carrying American-made weapons, either. There were no silhouettes on us that made us look like Americans. At a glimpse we looked like we were a group of men with some guns. Once again, the whole idea was to blend in like the Viet Cong, and at that time I was totally tuned to filling that role. Since I was the scout, I had to look more like a Viet Cong than anybody else.

I was the main point man for that unit. We carried a heavy-equipment person with us, carried an M-60 machine gun fully loaded, ready to knock through trees. We were prepared to hit anything. We hit regimental point units sometimes, just five of us. We were prepared to make contact with anything.

We'd be dropped off in an area that was probably pretty dangerous, in about four or five miles, and we patrolled two or three miles. Sometimes it would take an hour to go one hundred yards, the jungle was that thick. We'd have to crawl underneath it all. We were in there pretty deep. Once again, there were no front lines, but we were in an area that was very, very dangerous. Consequently, we had complete air support. When we were out on certain missions, the pilots had to be in their planes on our frequencies. We would scramble them that quickly. So it was, by military standards, very, very high-level missions we were going on.

On the Phoenix Program, we would go in . . . I had flown over the area the day before in a helicopter, so I knew exactly what it looked like in the daytime, and I'd translate that in my mind at nighttime. Usually I was the only one who knew where we were. Everybody had other specialties. The radio-person's specialty was a whole set of frequencies he had to deal with. The officer's specialty was to execute some of the orders. The medic had another specialty. Each person was an incredibly skilled technician.

I had to be totally tuned up. We were doing Dexedrine. When we'd go out on a mission, we'd take a whole handful of pills, and some of those were Dexedrine. When I hit Dexedrine I'd just turn into a pair of eyeballs and ears, That's probably why I don't remember too many of the details real well, because it was just like I was on a speed trip the whole time I was in the field. When I came in, the crash would be so hard it would totally wipe out anything I'd been through, and I'm sure that works when you need people to go out and do the kinds of things that we were doing, because it would be very hard to debrief us if we were ever wounded or captured. We had the morphine around our neck and we could shoot up immediately, which would make us incoherent for twenty-four hours at least, enough time to shift all the plans around that were predicated on that particular mission.

So when we would go in, I'd be barefoot, I would move up to a hootch. This is maybe during a real stormy night; they're not expecting Americans to be out there in the middle of a storm, they're not expecting them to come walking in at two o'clock in the morning in the middle of a Viet Cong stronghold. A stronghold is a village where they felt really secure. We would go into the hootch. I'd step in and I'd stand there and listen to everybody breathe. If I noticed any change in the breathing patterns of the people sleeping, then I was immediately on alert. I carried with me, more often than not, a duckbill shotgun. A duckbill throws your four-buck [buckshot] at a horizontal; you get a nice wide spray if you have to open fire. God. It was really intense, because you had a whole family sleeping in this one room and you're standing in the middle of them all.

What I would do is, around my head I wore a triangular green bandage. I'd take it off and tie it into a knot in the center and walk over to the bed – I knew exactly what bed this guy was sleeping in. I had a Navy K-bar knife, which is one of the best knives you can get. The blade is about seven or nine inches long, razor-sharp – you could shave with it. I would go over to the person and I would hold their nose shut so they'd take a breath with their mouth and I'd take this rag, which had a couple of knots in the middle of it, and cram it down their throat so it would get down to their larynx, at the same time bringing that knife up under their neck, so that if they moved at all they would be cutting their own throat.

So the person would obviously freeze. With that motion, I would take the gag, grab it from behind their head, the knife under the throat, and literally pick them up just by the head. They were small people, usually sleeping in their black pajamas, and I'd just pick them up and carry them out. Now, if anybody moved in the hootch, the other scout with me, who's Vietnamese, would start talking to them very quietly. He'd have them all lay down on the ground, face down. By then I'd have the person outside. I'd have his elbows secured behind his back. I would pass him to the prisoner-handler. All this time no words are spoken. We were incredibly well rehearsed. This has all taken about a minute, maybe a minute and a half. We would go back inside. The scout would then instruct these people that if they make a move, there's going to be a person at the door that will completely blow them away. Our little group would pull back. We'd only have five or six people and we were dispersed to cover ourselves. We would pull back and start to move for our exit. I would usually sit by the hootch for about five minutes and listen and, while I was doing that, hook a grenade on the door, flatten the pin and run a fishing line across the door so if anybody opened it up, they would drop the grenade and of course they would be killed.

I would sit by the doorway there and be very, very quiet and let them start mustering a bit, then I'd make a little noise outside so that they knew I was there. Once I did that, I'd leave and haul ass back to the unit to scout on the way back. If anybody came out, we could hear the grenade for about a mile if it went off. And these are like families, little kids and stuff. So it was something you just didn't think about. You just did it. It was that second you had to cover.

We did one mission, God, we spent half the night in a pigsty. We got into the area around one o'clock in the morning and climbed into a pigsty, a feeding area, and buried ourselves beneath all the manure and straw. We were looking through the wall. It was like a barn. There were little tiny cracks. We were waiting for our target to come in the marketplace, a tax collector who collected during market time, about eight o'clock in the morning. It was a sizable little village for Vietnam – must have been twenty hootches with a center courtyard – and he came into the area. I'll never forget that. He came walking into the area after we'd been sitting there all that time, and we just jumped up and knocked the entire wall down as we came out shooting. We just blasted everything, bodies were flying around. I just started running for the guy we wanted. It was my job to search him completely. I picked up an arm that had been blown across the courtyard and searched the sleeve. A lot of times they might carry a map that was sewn into the sleeve. I had to search all parts of the body. The body would be strewn all over the place, kicking and squirming and puking, eyeballs rolling around . . . It was like picking through a broken car . . . It wasn't like a human body any longer.

What blows me away is that my father is a meat-cutter. I couldn't stand the sight of blood as a kid and I still can't. And I can't stand the feeling of pain, either, for myself or somebody else. What's incredible is that I was able to do that so quickly, without hesitation and so calmly. I just did it. I don't think I made a habit of shooting people unnecessarily, but at the same time my fear level was so high that if it meant me being afraid or them being dead, usually the person was dead.

My Squad

Terry Whitmore

Whitmore served with the USMC in Vietnam. He later deserted.

In the Nam we blacks pretty much kept to ourselves, no matter how close we were to our squads. The real bullshitting was always done with other blacks. Jiving about our blocks. Sometimes gambling a little. But in combat the squad was the more important group. No matter what kinds of guys and colors were in the squad, it had to run smoothly if we were to stay alive. Of course we would jive each other about our backgrounds. We were still typical Americans.

This Polish cat and a brother from New York would always be jiving like that. Dumb nigger. Dirty polack. My grandfather used to own your grandfather and whip his ass every day. Shit like that. But just jiving. We even had a Mexican, Durand. We called him the wetback and he'd tell us how his boys kicked our asses at the Alamo. This kind of jiving went on all the time. It never got out of hand. Almost never.

One guy in my squad, Sully the Irishman, was very selfish. He'd get stuff from home and keep it all to himself. We had a little kitchen in the corner of our tent where we would pool all our goodies and eat together. But Sully would sit by himself, stuffing his face. And looking in his mirror. A real Gable. We'd sit around and sing together after chow. He'd be looking in his mirror. So we jumped in his shit whenever we could.

Out on Operation Medina, Charlie had us pinned down and we were dug in. Sully was radioman. Durand was squad leader. They hated each other, but they had to be together. Here we were in the middle of a battle. Durand was short, only a few days left in the Nam. So he was jumpy. Anything happened and he was on the ground fast. Sully became pissed. "Wetback motherfuckin' coward," and took off. Durand went after him. Tracers are flying over our heads and these two are swinging it out. The Mexican and the Puerto Ricans were hotheaded cats. Always ready to fight.

While I was in the Nam, a story appeared in *Stars and Stripes* about Dean Rusk's daughter marrying a Negro. That gave me a bit of the ass and I started to mock it. Sully piped up with his opinion that such a marriage was wrong. He was not jiving this time.

"Sully, it's their own business what they want to do." I was pissed.

Finally it came to the day when Sully and I almost drew on each other. We were way up north not too far from the DMZ. Charlie was everywhere. The monsoon season was ending. The day's rain had just stopped. We were hanging our clothes out to dry. From nowhere, for no reason, he started in with "I remember a name they used to call you a long time ago."

"Say it, motherfucker, just say it!" And I lowered my hand to my .45. I was ready to draw.

He had his .16 and went for it. Right on the trigger. We just stood there, staring at each other for about thirty seconds. If he had raised that .16, I damn sure was going to pull my .45, which was always half-cocked anyway. Not for bullshitting with the guys, but for Charlie. Loaded with a round always in the chamber. If he had raised that .16, one of us would be dead today. Sometimes it was that bad among us.

Otherwise we were a close squad. Even when it was really jumping back in the States, we would only jive each other about it. Especially when that priest was raising hell in Milwaukee. We had one cat from that town. We would fuck with him about his town catching hell.

"When you get home, you gonna have to keep up this

Nam shit. You'll be running a listening post just to go to the grocery store."

It was strange that we never jived like this when I first came to the squad. We had a black squad leader then, a real bull jive corporal. He was hit in an ambush a few weeks after I joined the squad. His third heart in the Nam. According to regulations, they had to send him home after three Purple Hearts. The squad changed after that.

We were a groovy squad, really tight when it came to combat. Rarely any bullshit jive then. Just fighting. And stealing. What we couldn't get from company supply, we stole from other squads, other companies. It didn't matter to us. We were very tight when it came to fighting and stealing. Of course if we couldn't steal what we needed, we'd just sell what we didn't want to the Vietnamese and buy back from them what we needed. They always had what we needed. Charlie's cousins always had everything.

If I Die in a Combat Zone

Tim O'Brien

Born in Minnesota in 1946, O'Brien was an army sergeant in
Vietnam, an experience he recorded in his 1973 memoir, *If I
Die in a Combat Zone*.

The summer of 1968, the summer I turned into a soldier, was
a good time for talking about war and peace. Eugene McCarthy was bringing quiet thought to the subject. He was
winning votes in the primaries. College students were listening to him, and some of us tried to help out. Lyndon Johnson
was almost forgotten, no longer forbidding or feared; Robert
Kennedy was dead but not quite forgotten; Richard Nixon
looked like a loser. With all the tragedy and change that
summer, it was fine weather for discussion.

And, with all of this, there was an induction notice tucked
into a corner of my billfold.

So with friends and acquaintances and townspeople, I
spent the summer in Fred's antiseptic cafe, drinking coffee
and mapping out arguments on Fred's napkins. Or I sat in
Chic's tavern, drinking beer with kids from the farms. I
played some golf and tore up the pool table down at the
bowling alley, keeping an eye open for likely-looking high
school girls.

Late at night, the town deserted, two or three of us would
drive a car around and around the town's lake, talking about
the war, very seriously, moving with care from one argument
to the next, trying to make it a dialogue and not a debate. We

covered all the big questions: justice, tyranny, self-determination, conscience and the state, God and war and love.

College friends came to visit: "Too bad, I hear you're drafted. What will you do?"

I said I didn't know, that I'd let time decide. Maybe something would change, maybe the war would end. Then we'd turn to discuss the matter, talking long, trying out the questions, sleeping late in the mornings.

The summer conversations, spiked with plenty of references to the philosophers and academicians of war, were thoughtful and long and complex and careful. But, in the end, careful and precise argumentation hurt me. It was painful to tread deliberately over all the axioms and assumptions and corollaries when the people on the town's draft board were calling me to duty, smiling so nicely.

"It won't be bad at all," they said. "Stop in and see us when it's over."

So to bring the conversations to a focus and also to try out in real words my secret fears, I argued for running away.

I was persuaded then, and I remain persuaded now, that the war was wrong. And since it was wrong and since people were dying as a result of it, it was evil. Doubts, of course, hedged all this: I had neither the expertise nor the wisdom to synthesize answers; most of the facts were clouded, and there was no certainty as to the kind of government that would follow a North Vietnamese victory or, for that matter, an American victory, and the specifics of the conflict were hidden away – partly in men's minds, partly in the archives of government, and partly in buried, irretrievable history. The war, I thought, was wrongly conceived and poorly justified. But perhaps I was mistaken, and who really knew, anyway?

Piled on top of this was the town, my family, my teachers, a whole history of the prairie. Like magnets, these things pulled in one direction or the other, almost physical forces weighting the problem, so that, in the end, it was less reason and more gravity that was the final influence.

My family was careful that summer. The decision was

mine and it was not talked about. The town lay there, spread out in the corn and watching me, the mouths of old women and Country Club men poised in a kind of eternal readiness to find fault. It was not a town, not a Minneapolis or New York, where the son of a father can sometimes escape scrutiny. More, I owed the prairie something. For twenty-one years I'd lived under its laws, accepted its education, eaten its food, wasted and guzzled its water, slept well at night, driven across its highways, dirtied and breathed its air, wallowed in its luxuries. I'd played on its Little League teams. I remembered Plato's *Crito*, when Socrates, facing certain death – execution, not war – had the chance to escape. But he reminded himself that he had had seventy years in which he could have left the country, if he were not satisfied or felt the agreements he'd made with it were unfair. He had not chosen Sparta or Crete. And, I reminded myself, I hadn't thought much about Canada until that summer.

The summer passed this way. Gold afternoons on the golf course, a comforting feeling that the matter of war would never touch me, nights in the pool hall or drug store, talking with towns-folk, turning the questions over and over, being a philosopher.

Near the end of that summer the time came to go to the war. The family indulged in a cautious sort of Last Supper together, and afterward my father, who is brave, said it was time to report at the bus depot. I moped down to my bedroom and looked the place over, feeling quite stupid, thinking that my mother would come in there in a day or two and probably cry a little. I trudged back up to the kitchen and put my satchel down. Everyone gathered around, saying so long and good health and write and let us know if you want anything. My father took up the induction papers, checking on times and dates and all the last-minute things, and when I pecked my mother's face and grabbed the satchel for comfort, he told me to put it down, that I wasn't supposed to report until tomorrow.

After laughing about the mistake, after a flush of red color and a flood of ribbing and a wave of relief had come and gone, I took a long drive around the lake, looking again at the place. Sunset Park, with its picnic table and little beach and a brown wood shelter and some families swimming. The Crippled Children's School. Slater Park, more kids. A long string of split level houses, painted every color.

The war and my person seemed like twins as I went around the town's lake. Twins grafted together and forever together, as if a separation would kill them both.

The thought made me angry.

In the basement of my house I found some scraps of cardboard and paper. With devilish flair, I printed obscene words on them, declaring my intention to have no part of Vietnam. With delightful viciousness, a secret will, I declared the war evil, the draft board evil, the town evil in its lethargic acceptance of it all. For many minutes, making up the signs, making up my mind, I was outside the town. I was outside the law, all my old ties to my loves and family broken by the old crayon in my hand. I imagined strutting up and down the sidewalks outside the depot, the bus waiting and the driver blaring his horn, the *Daily Globe* photographer trying to push me into line with the other draftees, the frantic telephone calls, my head buzzing at the deed.

On the cardboard, my strokes of bright red were big and ferocious looking. The language was clear and certain and burned with a hard, defiant, criminal, blasphemous sound. I tried reading it aloud.

Later in the evening I tore the signs into pieces and put the shreds in the garbage can outside, clanging the gray cover down and trapping the messages inside. I went back into the basement. I slipped the crayons into their box, the same stubs of color I'd used a long time before to chalk in reds and greens on Roy Rogers' cowboy boots.

I'd never been a demonstrator, except in the loose sense. True, I'd taken a stand in the school newspaper on the war, trying to show why it seemed wrong. But, mostly, I'd just listened.

"No war is worth losing your life for," a college acquaintance used to argue. "The issue isn't a moral one. It's a matter of efficiency: what's the most efficient way to stay alive when your nation is at war? That's the issue."

But others argued that no war is worth losing your country for, and when asked about the case when a country fights a wrong war, those people just shrugged.

Most of my college friends found easy paths away from the problem, all to their credit. Deferments for this and that. Letters from doctors or chaplains. It was hard to find people who had to think much about the problem. Counsel came from two main quarters, pacifists and veterans of foreign wars.

But neither camp had much to offer. It wasn't a matter of peace, as the pacifists argued, but rather a matter of when and when not to join others in making war. And it wasn't a matter of listening to an ex-lieutenant colonel talk about serving in a right war, when the question was whether to serve in what seemed a wrong one.

On August 13, I went to the bus depot. A Worthington *Daily Globe* photographer took my picture standing by a rail fence with four other draftees.

Then the bus took us through corn fields, to little towns along the way – Lismore and Rushmore and Adrian – where other recruits came aboard. With some of the tough guys drinking beer and howling in the back seats, brandishing their empty cans and calling one another "scum" and "trainee" and "GI Joe," with all this noise and hearty farewelling, we went to Sioux Falls. We spent the night in a YMCA. I went out alone for a beer, drank it in a corner booth, then I bought a book and read it in my room.

By noon the next day our hands were in the air, even the tough guys. We recited the proper words, some of us loudly and daringly and others in bewilderment. It was a brightly lighted room, wood paneled. A flag gave the place the right colors, there was some smoke in the air. We said the words, and we were soldiers.

I'd never been much of a fighter. I was afraid of bullies. Their ripe muscles made me angry: a frustrated anger. Still, I deferred to no one. Positively lorded myself over inferiors. And on top of that was the matter of conscience and conviction, uncertain and surface-deep but pure nonetheless: I was a confirmed liberal, not a pacifist; but I would have cast my ballot to end the Vietnam war immediately, I would have voted for Eugene McCarthy, hoping he would make peace. I was not soldier material, that was certain.

But I submitted. All the personal history, all the midnight conversations and books and beliefs and learning, were crumpled by abstention, extinguished by forfeiture, for lack of oxygen, by a sort of sleepwalking default. It was no decision, no chain of ideas or reasons, that steered me into the war.

It was an intellectual and physical stand-off, and I did not have the energy to see it to an end. I did not want to be a soldier, not even an observer to war. But neither did I want to upset a peculiar balance between the order I knew, the people I knew, and my own private world. It was not that I valued that order. But I feared its opposite, inevitable chaos, censure, embarrassment, the end of everything that had happened in my life, the end of it all.

And the stand-off is still there. I would wish this book could take the form of a plea for everlasting peace, a plea from one who knows, from one who's been there and come back, an old soldier looking back at a dying war.

That would be good. It would be fine to integrate it all to persuade my younger brother and perhaps some others to say no to wars and other battles.

Or it would be fine to confirm the odd beliefs about war: it's horrible, but it's a crucible of men and events and, in the end, it makes more of a man out of you.

But, still, none of these notions seems right. Men are killed, dead human beings are heavy and awkward to carry, things smell different in Vietnam, soldiers are afraid and often brave, drill sergeants are boors, some men think the war is proper and just and others don't and most don't care. Is that the stuff for a morality lesson, even for a theme?

Do dreams offer lessons? Do nightmares have themes, do we awaken and analyze them and live our lives and advise others as a result? Can the foot soldier teach anything important about war, merely for having been there? I think not. He can tell war stories.

In advanced infantry training, the soldier learns new ways to kill people.

Claymore mines, booby traps, the M-60 machine gun, the M-70 grenade launcher. The old 45-caliber pistol. Drill sergeants give lessons on the M-16 automatic rifle, standard weapon in Vietnam.

On the outside, AIT looks like basic training. Lots of push-ups, lots of shoe-shining and firing ranges and midnight marches. But AIT is not basic training. The difference is inside the new soldier's skull, locked to his brain, the certainty of being in a war, pending doom that comes in with each day's light and stays with him all the day long.

The soldier in advanced infantry training is doomed, and he knows it and thinks about it. War, a real war. The drill sergeant said it when we formed up for our first inspection: every swinging dick in the company was now a foot soldier, a grunt in the United States Army, the infantry, Queen of Battle. Not a cook in the lot, not a clerk or mechanic among us. And in eight weeks, he said, we were all getting on a plane that would fly to a war.

"I don't want you to mope around thinkin' about Germany or London," he told us. "Don't even think about it, 'cause there just ain't no way. You're leg men now, and we don't need no infantry in Piccadilly or Southampton. Besides, Vietnam ain't all that bad. I been over there twice now, and I'm alive and still screwin' everything in sight. You troops pay attention to the trainin' you get here, and every swingin' dick will be back in one piece, believe me. Just pay attention, try to learn something. The Nam, it ain't so bad, not if you got your shit together."

One of the trainees asked him about rumors that said we would be shipped to Frankfort.

"Christ, you'll hear the crap till it makes you puke. Every swingin' dick is going to Nam, every big fat swingin' dick."

During the first month, I learned that FNG meant "fuckin' new guy," and that I would be one until the Combat Center's next shipment arrived. I learned that GI's in the field can be as lazy and careless and stupid as GI's anywhere. They don't wear helmets and armored vests unless an officer insists; they fall asleep on guard, and for the most part, no one really cares; they throw away or bury ammunition if it gets heavy and hot. I learned that REMF means "rear echelon motherfucker"; that a man is getting "Short" after his third or fourth month; that a hand grenade is really a "frag"; that one bullet is all it takes and that "you never hear the shot that gets you"; that no one in Alpha Company knows or cares about the cause or purpose of their war: it is about "dinks and slopes," and the idea is simply to kill them or avoid them. Except that in Alpha you don't kill a man, you "waste" him. You don't get mangled by a mine, you get fucked up. You don't call a man by his first name – he's the Kid or the Water Buffalo, Buddy Wolf or Buddy Barker or Buddy Barney, or if the fellow is bland or disliked, he's just Smith or Jones or Rodríguez. The NCO's who go through a crash two-month program to earn their stripes are called "instant NCO's"; hence the platoon's squad leaders were named Ready Whip, Nestle's Quick, and Shake and Bake. And when two of them – Tom and Arnold – were killed two months later, the tragedy was somehow mitigated and depersonalized by telling ourselves that ol' Ready Whip and Quick got themselves wasted by the slopes. There was Cop – an Irish fellow who wanted to join the police force in Danbury, Connecticut – and Reno and the Wop and the College Joe. You can go through a year in Vietnam and live with a platoon of sixty or seventy people, some going and some coming, and you can leave without knowing more than a dozen complete names, not that it matters.

Mad Mark was the platoon leader, a first lieutenant and a Green Beret. It was hard to tell if the name or the reason for the name came first. The madness in Mad Mark, at any rate, was not a hysterical, crazy, into-the-brink, to-the-fore madness. Rather, he was insanely calm. He never showed fear. He was a professional soldier, an ideal leader of men in the field. It was that kind of madness, the perfect guardian for the Platonic Republic. His attitude and manner seemed perfectly molded in the genre of the CIA or KGB operative.

This is not to say that Mad Mark ever did the work of the assassin. But it was his manner, and he cultivated it. He walked with a lanky, easy, silent, fearless stride. He wore tiger fatigues, not for their camouflage but for their look. He carried a shotgun – a weapon I'd thought was outlawed in international war – and the shotgun itself was a measure of his professionalism, for to use it effectively requires an exact blend of courage and skill and self-confidence. The weapon is neither accurate nor lethal at much over seventy yards. So it shows the skill of the carrier, a man who must work his way close enough to the prey to make a shot, close enough to see the enemy's retina and the tone of his skin. To get that close requires courage and self-confidence. The shotgun is not an automatic weapon. You must hit once, on the first shot, and the hit must kill. Mad Mark once said that after the war and in the absence of other U.S. wars he might try the mercenary's life in Africa.

He did not yearn for battle. But neither was he concerned about the prospect. Throughout the first month, vacationing on the safe beaches, he did precisely what the mission called for: a few patrols, a few ambushes, staying ready to react, watching for signs of a rocket attack on Chu Lai. But he did not take the mission to excess. Mad Mark was not a fanatic. He was not gung-ho, not a man in search of a fight. It was more or less an Aristotelian ethic that Mad Mark practiced: making war is a necessary and natural profession. It is natural, but it is only a profession, not a crusade: "Hunting is a part of that art; and hunting might be practiced – not only against wild animals, but also against human beings who are intended by nature to be ruled by others and refuse to obey that intention – because war of this order is naturally just." And, like Aristotle, Mad Mark believed in and practiced the virtue of moderation, so he did what was necessary in war, necessary for an officer and platoon leader in war, and he did no more or less.

He lounged with us during the hot days, he led a few patrols and ambushes, he flirted with the girls in our caravan, and, with a concern for only the basics of discipline, he allowed us to enjoy the holiday. Lying in the shade with the children, we learned a little Vietnamese, and they learned words like "motherfucker" and "gook" and "dink" and "tit." Like going to school.

It was not a bad war until we sent a night patrol into a village called Tri Binh 4. Mad Mark led it, taking only his shotgun and five other men. They'd been gone for an hour. Then came a burst of fire and a radio call that they'd opened up on some VC smoking and talking by a well. In ten minutes they were out of the village and back with the platoon.

The Kid was ecstatic. "Christ! They were right out there, right in the open, right in the middle of the ville, in a little clearing, just sitting on their asses! Shit, I almost shit! Ten of 'em, just sitting there. Jesus, we gave 'em hell. Damn, we gave it to 'em!" His face was on fire in the night, his teeth were flashing, he was grinning himself out of his skin. He paced back and forth, wanting to burst.

"Jesus," he said. "Show 'em the ear we got! Let's see the ear!"

Someone turned on a flashlight. Mad Mark sat cross-legged and unwrapped a bundle of cloth and dangled a hunk of brown, fresh human ear under the yellow beam of light. Someone giggled. The ear was clean of blood. It dripped with a little water, as if coming out of a bathtub. Part of the upper lobe was gone. A band of skin flopped away from the ear, at the place where the ear had been held to a man's head. It looked alive. It looked like it would move in Mad Mark's hands, as if it might make a squirm for freedom. It seemed to have the texture of a hunk of elastic.

"Christ, Mad Mark just went up and sliced it off the dead dink! No wonder he's Mad Mark, he did it like he was cuttin' sausages or something."

"What are you gonna do with it? Why don't you eat it, Mad Mark?"

"Bullshit, who's gonna eat a goddamn dink. I eat women, not dead dinks."

"We got some money off the gook, too. A whole shitload." One of the men pulled out a roll of greasy piasters, and the members of the patrol split it up and pocketed it; then they passed the ear around for everyone to look at.

Mad Mark called in gunships. For an hour the helicopters strafed and rocketed Tri Binh 4. The sky and the trees and the hillsides were lighted up by spotlights and tracers and fires. From our position we could smell the smoke coming from Tri Binh 4. We heard cattle and chickens dying. At two in the morning we started to sleep, one man at a time. Tri Binh 4 turned curiously quiet and dark, except for the sound and light of a last few traces of fire. Smoke continued to billow over to our position all night, however, and when I awakened every hour, it was the first thing to sense and to remind me of the ear. In the morning another patrol was sent into the village. The dead VC was still there, stretched out on his back with his eyes closed and his arms folded and his head cocked to one side so that you could not see where the ear was gone. Little fires burned in some of the huts, and dead animals lay about, but there were no people. We searched Tri Binh 4, then burned most of it down.

The days in April multiplied like twins, sextuplets, each identical. We played during the days. Volleyball. Gin. Tag. Poker or chess. Mad Mark had fun with his riot gas grenades, tossing them into a bunker and watching the artillery officer scramble out in tears. Captain Johansen and the battalion commander, Colonel Daud, flew overhead in a helicopter, dumping gas grenades onto the LZ. It was a training exercise. The idea was to test our reaction time, to make sure our gas masks were functioning. Mostly, though, it was to pass away the month of April.

At night we were supposed to send out ambushes, orders of Colonel Daud. Sometimes we did, other times we did not. If the officers decided that the men were too tired or too restless for a night's ambush, they would prepare a set of grid coordinates and call them into battalion headquarters. It would be a false report, a fake. The artilleryman would radio phony information to the big guns in the rear. The 105's or 155's would blast out their expensive rounds of marking explosives, and the lieutenant would call back his bogus adjustments, chewing out someone in the rear for poor marksmanship. During the night's radio watch, we would call our nonexistent ambush, asking for a situation report. We'd pause a moment, change our voice by a decibel, and answer our own call: "Sit Rep is negative. Out." We did this once an hour for the entire night, covering the possibility that higher headquarters might be monitoring the net. Foolproof. The enlisted men, all of us, were grateful to Alpha's officers. And the officers justified it, muttering that Colonel Daud was a greenhorn, too damn gung-ho.

In the next days it took little provocation for us to flick the flint of our Zippo lighters. Thatched roofs take the flame quickly, and on bad days the hamlets of Pinkville burned, taking our revenge in fire. It was good to walk from Pinkville and to see fire behind Alpha Company. It was good, just as pure hate is good.

We walked to other villages, and the phantom Forty-eighth Viet Cong Battalion walked with us. When a booby-trapped artillery round blew two popular soldiers into a hedgerow, men put their fists into the faces of the nearest Vietnamese, two frightened women living in the guilty hamlet, and when the troops were through with them, they hacked off chunks of thick black hair. The men were crying, doing this. An officer used his pistol, hammering it against a prisoner's skull.

Scraps of our friends were dropped in plastic body bags. Jet fighters were called in. The hamlet was leveled, and napalm was used. I heard screams in the burning black rubble. I heard the enemy's AK-47 rifles crack out like impotent pop-guns against the jets. There were Viet Cong in that hamlet. And there were babies and children and people who just didn't give a damn in there, too. But Chip and Tom were on the way to Graves Registration in Chu Lai, and they were dead, and it was hard to be filled with pity.

The Bouncing Betty is feared most. It is a common mine. It leaps out of its nest in the earth, and when it hits its apex, it explodes, reliable and deadly. If a fellow is lucky and if the mine is in an old emplacement, having been exposed to the rains, he may notice its three prongs jutting out of the clay. The prongs serve as the Bouncing Betty's firing device. Step on them, and the unlucky soldier will hear a muffled explosion; that's the initial charge sending the mine on its one-yard leap into the sky. The fellow takes another step and begins the next and his backside is bleeding and he's dead. We call it "ol' step and a half."

More destructive than the Bouncing Betty are the boo-by-trapped mortar and artillery rounds. They hang from trees. They nestle in shrubbery. They lie under the sand. They wait beneath the mud floors of huts. They haunted us. Chip, my black buddy from Orlando, strayed into a hedgerow and triggered a rigged 105 artillery round. He died in such a way that, for once, you could never know his color. He was wrapped in a plastic body bag, we popped smoke, and a hel-icopter took him away, my friend. And there was Shorty, a volatile fellow so convinced that the mines would take him that he spent a month AWOL. In July he came back to the field, joking but still unsure of it all. One day, when it was very hot, he sat on a booby-trapped 155 round.

When you are ordered to march through areas such as Pinkville – GI slang for Song My, parent village of My Lai – the Batangan Peninsula or the Athletic Field, appropriately named for its flat acreage of grass and rice paddy, when you step about these pieces of ground, you do some thinking. You hallucinate. You look ahead a few paces and wonder what your legs will resemble if there is more to the earth in that spot than silicates and nitrogen. Will the pain be unbearable? Will you scream or fall silent? Will you be afraid to look at your own body, afraid of the sight of your own red flesh and white bone? You wonder if the medic remembered his morphine. You wonder if your friends will weep.

It is not easy to fight this sort of self-defeating fear, but you try. You decide to be ultracareful – the hard-nosed, realistic approach. You try to second-guess the mine. Should you put your foot to that flat rock or the clump of weed to its rear? Paddy dike or water? You wish you were Tarzan, able to swing with the vines. You try to trace the footprints of the man to your front. You give it up when he curses you for following too closely; better one man dead than two.

The moment-to-moment, step-by-step decision-making preys on your mind. The effect sometimes is paralysis. You are slow to rise from rest breaks. You walk like a wooden man, like a toy soldier out of Victor Herbert's *Babes in Toyland*. Contrary to military and parental training, you walk with your eyes pinned to the dirt, spine arched, and you are shivering, shoulders hunched. If you are not overwhelmed by complete catatonia, you may react as Philip did on the day he was told to police up one of his friends, victim of an antipersonnel mine. Afterward, as dusk fell, Philip was swinging his entrenching tool like a madman, sweating and crying and hollering. He dug a foxhole four feet into the clay. He sat in it and sobbed. Everyone – all his friends and all the officers – were very quiet, and not a person said anything. No one comforted him until it was very dark. Then, to stop the noise, one man at a time would talk to him, each of us saying he understood and that tomorrow it would all be over. The captain said he would get Philip to the rear, find him a job driving a truck or painting fences.

Once in a great while we would talk seriously about the mines. "It's more than the fear of death that chews on your mind," one soldier, nineteen years old, eight months in the field, said. "It's an absurd combination of certainty and uncertainty: the certainty that you're walking in mine fields, walking past the things day after day; the uncertainty of your every movement, of which way to shift your weight, of where to sit down.

"There are so many ways the VC can do it. So many configurations, so many types of camouflage to hide them. I'm ready to go home."

The kid is right:

The M-14 antipersonnel mine, nicknamed the "toe popper." It will take a hunk out of your foot. Smitty lost a set of toes. Another man who is now just a blur of gray eyes and brown hair – he was with us for only a week – lost his left heel.

The booby-trapped grenade. Picture a bushy shrub along your path of march. Picture a tin can secured to the shrub, open and directed toward the trail. Inside the can is a hand grenade, safety pin removed, so that only the can's metal circumference prevents the "spoon," or firing handle, from jumping off the grenade and detonating it. Finally, a trip wire is attached to the grenade, extending across the pathway, perhaps six inches above the dirt. Hence, when your delicate size-eight foot caresses that wire, the grenade is yanked from its container, releasing the spoon and creating problems for you and your future.

The Soviet TMB and the Chinese antitank mines. Although designed to detonate under the pressure of heavy vehicles, the antitank mine is known to have shredded more than one soldier.

The directional-fragmentation mine. The concave-faced directional mine contains from 450 to 800 steel fragments embedded in a matrix and backed by an explosive charge – TNT or petnam. The mine is aimed at your anticipated route of march. Your counterpart in uniform, a gentle young man, crouches in the jungle, just off the trail. When you are in range, he squeezes his electronic firing device. The effects of the mine are similar to those of a twelve-gauge shotgun fired at close range. United States Army training manuals describe this country's equivalent device, the Claymore mine: "It will allow for wider distribution and use, particularly in large cities. It will effect considerable savings in materials and logistics." In addition, they call the mine cold-blooded.

The corrosive-action-car-killer. The CACK is nothing more than a grenade, its safety pin extracted and spoon held in place by a rubber band. It is deposited in your gas tank. Little boys and men of the cloth are particularly able to maneuver next to an unattended vehicle and do the deed – beneath a universal cloak of innocence. The corrosive action of the gas-oline eats away the rubber band, releasing the spoon, blowing you up in a week or less. Although it is rarely encountered by the foot-borne infantryman, the device gives the rear-echelon mine finder (REMF) something to ponder as he delivers the general's laundry.

In the three days that I spent writing this, mines and men came together three more times. Seven more legs were out on the red clay; also, another arm.

The immediacy of the last explosion – three legs, ten min-utes ago – made me ready to burn the midsection of this report, the flippant itemization of these killer devices. Hear-ing over the radio what I just did, only enough for a flashing memory of what it is all about, makes the *Catch-22* jokes into a cemetery of half-truths. "Orphan 22, this is . . . this is Yankee 22 . . . mine, mine. Two guys . . . legs are off . . . I say again, legs off . . . request urgent dust-off, grid 711888 . . . give me ETA . . . get that damn bird." Tactical Operations Center: "You're coming in distorted . . . Yankee 22? Say again . . . speak slowly . . . understand you need dust-off helicopter?" Pause. "This is Yankee 22 . . . for Chri . . . ake . . . need chop-per . . . two men, legs are . . ."

But only to say another truth will I let the half-truths stand.

The catalog of mines will be retained, because that is how we talked about them, with a funny laugh, flippantly, with a chuckle. It is funny. It's absurd.

Patent absurdity. The troops are going home, and the war has not been won, even with a quarter of the United States Army fighting it. We slay one of them, hit a mine, kill another, hit another mine. It is funny. We walk through the mines, trying to catch the Viet Cong Forty-eighth Battalion like an unexperienced hunter after a hummingbird. But he finds us far more often than we do him. He is hidden among the mass of civilians or in tunnels or in jungles. So we walk to find him, stalking the mythical, phantomlike Forty-eighth Battalion from here to there to here to there. And each piece of ground left behind is his from the moment we are gone on our next hunt. It is not a war fought for territory, not for pieces of land that will be won and held. It is not a war fought to win the hearts of the Vietnamese nationals, not in the wake of contempt drawn on our faces and on theirs, not in the wake of a burning village, a trampled rice paddy, a battered detainee. If land is not won and if hearts are at best left indifferent; if the only obvious criterion of military success is body count and if the enemy absorbs losses as he has, still able to lure us amid his crop of mines; if soldiers are being withdrawn, with more to go later and later and later; if legs make me more of a man, and they surely do, my soul and character and capacity to love notwithstanding; if any of this is truth, a soldier can only do his walking laughing along the way and taking a funny, crooked step.

It Made You Feel Omni

Michael Herr

Herr covered the Vietnam War for *Esquire* and *Rolling Stone*. He
wrote the screenplay for Coppola and Milius' *Apocalypse Now*.
From Herr's *Dispatches*, published in 1977.

Airmobility, dig it, you weren't going anywhere. It made you
feel safe, it made you feel Omni, but it was only a stunt, technology. Mobility was just mobility, it saved lives or took them
all the time (saved mine I don't know how many times, maybe
dozens, maybe none), what you really needed was a flexibility
far greater than anything the technology could provide, some
generous, spontaneous gift for accepting surprises, and I
didn't have it. I got to hate surprises, control freak at the
crossroads, if you were one of those people who always
thought they had to know what was coming next, the war
could cream you. It was the same with your ongoing attempts
at getting used to the jungle or the blow-you-out climate or
the saturating strangeness of the place which didn't lessen
with exposure so often as it fattened and darkened in accumulating alienation. It was great if you could adapt, you had
to try, but it wasn't the out as you were. If it looked like they
weren't you thought they were insane, if it looked like they
were it made you feel a lot worse.

I went through that thing a number of times and only got
a fast return on my fear once, a too classic hot landing with
the heat coming from the trees about 300 yards away, sweeping machine-gun fire that sent men head down into swampy

water, running on their hands and knees toward the grass where it wasn't blown flat by the rotor blades, not much to be running for but better than nothing. The helicopter pulled up before we'd all gotten out, leaving the last few men to jump twenty feet down between the guns across the paddy and the gun on the chopper door. When we'd all reached the cover of the wall and the captain had made a check, we were amazed to see that no one had even been hurt, except for one man who'd sprained both his ankles jumping. Afterward, I remembered that I'd been down in the muck worrying about leeches. I guess you could say that I was refusing to accept the situation.

"Boy, you sure get offered some shitty choices," a Marine once said to me, and I couldn't help but feel that what he really meant was that you didn't get offered any at all. Specifically, he was just talking about a couple of C-ration cans, "dinner," but considering his young life you couldn't blame him for thinking that if he knew one thing for sure, it was that there was no one anywhere who cared less about what *he* wanted. There wasn't anybody he wanted to thank for his food, but he was grateful that he was still alive to eat it, that the motherfucker hadn't scarfed him up first. He hadn't been anything but tired and scared for six months and he'd lost a lot, mostly people, and seen far too much, but he was breathing in and breathing out, some kind of choice all by itself.

He had one of those faces, I saw that face at least a thousand times at a hundred bases and camps, all the youth sucked out of the eyes, the color drawn from the skin, cold white lips, you knew he wouldn't wait for any of it to come back. Life had made him old, he'd live it out old. All those faces, sometimes it was like looking into faces at a rock concert, locked in, the event had them; or like students who were very heavily advanced, serious beyond what you'd call their years if you didn't know for yourself what the minutes and hours of those years were made up of. Not just like all the ones you saw who looked like they couldn't drag their asses through another day of it. (How do you feel when a nineteen-year-old kid tells you from the bottom of his heart that he's gotten too old for this kind of shit?) Not like the faces of the dead or wounded either, they could look more released than overtaken. These were the faces of boys whose whole lives seemed to have backed up on them, they'd be a few feet away but they'd be looking back at you over a distance you knew you'd never really cross. We'd talk, sometimes fly together, guys going out on R&R, guys escorting bodies, guys who'd flipped over into extremes of peace or violence. Once I flew with a kid who was going home, he looked back down once at the ground where he'd spent the year and spilled his whole load of tears. Sometimes you even flew with the dead.

Once I jumped on a chopper that was full of them. The kid in the op shack had said that there would be a body on board, but he'd been given some wrong information. "How bad do you want to get to Danang?" he'd asked me, and I'd said, "Bad."

When I saw what was happening I didn't want to get on, but they'd made a divert and a special landing for me, I had to go with the chopper I'd drawn, I was afraid of looking squeamish. (I remember, too, thinking that a chopper full of dead men was far less likely to get shot down than one full of living.) They weren't even in bags. They'd been on a truck near one of the firebases in the DMZ that was firing support for Khe Sanh, and the truck had hit a Command-detonated mine, then they'd been rocketed. The Marines were always running out of things, even food, ammo and medicine, it wasn't so strange that they'd run out of bags too. The men had been wrapped around in ponchos, some of them carelessly fastened with plastic straps, and loaded on board. There was a small space cleared for me between one of them and the door gunner, who looked pale and so tremendously furious that I thought he was angry with me and I couldn't look at him for a while. When we went up the wind blew through the ship and made the ponchos shake and tremble until the one next to me blew back in a fast brutal flap, uncovering the face. They hadn't even closed his eyes for him.

The gunner started hollering as loud as he could, "Fix it! Fix it!" Maybe he thought the eyes were looking at him, but there wasn't anything I could do. My hand went there a couple of times and I couldn't, and then I did. I pulled the poncho tight, lifted his head carefully and tucked the poncho under it, and then I couldn't believe that I'd done it. All during the ride the gunner kept trying to smile, and when we landed at Dong Ha he thanked me and ran off to get a detail. The pilots jumped down and walked away without looking back once, like they'd never seen that chopper before in their lives. I flew the rest of the way to Danang in a general's plane.

We were all strapped into the seats of the Chinook, fifty of us, and something, someone was hitting it from the outside with an enormous hammer. How do they do that? I thought, we're a thousand feet in the air! But it had to be that, over and over, shaking the helicopter, making it dip and turn in a horrible out-of-control motion that took me in the stomach. I had to laugh, it was so exciting, it was the thing I had wanted, almost what I had wanted except for that wrenching, resonant metal echo; I could hear it even above the noise of the rotor blades. And they were going to fix that, I knew they would make it stop. They had to, it was going to make me sick.

They were all replacements going in to mop up after the big battles on Hills 875 and 876, the battles that had already taken on the name of one great battle, the battle of Dak To. And I was new, brand new, three days in-country, embarrassed about my boots because they were so new. And across from me, ten feet away, a boy tried to jump out of the straps and then jerked forward and hung there, his rifle barrel caught in the red plastic webbing of the seat back. As the chopper rose again and turned, his weight went back hard against the webbing and a dark spot the size of a baby's hand showed in the center of his fatigue jacket. And it grew – I knew what it was, but not really – it got up to his armpits and then started down his sleeves and up over his shoulders at the same time. It went all across his waist and down his legs, covering the canvas on his boots until they were dark like everything else he wore, and it was running in slow, heavy drops off of his fingertips. I thought I could hear the drops hitting the metal strip on the chopper floor. Hey! . . . Oh, but this isn't anything at all, it's not real, it's just some *thing* they're going through that isn't real. One of the door gunners was heaped up on the floor like a cloth dummy. His hand had the bloody raw look of a pound of liver fresh from the butcher paper. We touched down on the same lz we had just left a few minutes before, but I didn't know it until one of the guys shook my shoulder, and then I couldn't stand up. All I could feel of my legs was their shaking, and the guy thought I'd been hit and helped me up. The chopper had taken eight hits, there was shattered plastic all over the floor, a dying pilot up front, and the boy was hanging forward in the straps again, he was dead, but not (I knew) really dead.

It took me a month to lose that feeling of being a spectator to something that was part game, part show. That first afternoon, before I'd boarded the Chinook, a black sergeant had tried to keep me from going. He told me I was too new to go near the kind of shit they were throwing around up in those hills. ("You a reporter?" he'd asked, and I'd said, "No, a writer," dumbass and pompous, and he'd laughed and said, "Careful. You can't use no eraser up where you wanna go.") He'd pointed to the bodies of all the dead Americans lined in two long rows near the chopper pad, so many that they could not even cover all of them decently. But they were not real then, and taught me nothing. The Chinook had come in, blowing my helmet off, and I grabbed it up and joined the replacements waiting to board. "Okay, man," the sergeant said. "You gotta go, you gotta go. All's I can say is, I hope you get a clean wound."

The Interrogation of the Prisoner Bung by Mister Hawkins and Sergeant Tree

David Huddle

David Huddle served with military intelligence in Vietnam. His short story "The Interrogation of the Prisoner Bung" was originally published in 1971 in *Esquire*.

THE LAND IN THESE PROVINCES to the south of the capital city is so flat it would be possible to ride a bicycle from one end of this district to the other and to pedal only occasionally. The narrow highway passes over kilometers and kilometers of rice fields, laid out square and separated by slender green lines of grassy paddy-dikes and by irrigation ditches filled with bad water. The villages are far apart and small. Around them are clustered the little pockets of huts, the hamlets where the rice farmers live. The village that serves as the capital of this district is just large enough to have a proper marketplace. Close to the police compound, a detachment of Americans has set up its tents. These are lumps of new green canvas, and they sit on a concrete, French-built tennis court, long abandoned, not far from a large lily pond where women come in the morning to wash clothes and where policemen of the compound and their children come to swim and bathe in the late afternoon.

The door of a room to the rear of the District Police Head-quarters is cracked for light and air. Outside noises – chickens quarreling, children playing, the mellow grunting of the pigs owned by the police chief – these reach the ears of the three men inside the quiet room. The room is not a cell; it is more like a small bedroom.

The American is nervous and fully awake, but he forces himself to yawn and sips at his coffee. In front of him are his papers, the report forms, yellow notepaper, two pencils and a ball-point pen. Across the table from the American is Sergeant Tree, a young man who was noticed by the government of his country and taken from his studies to be sent to inter-preter's school. Sergeant Tree has a pleasant and healthy face. He is accustomed to smiling, especially in the presence of Americans, who are, it happens, quite fond of him. Sergeant Tree knows that he has an admirable position working with Mister Hawkins; several of his unlucky classmates from inter-preter's school serve nearer the shooting.

The prisoner, Bung, squats in the far corner of the room, his back at the intersection of the cool concrete walls. Bung is a large man for an Asian, but he is squatted down close to the floor. He was given a cigarette by the American when he was first brought into the room, but has finished smoking and holds the white filter inside his fist. Bung is not tied, nor restrained, but he squats perfectly still, his bare feet laid out flat and large on the floor. His hair, cut by his wife, is cropped short and uneven; his skin is dark, leathery, and there is a bruise below one of his shoulder blades. He looks only at the floor, and he wonders what he will do with the tip of the cig-arette when the interrogation begins. He suspects that he ought to eat it now so that it will not be discovered later.

From the large barracks room on the other side of the building comes laughter and loud talking, the policemen changing shifts. Sergeant Tree smiles at these sounds. Some of the younger policemen are his friends. Hawkins, the Amer-ican, does not seem to have heard. He is trying to think about sex, and he cannot concentrate.

"Ask the prisoner what his name is."

"What is your name?"

The prisoner reports that his name is Bung. The language startles Hawkins. He does not understand this language, except the first ten numbers of counting, and the words for yes and no. With Sergeant Tree helping him with the spelling, Hawkins enters the name into the proper blank.

"Ask the prisoner where he lives."

"Where do you live?"

The prisoner wails a string of language. He begins to weep as he speaks, and he goes on like this, swelling up the small room with the sound of his voice until he sees a warning twitch of the interpreter's hand. He stops immediately, as though corked. One of the police chief's pigs is snuffing over the ground just outside the door, rooting for scraps of food.

"What did he say?"

"He says that he is classed as a poor farmer, that he lives in the hamlet near where the soldiers found him, and that he has not seen his wife and his children for four days now and they do not know where he is.

"He says that he is not one of the enemy, although he has seen the enemy many times this year in his hamlet and in the village near his hamlet. He says that he was forced to give rice to the enemy on two different occasions, once at night, and another time during the day, and that he gave rice to the enemy only because they would have shot him if he had not.

"He says that he does not know the names of any of these men. He says that one of the men asked him to join them and to go with them, but that he told this man that he could not join them and go with them because he was poor and because his wife and his children would not be able to live without him to work for them to feed them. He says that the enemy men laughed at him when he said this but that they did not make him go with them when they left his house.

"He says that two days after the night the enemy came and took rice from him, the soldiers came to him in the field where he was working and made him walk with them for many kilometers, and made him climb into the back of a large truck, and put a cloth over his eyes, so that he did not see where the truck carried him and did not know where he was until he was put with some other people in a pen. He says that one of the soldiers hit him in the back with a weapon, because he was afraid at first to climb into the truck.

"He says that he does not have any money but that he has ten kilos of rice hidden beneath the floor of the kitchen of his house. He says that he would make us the gift of this rice if we would let him go back to his wife and his children."

When he has finished his translation of the prisoner's speech, Sergeant Tree smiles at Mister Hawkins. Hawkins feels that he ought to write something down. He moves the pencil to a corner of the paper and writes down his service number, his Social Security number, the telephone number of his girl friend in Silver Spring, Maryland and the amount of money he has saved in his allotment account.

"Ask the prisoner in what year he was born?"

Hawkins has decided to end the interrogation of this prisoner as quickly as he can. If there is enough time left, he will find an excuse for Sergeant Tree and himself to drive the jeep into the village.

"In what year were you born?"

The prisoner tells the year of his birth.

"Ask the prisoner in what place he was born."

"In what place were you born?"

The prisoner tells the place of his birth.

"Ask the prisoner the name of his wife."

"What is the name of your wife?"

Bung gives the name of his wife.

"Ask the prisoner the names of his parents."

Bung tells the names.

"Ask the prisoner the names of his children."

"What are the names of your children?"

The American takes down these things on the form, painstakingly, with the help in the spelling from the interpreter, who has become bored with this. Hawkins fills all the blank spaces on the front of the form. Later, he will add his summary of the interrogation in the space provided on the back.

"Ask the prisoner the name of his hamlet chief."

"What is the name of your hamlet chief?"

The prisoner tells this name, and Hawkins takes it down on the notepaper. Hawkins has been trained to ask these questions. If a prisoner gives one incorrect name, then all names given may be incorrect, all information secured unreliable.

Bung tells the name of his village chief, and the American takes it down. Hawkins tears off this sheet of notepaper and gives it to Sergeant Tree. He asks the interpreter to take this paper to the police chief to check if these are the correct names. Sergeant Tree does not like to deal with the police chief because the police chief treats him as if he were a farmer. But he leaves the room in the manner of someone engaged in important business. Bung continues to stare at the floor, afraid the American will kill him now that they are in this room together, alone.

Hawkins is again trying to think about sex. Again, he is finding it difficult to concentrate. He cannot choose between thinking about sex with his girl friend Suzanne or with a plump girl who works in a souvenir shop in the village. The soft grunting of the pig outside catches his ear, and he finds that he is thinking of having sex with the pig. He takes another sheet of notepaper and begins calculating the number of days he has left to remain in Asia. The number turns out to be one hundred and thirty-three. This distresses him because the last time he calculated the number it was one hundred and thirty-five. He decides to think about food. He thinks of an omelet. He would like to have an omelet. His eyelids begin to close as he considers all the things that he likes to eat: an omelet, chocolate pie, macaroni, cookies, cheeseburgers, black-cherry Jell-O. He has a sudden vivid image of Suzanne's stomach, the path of downy hair to her navel. He stretches the muscles in his legs, and settles into concentration.

The clamor of chickens distracts him. Sergeant Tree has

caused this noise by throwing a rock on his way back. The police chief refused to speak with him and required him to conduct his business with the secretary, whereas this secretary gloated over the indignity to Sergeant Tree, made many unnecessary delays and complications before letting the interpreter have a copy of the list of hamlet chiefs and village chiefs in the district.

Sergeant Tree enters the room, goes directly to the prisoner, with the toe of his boot kicks the prisoner on the shinbone. The boot hitting bone makes a wooden sound. Hawkins jerks up in his chair, but before he quite understands the situation, Sergeant Tree has shut the door to the small room and has kicked the prisoner's other shinbone. Bung responds with a grunt and holds his shins with his hands, drawing himself tighter into the corner.

"Wait!" The American stands up to restrain Sergeant Tree, but this is not necessary. Sergeant Tree has passed by the prisoner now and has gone to stand at his own side of the table. From underneath his uniform shirt he takes a rubber club, which he has borrowed from one of his policeman friends. He slaps the club on the table.

"He lies!" Sergeant Tree says this with as much evil as he can force into his voice.

"Hold on now. Let's check this out." Hawkins' sense of justice has been touched. He regards the prisoner as a clumsy, hulking sort, obviously not bright, but clearly honest.

"The police chief says that he lies!" Sergeant Tree announces. He shows Hawkins the paper listing the names of the hamlet chiefs and the village chiefs. With the door shut, the light in the small room is very dim, and it is difficult to locate the names on the list. Hawkins is disturbed by the darkness, is uncomfortable being so intimately together with two men. The breath of the interpreter has something sweetish to it. It occurs to Hawkins that now, since the prisoner has lied to them, there will probably not be enough time after the interrogation to take the jeep and drive into the village. This vexes him. He decides there must be something unhealthy in the diet of these people, something that causes this sweet-smelling breath.

Hawkins finds it almost impossible to read the columns of handwriting. He is confused. Sergeant Tree must show him the places on the list where the names of the prisoner's hamlet chief and village chief are written. They agree that the prisoner has given them incorrect names, though Hawkins is not certain of it. He wishes these things were less complicated, and he dreads what he knows must follow. He thinks regretfully of what could have happened if the prisoner had given the correct names: the interrogation would have ended quickly, the prisoner released; he and Sergeant Tree could have driven into the village in the jeep, wearing their sunglasses, with the cool wind whipping past them, dust billowing around the jeep, shoeshine boys shrieking, the girl in the souvenir shop going with him into the back room for a time.

Sergeant Tree goes to the prisoner, kneels on the floor beside him, and takes Bung's face between his hands. Tenderly, he draws the prisoner's head close to his own, and asks, almost absentmindedly, "Are you one of the enemy?"

"No."

All this strikes Hawkins as vaguely comic, someone saying, "I love you," in a high-school play.

Sergeant Tree spits in the face of the prisoner and then jams the prisoner's head back against the wall. Sergeant Tree stands up quickly, jerks the police club from the table, and starts beating the prisoner with random blows. Bung stays squatted down and covers his head with both arms. He makes a shrill noise.

Hawkins has seen this before in other interrogations. He listens closely, trying to hear everything: little shrieks coming from Sergeant Tree's throat, the chunking sound of the rubber club makes. The American recognizes a kind of rightness in this, like the final slapping together of the bellies of a man and a woman.

Sergeant Tree stops. He stands, legs apart, facing the

prisoner, his back to Hawkins. Bung keeps his squatting position, his arms crossed over his head.

The door scratches and opens just wide enough to let in a
policeman friend of Sergeant Tree's, a skinny, rotten-toothed
man, and a small boy. Hawkins has seen this boy and the
policeman before. The two of them smile at the American
and at Sergeant Tree, whom they admire for his education
and for having achieved such an excellent position. Hawkins
starts to send them back out, but decides to let them stay. He
does not like to be discourteous to Asians.

Sergeant Tree acknowledges the presence of his friend and
the boy. He sets the club on the table and removes his uniform shirt and the white T-shirt beneath it. His chest is
powerful, but hairless. He catches Bung by the ears and jerks
upward until the prisoner stands. Sergeant Tree is much
shorter than the prisoner, and this he finds an advantage.

Hawkins notices that the muscles in Sergeant Tree's buttocks are clenched tight, and he admires this, finds it attractive.
He has in his mind Suzanne. They are sitting on the back seat
of the Oldsmobile. She has removed her stockings and garter
belt, and now slides the panties down from her hips, down
her legs, off one foot, keeping them dangling on one ankle,
ready to be pulled up quickly in case someone comes to the
car and catches them. Hawkins has perfect concentration. He
sees her panties glow.

Sergeant Tree tears away the prisoner's shirt, first from
one side of his chest and then the other. Bung's mouth sags
open now, as though he were about to drool.

The boy clutches at the sleeve of the policeman to whisper
in his ear. The policeman giggles. They hush when the American glances at them. Hawkins is furious because they have
distracted him. He decides there is no privacy to be had in
the entire country.

"Sergeant Tree, send these people out of here, please."

Sergeant Tree gives no sign that he has heard what
Hawkins has said. He is poising himself to begin. Letting out
a heaving grunt, Sergeant Tree chops with the police club,

catching the prisoner directly in the center of the forehead. A flame begins in Bung's brain; he is conscious of a fire, blazing, blinding him. He feels the club touch him twice more, once at his ribs and once at his forearm.

"Are you the enemy?" Sergeant Tree screams.

The policeman and the boy squat beside each other near the door. They whisper to each other as they watch Sergeant Tree settle into the steady, methodical beating. Occasionally he pauses to ask the question again, but he gets no answer.

From a certain height, Hawkins can see that what is happening is profoundly sensible. He sees how deeply he loves these men in this room and how he respects them for the things they are doing. The knowledge rises in him, pushes to reveal itself. He stands up from his chair, virtually at attention.

A loud, hard smack swings the door wide open, and the room is filled with light. The Police Chief stands in the doorway, dressed in a crisp, white shirt, his rimless glasses sparkling. He is a fat man in the way that a good merchant might be fat – solid, confident, commanding. He stands with his hands on his hips, an authority in all matters. The policeman and the boy nod respectfully. The Police Chief walks to the table and picks up the list of hamlet chiefs and village chiefs. He examines this, and then he takes from his shirt pocket another paper, which is also a list of hamlet chiefs and village chiefs. He carries both lists to Sergeant Tree, who is kneeling in front of the prisoner. He shows Sergeant Tree the mistake he has made in getting a list that is out of date. He places the new list in Sergeant Tree's free hand, and then he takes the rubber club from Sergeant Tree's other hand and slaps it down across the top of Sergeant Tree's head. The Police Chief leaves the room, passing before the American, the policeman, the boy, not speaking or looking other than to the direction of the door.

It is late afternoon and the rain has come. Hawkins stands inside his tent, looking through the open flap. He likes to look out across the old tennis court at the big lily pond. He has been fond of water since he learned to water-ski. If the rain stops before dark, he will go out to join the policeman and the children who swim and bathe in the lily pond.

Walking out on the highway, with one kilometer still to go before he comes to the village, is Sergeant Tree. He is alone, the highway behind him and in front of him as far as he can see and nothing else around him but rain and the fields of wet, green rice. His head hurts and his arms are weary from the load of rice he carries. When he returned the prisoner to his hamlet, the man's wife made such a fuss Sergeant Tree had to shout at her to make her shut up, and then, while he was inside the prisoner's hut conducting the final arrangements for the prisoner's release, the rain came, and his policeman friends in the jeep left him to manage alone.

The ten kilos of rice he carries are heavy for him, and he would put his load down and leave it, except that he plans to sell the rice and add the money to what he has been saving to buy a .45 caliber pistol like the one Mister Hawkins carries at his hip. Sergeant Tree tries to think about how well-received he will be in California because he speaks the American language so well, and how it is likely that he will marry a rich American girl with very large breasts.

The prisoner Bung is delighted by the rain. It brought his children inside the hut, and the sounds of their fighting with each other make him happy. His wife came to him and touched him. The rice is cooking, and in a half hour his cousin will come, bringing with him the leader and two other members of Bung's squad. They will not be happy that half of their rice was taken by the interpreter to pay the American, but it will not be a disaster for them. The squad leader will be proud of Bung for gathering the information that he has – for he has memorized the guard routines at the police headquarters and at the old French area where the Americans are staying. He has watched all the comings and goings at these places, and he has marked out in his mind the best avenues of approach, the best escape routes, and the best places to set up ambush. Also, he has discovered a way that they can lie in wait and kill the Police Chief. It will occur at the place where the Police Chief goes to urinate every morning at a certain time. Bung has much information inside his head, and he believes he will be praised by the members of his squad. It is even possible that he will receive a commendation from someone very high.

His wife brings the rifle that was hidden, and Bung sets to cleaning it, savoring the smell of the rice his wife places before him and of the American oil he uses on the weapon. He particularly enjoys taking the weapon apart and putting it together again. He is very fast at this.

A Viet Cong Memoir

Truong Nhu Tang

Truyong Nhu Tang was an economics advisor for the South Vietnamese government while covertly serving as a member of the Viet Cong. Following the fall of Hanoi he became disillusioned with Communism and escaped to France.

Infiltrating into areas under secure government control to see wives and children who had often been marked as Vietcong dependents was a chance business. To get around this, from time to time we would be able to bring families out to the jungle, something that was done for soldiers as well as cadres. But such meetings were necessarily brief and dangerous themselves. (Vo Van Kiet's wife and children were killed on their way to one such rendezvous, when they were caught in a B-52 raid.) More often than not these men went for extended periods without any contact at all with their families.

But for all the privations and hardships, nothing the guerrillas had to endure compared with the stark terrorization of the B-52 bombardments. During its involvement, the United States dropped on Vietnam more than three times the tonnage of explosives that were dropped during all of World War II in military theaters that spanned the world. Much of it came from the high altitude B-52s, bombs of all sizes and types being disgorged by these invisible predators. The statistics convey some sense of the concentrated firepower that was unleashed at America's enemies in both North and

South. From the perspective of those enemies, these figures translated into an experience of undiluted psychological terror, into which we were plunged, day in, day out for years on end.

From a kilometer away, the sonic roar of the B-52 explosions tore eardrums, leaving many of the jungle dwellers permanently deaf. From a kilometer, the shock waves knocked their victims senseless. Any hit within a half kilometer would collapse the walls of an unreinforced bunker, burying alive the people cowering inside. Seen up close, the bomb craters were gigantic – thirty feet across and nearly as deep. In the rainy seasons they would fill up with water and often saw service as duck or fishponds, playing their role in the guerrillas' never-ending quest to broaden their diet. But they were treacherous then too. For as the swamps and lowland areas flooded under half a foot of standing water, the craters would become invisible. Not infrequently some surprised guerrilla, wading along what he had taken to be a familiar route, was suddenly swallowed up.

It was something of a miracle that from 1968 through 1970 the attacks, though they caused significant casualties generally, did not kill a single one of the military or civilian leaders in the headquarters complexes. This luck, though, had a lot to do with accurate advance warning of the raids, which allowed us to move out of the way or take refuge in our bunkers before the bombs began to rain down. B-52s flying out of Okinawa and Guam would be picked up by Soviet intelligence trawlers plying the South China Sea. The planes' headings and air speed would be computed and relayed to COSVN headquarters, which would then order NLF or Northern elements in the anticipated target zones to move away perpendicularly to the attack trajectory. Flights originating from the Thai bases were monitored both on radar and visually by our intelligence nets there and the information similarly relayed.

Often the warnings would give us time to grab some rice and escape by foot or bike down one of the emergency routes.

Hours later we would return to find, as happened on several occasions, that there was nothing left. It was as if an enormous scythe had swept through the jungle, felling the giant teak and go trees like grass in its way, shredding them into billions of scattered splinters. On these occasions – when the B-52S had found their mark – the complex would be utterly destroyed: food, clothes, supplies, documents, everything. It was not just that things were destroyed; in some awesome way they had ceased to exist. You would come back to where your lean-to and bunker had been, your home, and there would simply be nothing there, just an unrecognizable landscape gouged by immense craters.

Equally often, however, we were not so fortunate and had time only to take cover as best we could. The first few times I experienced a B-52 attack it seemed, as I strained to press myself into the bunker floor, that I had been caught in the Apocalypse. The terror was complete. One lost control of bodily functions as the mind screamed incomprehensible orders to get out. On one occasion a Soviet delegation was visiting our ministry when a particularly short-notice warning came through. When it was over, no one had been hurt, but the entire delegation had sustained considerable damage to its dignity – uncontrollable trembling and wet pants the all-too-obvious outward signs of inner convulsions. The visitors could have spared themselves their feelings of embarrassment; each of their hosts was a veteran of the same symptoms.

It was a tribute to the Soviet surveillance techniques that we were caught above-ground so infrequently during the years of the deluge. One of these occasions, though, almost put an end to all our endeavors. Taken by surprise by the sudden earthshaking shocks, I began running along a trench toward my bunker opening when a huge concussion lifted me off the ground and propelled me through the doorway toward which I was heading. Some of my Alliance colleagues were knocked off their feet and rolled around the ground like rag dolls. One old friend, Truong Cao Phuoc, who was working in the foreign relations division, had jumped into a shelter that collapsed on him, somehow leaving him alive with his head protruding from the ground. We extricated him, shoveling the dirt out handful by handful, carefully removing the supporting timbers that were crisscrossed in the earth around him. Truong had been trapped in one of the old U-shaped shelters, which became graves for so many. Later we learned to reinforce these dugouts with an A-frame of timbers that kept the walls from falling in. Reinforced in this manner, they could withstand B-52 bomb blasts as close as a hundred meters.

Sooner or later, though, the shock of the bombardments wore off, giving way to a sense of abject fatalism. The veterans would no longer scrabble at the bunker floors convulsed with fear. Instead people just resigned themselves – fully prepared to "go and sit in the ancestors' corner." The B-52s somehow put life in order. Many of those who survived the attacks found that afterward they were capable of viewing life from a more serene and philosophical perspective. It was a lesson that remained with me, as it did with many others, and helped me compose myself for death on more than one future occasion.

But even the most philosophical of fatalists were worn to the breaking point after several years of dodging and burrowing away from the rain of high explosives. During the most intense periods we came under attack every day for weeks running. At these times we would cook our rice as soon as we got out of our hammocks, kneading it into glutinous balls and ducking into the bunkers to be ready for what we knew was coming Occasionally, we would be on the move for days at a time, stopping only, to prepare food, eating as we walked. At night we would sling our hammocks between two trees wherever we found ourselves, collapsing into an exhausted but restless sleep, still half-awake to the inevitable explosions.

Pursued relentlessly by such demons, some of the guerrillas suffered nervous breakdowns and were packed off for hospital stays; others had to be sent home. There were cases too of fighters rallying to the Saigon government, unable to cope with the demands of life in the jungle. Times came when nobody was able to manage, and units would seek a hopeful refuge across the border in Cambodia.

The first months of 1970 were a precarious time. Even before the new year began, intelligence sources in Phnom Penh informed us that Cambodia's Prince Sihanouk was coming under increased American pressure to allow stepped-up bombing of our Cambodian sanctuaries. Through the years of war, Sihanouk had bravely and ingeniously maintained Cambodia's neutrality, in part by turning a blind eye toward happenings in the border region. Indications that the Americans were looking for a more formal acquiescence to their strikes against our bases and supply routes were ominous indeed. Coupled with this information, Soviet and Chinese sources inside the Cambodian government were now sharing with us intimations they had been receiving of a possible anti-Sihanouk coup.

In preparation for whatever might eventuate, all our headquarters units began fine-tuning their contingency plans. The escape routes we would use if necessary led west across the Vam Co River and into Cambodia's Prey Veng Province, then north toward Kratie. Depending on circumstances, we could take up positions there, on the west bank (the far side) of the Mekong, or continue north up the Ho Chi Minh Trail toward Laos. Strong elements of the NLF's 5th, 7th, and 9th Divisions were brought into the area to provide security for any movements we might be forced to make.

Then, on March 18, 1970, while Sihanouk was vacationing in France, his opponents struck, deposing him as head of the Cambodian government. Sihanouk's removal was for us a cause of instant anxiety, as we now looked over our shoulders at Cambodia, not as a refuge but as a potential danger. With Sihanouk's less-than-farsighted minister Lon Nol in power, Phnom Penh immediately began to stare in our direction with undisguised hostility. Sensing the possibility of entrapment between a Saigon/American offensive from the east and Royal Cambodian Army pressure from the west, COSVN did not wait to monitor developments in the Cambodian capital. On March 19 the permanent staff moved out toward positions that had been readied deep inside Kratie. By the time troops from the American 25th Division struck the headquarters area during the American/Cambodian incursion, the COSVN command staff had been gone almost two months.

With these portentous events as background, the NLF, PRG, and Alliance complexes readied themselves for emergency withdrawal. As we reviewed defensive measures and logistical planning, the B-52 raids reached a peak of frequency. Each day massive explosions rumbled in the distance, shaking the ground under us as the bombers incessantly probed the surrounding jungle. Then on March 27 at four in the morning, we were awakened by the familiar thunder – nearer now than it had been in recent days. All the officials and guards made for the shelters, listening intently. The concussive *whump-whump-whump* came closer and closer, moving in a direct line toward our positions. Then, as the cataclysm walked in on us, everyone hugged the earth – some screaming quietly, others struggling to suppress attacks of violent, involuntary trembling. Around us the ground began to heave spasmodically, and we were engulfed in a monstrous roar. Then, abruptly, it stopped, leaving behind it nearly a hundred dazed Maquis, shaking their heads in an attempt to clear the pressure from their ears. The last of the bomb craters had opened up less than a kilometer away. Again, miraculously, no one had been hurt. But we knew that the time had come. Following advance groups, which had already crossed the Vam Co, the main body – all the ministries and command units spread out over a fifty- or sixty-kilometer arc – began the trek into Cambodia.

By March 30 the Justice Ministry was already established in one of the sanctuary complexes, working and sleeping inside bunkers. Early that morning, three days after the near miss by the B-52s, I was thrown out of my cot onto the bunker floor by a series of explosions rocking the area. Glancing quickly out through the bunker opening, my guards and I saw helicopters hovering just above the trees, maneuvering in to land. I could make out the faces of ARVN soldiers and gun barrels protruding from the open doorways. By this time, fire was stuttering out from the dugouts and shelters as our security people began loosing a fusillade of small-arms and machine gun fire at the attackers. Over the radio, voices crackled through with news that the other ministries were also under attack.

Hour followed hour as the firing surged, died down, then flared up again. All day long I hunkered down in the shelter, my two bodyguards watching the fighting closely, occasionally letting off a volley from their AK47s through the embrasures. Squirming around on my stomach, I gathered together the most important papers, knowing that, whatever the cost, we would have to break through the encirclement when night came. It was a matter of desperation; none of us had any question that we would be captured the following day if we were still in the complex.

With darkness, pressure from the Saigon troops eased off. They undoubtedly knew that our main force units were in the area, and they were afraid of being trapped themselves. At the signal, my guards and I slipped out of the bunker under the dying glow of a flare. There was no firing as we headed westward into the jungle along one of the prearranged escape routes toward the security corridor the 7th Division was setting up. I ran as far as I was able, then slowed into a kind of shuffling trot, gasping for breath. Some of the ministry officials were on the trail in front of me. I could hear other people hurrying behind. From the bunker complex the firing was picking up, filling the night with the staccato bursts of AK47s and M-16s.

Behind us the security teams fanned out, screening our flight and deflecting pursuit. Half-running, half-walking between my guards, I made my way along the trail, unable to see a thing in the blackness of the jungle. All night we slogged along, unsure of what was happening in back of us but determined to keep moving. As the initial rush of adrenalin wore off, my legs began to feel leaden, and my throat ached with thirst. When word was finally passed that we could stop, I slumped to the ground where I was, stupefied with exhaustion. Just before I passed out, I managed to scoop up a few handfuls of water from a stagnant pool next to the trail.

When I awoke it was 6 A.M. The first thing I noticed was that the swampy puddle from which I had drunk the previous night was the repository of several large piles of buffalo excrement. But I hardly had time to reflect on this unpleasant surprise before we heard the shriek of approaching jets. We dived into the jungle just as several American planes shot by, machine-gunning the trail. Under sporadic bombing and strafing attacks, we moved ahead all morning, an entire column by this time made up of the NLF, PRG, and Alliance ministries and support personnel. Though it was impossible to get firm information, it seemed as if we had not incurred any serious losses in the maelstrom of the previous day's assault.

As we walked, our troop strength was more and more in evidence. General Hoang Van Thai had deployed his defense forces to create a secure corridor from the rendezvous point (the place we had stopped for a few hours of sleep) and the Cambodian province of Kratie, our destination to the north. Though as we trudged along, the situation was unclear, there was no doubt at all that Thai's arrangements were undergoing a serious test. We knew that the Saigon troops had launched a thrust against us from the east while Lon Nol's Royal Cambodian forces were moving in from the west along Route 7, a road that intersected the corridor. Knowing that we were in great danger, we walked as fast as we could all day, our only food the cold rice balls we ate as we marched. Meanwhile, the 9th Division threw up a screen against the ARVN drive, while the 5th moved to block the Cambodians on our left. Along the corridor between them the headquarters and government personnel fled, closely shielded by units from the 7th.

Toward the end of the next day, April 2, a motorcycle driver picked me out of the line of march. He had been sent by PRG President Phat to take me to the 7th Division's headquarters farther to the north, where the rest of the NLF, PRG, and Alliance leadership was already assembled, including Mme. Nguyen Thi Dinh, deputy commander of the NLF armed forces. Early the following morning, we all moved out toward Route 7 only a few miles to our north, aware now that the highway was already under attack.

Fighting to break through the PLAF blocking forces, the ARVN and Cambodian vanguards were struggling to gain control of the highway before we could get there, which would cut off our escape and seal us into southern Cambodia, where we could be surrounded and cut apart. We were not sure whether the forces trying to head us off were aware of exactly who or what they were after, and to this day I do not know whether American and Saigon government military analysts realized how close they were to annihilating or capturing the core of the Southern resistance – elite units of our frontline fighters along with the civilian and much of the military leadership. But as we hurried through the corridor, *we* at least were quite clear about the stakes involved in breaking out. Our efforts were thus tinged not only with the desperation of men fleeing the grasp of a merciless foe, but with anxiety for the very existence of our struggle.

It was at this point that Dr. Hoa, seven months pregnant and supported on one side by her husband, on the other by a bodyguard, went into labor. It had been expected that she would require a cesarean section, so a surgical team had accompanied her on the move into Cambodia. But as it turned out, whether because of the constant walking or for some other reason, the birth came normally – and precipitously. On a square of nylon laid out on the jungle floor, the minister of health gave birth to a baby boy, noisy and apparently well, despite his ill-timed appearance and the confusion into which he had been born. Carrying this new addition to the revolutionary forces, we neared Route 7, listening intently for incoming artillery rounds amidst the sounds of battle to our right and left.

Just before we got to the highway, word passed down the column that our line blocking the Cambodians was holding – at least for the moment – and that the 9th Division had counterattacked Saigon forces at Krek, about ten kilometers to the east. Buoyed by this news we crossed 7 and pushed northward in the first of what would become a series of forced marches.

Before long our relief at having avoided entrapment was submerged in an exhaustion beyond description. As day, then night, then day again passed with constant harassment, little sleep, and cold dinners eaten for the most part on the trail, the middle-aged and elderly ministers, with their middle-aged civilian staffs, all of them weakened by disease and half-famished, began to break down physically. As we walked, the rains, typical for that time of year, poured down continuously, turning the red Cambodian earth to a sticky clay that sucked at our rubber sandals, until the last of them had been lost or discarded. Barefoot, pants rolled up above our knees, we shuffled ahead in the ankle-deep mud, each step an energy-draining struggle. Those who had bicycles abandoned them beside the muck of the trail. Like robots, we made our way through the downpour, each man grasping the shirt of the man in front of him for support and direction.

For five days it rained without letup. By this time I could barely stand, let alone walk. I moved along in a slow-motion daze, conscious only of the man in front of me – whose shirt I continued to clutch – and the mortar rounds and artillery shells that crashed sporadically into the jungle alongside our column, from time to time sending us sprawling face first into the mud. At night we slung our hammocks from the rubber trees, propping our nylon squares over us in a useless attempt to keep off the torrents of water. When morning came, it was difficult for any of us to tell if we had slept or had simply lapsed temporarily comatose.

But as we continued northward, we all sensed that there was less urgency to our movement. At some unidentifiable point we realized that no more shells were exploding dully in the sodden trees. At last, in the jungles outside Kratie, 150 kilometers or so north of Route 7, we were able to stop and rest. For several days we did little other than sleep and enjoy the luxuries of hot tea and prepared food, items we hadn't seen for a week and a half. With an opportunity to relax and begin recuperating from this ordeal, spirits started to revive. COSVN's Pham Hung and General Trung joked that "Even though we ran like hell, still we'll win," sentiments that Henry Kissinger anticipated in his 1968 *Foreign Affairs* article: "Guerrillas win if they don't lose. A standard army loses if it does not win."

In taking stock of the situation, we had not in fact lost a great deal. In terms of casualties, our luck had continued to hold. Despite the close escape and the rigors of the march, all of the leadership had managed to arrive at Kratie unharmed. Here we linked up with the COSVN staff, which had previously been evacuated to the region, also without loss. In the expanses of Cambodia's northern provinces, we were less vulnerable to the B-52S and relatively immune to assault, since our forces had de facto control over the region (and had had for some time).

The ARVN attacks that we had so narrowly survived were a precursor to the large-scale American incursion into Cambodia that jumped off a month later. The wider war that resulted from these actions was an almost immediate benefit to us. The American/ARVN attack indeed caused damage and disrupted supply lines. But our antagonists had no staying power in Cambodia. The United States at this point was already in the process of a staged unilateral withdrawal, which could not be truly compensated for by increased air activity. The Saigon forces by themselves were hard-pressed to meet the military challenge they faced in South Vietnam, without adding Cambodia to their burden, while Lon Nol's army was quite simply unprepared for the kind of warfare it now had to face.

Nixon and Kissinger had gambled that a limited foray into our base areas and supply routes would have a telling effect. But they had seriously exaggerated their own ability to inflict damage relative to their opponents' elasticity and durability. Unwisely, they had traded a few immediate and short-term military gains for the unpredictable consequences of intruding into an already volatile Cambodia and for severe, long-term political debits at home. To our analysts, monitoring the American domestic scene, it seemed that the Cambodian invasion had stimulated a divisiveness equaled only perhaps by the Tet Offensive two years earlier. We had indeed, as Pham Hung said, run away, but Nixon had paid dearly for our temporary discomfiture by sustaining major political losses. Kissinger's argument that the invasion had gained a year may be true. But to our way of looking at it – from a political and diplomatic perspective as well as militarily – the United States action had resulted in a resounding victory for the Front.

One Woman's Vietnam

Doris Allen

Doris "Lucki" Allen, a black WAC, was a warrant officer in
military intelligence in Vietnam.

I volunteered to go to Vietnam. I was working in strategic
intelligence at that time. I wanted to go because I kept hearing what I thought must have been lies – all of this couldn't
be true, the information that was coming back to me. And I
got information not only through regular intelligence channels, but also from overseas newspapers and the regular
media. There was a lot of conflict for me in knowing who was
telling the truth, so I said, "Well, I know whatever it is I know,
and I may as well be there too. I'm gonna be a part of this."
Instead of just sitting back here and knowing that I had an
expertise that was needed, it was better for me to be there.
Not to fight and not to shoot guns and not to kill people, but
I looked at it rather that my intelligence would save lives, as
opposed to taking lives. Two months prior to the time that I
left Fort Bragg, I did not read anything having to do with
Vietnam. I didn't read reports; I didn't read newspapers; I
almost didn't listen to the news. I'd kind of close it off when
it came to what was happening in Vietnam. The reason I did
this is because when I got to Vietnam, I wanted to be open-
minded and unbiased and be able to work from there.

When I got to Vietnam, my paranoia started really showing. I don't remember the day I got to Vietnam, but it was
either the thirteenth, fourteenth, or fifteenth of October,

1967. Going over, I was the only woman on the plane with all the other GIs. What I spent my time doing while I was on the plane is reading newspapers and doing the entire order of battle. This was possible because in newspapers they had given locations of all of the American troops from division headquarters down to platoon-size units, exactly where they were in all of Vietnam. So I kept saying to myself, "Here I am sitting on the plane being able to figure out where all of our troops are." I said, "My God, the enemy must be . . . They know!" I think I got paranoid reading that paper, you know. But I already had my cover story – "When I get to Vietnam I won't know anything about anything, and if I get captured, I'll be okay." The cover story I had made up was that I was an expert on the M-16. I knew why it jammed, when it jammed, what was wrong with it; I knew everything about it. I don't know a thing about the M-16 right now, but I had that weapon so heavy in my mind . . . And if they got me I was going to tell them that the only thing I did was take complaints about the M-16. I was going to say, "You know yourself it's a horrible weapon and that your AK-47 is much better than our M-16." Wow, listen to that fantasy!

When I got to Saigon, to Tan Son Nhut airport, dressed in my nice, clean cord uniform, I was looking sharp. They were calling off all these units and all these names, and I did not hear my name once. I don't care where you are, you hear your own name. I was just standing here, and all of a sudden the airport was clearing out, right? But I don't see it clearing out because I'm standing with head against the wall, because when I got there I see all these people that I knew were Vietnamese, okay? For whatever reason, I knew they were Vietnamese, and I saw these cameras, and people are clicking their cameras, and why are these people in here taking pictures? Oh, my God. Not realizing this is their airport – it wasn't military; we just happened to land there. I was standing with my face against the wall – "I hope they don't take a picture of me, oh, God." And that kind of wore out, but that was my introduction. Then I finally found somebody, and I said, "Listen, I'm here, you know, you must have a place for me." And I didn't want to tell them I was military intelligence. . . . Well, anyway, that was all my own anxiety.

They finally decided where I belonged, and I went down to wherever that place was where all the other Army women were sent, and they'd given me this white towel and white washcloth, so I could take a shower. And I think I have a beautiful brown color, right? I got in the shower and started washing, and I said, "Oh, my God, what's happening?!" My washcloth, absolutely, so help me God, was brown, and I thought I was turning white. You don't know how panicky that is – this is the honest truth. I just got panicky, and I almost started crying. . . . Do you realize how dusty and dirty Vietnam was? And this was a matter of being there just a few hours. Imagine, the first day there, and all my black's coming off. Well, I got over that.

The next day I started working. I was in intelligence. For my first year in Vietnam, I worked in the Army Operations Center (AOC), Headquarters, United States Army, Vietnam (USARV). I was the only specialist-7 at the time; there were only twenty-two spec-7s in the military. I was in the "Two Shop" in the AOC and was the only woman in there. I remember one of my humors came up one day. When the general walked in, nobody, none of the men in there, wanted to tell him that his fly was open. I told him his fly was open, and everybody glared at me. I don't think they liked that. The general says, "Oops, thank you," and zips his pants up.

Another general, Air Force General Ryan from Pacific Command in Hawaii, came for an orientation. I was directed to give the orientation, which included a complete rundown of the current military operations throughout Vietnam. I remember it kind of disturbed me, because they put five very plush chairs for the general and his staff to sit in, and I was wondering, "This is Vietnam. Why are you putting plush chairs there for somebody to sit in? I'm talking about war!" When I finished briefing General Ryan, he walked over to me and said, very loudly so that everybody in the AOC could hear it, "I've been CINCPAC for" – whatever time it was – "and I've had lots of reports from over here in Vietnam and been all over Vietnam, and this is the best and most honest report I've had yet, because you stood up here and dared to tell the truth." And everybody else was very excited about this. I think there was a lot of anxiety behind the fact that I was the only spec-7 in there. Well, being spec-7 had the connotation of, you're either really great or you're something special. Being a woman had lots to do with that. My credibility was with me – I had it – but a lot of people couldn't believe, or didn't want to believe, that a woman could actually be making decisions or analyses – and their being correct.

I think the first time I was really tested was when I called the Tet offensive. I had been looking at my notes and reading everything. I had all these reports that I'd read through; I was pouring over them and really into it. Then I wrote a paper, and I titled it "50,000 Chinese." What it said was, we had better get our stuff together because this is what is facing us, this is what is going to happen, and it's going to happen on such and such a day, around such and such a time. I had never heard the word *Tet*; it just wasn't part of my vocabulary. I didn't know that there was a Tet celebration, like maybe a lot of people in foreign countries don't know that we celebrate Easter or Christmas. But I put the date down and said it's going to happen around this particular date. When I took it in to the G-2, the intelligence officer said, "Well, I don't know about this." And I said, "We need to disseminate this. It's got to be told." Well, he sort of believed it and said, "I'll tell you what to do. I want you to take it up to Saigon and run it through and see what they think there, what the G-2 at MACV thinks about it." I said okay, and I got in my jeep and went on up to Saigon.

When I walked in I knew that it had to go through and be scrutinized by about fifteen people. It seemed like that, but it really went through only four or five. When I walked in there, the sergeant came up to me and said, "Can I help you?" And I said, "Yes, I'd like to see the G-2. I have something et cetera, et cetera."The captain came out: "What do you have?" I said, "I'd like to see the G-2 et cetera, et cetera." And he said, "Just a minute." A major came out, and I showed it to the major, and he said, "Well, just a minute." He handed it back to me, this paper I'd written. I guess it was a page and a half. He walked back in there and said, "Maybe you better go talk to the colonel." The colonel came out, got the paper, took it back in the back, they discussed it, I imagine, and they came back out and said, "Well, we really don't know if this is ... No, I don't think we better, no ..." I know that they knew there was substance in it. ... I don't know why I said that – I don't know, but they must have, because too many people took too much time to discuss it, whatever it was. Maybe they just saw it as logic, I don't know. I did this at least thirty days ahead of when this was supposed to be, and I think one of the things that might have scared them off was that I titled the report "50,000 Chinese," and there were not supposed to be any Chinese in the country; these were supposed to be Vietnamese, Viet Cong, North Vietnamese Army, okay? Maybe calling them Chinese made it unacceptable to our headquarters. At any rate, the date came, and I was right ... but Tet, believe me, is history. Tet is history. Well, I'm not an "I told you so" person, but I most certainly felt very good for having at least tried to warn our brass, and even though we lost so much, I felt inside myself that I had done what I was supposed to do.

Another incident. The order came to send a convoy up to Song Be, and I warned the colonel that they shouldn't because of a possible ambush. I outlined enemy locations and the site of a possible ambush. "Well, ahh, I'm sorry, we're going to send it anyway." They sent the convoy up. ... We're talking about five flatbed trucks blown up, nineteen wounded, and three killed. We lost a lot. You know, when you're talking about a flatbed, you're talking about lots and lots of ammunition that gets wasted because it got caught in an ambush. I even told them the probable location of the ambush. About two days later, when it was time to send out another convoy, the colonel came in and asked me, "Hey, by the way, do you think we ought to send this convoy up there today?" What happens with that is, somewhere your credibility is being questioned. Not that I had to establish any more credibility. As far as I was concerned, I was doing a sincere, caring, very professional job. So the onus was not on me to prove my credibility; the onus was on them to listen.

I guess the things that really stick about Vietnam is knowing you give them something and what you give is reliable and valid, but biases can creep through. There are a lot of things that they might have been biased about me with. I was a specialist as opposed to being a sergeant. I was black instead of being something else. I was enlisted instead of being an officer – especially in the milieu where there were only two enlisted people, and I was one of them. There was a master sergeant and myself; the other twenty-eight were officers. Being a WAC, whew! You know, "Women have no business over here, WACs especially." You know, there were a lot of things at my age – let me see how old I was, about ten blacks were into their black-power salute and a few whites had their confederate flags and stuff, there was a togetherness that I think you can only get in times of peril, if I can use that term.

I kept getting orders to go to Fort Bragg, North Carolina. I got five sets of orders to go to Fort Bragg while I was in Vietnam. I kept telling them, "I'm not going to Fort Bragg. I'll stay here." I was living in a hotel in Saigon my last six or seven months, and I had to walk to work. That was a trip, a combat tour in itself, walking up and down the streets of Saigon. But it got so bad I used to . . . They didn't want us to carry weapons in Vietnam; women couldn't carry weapons. Doris I. Allen carried her weapon. Make no mistake, I carried a .45. A couple others of us, friends of mine, carried weapons. That .45 was mine and I loved it, and I'm going to say it now: I still have it. I used to be able to cock that thing behind my back – maybe I was getting skittish or whatever. I had seen my name on captured enemy documents as one of the persons to be eliminated, and that's scary. The first time they told me that they had found a document with my name on it, it was on a list of intelligence personnel to be done away with, to be eliminated. I felt kind of, well, important – "Hey, tell all your friends how important you are," you know. Then the second time, I actually saw it. It was on a captured enemy document. The third time I saw it I happened to be assigned to the translation branch, in charge of the interpreters section at the Combined Documents Exploitation Center (CDEC) in Saigon. And one of my supervisors said, "Come here, Ms. Allen," and he put the captured document in my hand. I told him two and a half months later I was going home. It really got kind of scary. Then when cowboys on motor-bikes would come by me and try to rip off my briefcase, it was just time to come home. I was getting skittish, getting nervous, and I might have blown somebody's head off. . . .

But at any rate, they finally got me back to Fort Bragg anyway. You know, when people want you, they get you. When I got back to Fort Bragg, I put on my uniform and I walked in, and I know I was looking good – a new warrant officer, WO-1. I had three rows of good stuff here on my chest – you know, all those pretty little five-cent ribbons you put on your chest on this side – and I had three ribbons over here. I walked into the office, and the colonel was sitting behind his desk, and in his office were sitting five other colonels. He says, "We have just the place for you. We're going to put you in CONTIC." The same outfit I was in before! I said, "Just a moment, sir," and he says, "Yes?" I said, "I must say this: I'm not given to vulgarity, and I'm not given to profanity, but I think I've spent my time in hell." And he says, "What? What do you mean?" I said, "I just got back here from Vietnam, where I spent three years. Before I went to Vietnam, I spent four years at Fort Bragg, North Carolina, and I think that's enough time in hell." He said, "Oops. Okay, where do you want to go?" Okay, that was another example of "if you don't tell him, you don't get it." I'm not saying that other women haven't told what they wanted, you know, and been assertive, but I'm saying that if we don't do that, then we are doomed as far as I'm concerned. And I think that's one of the reasons that I was able to do thirty years in the military – because had I not been able to talk for myself and not feel afraid to do that, then I think I could not have survived as well.

When I got back from Vietnam, I guess I did not have the problems that some people had. Maybe that was because, as I told you, my sister had been my commanding officer back at Camp Stoneman and she was very in tune to me. I became an instructor at the intelligence school in Fort Holabird, Maryland. About a year later we moved the intelligence school to Fort Huachuca, Arizona, and within a matter of a year, I became a full-time special agent. So my life was all working when I got back, as opposed to being put out on the street – put out to pasture, so to speak – and being left to the mercies and the tenderness of those people who did not like Vietnam vets, especially here in the state of California. Some people went home to some places, and they were heroes, and that's not that they were looking to be heroes, they were just looking to come home and – "Please welcome me home. I've been away." I think it was easier for me because of my sister on the one hand and the fact that I was really working on the other.

Actually one of the biggest shocks to me was that I had less money to spend. Within a month of leaving Vietnam I had been promoted to warrant officer. As a spec-7 having as much time in service as I did, I made more money than a warrant officer-one, newly promoted. So I lost that money. I was also collecting combat pay and interrogator specialty pay, so my shock was more like coming back and "Geez, I'm broke!" I wasn't eating as well – over there it was good steaks. Make no mistake, I ate very well in Vietnam. All that heat – I had an air conditioner in my room. I worked hard but I played hard. I had a nice, nice fellow who thought the world of me, and I thought the world of him. Every day he'd bring me a quart of Crown Royal. I didn't usually drink the whole bottle every day – unless I had to go to the bunker.

But that was a different time. . . . You had to sort of get crazy over there. Then when you got home, there was a lot of camaraderie lost. Nobody even really rapped about these things, and then things start going through your head. A good friend of mine, a nurse, told me that when she got back and saw that she was not being welcomed back, she internalized it and put it upon herself and said, "The only reason I'm feeling that way is 'cause I left that guy on the gurney, and I got to go back and take care of him." I think a lot of Vietnam vets have not been able to air and say what was happening. Again I'm very fortunate to have my sister that, even right now when I try to get crazy or whatever, says, "Come on, knock it off" or "Hey, this is what's happened to you." I think we all needed that somewhere.

After I retired in 1980, I never had to go out there on the street and look for a job. A friend of mine called me a month before I got out. I hadn't talked to him for five years, and he says, "Congratulations on your retirement." We had a nice conversation, and he said, "By the way, what I really called about is, I'd like you to come work for me." So the bottom line of that is that I did become a private investigator with his company, and we still work together. The other thing that really helped me is that I'm working on my Ph.D. So what I've been doing – I've been working; I haven't given myself a chance to fall. . . . It's still there in my mind, but it has not come out to really haunt me, okay? Like I say, I keep busy, and now that I'll finish my Ph.D. next year, I'll have to find something to do, something to keep me going. Another thing I haven't been willing to do in one sense is to walk the picket line, but I might have to go start doing that.

Now you have the story of my life, my entire life.

Winners and Losers

Gloria Emerson

Emerson went to Vietnam in 1970 as a reporter for the *New York Times*.

When American troops first arrived in Vietnam most of them were sent to the 90th Replacement Battalion at Bien Hoa, twenty-two miles northeast of Saigon, for what the Army called "in-country processing." One of the first things they were ordered to do was to write their parents immediately saying they had arrived safely in Vietnam. Later, when they were no longer new troops, soldiers wrote home to their mothers to send them all sorts of things: garlic salt, machetes, wire cutters, wading boots, tennis socks, pickles and certain knives. Many of the mothers sent cookies; I saw a lot of chocolate chip cookies. In the rear, on the big bases, the PXs seemed bloated; at Cam Ranh Bay soldiers could buy Koolfoam pillows, Shag Time bath mats, brightly colored oversized beach towels, Chun King chow mein and garlic sausage. Vietnam was never the same place for the two million, six hundred thousand men who were sent to Vietnam.

There were always soldiers who found it hard to write home; it required too much concentration, it was too hard to explain what was happening or not happening, they did not know how to say it. In the field the soldiers wrote the names of their girl friends and their wives on their helmet liners or on the soft jungle hats – they were Phyllis, Monica, Susie, Wendy, Linda, Maryanne. They wrote too on the camouflage covers of their helmets: F.T.A. meant Fuck the Army. Peace, Peace, Peace, said the helmet covers, Love, Love, Love. It was sometimes a gaudy army: the soldiers wore love beads and peace symbols, crosses and bracelets woven out of black bootlaces, folded scarves or woven head-bands around their foreheads, tinted sunglasses.

It was a defiant yet dispirited army. They were against the war, not because of political perceptions, but because it took away too much, it put them in danger, and they hated the nagging, the bullying, the hassling of the military. Everywhere we waved to each other by giving the peace symbol, the V, which meant getting out. The infantrymen – the II Bravos – liked to wear soft camouflaged hats; some hung the rings of grenades above the brim to show how many they had thrown. It was not permitted for the men to wear these hats when they went to a stand-down area or to the big bases. It meant they were out of uniform. It made them hate their superiors, who became the immediate, the visible enemy. On a C-130 from Cam Ranh to Saigon, just after Christmas, a Specialist 4 named James Blunt in the 23d Division, the Americal, kept talking about his boonie hat, as the infantrymen called it. Nothing he owned was so important. We were packed in as usual, shoulder to shoulder, knees almost touching in the long rows of web seats facing each other. Almost everyone except Blunt was going to sleep; there was no snoring, they all dozed quietly, like men who had been chloroformed.

"They're always trying to take it away from me but I won't let them," he said. Blunt was twenty-six and his platoon had called him the Old Man. The hat was discoloured and smelled damp. "One lifer at Long Binh said to me that I couldn't wear it on the base and I told him I'd kill him on the spot if he tried to make me. He looked kind of startled. They won't let me wear it lots of places but I don't give a fuck. I do my job – I won't let anyone else walk point, only me, that's the way it is.

This here" – the little hat was lifted up for me to see again – "is a kind of memento. There's my wife's name. She's my second wife. It's Donna, see. Well, when I wear it walking point, she's kind of leading me, see."

When Blunt the Old Man was wounded the platoon got the hat to him in the hospital.

In Saigon, I sent a telegram to the United States for a Lieutenant Alsup from Asheboro, North Carolina, whose wife had just given birth to a daughter whose name he did not know. The lieutenant was worried; his tour in Vietnam was almost over but he felt he should stay longer to be with his platoon to keep them alive. If the platoon got a new officer, a fool, or one who wanted medals, the men might be pushed hard to find the enemy and engage them. The lieutenant did not want any of his men put in greater risk. No one used the words "die" and "death." A man was hit, not wounded. If he was killed, they said wasted or blown away. He bought it, or he bought the farm. He was greased or lit-up. Death was the Max. Each year the language of the soldiers changed a little as the new bunch came in.

Even now, so many years later, I still have the scrap of paper the lieutenant wrote his message on. It says: "Michelle, I am thrilled about the baby stop I live day to day thinking of you stop I cannot bear to even peek two days ahead for there are so many left but not as many as before stop I love you Bill." But that day he could not make up his mind: to stay with the platoon or to go home to his wife.

The soldiers had a year in Vietnam, sometimes a little less. Over and over they counted each day gone and all the days left to get through. They counted all the time and told you fifty days were left, ten days, three days. The Army counted everything else, insisted that all things be counted, until the numbers meant nothing – but still the counting kept on. Sometimes there were contests for the troops which were based on points to be won and points that could be taken away. One contest in the 25th Division in 1969, called "Best of the Pack," was for the best rifle and the best weapons platoon in the 1st Battalion, 27th Infantry, which was known as the Wolfhounds. One award was a two-day pass for best weapons in Dau Tieng; the other, for best rifles a three-day pass in Cu Chi. "The platoon will also have exclusive permission to wear a special marked camouflaged jungle hat when not on operations," the announcement said. "Points will be awarded for the following":

5	Per man per day above 25 on an operation
10	Each possible body count
10	Each 100 lbs. of rice
15	Each 100 lbs. of salt
20	Each mortar round
50	Each enemy individual weapon captured
100	Each enemy crew served weapon captured
100	Each enemy Body Count
200	Each tactical radio captured
500	Each individual weapon captured
500	Perfect score on CMMI (inspection)
1,000	Each prisoner of war

Points will be deducted for the following:

50	Each U.S. WIA (wounded)
500	Each U.S. KIA (killed)

If a man was killed, his platoon was penalized and had less of a chance to win the pass.

Many men were desperate to get out of the field, but until they were sick or wounded there was nothing they could do except go crazy, but there was punishment for doing that. I knew some who drank bad water hoping to get a fever of unknown origin, others would not take their malaria pills. There were men who felt terrible, but it had nothing to do with their bodies. At Chu Lai, headquarters of the Americal, there was a mental hygiene clinic and a psychiatrist who saw men on the base and those who had been on the line.

He had a tiny room: a table, two chairs, and another chair where I was allowed to sit in a corner. Each man had ten or fifteen minutes with the psychiatrist – a captain – who was young and had never seen combat. He had been drafted under the Berry Plan, which allowed him to finish his residency in psychiatry before induction. At any rate, the doctor let me sit in the room and take notes. The soldiers were asked if they minded this, but all they cared about was talking to him. Not one of them said they were ill from facing their own deaths, they only said how something was wrong. It did not take long to realize the doctor could only follow Army procedures, assure them that it was normal to be under stress, and let them be sent out again. Perhaps there was nothing he could do but give them ten or fifteen minutes, and some pills.

A platoon leader said he had been very dizzy and almost fainted during an attack and that an enlisted man had taken over. The doctor said that when you suffered from hyperventilation, it was good to do breathing exercises with your face inside a paper bag. The soldier looked hard at the doctor, turned his head to look at me, then we both looked at the doctor again.

He said: "Doc, we were taking fire."

"Yes, I understand, but how do you know this won't work unless you try it?" the doctor said. He told the platoon leader how to do the breathing – puff puff out, puff puff in – and that was that.

There was a very pale boy with blond hair that stuck up in back. He could not speak distinctly and for quite some time the three of us sat in the little room waiting for him to be able to begin. His trouble was that his best friend had been killed, but since then he had seen the best friend twice, standing close to him, smiling, looking as he had once looked. The doctor decided the boy should be put to bed for one day and one night and sedated so he could sleep.

"I want to call my parents," the boy said. He was not told yes or no. The psychiatrist said it was okay to let the boy go to bed for a while, but that was as far as the Army could let him regress. After that, the boy would have to go back on the line again.

Life on the Line

Bill Frazer

Frazer was a helicopter pilot with 1st Squadron, 9th Cavalry.

I went through flight school at nineteen and had turned twenty just prior to going to Vietnam in February 1970. I was assigned to the First Cavalry Division, or, to be more specific, an elite unit of the First Cav known as the First of the Ninth. I served with both Charlie Troop in Phuc Vinh and Alpha Troop at Song Be, or Firebase Buttons.

The First of the Ninth operated primarily as a separate unit: we worked the hot-spots in our area in northern III Corps along the Cambodian border. I flew as a scout pilot, and my job primarily was to get up every morning at four-thirty, go through a quick briefing, pick up my codes for the day, go out to my aircraft, fly out to the AO (area of operations) up on the Cambodian border and shoot people.

I flew a Hughes OH-6 Loach scout helicopter and my job was to hover around above the trees, and when I say hover I mean hover: we didn't fly above 20 knots, and stayed just inside translational lift. We worked in an area that was primarily triple-canopy jungle where the trees were about 150 feet high.

I always had a cover ship, a Cobra, which flew circles above me at 3,500 feet, taking spot reports as I flew around and saw signs of enemy activity, whether it be trails, hooches or equipment. The copilot of the high bird would write the spot reports down on the plexiglass of the Cobra and later relay them to headquarters.

Because we covered the hot-spots there were very few days when we didn't take any fire. I can only remember a few times during the 370 days that I was in Nam when I didn't come under fire or get involved in a firefight. We flew from first light to last light and generally put in twelve to sixteen hours a day, seven days a week.

We usually flew in a Pink Team which comprised a Cobra from the Red Platoon and a Loach from the White Platoon. We would normally fly out to the AO at about 3,500 feet to stay above small-arms fire, and when we reached the AO I would put the Loach into a slip, kick it out of trim and let it fall like a rock, to decrease my exposure to small-arms fire between 3,500 feet and the tops of the trees. I would then recover power on top of the trees and start working in tight right-hand circles.

Our crew comprised three people, a warrant officer pilot, an observer (usually an enlisted man who sat on the left side in the front) and a crew chief. The observer carried an M-16 rifle and a smoke grenade to mark targets, and the crew chief, whom we called "Torq," sat on the floor in the back. In our unit we did not have bungee cords, seat belts or safety harnesses for the torq. We also took out everything we could to lighten the aircraft. This was so we could carry more frag grenades, 30-caliber ammunition for our machine gun, home-made bombs, white phosphorous grenades ("Willy Petes") and smokes.

If we saw a gook as we were flying in tight right circles, I would shout "I got gooks." Immediately, the crew chief in the back would lean out the doorway and pull the trigger on the machine gun. Now quite often he would not see the target until after the pilot had seen it, so his job was just to pull the trigger, ensure that we didn't fly into our own bullets, keep the bullets away from the main rotor and let the pilot walk the bullets into the target.

When you first start flying scouts, the pilot is pretty worthless. You can't see anything. You're a new pilot and so tied up trying to fly the aircraft and keep from hitting things that you haven't yet developed the highly skilled vision that it takes to pick up trails or individuals hiding on the ground and so forth. So for the first couple of months the crew chief does most of the work.

Our crew chiefs were probably some of the gutsiest people you could imagine. We reconned by target – we made ourselves such a real meaty target that the gooks on the ground could not resist shooting at us. They had the advantage because they could hear and see us before we could see them. Usually they would open up as we flew over the top of them and we would have to break and come around again. The only way you could cover yourself would be for the crew chief to step out onto the skids and hold on to the door rim with one hand and fire the M-60 with the other to cover your tail.

As we would make our break the observer would throw out a red smoke to mark the gooks' position. The Cobra would then roll in and saturate the area with rockets and minigun fire. After he made one or two passes we would move back into the area to do a BDA, a bomb damage assessment, to check the kills. Because we used point-detonating rockets and were working in triple-canopy jungle, many times the rocket fire from the Cobra was ineffective because it would blow up in the tops of the trees and the shrapnel would not penetrate to the ground. However, it did keep their heads down long enough, so we could come back in and shoot them. Our job was to stay on top of them, shoot them, or get shot down ourselves. It was as simple as that. When we got in a firefight we stayed there until it ended.

Many times when we hit a hot-spot like that we would work it for hours, sometimes an entire day. It would be a constant running battle and the only time we would break station would be to refuel or rearm. In these situations a second Pink Team would cover our breaks and we would relieve them when they had to leave. Often an Air Force OV-10 FAC would follow us out to the AO, because they knew that one of our troops would be getting into trouble that day. They would orbit around 5,000–7,000 feet and hope that they could direct a team of Air Force fighters into the area.

You couldn't ask for a better unit to be around than the First Cav or the First of the Ninth. I had heard back when I was stateside that if you've got to go to a combat unit the First Cav was a stand-up unit and they were that. The First of the Ninth lived up to that reputation. It's unbelievable some of the situations we got into and the fact that you never backed away from them. I can remember when I first got in-country just how scared I was. I was a 20-year-old kid and I couldn't imagine myself killing anybody, and the idea of someone trying to kill me during the 365 days of my tour was more than I could handle. I went through a period of about a month and a half when I was so scared I just couldn't handle it, but eventually you get used to it. Its amazing what the mind can adjust to. The only thing I can equate it to is a form of insanity, but it's an insanity that helps you survive. You literally become the meanest person out there.

The mortality rate amongst scout pilots was incredibly high, especially in units like the First of the Ninth or the Second of the Seventeenth with the 101st Airborne. Because of our missions and the areas that we worked pilots just didn't last long. Chuck Frazier and I finished our first six months as scout pilots at the same time. We were told by our platoon leader that we were only the fifth and sixth scout pilots in Charlie Troop ever to complete six months. Chuck and I went on to fly for a full year and were only number two and three to do so. There had only been one other pilot before us who had flown for a complete year and survived to tell the story.

My CO, Major Rosher, would not let me do an additional six months in scouts, because he was sure I would get killed. Instead, I was forced to attend Cobra school, and when I came back they put me in the red platoon as a copilot in a Cobra. I lasted two weeks there; I couldn't stand the job. We were flying around at 3,500 feet and shooting rockets at the trees, whereas in scouts we were looking the gooks in the face.

The level of intensity was just like a drug. I can tell you there is nothing that can get you as high as that kind of life-and-death intensity on a day-to-day basis – when you are riding the thin edge of being wiped out, when they are shooting your helicopter up, and glass and crap is flying everywhere and tracers are flying in one door and out the other. The adrenalin high is such that there is not a dope or a booze made that can give you that kind of intense high.

All of us were that way in scouts. The ones who weren't like that you knew weren't going to make it. You needed that level of intensity. In my mind I would have damn near crashed the helicopter on top of them rather than let them get away. You wanted them so bad I felt sure that that desire radiated itself to the enemy and kept them scared and ducking, and I think this is the reason that I survived a year of nonstop battles.

After two weeks of flying Cobras I knew it was not for me. I had to get back down on the deck again. One day Major Harris, the CO of Alpha Troop, came into our squadron headquarters at Phuc Vinh. They had just moved from Tay Ninh to Firebase Buttons, up around Song Be. I asked him if he had a slot open for a scout pilot in his unit. It was a kind of stupid question because there was always a slot open for a scout pilot anywhere in the First of the Ninth. He couldn't believe it and said "Pack your bags – you can come with me tonight."

The accommodation at Firebase Buttons was the bottom of the heap. It was knee-deep in mud and we were living twenty men in a ten-man tent. We didn't have mess facilities, and if you couldn't steal C rations or had a care package from home you didn't eat! Everything stayed wet and had mold on it. We couldn't get water to shower or wash your clothes in. We would wear the same uniform for four or five days and we just stank. The only luxury we had was coffee in the morning, and we had to use it to brush our teeth with!

I can remember the day I joined the First of the Ninth at Phuc Vinh and went to my first scout meeting that night.

Nothing impressed me more than walking in there and seeing these guys. They were grungy and haggard, and had a look in their eye that I had never seen before, a result of being in combat day in day out. In the previous five days they had lost seven pilots, either killed or badly wounded. My platoon leader had been shot down that day, got another aircraft and went out again and had two crew members injured – and that was all in a day's work.

As a new guy, or "f***ing new guy" (FNG) as we were known, I sat in my newly pressed uniform and listened to them discuss the day's events. It scared the hell out of me. After the meeting I went back to my hooch and a couple of wild-looking crew chiefs came in and said, "Is there a Mister Frazer in here?" I said "Yeah, that's me." They said "Good to meet you Sir. My name's Neff and this is Rankin." Then they said, "Could we have your initials please?" I said "Well, yeah, it's W. C. F." They asked me to come over and stand next to the wall, and when I did so one of them pulled out a tape measure and he measured me. I said "What in the hell are you doing?" He looked me right in the eye and said "We're measuring you for a body bag motherf***er, 'cos you ain't goin' to make it!"

The first time that you kill somebody stands out in your memory for life. I can remember it vividly. As a new scout pilot they send you out on what are referred to as rat-f*** missions, in areas where you don't expect to see much. This is to keep the new pilots out of trouble until they learn the job and the aircraft. This day we were working an area to the east of Firebase Buttons close to an area known as Elephant Flats. Apparently there hadn't been much enemy activity up there for a while and they thought that was a safe place to put me.

My high-bird pilot that day was on his second tour in Vietnam and was not much less than an alcoholic. Nobody wanted to fly with him and they generally sent him on the rat-f***s so that no one would have to depend on him in a bad situation. We were working along a river surrounded with open fields and we came across what looked like a rocket pod jettisoned by a Cobra. As we came down to check it out I looked across the river and saw a sampan tied up in some trees. I told the high bird about it and went on over for a look. I assumed he was watching me and covering me, but what I didn't realize was that he was sitting over there messing about with that pod.

As I went on over to the sampan he told me "If you see gooks, shoot 'em," but I was new and did not want to open fire indiscriminately and shoot some innocent civilian. As I flew over the cornfield I saw two guys squatting down on their haunches, right next to two pottery kilns. It was a part of a VC base camp and these guys had their AK-47s beneath them, although I couldn't see this from 20–30 feet above them. I told the Cobra "I have gooks," and he replied "Shoot 'em!" As I was thinking that they might be friendly they stood up, took aim and opened up at me.

We took about fifteen hits all over the aircraft and at that point my crew chief pulled the trigger on the machine gun. It fired about three rounds and then jammed. The observer got shook and dropped the smoke in the cabin and we went IFR with red smoke. He began to fish around trying to kick it out and I threw the aircraft out of trim to try to blow the smoke out of the door, so I could see where we were going. In all the confusion and hollering, my high bird, who hadn't been watching me (an unforgivable sin), spotted my red smoke. The pilot wasn't thinking straight and locked in on the red smoke. It didn't register that the smoke was flying along at 150 miles an hour, and he began shooting rockets at it!

Finally we got everything sorted out and I went back in again to try to find the two gooks who had now disappeared. I noticed a guy lying on the ground pointing an M-16 up at me, but before he could fire, my torq ran a path of bullets across the top of him. This was the first time I had seen a guy killed and it isn't like you see on TV: the guy kept crawling and looking up at me. My torq had been in Nam for two years and he knew he was dead. I could have sworn he was still alive; I hollered at him to shoot him again, but he said

"He's dead." I said "Bull**** – he's still moving: shoot him, just open up on him." So he did and he put about thirty rounds into him, but he still kept moving.

I ended up killing ten people in the open that day – ten people. I can remember that my fuel-low warning light came on and we were just about out of ammo, but there was the one guy dressed in white who had been standing at the pottery kiln and I had not yet found him. We had just about given up on him and were ready to leave as soon as a team from the Blue Max arrived. Just then we flew over a clump of head-high vegetation, and standing in the middle of it was this guy. As he stuck his gun up in the air to shoot at us, we dropped a grenade on him and blew him to pieces.

For the next three or four nights I couldn't sleep. I would go over that entire battle time and time again in my dreams, but after that I became accustomed to it and it didn't bother me any more.

I remember a story that Chuck Frazier told about a mission he was on. He had stumbled across several gooks in the open and killed some of them, but over about an hour and a half period they would keep coming across them as they broke from cover to run. They were taking a little fire, but not much because the gooks were just ducking and hiding and running. Eventually they began to run out of everything. Torq was in the back, firing the machine gun, when it suddenly stopped. Chuck said "What are you doing? Keep shooting at 'em." Torq said "I can't – I'm out of ammo." So Chuck said "Well, throw something at 'em." Torq replied "I can't – we're out of grenades." He said "Well, for Christ's sake shoot something at them," thinking that he may have had an M-79 Chunker (grenade launcher) or something. He turned around and looked and the crew chief was standing out on the skids, shooting them the finger. It was all he had left. He told him "Dammit, shoot something at them," so he stood on the skids and flipped them the bird.

Leaving the Nam

Anonymous

Me and my buddy Al rotated out at the same time. We left from a place called Freedom Hill. A big chopper came down and picked us up and dropped us on the flight deck of the *New Orleans*, a small carrier out in the middle of Da Nang Harbor. We looked back in at land, where we spent a year. I had never thought about getting killed, but I never thought about coming back either. I knew if you thought about coming back, you'd buy it, for sure.

I looked at Al and I started laughing. I said, "Al, I think we made it." He started laughing. We laughed so hard that we were crying. We couldn't stand up. My sides ached. We made it.

Yet people we'd hung around with for months were gone, gone forever. You were real glad that you were you and not them. You felt so good to see the people that had survived with you. It felt so good to look into their faces after it was all over and you could just exhale, take a breather, just taste the time, taste the life.

It was love. It was true love of being alive and being thankful for the joy of looking into their faces. It almost made what you had been through worthwhile. But, I guess, not quite.

After rolling across the Pacific for sixteen days, seeing this country was amazing. I cried. I wanted to kiss the dirt. It was home. I had been a foreigner in a strange place. Out there, outside the United States, you're in Indian Country. There was only one place that meant anything and that was my home.

I was really looking forward to coming home, but after three or four days, I was climbing the walls. I dropped back into the old neighbourhood and nothing had changed. They were the same people in the same situation with the same head. There's been no time passing for them. It was like I never left. But I *did* leave. I wasn't the same anymore. I didn't feel comfortable doing what I used to do. I didn't know how to *spend* time.

I was geared up for dealing with a hundred thousand dollars' worth of equipment and a lot of responsibility for human life. I've come back here . . . to do what?

Civilian level is bullshit. You make a mistake, nobody's going to die. Big fucking deal. It's really hard to get excited about what's going on over here. You see politicians lying to you, it makes you want to throw up. Send them over there. I see people in business who never had to put their ass on the line or really extended themselves and they're making it. It's not fair.

In Nam, they called grunts kings. I walked with kings. These people were going to get shit on when they came back here, but in Vietnam they were kings. There was no bullshit. You get in a fire fight and you see exactly who's who. There wasn't anything phony. It was all very real, the realest thing I've ever done. Everything since seems totally superfluous. It's horseshit.

People don't understand. They hate you for being there, like you should feel guilty for it. "You went to Vietnam? Oh, wow, man, where's your head at?"

"Go throw some wheat germ on your yogurt. Fuck you, I don't want to hear your bullshit."

When we were over there, I thought, "My God, if I ever get back to the World, I'm going to tear the place apart. The World will be my oyster and *nothing* is going to stop me. I'll have it all." Here it is going on twelve years later and what the fuck have I done?

*   *   *

I'd been living in the boonies for six months and flew right back to the States. So I was disoriented. At El Toro Air Force Base a guy says to me, "Where you want to get stationed?"

"Marine barracks, Brooklyn," I says fucking around with him.

"We got one in New London, Connecticut."

"That's close enough." Bang, bang, bang, he stamps everything on my papers. I had no idea what Marine barracks was. I just wanted to be near the neighbourhood, hang out. I was a hot nineteen years old and been to Vietnam.

I went to the Marine barracks in Connecticut and I found out – uh-oh, it's all embassy Marines. They're all covered in blue with red stripes down their pants, spit-shined boots, orders. None of them has been to Vietnam and this ain't grunt stuff. These guys may be the finest in discipline, but they don't look out for each other. In Nam the grunts learned to look out for each other. You look out for your boys, you fuck over the officers. Here, it's just the opposite. Everybody is doing everything they can to nail you. The Marine Game – you *will* obey regulations or you *will* be written up and you *will* go to the brig. I didn't want to hear that, I just came back from a war.

I signed in wearing my civilian clothes. I'm all alone and I was feeling discombobulated. It was just too much, too quick for me. I said to myself, "No, man. I don't want no part of this." There was only one thing in my mind: Get back to Vietnam where I felt at home.

I was there two hours and I flipped out. I started walking down the corridor knocking all the frames full of rules and regulations off the walls, throwing down all their little trophies and commendations. No words. Nothing.

There were about ten guys there coming towards me, and I started going at blows with them. They beat the shit out of me, cuffed me and threw me in the brig. They gave me a shot of dope which fucked me up, too.

After I got out of the hospital, I went over to see the major.

He looked at my records and said, "You're a grunt. What are you doing here?"

"I don't know."

"Do you want to leave this unit?"

"Yes, sir."

"Do you want to go back to West Pac?"

"Yes, sir, I just want to get back to Vietnam, where I belong." I really felt that I belonged there.

No problem. I was out of that barracks in record time.

My second year in Nam I got into the Air Wing. All I fucking did was smoke pot and ride gunner on helicopters. But they were beginning to send Marines back, and they were trying to push me back to the States again. I wasn't having any of that. I had to go up in front of a full bird colonel and lie to him about why I had to stay in Vietnam. Here I am, an Italian boy from Brooklyn, New York. I told the colonel that I took some money from loan sharks back home and I'm in trouble, they're going to kill me and hurt my family. As the colonel can see, if he checks my records, I've been saving my money and I ain't been on R&R – which luckily was true. He fell for it. What does he know? He's from Fishbite Falls somewheres, right? He let me stay.

I was going to stay a third year, but they gave me a year early-out and made me go back home. Some guys they had to lock up because they wouldn't leave Vietnam. A lot of guys wanted to die there. I mean, I wanted to die there. All my fucking friends died there.

I felt so much like I didn't belong in America. What are you going to do? How are you going to talk to somebody? I went back there to get it over quick, but it never came. It was suicide, trying to kill myself, going back. I didn't know that's what it was then. I just wanted to get back and be around people I knew. I didn't care if I died around people I knew.

Finally my day came and I made the big swoop. Big Bird to Paradise, we used to call it. They said it was time to go and I started crying. One dude gave me a bracelet. I said, "I'm going home to the States, but you fucking dudes are still going to be here." I got my shit and throwed it on the truck and said, "Let's go." I left the fuckers $20. "Go ahead and buy a case of beer on me whenever you can."

On my way out I was assigned to some rinky-dink headquarters battalion where the office pogues sit around on their fat asses. They took all my stuff away from me. I reported in the field hat that I had had made by some of the villagers. A sergeant takes it away from me and gives it to some other dude sitting in the office. They didn't want me to be too salty. If I'd have had that motherfucker in the field, I'd have had his ass. But I didn't want to make trouble. I was going home.

Then on Okinawa, they took all our gear away and gave us new fatigues, all too big and didn't fit. Put us in some big old barracks somewheres and wouldn't let us go into town. Just out of fucking combat and you can't even go and get a few beers, have a little fun. They had us picking up cigarette butts for three days. That was "rehabilitation", so we would come to our senses. This chickenshit staff sergeant, younger than we were, who was making us pick up cigarette butts, said, "Just because you been to Vietnam, you ain't no God damn heroes."

We didn't want to be picking up cigarette butts, we been picking up bodies for fifteen months. Give us a little slack. We practised marching. We had formations. All's we wanted to do was go home.

When I first got back, I was at my brother's house in California. The first week I was there, I slept on the floor because I couldn't get comfortable in a bed. I'd drink cold beer and get a sore throat. I had to wait for my beer to get warm before I could drink it. I ain't shitting you. I ate like a fucking animal. They asked me all kinds of questions. "How many did you kill?" "How does it feel to kill somebody?" A hell of a lot better than if he had shot me, that's what I told them.

I was an MP for a while at Quantico after that. I wanted to be a cop when I got out of the service. But the police told me I was too small. Hell, they didn't tell me I was too small when they sent me over to Nam. They didn't tell me I couldn't fight. They don't give nobody a chance to do nothing.

I didn't know how to act, didn't know what kind of clothes to buy, didn't like long-haired people, didn't like nothing. I carried a gun on me. People seemed to be messing with me all the time. Hey, I'd seen enough of that fighting shit. I didn't need that. You get back though and they say, "I see you made it all right. Big fucking deal." Some fucking ass asked me, "How come you didn't get killed?"

When I got discharged, they had the nerve to demand $600 from me. They were saying that they overpaid me in Vietnam. How the hell was I supposed to know they were overpaying me? They said, "Well, you was getting rank." But we didn't know what the pay scale was over there. An officer came up and said you were due this amount of money. You'd sign the chit. They would give you so much in Vietnamese money or scrip and then you would put the rest in a bank down in the Da Nang area. You'd send X amount home. That was it. I'd send $100 home, take $20 out in the bush and the rest I send down to the rear. It was a set pattern with me. I had to threaten to get civilian lawyers. We settled on $300. I had to pay to get discharged.

When I got my honourable discharge, I thought it would be really nice. It comes in the mail and it's a computer printout with my Social Security number on a piece of cardboard, so I just threw it away. I was really disappointed. I thought I'd at least get a little plaque or something.

When I came back about six of us were walking through the airport and a girl – maybe eighteen or nineteen, about the same age as me really – she asked me how many women and children did I kill. I told her, "Nine. Where's your mother at?" I thought it was great fun putting her down like that! But inside I felt, "Gees, why is she treating me like that?"

I thought I would come home as a war hero, you know. I

didn't really want to be a war hero, but I thought I'd get a lot of respect, because I'd done something for my country. Somewhere deep in my psyche I thought that people would react to what I'd done, and say, "Hey, good job. Good work."

My family did. "Hey, great. How many people did you kill?" That wasn't right either. I didn't tell them when I was getting home, because I didn't want a party. But it happened anyway. I couldn't stay at that. I hung out an hour or two. Then I went out with my friends and got fucked up out of my face.

The Fall of Saigon: Evacuation of the American Embassy

John Pilger

The capital of South Vietnam fell to communist forces on 30 April 1975. Pilger, an Australian, reported on Vietnam for the *Daily Mirror* of London.

People were now beginning to come over the wall. The Marines, who had orders not to use their guns, had been up all night and were doped with "speed" – methedrine – which provides a "high" for twenty-four hours before the body craves sleep. But methedrine also whittles the nerve ends, and some of the young Marines were beginning to show the effects. As the first Chinook helicopter made its precarious landing, its rotors slashed into a tree, and the snapping branches sounded like gunfire. "*Down! Down!*" screamed a corporal to the line of people crouched against the wall, waiting their turn to be evacuated, until an officer came and calmed him.

The helicopter's capacity was fifty, but it lifted off with seventy. The pilot's skill was breathtaking as he climbed vertically to two hundred feet, with bullets pinging against the rotors and shredded embassy documents playing in the downdraft. However, not all the embassy's documents were shredded and some were left in the compound in open plastic bags. One of these I have. It is dated 25 May, 1969 and reads,

"Top Secret ... memo from John Paul Vann, counter
insurgency":
... 900 houses in Chau Doc province were destroyed by
American air strikes without evidence of a single enemy
being killed ... the destruction of this hamlet by friendly
American firepower is an event that will always be
remembered and never forgiven by the surviving population ...

From the billowing incinerator on the embassy roof rained
twenty, fifty and one hundred dollar bills. Most were charred;
some were not. The Vietnamese waiting around the pool
could not believe their eyes; former ministers and generals
and torturers scrambled for their bonus from the sky or sent
their children to retrieve the notes. An embassy official said
that more than five million dollars were being burned. "Every
safe in the embassy has been emptied and locked again," said
the official, "so as to fool the gooks when we've gone."

The swishing of rotors now drowned the sounds of the
dusk: the crump of artillery, the cries of women attempting to
push young children over the wall. Two Marines watched a
teenage girl struggle through the barbed wire. At first they
did nothing, then as her hands clawed the last few inches one
of them brought his rifle butt down on one hand, while the
other brought his boot down on the other. The girl fell, crying,
back into the mob. Somehow, most of one family had managed to get over the wall: a man, his wife, and her father.
Their sons and his grandmother were next, but the barrel of
an M-16 spun them back to the other side. The wife pleaded
with a Marine to let the rest of her family over, but he did not
hear her.

At least a thousand people were still inside the embassy,
waiting to be evacuated, although most of the celebrities, like
"Giggles" Quang, had seen themselves on to the first helicopters; the rest waited passively, as if stunned. Inside the
embassy itself there was champagne foaming on to polished
desks, as several of the embassy staff tried systematically to

wreck their own offices: smashing water coolers, pouring bottles of Scotch into the carpets, sweeping pictures from the wall. In a third-floor office a picture of the late President Johnson was delivered into a wastepaper basket, while a framed quotation from Lawrence of Arabia was left on the wall. The quotation read:

> Better to let them do it imperfectly, than to do it perfectly yourself, for it is their country, their war, and your time is short.

From the third floor I could see the British embassy across the road. It was being quietly ransacked now. The Union Jack, which had been spread across the main entrance, perhaps to ward off evil spirits, had been torn away and looters were at work with little interference from the police. I derived some small satisfaction from the sight of this. It was there, a few days earlier, that the British Ambassador, a spiffy chap called John Bushell, had shredded his own papers and mounted his own little evacuation without taking with him a dozen very frightened British passport holders. Before he drove away, Mr Bushell gave an impromptu press conference.

"We are pulling out for reasons of safety," he said. "Our main responsibility is the safety of the British community in Saigon."

I asked him about people who were waving their British passports outside the gates of the British embassy. Why were they not even allowed into the compound?

"Look here," he replied, "we gave ample warning. We put advertisements in the local papers. The trouble with these people, as I understand it, was that they didn't have tax clearance, which takes ten days, as well as exit visas from the Vietnamese government."

Exit visas? Tax clearances? But wasn't this an emergency evacuation for reasons, as he had just said, of protecting life?

"Well, yes," he replied, "but we really can't break the rules laid down by government, can we?"

But surely this government had ceased to exist and there might be anarchy and a great deal of danger, which was why he was getting out?

"That may be true," said the Ambassador, "but we gave these people a reasonable time to get the paperwork done, and you really can't expect us to help them at such short notice . . . look here, the Americans surely will pick up any stray palefaces."

But "these people" were Indians and Chinese. The Ambassador looked confused.

"Oh, you mean Hong Kongers," he said. "They should have heeded our warnings . . . they'll have just to work hard at it, won't they?" At this, he turned to another British official and said, "How many coolies . . . Vietnamese . . . are we leaving, do you know?"

The official replied, "Coolies? Oh, about thirty-six in all."

At six-fifteen p.m. it was my turn for the Jolly Green Giant as it descended through the dark into the compound. The loadmaster stopped counting at sixty; people were in each other's arms. The helicopter tilted, rose, dropped, sharply, then climbed as if laden with rocks; off to the starboard there were shots. We flew low over the centre of the city, over the presidential palace where "Big" Minh awaited his fate, and the Caravelle Hotel, where I owed for two days, then out along the Saigon River, over the Rung Sat, the "swamp of death" which lay between the city and the sea. The two gunners scanned the ground, as they always used to, looking for "Charlie". Some of us had on our minds the heat-seeking missile which had brought a helicopter down as we watched in the early hours. There was small arms fire around us, but they were letting us go; and when the South China Sea lay beneath us, the pilot, who was red-eyed with fatigue and so young he had acne, lit up a cigarette and handed the packet around. In the back of the helicopter there was a reminder of what we had left: a woman, who had left her daughter on the other side of the wall, cried softly.

Memorial

Bobbie Ann Mason

Mason was born in Mayfield, Kentucky. In this extract from her novel *In Country* seventeen-year-old Sam, her uncle Emmett and her grandmother Mamaw visit the Vietnam Veterans' Memorial in Washington, DC. The year in 1984.

As THEY DRIVE INTO WASHINGTON a few hours later, Sam feels sick with apprehension. She has kept telling herself that the memorial is only a rock with names on it. It doesn't mean anything except they're dead. It's just names. Nobody here but us chickens. Just us and the planet Earth and the nuclear bomb. But that's O.K., she thinks now. There is something comforting about the idea of nobody here but us chickens. It's so intimate. Nobody here but us. Maybe that's the point. People shouldn't make too much of death. Her history teacher said there are more people alive now than dead. He warned that there were so many people alive now, and they were living so much longer, that people had the idea they were practically immortal. But everyone's going to die and we'd better get used to the notion, he said. Dead and gone. Long gone from Kentucky.

Sometimes in the middle of the night it struck Sam with sudden clarity that she was going to die someday. Most of the time she forgot about this. But now, as she and Emmett and Mamaw Hughes drive into Washington, where the Vietnam Memorial bears the names of so many who died, the reality of death hits her in broad daylight. Mamaw is fifty-eight. She is going to die soon. She could die any minute, like that race-horse that keeled over dead, inexplicably, on Father's Day. Sam has been so afraid Emmett would die. But Emmett came to Cawood's Pond looking for her, because it was unbearable to him that she might have left him alone, that she might even die.

The Washington Monument is a gleaming pencil against the sky. Emmett is driving, and the traffic is frightening, so many cars swishing and merging, like bold skaters in a crowded rink. They pass cars with government license plates that say FED. Sam wonders how long the Washington Monument will stand on the Earth.

A brown sign on Constitution Avenue says VIETNAM VETERANS MEMORIAL. Emmett can't find a parking place nearby. He parks on a side street and they walk toward the Washington Monument. Mamaw puffs along. She has put on a good dress and stockings. Sam feels they are ambling, out for a stroll, it is so slow. She wants to break into a run. The Washington Monument rises up out of the earth, proud and tall. She remembers Tom's bitter comment about it – a big white prick. She once heard someone say the U.S.A. goes around fucking the world. That guy who put pink plastic around those islands should make a big rubber for the Washington Monument, Sam thinks. She has so many bizarre ideas there should be a market for her imagination. These ideas are churning in her head. She can hardly enjoy Washington for these thoughts. In Washington, the buildings are so pretty, so white. In a dream, the Vietnam Memorial was a black boomerang, whizzing toward her head.

"I don't see it," Mamaw says.

"It's over yonder," Emmett says, pointing. "They say you come up on it sudden."

"My legs are starting to hurt."

Sam wants to run, but she doesn't know whether she wants to run toward the memorial or away from it. She just wants to run. She has the new record album with her, so it won't melt in the hot car. It's in a plastic bag with handles. Emmett is carrying the pot of geraniums. She is amazed by him, his impressive bulk, his secret suffering. She feels his anxiety. His heart must be racing, as if something intolerable is about to happen.

Emmett holds Mamaw's arm protectively and steers her across the street. The pot of geraniums hugs his chest.

"There it is," Sam says.

It is massive, a black gash in a hillside, like a vein of coal exposed and then polished with polyurethane. A crowd is filing by slowly, staring at it solemnly.

"Law," says Sam's grandmother quietly. "It's black as night."

"Here's the directory," Emmett says, pausing at the entrance. "I'll look up his name for you, Mrs Hughes."

The directory is on a pedestal with a protective plastic shield. Sam stands in the shade, looking forward, at the black wing embedded in the soil, with grass growing above. It is like a giant grave, fifty-eight thousand bodies rotting here behind those names. The people are streaming past, down into the pit.

"It don't show up good," Mamaw says anxiously. "It's just a hole in the ground."

The memorial cuts a V in the ground, like the wings of an abstract bird, huge and headless. Overhead, a jet plane angles upward, taking off.

"It's on Panel 9E," Emmett reports. "That's on the east wing. We're on the west."

At the bottom of the wall is a granite trough, and on the edge of it the sunlight reflects the names just above, in mirror writing, upside down. Flower arrangements are scattered at the base. A little kid says, "Look, Daddy, the flowers are dying." The man snaps, "Some are and some aren't."

The walkway is separated from the memorial by a strip of gravel, and on the other side of the walk is a border of dark gray brick. The shiny surface of the wall reflects the Lincoln Memorial and the Washington Monument, at opposite angles.

A woman in a sunhat is focusing a camera on the wall. She says to the woman with her, "I didn't think it would look like this. Things aren't what you think they look like. I didn't know it was a wall."

A spraddle-legged guy in camouflage clothing walks by with a cane. Probably he has an artificial leg, Sam thinks, but he walks along proudly, as if he has been here many times before and doesn't have any particular business at that moment. He seems to belong here, like Emmett hanging out at McDonald's.

A group of schoolkids tumble through, noisy as chickens. As they enter, one of the girls says, "Are they piled on top of each other?" They walk a few steps farther and she says, "What are all these names anyway?" Sam feels like punching the girl in the face for being so dumb. How could anybody that age not know? But she realizes that she doesn't know either. She is just beginning to understand. And she will never really know what happened to all these men in the war. Some people walk by, talking as though they are on a Sunday picnic, but most are reverent, and some of them are crying.

Sam stands in the center of the V, deep in the pit. The V is like the white wings of the shopping mall in Paducah. The Washington Monument is reflected at the center line. If she moves slightly to the left, she sees the monument, and if she moves the other way she sees a reflection of the flag opposite the memorial. Both the monument and the flag seem like arrogant gestures, like the country giving the finger to the dead boys, flung in this hole in the ground. Sam doesn't understand what she is feeling, but it is something so strong, it is like a tornado moving in her, something massive and overpowering. It feels like giving birth to this wall.

"I wish Tom could be here," Sam says to Emmett. "He needs to be here." Her voice is thin, like smoke, barely audible.

"He'll make it here someday. Jim's coming too. They're all coming one of these days."

"Are you going to look for anybody's name besides my daddy's?"

"Yeah."

"Who?"

"Those guys I told you about, the ones that died all around me that day. And that guy I was going to look up – he might be here. I don't know if he made it out or not."

Sam gets a flash of Emmett's suffering, his grieving all these years. He has been grieving for fourteen years. In this dazzling sunlight, his pimples don't show. A jet plane flies overhead, close to the earth. Its wings are angled back too, like a bird's.

Two workmen in hard hats are there with a stepladder and some loud machinery. One of the workmen, whose hat says on the back NEVER AGAIN, seems to be drilling into the wall.

"What's he doing, hon?" Sam hears Mamaw say behind her.

"It looks like they're patching up a hole or something." *Fixing a hole where the rain gets in.*

The man on the ladder turns off the tool, a sander, and the other workman hands him a brush. He brushes the spot. Silver duct tape is patched around several names, leaving the names exposed. The names are highlighted in yellow, as though someone has taken a Magic Marker and colored them, the way Sam used to mark names and dates, important facts, in her textbooks.

"Somebody must have vandalized it," says a man behind Sam. "Can you imagine the sicko who would do that?"

"No," says the woman with him. "Somebody just wanted the names to stand out and be noticed. I can go with that."

"Do you think they colored Dwayne's name?" Mamaw asks Sam worriedly.

"No. Why would they?" Sam gazes at the flowers spaced along the base of the memorial. A white carnation is stuck in a crack between two panels of the wall. A woman bends down and straightens a ribbon on a wreath. The ribbon has gold letters on it, "VFW Post 7215 of Pa."

They are moving slowly. Panel 9E is some distance ahead. Sam reads a small poster propped at the base of the wall: "To those men of C Company, 1st Bn. 503 Inf., 173rd Airborne who were lost in the battle for Hill 823, Dak To, Nov. 11, 1967. Because of their bravery I am here today. A grateful buddy."

A man rolls past in a wheelchair. Another jet plane flies over.

A handwritten note taped to the wall apologizes to one of the names for abandoning him in a firefight.

Mamaw turns to fuss over the geraniums in Emmett's arms, the way she might fluff a pillow.

The workmen are cleaning the yellow paint from the names. They sand the wall and brush it carefully, like men polishing their cars. The man on the ladder sprays water on the name he has just sanded and wipes it with a rag.

Sam, conscious of how slowly they are moving, with dread, watches two uniformed marines searching and searching for a name. "He must have been along here somewhere," one says. They keep looking, running their hands over the names.

"There it is. That's him."

They read his name and both look abruptly away, stare out for a moment in the direction of the Lincoln Memorial, then walk briskly off.

"May I help you find someone's name?" asks a woman in a T-shirt and green pants. She is a park guide, with a clipboard in her hand.

"We know where we are," Emmett says. "Much obliged, though."

At panel 9E, Sam stands back while Emmett and Mamaw search for her father's name. Emmett, his gaze steady and intent, faces the wall, as though he were watching birds; and Mamaw, through her glasses, seems intent and purposeful, as though she were looking for something back in the field, watching to see if a cow had gotten out of the pasture. Sam imagines the egret patrolling for ticks on a water buffalo's back, ducking and snaking its head forward, its beak like a punji stick.

"There it is," Emmett says. It is far above his head, near the top of the wall. He reaches up and touches the name. "There's his name, Dwayne E. Hughes."

"I can't reach it," says Mamaw. "Oh, I wanted to touch it," she says softly, in disappointment.

"We'll set the flowers here, Mrs Hughes," says Emmett. He sets the pot at the base of the panel, tenderly, as though tucking in a baby.

"I'm going to bawl," Mamaw says, bowing her head and starting to sob. "I wish I could touch it."

Sam has an idea. She sprints over to the workmen and asks them to let her borrow the stepladder. They are almost finished, and they agree. One of them brings it over and sets it up beside the wall, and Sam urges Mamaw to climb the ladder, but Mamaw protests. "No, I can't do it. You do it."

"Go ahead, ma'am," the workman says.

"Emmett and me'll hold the ladder," says Sam.

"Somebody might see up my dress."

"No, go on, Mrs Hughes. You can do it," says Emmett. "Come on, we'll help you reach it."

He takes her arm. Together, he and Sam steady her while she places her foot on the first step and swings herself up. She seems scared, and she doesn't speak. She reaches but cannot touch the name.

"One more, Mamaw," says Sam, looking up at her grandmother – at the sagging wrinkles, her flab hanging loose and sad, and her eyes reddened with crying. Mamaw reaches toward the name and slowly struggles up the next step, holding her dress tight against her. She touches the name, running her hand over it, stroking it tentatively, affectionately, like feeling a cat's back. Her chin wobbles, and after a moment she backs down the ladder silently.

When Mamaw is down, Sam starts up the ladder, with the record package in her hand.

"Here, take the camera, Sam. Get his name." Mamaw has brought Donna's Instamatic.

"No, I can't take a picture this close."

Sam climbs the ladder until she is eye level with her father's name. She feels funny, touching it. A scratching on a rock. Writing. Something for future archaeologists to puzzle over, clues to a language.

"Look this way, Sam," Mamaw says. "I want to take your picture. I want to get you and his name and the flowers in together if I can."

"The name won't show up," Sam says.

"Smile."

"How can I smile?" She is crying.

Mamaw backs up and snaps two pictures. Sam feels her face looking blank. Up on the ladder, she feels so tall, like a spindly weed that is sprouting up out of this diamond-bright seam of hard earth. She sees Emmett at the directory, probably searching for his buddies' names. She touches her father's name again.

"All I can see here is my reflection," Mamaw says when Sam comes down the ladder. "I hope his name shows up. And your face was all shadow."

"Wait here a minute," Sam says, turning away her tears from Mamaw. She hurries to the directory on the east side. Emmett isn't there anymore. She sees him striding along the wall, looking for a certain panel. Nearby, a group of marines is keeping a vigil for the POWs and MIAs. A double row of flags is planted in the dirt alongside their table. One of the marines walks by with a poster: "You Are an American, Your Voice Can Make the Difference." Sam flips through the directory and finds "Hughes." She wants to see her father's name there too. She runs down the row of Hughes names. There were so many Hughes boys killed, names she doesn't know. His name is there, and she gazes at it for a moment. Then suddenly her own name leaps out at her.

SAM ALAN HUGHES PFC AR 02 MAR 49 02 FEB 67 HOUSTON TX 14E 104

Her heart pounding, she rushes to panel 14E, and after racing her eyes over the string of names for a moment, she locates her own name.

SAM A HUGHES. It is the first on a line. It is down low enough to touch. She touches her own name. How odd it feels, as though all the names in America have been used to decorate this wall.

Permissions and Acknowledgements

Jules Roy, "Dien Bien Phu", is an extract from *Dien Bien Phu*, Faber & Faber, 1967. Copyright © 1963 Jules Roy. English translation copyright © 1967 Harper & Row and Faber & Faber. Reprinted by permission of Faber & Faber.

Malcolm W Browne, Death in the Rice Fields', is an extract from *The New Face of War*, Bobbs-Merrill, 1965. Copyright © 1965, 1968 Malcolm W. Browne. Reprinted by permission of Simon & Schuster Inc.

James Stockdale, "Tonkin Gulf: Eyewitness" is an extract from *The Bad War: An Oral History*, ed. Kim Williamson & Newsweek correspondents, New American Library, 1987. Copyright © Newsweek, Inc. Reprinted by permission of Penguin Books USA Inc.

James Crumley, "One to Count Cadence" is an extract from *One To Count Cadence*, Vintage, 1987. Copyright © 1969 James Crumley.

John Laurence, "First Blood", is an extract from *The Cat From Hue*, PublicAffairs Ltd, 2002. Copyright © 2002 John Laurence

Charlie Beckwith, "The Relief of Plei Mei" is an extract from *Delta Force*, Avon Books, 1983. Copyright © 1983 Charles A. Beckwith. Reprinted by permission of HarperCollins

Harold G. Moore & Joseph L Galloway, "la Drang" is an extract from *We Were Soldiers Once . . . And Young*, Airlife, 1994. Copyright © 1992 Lt. General H.G. Moore and Joseph L. Galloway

Various, "Voices to America: Letters Home" is extracted from *Letters from America*, ed. Bill Adler, 1967, and *Dear America: Letters Home from Vietnam*, ed. Bernard Edelman, 1985. Copyright © 1985 The New York Vietnam Veterans Memorial Commission

Charlie A Beckwith, " 'You're in Bad Shape, Boss' " is an extract from *Delta Force*, Avon Books, 1983. Copyright © 1983 Charles A. Beckwith. Reprinted by permission of HarperCollins

Nicholas Tomalin, "The General Goes Zapping Charlie Cong", *Sunday Times*, 5 June, 1966. Copyright © 1966 Times Newspapers/News International

Harrison E Salisbury, "Hanoi: The Museum of the Revolution" is an extract from *Behind the Lines*, Secker & Warburg, 1987.

John McCain III, "Killed" is an extract from *Faith of My Fathers*, Random House, 1999. Copyright © 1999 John McCain and Mark Salter

Peter Arnett, "Hill 875", Associated Press wire copy, 22 November, 1967. Copyright © 1967 Associated Press. Reprinted by permission of Associated Press.

John Ketwig, "And a Hard Rain Fell" is an extract from *And a Hard Rain Fell*, Macmillan, 1985. Copyright © 1985 John Ketwig. Reprinted by permission of Macmillan.

Frank Camper, "Recon" is an extract from *LRRP: The Professionals*, Dell Publishing, 1988. Copyright © 1988 Frank Camper

Robert Mason, "R&R", is an extract from *Chickenhawk*, Corgi 1984. Copyright © 1983 Robert C Mason

John Fetterman, "Little Duck Comes Home" (originally "Pfc Gibson Comes Home"), *Louisville Times*, July, 1968. Copyright © *Louisville Times* 1968.

Studs Terkel, "Police Break Up Anti-War Protest" is an extract from *Talking to Myself*, Pantheon Books, 1977. Copyright © 1977 Studs Terkel

Abbie Hoffman, "The Chicago Seven Trial: The Testimony of Abbie Hoffman, Yippie" is from Famous American

Trials, http://law2.umkc.edu/faculty/projects/ftrials/chi-cago7/chicago7.html

Charlie Stephens & Mike Misiaszek, "Winter Soldiers", copyright © the Vietnam Generation, Inc.

John Kifner, "The shootings at Kent State", *New York Times*, May 5, 1970. Reprinted by permission of the New York Times.

Ron Kovic, "Born on the Fourth of July" is an extract from *Born on the Fourth of July*, Akashic Books, 2005. Copyright © 1976 Ron Kovic. Reprinted by permission of Akashic Books.

Micki Voisard, "I'm Micki, Fly Me" is an extract from *A Piece of My Heart*, ed. Keith Walker, Presidio Press. Reprinted by permission.

Gustav Hasford, "Spirit of the Bayonet" is an extract from *The Short-Timers*, Bantam Books, Inc., 1979. Copyright © 1979 Gustav Hasford. Reprinted by permission of Bantam Books Inc.

Anonymous, "Voices in America: Enlistment" is an extract from *Nam*, Mark Baker, Abacus, 1982. Copyright © Mark Bates, 1987.

Donald Bodey, "This is War, Man" is an extract from *FNG*, Headline, 1984. Copyright © 1984 Donald Bodey. Reprinted by permission of Headline.

John T Wheeler, "Khe Sanh: Life in the V Ring", Associated press wire copy, 12 February, 1968. Reprinted by permission.

Seymour Hersh, "My Lai" is an extract from *My Lai 4*. Copyright © 1970 Seymour Hersh.

Maureen Walsh, "Burning Flesh" is an extract from *A Piece of My Heart*, ed. Keith Walker, Presidio Press. Reprinted by permission.

Lewis B Puller, "Fortunate Son" is an extract from *Fortunate Son*, Grove Press, 1991. Copyright © 1991 Lewis B. Puller, Jr. Reprinted by permission Grove/Atlantic, Inc.

Various, "Voices from Vietnam" are extracts from *Letters from America*, ed. Bill Adler, 1967, and *Dear America:*

Country, Alfred Knopf, 1987. Copyright © 1987 Bobbie Ann Mason. Reprinted by permission of HarperCollins.

My thanks are due to Charlie Trietline and Jonathan Ball for suggestions for inclusion in this volume.